Chinese Blockbu

CHINESE BLOCKBUSTER

Learn to read simplified and traditional Chinese characters and to pronounce them in Mandarin by bringing their building blocks to life with comedy, drama and a few memory tricks

Book 1

Gilbert-C. Rémillard

Illustrated by the author

Chineseblockbuster.com

ISBN: 978-1540796523

To France, without whom this work would not have been possible. It is a privilege to share my life and love with you.

CONTENTS

INTRODUCTION

Two friends are having a discussion:
"You did what? You nailed the guy's RIGHT HAND with your STAPLE GUN?"
"*That's right!* Here's why…
["This presumed **postgraduate** in oenology owns the WINERY *opposite* my house. I had asked him many times not to park his delivery truck in front of my driveway, because it blocks my exit. He was always *opposed* to that idea and never *replied.* So, when I saw him park his truck at the same place once again, I ran out and nailed him to the dashboard, using only ONE STAPLE. Or maybe *a couple…*"]

By reading this story above and picturing it in your mind, you can learn and remember all there is to know about the Chinese character 对 [對], that is:

1. Its various meanings, shown in *italics* in the story (**1** *That's right!* **2** Measure word for a *couple*, a *pair.* **3** To *be opposite, oppose, face.* **4** To *answer, reply.*)
2. Its pronunciation and tone in Mandarin, **duì**, with the help of a sound word, **postgraduate**, shown in bold in the story. In this book, sound words are used to help you remember the pronunciation of Chinese characters.
3. The building blocks that make up both versions, simplified and [traditional], of the Chinese character 对 [對]. The part of the story dealing with the structure of the traditional character is easy to recognize as it is written between [square brackets]. Similarly, the building blocks for the traditional character are written between [square brackets] when they are introduced. For this story, we have:

   Simplified character: 又 RIGHT HAND + 寸 STAPLE GUN

   Traditional character: [丵 WINERY + 一 ONE + 寸 STAPLE]
4. A story may contain factual and fictitious building blocks, all written in small caps. The factual building blocks are underscored with a SOLID LINE and the fictitious ones with a DOTTED LINE. The character 寸 carries both fictional meanings of STAPLE and STAPLE GUN in the story above. Note that, where applicable, the factual meaning will also be indicated beside any fictitious meaning when the components are listed. In this case, the factual meaning of 寸 is a Chinese INCH.

If you are new to Chinese and are overwhelmed by this brief description above, this is normal. Read on.

LEARNING CHINESE

In our days and age, the Chinese language is rapidly gaining in importance. With over 1 billion users, it is the most widely spoken language in the world. Add to that the importance of China in the world economy and you end up with a situation where knowing Chinese is a big advantage.

Here's the big hurdle: to be able to read Chinese, one needs to recognize a few thousand Chinese characters and to memorize their definitions and their pronunciations. This is the most important step. Chinese characters represent the Chinese alphabet and, as you know, you must learn the alphabet before being able to read in any language.

But first things first. What are those funny symbols that we call Chinese characters?

CHINESE CHARACTERS

At the dawn of civilization, writing systems were composed of pictograms and ideograms symbols. The sun was represented by a drawing of the sun, a man by a drawing of a man, an idea by the drawing of an action, etc. In many early civilizations, it was later deemed too difficult to express a full range of ideas that way and alphabetic systems based on a set of letters were invented, each letter representing a sound. By learning just a few letters, they could write all the words in their language.

The Chinese, however, stuck to their pictograms, which, after a few thousand years of evolution and simplifications, became those beautiful logograms[1] that we call Chinese characters. The beauty of this system is that characters do not need to change as people's pronunciation evolves through time because the meaning of a character is not linked to its pronunciation. It is therefore possible to read and make sense of ancient texts written a few thousand years ago, something much more difficult to do with the alphabetic systems, which must evolve with the changes in pronunciation. This is the reason why, for instance, the spelling of old English and Latin is so different than the spelling of modern English and modern Italian.

Another advantage of the Chinese system is that one does not need to understand the dialect of a writer to understand his or her prose. For example, a Chinese from mainland China who speaks Mandarin may have difficulty to understand a Chinese from Hong Kong who speaks Cantonese, but they both can read the same Chinese text.[2]

The price to pay for this, though, is relatively high:

1. You need to memorize a great number of characters when learning to read

---

[1] A logogram is a written character that represents a concept and not a sound.
[2] Numbers (1, 2, 3…) are an example where we have a similar situation with other languages. All numbers can be read and understood almost everywhere, but they are pronounced differently in each language.

and write. So, instead of learning, let's say, 26 letters to be able to read and communicate by writing in the English language, you must memorize a few thousand characters.

2. If you want to be able to read anything in Chinese that comes your way, you need to learn two versions, simplified and traditional, of some of the characters.
3. A character often has more than one definition or meaning. Earliest Chinese characters were initially associated with a single concept or meaning. With time, each character developed more connotations, sometimes totally unrelated to the first meaning.
4. When learning to speak, you need to associate a pronunciation to each of these characters and quite a few have more than one pronunciation.

SIMPLIFIED AND TRADITIONAL CHARACTERS

There are two standard versions of written Chinese: simplified and traditional.

When Chairman Mao came into power in 1949, he decided to do something about the low national literacy rates by decreasing the complexity of the traditional characters. So, with the help of a few linguists, a first list of simplified characters was produced in 1956 and a second list in 1964[3]. This simplification process was applied to a subset of about 2,000 characters amongst all the characters in common use. As such, many characters still only have their traditional form.

Hong Kong, Taiwan, Macau and the Chinese immigrant communities established overseas did not adopt the simplified characters as readily and kept using the traditional characters. This explains why signs in the Chinatowns of the world are most often seen written with traditional characters.

To be able to read everything, like Classical Chinese, texts written before the simplification process or published outside of China, street signs in Chinatowns or recent novels as well as newspapers published in mainland China, you need to learn both forms. It is like learning block letters and cursive writing in English. Both should be learned to be fluent in the language.

PRONUNCIATIONS, TONES AND PINYIN

For westerners, Chinese has a peculiar sonority, as it does not sound like anything else on earth! Over the years, a few romanization systems have been created that make use of the Roman alphabet to describe the sound of Chinese, starting with the Jesuit missionary Matteo Ricci in 1605. The latest system, pinyin (拼音),

---

[3] For example, the traditional character for the verb listen, 聽, was simplified to 听 and the character for horse, 馬, was simplified to 马.

was developed in the 1950s by the Chinese government. Pinyin is now used everywhere in the world as the romanization standard for Chinese sounds. It is very important for a learner to be familiar with it[4].

In a nutshell, each Chinese character is pronounced using one syllable, which consists of an optional initial phoneme that has one or two consonants, followed by a final phoneme which may contain one or two vowels, with the possible addition of a 'n' or 'ng' at the end. Therefore, a Chinese pronunciation written in pinyin looks like this: ai (no initial, final 'ai'), ma (initial 'm,' final 'a'), yin (initial 'y,' final 'in'), quan (initial 'q,' final 'uan'), huang (initial 'h,' final 'uang'), zhang (initial 'zh,' final 'ang'), etc.

In addition to learning the sound of a character, you also need to learn its tone. Mandarin uses four tones to differentiate characters having the same pinyin spelling, the tone being the pitch of the voice a speaker uses when articulating the character. The tone is very important because it determines the meaning of the character and it allows your ears to distinguish amongst other characters that have the same pronunciation. If you ignore it, you may create funny or embarrassing situations when you try to speak Chinese. In pinyin, the tone is indicated by an accent over one of the vowels in the syllable. The four tones are:

First tone: A high-level pitch with the volume held constant. Example: mā.

Second tone: The pitch rises sharply from the middle register, increasing in volume. Example: má.

Third tone: The pitch falls then rises. It starts low and falls lower before rising again. In practice, it sounds more like a low register pitch. Example: mǎ.

Fourth tone: Falling pitch. It starts high and drops sharply. Example: mà.

There is also a neutral tone, much shorter and subtler than the other four. A neutral tone sounds like a toned down fourth tone. Some characters are pronounced in the neutral tone when they become part of certain words. There is also a small number of characters that are always pronounced in the neutral tone. In pinyin, it is written with no accent: ma[5].

---

[4] Pinyin is useful for learning how to pronounce the characters, but not sufficient to understand the meaning of the text if you rely solely on it. The reason is that many Chinese characters are pronounced the same. The only way to understand what the text you are reading is about is to see the character itself. There is no way around it. This is the basis and arguably the hardest part when learning Chinese: to be able to recognize and pronounce the characters you see.

[5] I encourage you to browse the Web and look for 'pinyin charts.' A few websites allow the reader to hear the proper pinyin pronunciation by clicking on each one. It will be very helpful for you to hear what these syllables sound like.

A NEW APPROACH TO YOUR RESCUE

A Chinese learner needs to remember not only the structure of a character along with its definitions, but also the various other pronunciations and tones it may have, along with their connected meanings. No wonder many people think it is impossible to learn Mandarin and they quit before even trying. But take heart; learning Chinese is not as difficult as it may seem.

First, Chinese grammar is relatively simple compared to other languages. There are no tense modifications, no case inflections, no gender affixes, no plurals. Most of these grammatical elements are managed by way of sentence structure and the use of particles.

Secondly, most Chinese characters are composed of building blocks or components[6] that form part of a character and which are seen repeated in other characters. This way, the number of symbols to learn is drastically reduced. In other words, Chinese characters are not arbitrary symbols; they are composed of familiar building blocks, and there is an underlying logical structure guiding their construction. It is as if you had a box of Lego blocks containing yellow, blue, green and red bricks with a limited number of shapes, allowing you to create an almost unlimited number of structures with them.

Finally, the approach used in this book is to offer a complete method based on building blocks, sound words and mnemonics that will leave no stones unturned. Each character (both its traditional and simplified versions) is associated with its own story, like the one illustrated at the top of this chapter, allowing you to remember all aspects of the said character in one fell swoop. This innovative approach will help you overcome the challenges of learning the Chinese language and make you achieve the 'impossible.'

BUILDING BLOCKS

Chinese characters are composed of building blocks. While a few characters represent actual pictures (日 for sun, 月 for moon, 山 for mountain, 木 for tree) and symbols (一 for one, 二 for two, 三 for three), the great majority of Chinese characters are what we call sound-meaning compounds. They usually consist of a component taken from a list of 214 elements called radicals[7], that gives a hint to the meaning of the character, combined to another part that gives a hint to its pronunciation. Most of the time, these two parts are also characters themselves.

[6] Both terms, 'building blocks' and 'components', are used interchangeably in this book.
[7] Radicals, or more precisely Kangxi radicals, are used by most Chinese dictionaries to organize their content, a bit like the 26 letters of the alphabet are used to order words in a Western dictionary.

Take for instance the following three characters:

1 根 **gēn** (root of a plant) **2** 校 **xiào** (school) **3** 村 **cūn** (village, hamlet)

They all have on the left side the character 木, a radical which means 'tree, wood.' It is used here to indicate that the character to which it belongs has something to do with wood: **1** the root of a plant, of a tree; **2** a wooden structure where you study; **3** a village with houses made of wood.

Written on the right side of the tree radical are components (and characters in their own rights) which give an indication to the sound of the main character.

1 艮 **gěn** (tough; stubborn) **2** 交 **jiāo** (to deliver, hand over; to intersect)

3 寸 **cùn** (Chinese inch)

Their meaning, in this case, does not contribute to the sense of the character to which they belong.

There are also what we call meaning-meaning compounds, where two or more semantic components are joined to create a new character that has a meaning derived from the sum of the meanings of all the components. For example, still using 木 as a radical, we have 析 **xī** (to separate, divide, split) where the right part 斤 **jīn** represents an ax, hence to separate, split wood with an ax; the character 林 **lín**, where two trees are put next to each other to mean 'grove, woods'; or the character 森 **sēn**, where three trees are grouped to mean 'forest.'

With time, the characters underwent gradual changes, mostly phonetic changes but also shifts in meanings and structure to the point that lexicographers are not always able to trace them back to the original character. Therefore, some characters no longer appear on their own and do not have a meaning or a pronunciation of their own. They have essentially become 'non-characters,' but they continue to be used as building blocks to form more complex characters. In such cases, a fictitious meaning is given in this series to help memorize a non-character, often based on its shape for a better recall.

Why Are Fictitious Meanings Useful?

Fictitious meanings are not only useful to help memorize non-characters. This book capitalizes on their power as an important mnemonic tool to help make the stories more vivid, allowing you to use many of your senses when you read them and help them stick. Fictitious meanings are used in this book when:

- An abstract concept needs to be transformed into a concrete object to be able to visualize it. If we go back to the example given at the beginning of the book for character 寸, it is much easier for your brain to visualize a STAPLE GUN than a length measurement of one INCH.

- The shape or structure of a character reminds us of a physical object, making it easier for our brain to make the association with the character and the said object. If we take the character 十 for number TEN as an example, it is easier to picture a CROSS than to try to picture a number 10 in our mind.
- A character needs to be differentiated from other characters having the same meaning. For example, both 丈 and 老 mean 'old man.' With the appearance of one leg being longer than the other, the fictitious meaning of LIMPING MAN is given to the first character to help your brain differentiate between these two characters.

In all these instances, the real meaning of the character is mentioned in the text or appended to the fictitious meaning when used so that its real meaning also gets registered.

SOUND SYSTEM

Learning a language requires to be able to pronounce its words, and for Chinese characters, it means learning to pronounce pinyin syllables made up of initial and final phonemes.

Since not all initials can be combined to all finals, the total number of possible syllables is limited to 404. Also, not all syllables are pronounced in the four tones. The net result is that we get a total of about 1300 distinct syllables, which is far smaller than in a language such as English. Considering that there are roughly 6,000 Chinese characters still commonly used, this amounts to a lot of homophones, that is, different characters that are pronounced with the exact same sound and tone. It is therefore imperative to develop a system that would allow us to reduce the confusion and differentiate between all these homophones.

When I devised my own system to learn and remember Chinese characters, I wanted to use mnemonics to reproduce the sound of Mandarin. I then quickly realized that it was close to impossible to reproduce all Chinese sounds with enough precision by relying only on English sounds. For example, the letter 'u' in a pinyin syllable is pronounced as the English 'u' in some cases and as the German 'ü' or the French 'u' in some other cases (like in the pinyin **yu**). The 'c' in the pinyin **cun** is best remembered as a German 'z' (which sounds like 'ts') while the 'z' of **zan** sounds more like the Italian 'z' letter (sounds like 'ds'). The initial 'ch' is a good match for the Spanish 'ch' sound and the initial 'r' sounds almost like the French 'j.'

This was when I realized that by using five European languages (English, French, Italian, Spanish and German) to create 'sound words' mimicking Chinese sounds,

I had a fighting chance to better remember the pronunciation of the characters I was studying! This system allowed me to differentiate between similarly sounding initials (like the 'c' sound and the 'z' sound above), a frequent source of confusion for Chinese learners because some of them sound almost the same to our ears but they are in fact quite different. To learn characters well, you need to be able to make the difference and know which pinyin sound a character belongs to.

Some of you may point out that they wish to learn Chinese, not German or the other romance languages. Firstly, most 'sound words' defined in this book (i.e. a single word, an expression or part of an expression that sounds like the pinyin we are trying to remember) are in English. Secondly, just consider learning a few simple words in another language as an additional bonus. It is fun and useful, the words selected are very simple and you may know them already. And it gives us access to a greater stock of images and meanings we can pick from[8].

I invite you to consult Appendix 1: Chinese Initials and Finals where you will find two tables describing the approximate sound of each initial and final in pinyin and how they are reproduced using the five European languages.

The approach in this book is to assign a sound word to each of these unique syllables, along with its tone. Part of this sound word, let's call it the 'sound part,' stands for the Chinese pronunciation of the character under study. Sound words are designed to create an image in your mind that will become part of a story and will help you remember the proper pronunciation and tone of a character. Chinese sounds are reproduced in a variety of ways and the sound words selected may sometimes remain rough approximations in the case of sounds that are 'very Chinese.' Your brain won't mind, though, because it will know after a while that a sound word is used to represent a specific pinyin and not another.

"Fine," you might say, "but how do I know if a sound word is for a first, a second, a third or a fourth tone? And which part of the sound word should I focus on?" Here is how I solved this problem:

- One-syllable sound words beginning with the sound part are used for the first tone.
- Two-syllables sound words beginning with the sound part are used for the second tone.
- Sound words with three or more syllables beginning with the sound part are used for the third tone.
- Since four-syllable words are hard to come by, sound words ending with the sound part or having the sound part anywhere except at the beginning are used for the fourth tone.

---

[8] When in doubt about the pronunciation of a foreign sound word, I invite you to visit Forvo (https://forvo.com), the pronunciation dictionary online. It is a fantastic tool where you can hear native people pronounce a word in their language and it's free.

- The neutral tone is treated as a fourth tone as far as its sound word is concerned.

It is important to realize that what I mean by one syllable, two syllables and three syllables is not the actual number of grammatical syllables a word contains, but the number of pronounced syllables it has. For example, the English verb 'choke' has two grammatical syllables but is pronounced as a one-syllable word. It would therefore represent a first tone. On the other hand, Germans are known to pronounce all the syllables of their words. For example, the word 'Zeuge,' meaning 'witness,' is pronounced zeu-ge (with the 'ge' syllable clearly heard) and is used for a second tone.

As an example, here are the sound words selected for pinyin fa, ji and peng. The sound part of each sound word is double-underlined.

Pinyin	First tone	Second tone	Third tone	Fourth tone
fa	Fax	Fallen	Faraday	Sofa
ji	Jeep	Jitters	Jigsaw puzzle	Fiji
peng	Punk	Penguin	Penghulu	Alpenglow

As the example for peng demonstrates, the spelling of the sound word does not have to match the pinyin spelling. It just needs to sound like it. 'Punk' is not spelled like 'peng,' but the pronunciation is similar. I have attempted to select sound words that are a good phonetic representation of their Chinese counterparts, although they are not always a perfect match.

This book uses many conventions for the creation of sound words. For instance, since there are not many European words containing the letters 'ao,' this combination is often replaced by 'ar' since it sounds similar. For example, for pinyin bao, we have:

Pinyin	First tone	Second tone	Third tone	Fourth tone
bao	Bar	Barber	Barbarians	Fubar

Many of these conventions are described in Appendix 2: Special Sound Mnemonics, which provides a listing of special sound words that have been selected to be a good representation of the pinyin sound they stand for. And as in any rule, there are exceptions. Appendix 2 will help you understand those few exceptions and how they are addressed.

MNEMONICS

A working memory is based on associations. Most of what you learn in life, even if you do not realize it, is done by way of mnemonics and connections between ideas and thoughts. You associate the new concept you are trying to learn with something you already know. After a while, the connections tend to disappear and the new idea or word is transferred to the long-term memory.

It has been shown that humans more easily remember surprising, humorous, silly and shocking stories. The more absurd, the better. Also, strong emotions help things stick. Most people remember where they were on September 11 or, for the older generation, when John F. Kennedy was shot. And you would probably remember better when your friend Joe decided to run naked in the street after having drunk too much than when he was average Joe on a typical day.

STORIES

The stories are the glue to help you remember all there is to know about each character. They may refer to historical facts and events, but most of them are totally fabricated. Some stories may also deal with harsh themes, as strong images are necessary for impressing our brain. Political correctness is not good to remember stuff. In fact, if we are shocked, we will remember the characters, their pronunciation and their building blocks better!

You will also notice that the stories often use 'I' in the present tense. This usage of the first person is not about me but about you. I want you to imagine yourself at the center of the action. You become the main character in the story. Also, most stories are written with the masculine gender, only to lighten the text.

Furthermore, if a German or Italian word is used as a sound word, the story may concern a German or an Italian person or it may place you somewhere in Germany or Italy, just to help you remember the proper sound word.

The stories are only examples of what is possible to achieve with this method. I even encourage you to make your own stories with the building blocks I provide. If you have more personal stories you can relate to, use them. They would work even better. Think of this book as a box of Lego blocks, where you can build the model shown on the box cover or make your own toy. For some of you, my madness may suit you just fine and that's alright!

Finally, to make the stories work better, use as many senses as you can. When reading a story, close your eyes and see the building blocks with vivid colors (visual sense), odors (sense of smell) or as humongous objects when they are concrete things or as a struggling action when it is a verb, all the while hearing the sound word resonate or reverberate in your mind (audio). See the definitions as repeated, incessant actions when they concern verbs and adverbs, or as a swarm of objects when they represent concrete things.

For example, let's return to the story presented at the beginning of the book for the character 对 [對].

Two friends are having a discussion:
"You did what? You nailed the guy's RIGHT HAND with your STAPLE GUN?"
"*That's right*! Here's why…
["This presumed **postgraduate** in oenology owns the WINERY *opposite* my house. I had asked him many times not to park his delivery truck in front of my driveway, because it blocks my exit. He was always *opposed* to that idea and never *replied*. So, when I saw him park his truck at the same place once again, I ran out and nailed him to the dashboard, using only ONE STAPLE. Or maybe *a couple*…"]

For the building blocks, you could visualize a huge, flashy yellow STAPLE GUN and a bloodied RIGHT HAND. The WINERY could be completely pink (they make rosés…) and you could smell the pungent fermentation odors coming out of the place. The ONE STAPLE that you hold between your fingers could be shiny gray.

For the meaning *That's right*, the friend could answer "*That's right*! *That's right*! *That's right*!" when asked about what he did (repeated action).

For the meanings *opposite* and *opposed*, you could imagine a surveyor knocking at your door to inform you that after precise measurements, he can attest that the WINERY is exactly *opposite* your house, while you see the WINERY owner rushing towards you, shouting, "Objection! I am *opposed* to that affirmation!"

For the meaning to *reply*, after asking your neighbor not to park his delivery truck in front of your driveway, you could visualize him looking straight at you while he puts a duct tape over his mouth with the words 'No *reply*' written on it.

As for *a couple*, you can imagine a married *couple* walking by in the street and watching in horror as you staple the guy to the dashboard.

While all this action is going on, you hear the word **postgraduate** resonate in your mind: **postgraduate… graduate… duate… duì …duì …duì…**

It takes much longer to explain the method than to process all these elements in your mind. But I assure you that if you spend the extra effort to make the stories as vivid as you can, the characters will be yours.

LAST WORDS

Learning Chinese is a complex endeavor and it must rely on a few parallel activities to be successful. Learning to recognize and pronounce Chinese characters is arguably the hardest part in learning Chinese for a foreign person, but also the most important if you want to become fluent in the language. Thankfully, the book you are reading right now takes good care of that part. Once you have crossed that hurdle, the rest is relatively smooth sailing.

Fluency will not come to you magically, though, without effort on your part. You will still need to come back to the stories occasionally to make them stick. You will need to review, review and review some more, as with any other languages you wish to learn. But the first time you realize that you can read and understand Chinese texts, the feeling is amazing!

I invite you to visit my website at **ChineseBlockbuster.com**, which provides useful information about learning Chinese.

A Chinese proverb often cited says that 'A trip of one thousand miles starts with the first step.' Likewise, a trip of a few thousand characters starts with the first one. Come aboard! As an aerospace engineer, I am here to prove to you that learning Chinese is not rocket science!

USER GUIDE

This book is the first of a series that intend to cover some 4000 characters and building blocks in both simplified or traditional format. These characters were selected using the top entries of the Modern Chinese Character Frequency List produced by Jun Da 笪骏, Director of the Media Center for Language Acquisition Department of Foreign Languages and Literatures at the Middle Tennessee State University[9]. The list was generated from a large corpus of Chinese texts collected from online sources. The characters covered in the series are essentially all you need to be able to read most documents in modern Chinese. You may still tumble over a few characters not covered in this series if you read ancient or very advanced texts, but you will have at your disposal all the building blocks needed to create your own mnemonics.

The characters are presented in a logical order, roughly following the order of their frequency of use. I say roughly because a character is composed of other characters or building blocks that may be further down the frequency list. These building blocks logically need to be introduced first. Also, characters with similar shapes or having a similar role (like numbers) tend to be presented together. This is what I mean by 'logical order.' The book you are holding introduces the first few hundred characters necessary to set you on your way for mastering Chinese.

If you are impatient to learn, you can jump immediately to the section dealing with characters and building blocks on page 23 as the presentation of each character follows a standardized approach that is relatively easy to understand. The first few characters will include some details on the system (grayed-out text between parentheses) to get you started. As exceptions are often the rules in any standardized approach, especially to address a language as complex as Chinese, I recommend that you first go through this User Guide that describes the various sections in the presentation of each character.

Now, let's look at the various elements of the presentation by using four characters which together present most of the different arrangements you may encounter.

[9] Da, Jun. 2004. Chinese text computing. <http://lingua.mtsu.edu/chinese-computing>

Figure 1

14 ① 乞 ② ③ 3rd

DEFINITION ④

To *beg, plead for.*

PRONUNCIATION ⑤

qǐ

SOUND WORD ⑥

Chihuahua
The smallest dog.

⑦

COMPONENTS ⑧

𠂉 RIFLE[8] + 乙 HOOK[13] SECOND

MNEMONICS ⑨

- Here is your very first composite Chinese character, made of two building blocks, that you were *begging* for!
- The ancient form, , looks like a hand *begging* for food or money.

STORY ⑩

Today, I saw a man sitting in the street, with a **Chihuahua** in his lap, a HOOK in place of his left hand, *begging* for money. When he asked me to spare some change, I refused, until he pulled out a RIFLE and his **Chihuahua** started growling!

EXAMPLES ⑪

乞求(qǐ qiú) To beg. 乞丐(qǐ gài) Beggar.

WANT A LITTLE MORE? ⑫

Usage frequency: Middle third.

Figure 2

187 ① **对[對]** ② ③ 4th

DEFINITION ④

1. *That's right!*
2. Measure word for a *couple*, a *pair*.
3. To *be opposite, oppose, face*.
4. To *answer, reply*.

PRONUNCIATION ⑤

duì

SOUND WORD ⑥

Postgraduate
A student who continues to study for an advanced degree after earning a bachelor's degree.

⑦

SIMPLIFIED COMPONENTS ⑧

又 RIGHT HAND[71] +
寸 STAPLE GUN[160] INCH

TRADITIONAL COMPONENTS

[丵 WINERY[186] + 一 ONE[15] +
寸 STAPLE[160] INCH]

STORY ⑩

"You did what? You nailed the guy's RIGHT HAND with your STAPLE GUN?"
"*That's right*! Here's why...

["This presumed **postgraduate** in oenology owns the WINERY *opposite* my house. I had asked him many times not to park his delivery truck in front of my driveway, because it blocks my exit. He was always *opposed* to that idea and never *replied*. So, when I saw him park his truck at the same place once again, I ran out and nailed him to the dashboard, using only ONE STAPLE. Or maybe *a couple*..."]

EXAMPLES ⑪

1. 对了 (duì le) That's correct, right.
2. 一对夫妻 (yī duì fū qī) A married couple.
3. 反对 (fǎn duì) To oppose, be against. 对面 (duì miàn) Across from.
4. 对答 (duì dá) To answer.

WANT A LITTLE MORE? ⑫

Usage frequency: Top 100.

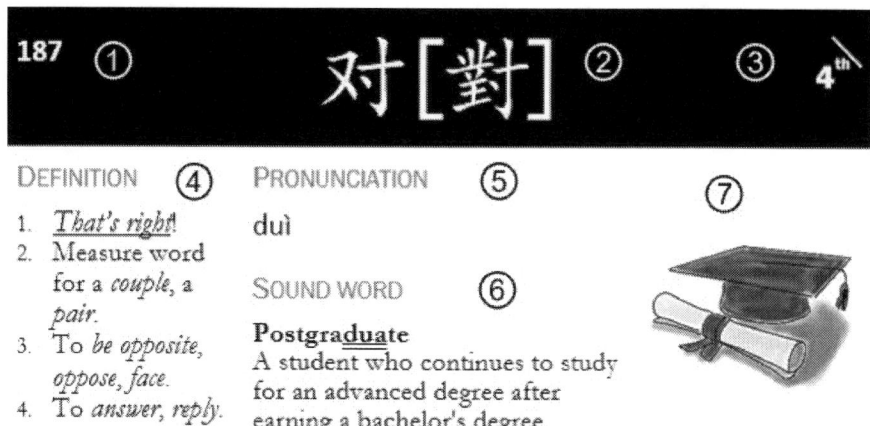

Figure 3

104 ① 辶[辵] ② ③ 4th

DEFINITION ④

† To go hesitantly, moving forward and being halted.

PRONUNCIATION ⑤

chuò

SOUND WORD ⑥

Chanchullo /tʃaɲtʃuʎo/
Spanish word for 'scam', 'racket', 'dirty tricks'.

⑦

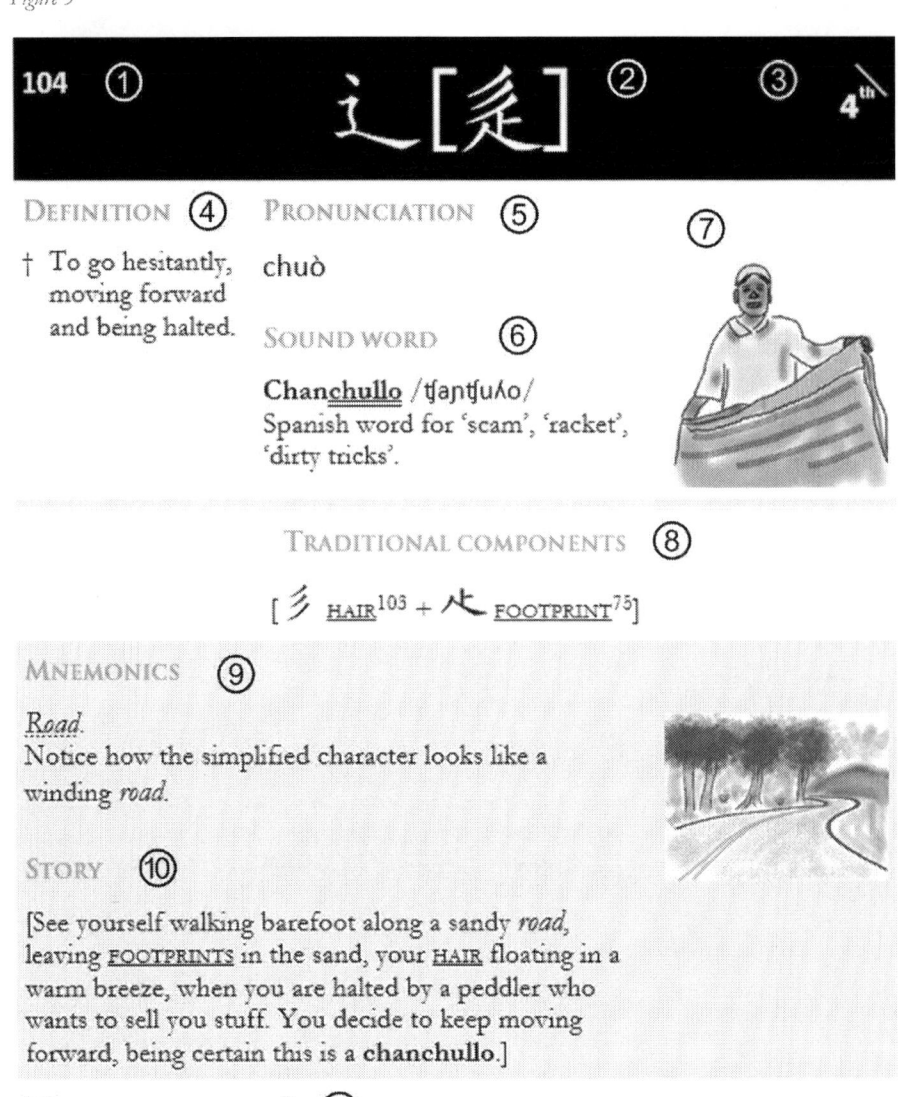

TRADITIONAL COMPONENTS ⑧

[彡 HAIR[103] + 龰 FOOTPRINT[75]]

MNEMONICS ⑨

Road.
Notice how the simplified character looks like a winding *road*.

STORY ⑩

[See yourself walking barefoot along a sandy *road*, leaving FOOTPRINTS in the sand, your HAIR floating in a warm breeze, when you are halted by a peddler who wants to sell you stuff. You decide to keep moving forward, being certain this is a **chanchullo**.]

WANT A LITTLE MORE? ⑫

This is the 162nd of the 214 Kangxi radicals.

Figure 4

159A ① **说[說]** ② ③ 1st

DEFINITION ④

To *speak, say.*

PRONUNCIATION ⑤

shuō

SOUND WORD ⑥

Shoo off
To expel, chase away.

⑦

COMPONENTS ⑧

讠[言] SPEECH[102] + 兑[兌] to CASH[158]

STORY ⑩

This fraudulent preacher is trying to CASH in big by giving SPEECHES. More often than not, however, they **shoo off** the guy from the stage, not allowing him to *speak.*

EXAMPLES ⑪

听说(tīng shuō) To hear, understand that… 小说(xiǎo shuō) Fiction, novel. 说中文(shuō zhōng wén) To speak Chinese.

WANT A LITTLE MORE? ⑫

- Usage frequency: Top 100.

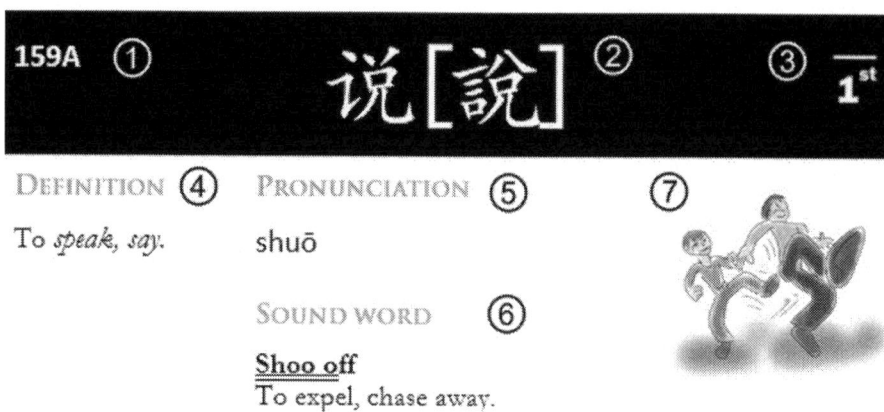

1. This is the sequence number, reflecting the order of presentation of the character in this series.

   If a character has two different pronunciations and each pronunciation means something different, two separate entries are created for the same character. The corresponding entries follow each other. Figure 4 is such an example where the letter 'A' after the number indicates that this character has at least another entry following this one, with the same number followed by the next sequential letter. Likewise, if a simplified character represents the simplification of two different traditional characters, both entries follow each other.

2. Chinese character. In Figure 1, there exists only one version of the character. Figure 2, Figure 3 and Figure 4 show characters with both a simplified and a traditional format, the traditional one being written between square brackets.

3. The tone used (first, second, third or fourth tone) when the character is pronounced. An accent is indicated above the number, as an additional reminder of how the tone is written in pinyin. This space is left empty for characters pronounced in the neutral tone and for building blocks having no pronunciation of their own.

4. The real, actual definitions of the character, written in *italics* and presented as a numbered list. Some of these are also underscored with a solid line; they are the values selected in this series to be associated with the character when it is used as a building block in other characters. All the values written in *italics* should be learned. If a definition is indicated but is not written in *italics*, it is a definition that is no longer used in modern Chinese. This section may also list, next to the symbol †, ancient or obsolete meanings worthy of mention. Figure 3 shows such an instance. These ancient meanings may sometimes be used as building block values in this book. For non-characters that only serve as a building block in other characters, they are indicated as such.

5. The pronunciation of the character, in pinyin. For non-characters, "Not applicable" will be indicated since they no longer have a pronunciation.

6. The sound word used that best represents the character pronunciation, written in bold. The part of the sound word which reproduces the Chinese sound is doubly underlined in that section. In the case of a non-English sound word, as shown in Figure 3, its phonetic is indicated between /slashes/ using the International Phonetic Alphabet[10]. A definition of the

[10] International Phonetic Alphabet: https://en.wikipedia.org/wiki/International_Phonetic_Alphabet

sound word follows, when deemed useful. In some cases, you will also see a reference to Appendix 2: Special Sound Mnemonics in this section, that provides additional details to help you understand the choice of a sound word. For non-characters, "Not applicable" will be indicated.

7. An image used to reinforce the meaning of the sound word.

8. The list of components or building blocks making up the character. Here are a few important points regarding this section:

   For characters having both a simplified and a traditional format, the building blocks of each are represented under separate headings, with the traditional ones between brackets. When both formats of a character are composed of the same building blocks, each format using either the simplified or the traditional version of the said building blocks, only one heading is provided, as shown in Figure 4.

   In some other cases, only the simplified or the traditional character is decomposed into its building blocks, its counterpart being too simple to decompose or its shape being better represented by a fictitious meaning. Figure 3 shows an example of just the traditional character being broken up.

   Another important point concerns the difference between real and fictitious meanings. Building blocks are always written in UNDERLINED SMALL CAPS (hint: blocky letters) where they appear. The building blocks underscored with a SOLID LINE represent real meanings while those underscored with a DOTTED LINE signify fictitious meanings. When a component is slightly different than its manifestation in the character under study, it is preceded by a ~ tilde.

   In Figure 2, you can also see that the word INCH is appended as a superscript to the building blocks for STAPLE GUN and STAPLE. When a corresponding real value exists for a fictitious building block, it is indicated as such. In this case, inch is written in UNDERLINED SMALL CAPS because 'inch' is also a value selected to represent character 寸 when it is used as a building block. Otherwise, one of the real values (that are written in italics and not underlined when presented in the Definition section of the character) is appended as a superscript and written with normal font. When no real meaning superscript is written besides a building block, as is the case for WINERY in Figure 2, it means that there is no longer an actual value associated with it.

   The superscript number written to the right of the building block corresponds to its sequence number in the book and allows you to quickly reference the character or building block.

Finally, the components making up a character are listed in the order in which they would be written. Appendix 5: Order for Writing Chinese Characters provides further details.

9. You will find in this part memory hints and mental images to help you memorize the character as well as other important things, presented as a bullet list when there are more than one, as in Figure 1.

   In some instances, the ancient form of the character is provided when it may help you understand and remember the character under study, as is the case in Figure 1, where  shows a hand begging for money. For this ancient form, we go back to the small seal script, created in the latter half of the 1st millennium BC, when the first emperor of China promulgated the standardization of Chinese calligraphy. Yes, the same emperor who had an army of terracotta soldiers built for his afterlife; a fascinating period in China's history.

   This section also presents the fictitious meanings given to some characters in the book. In Figure 3, the character is given the fictitious meaning of *road*. The fictitious values are always written in italics and underscored with a dotted line when introduced. This is to remind you that when this character serves as a building block in another character, its value will appear in small caps and will be underscored with a dotted line as well (like ROAD in this case).

   A quick way to know if a character will ever be used as a building block is to look at its Definition and Mnemonics (if present) sections. If no values are underscored by a solid line or a dotted line in both sections, as is the case in Figure 4, the character will never be used as a building block.

   Finally, illustrations often accompany the fictitious definitions in this section, as shown in Figure 3.

10. The Story section is the centerpiece of the whole presentation. This is where all the elements of a character (meanings, building blocks, pronunciation) are brought together in a memorable narrative. The part of the story dealing with the traditional characters is written between brackets. The meanings are written in *italics*, the components in UNDERLINED SMALL CAPS (solid or dotted line) and the sound word in **bold**.

    In certain situations, these various formats may be combined in a story. For instance, when a BUILDING BLOCK has the same value as one of the *meanings* for the character under analysis, it is written in *ITALICS SMALL CAPS*. Likewise, if the **sound word** has the same value as one of the *meanings*, it is written in ***bold italics***.

There may be cases where either the Mnemonics or the Story section is sufficient to convey a memorable narrative. Typically, only the Mnemonics section is used for 'non-characters' and very rare characters.

11. Seeing Chinese characters in combination with other characters is very useful to be able to read Chinese texts. As such, this section provides, except for very rare characters and non-characters, examples of usage to form words in modern Chinese, presented in a numbered list that corresponds to the numbered list in the Definition section. Most of the examples provided consist of two-character words (as most modern Chinese words are now written), but expressions and sentences are given as well. For economy of space, only simplified characters are used in the examples. Also, although it is usual practice to glue together the pinyin of each character forming a word, the pinyin pronunciation of each character is separated by a space in this series, to help you distinguish them better.

    In a few cases, a character is pronounced in the neutral tone when used in a specific word. For instance, one such example is the word 儿子 (ér zǐ) which means 'Son.' While the character 子 is usually pronounced in the third tone (as shown by the accent above its pinyin), it is pronounced in this word in the neutral tone. To help you notice these special cases, the pinyin of such characters will be underscored with a dotted line.

12. Because learning Chinese characters is so interesting, I am betting you will 'want a little more.' This last section indicates:

    - Whether the character is one of the 100 most common Chinese surnames, based on a report on the household registrations released by the Chinese Ministry of Public Security on April 24, 2007, for Mainland China, Hong Kong and Macau.
    - Whether the character is a heavenly stem or an earthly branch. Chinese people make use of ten 'heavenly stems' and twelve 'earthly branches,' i.e. characters that are used in enumerations (like we use A, B, C … or 1, 2, 3…) or in date calculations. If you are interested in Chinese history or want to understand the meaning of these characters that you may encounter in Chinese texts as bullet lists, it is very useful to know them. They are listed in Appendix 4: Heavenly Stems & Earthly Branches.
    - Whether the character is one of the 214 Kangxi radicals, listed in Appendix 3: 214 Kangxi Radicals.
    - The frequency of use of each character. Going from the most to the least frequent, we have: Top 10, Top 100, Top 500, Top third (1-2000), Middle third (2000-4000) and Bottom third (4000-6000). For non-characters, i.e. pure elements of the Chinese writing system, for

characters that are no longer used to form words but which are still used as building blocks and for rare characters with a frequency of use above 6000, no frequency of use is indicated, as is the case for Figure 3.

- Any additional points worthy of mention and other fascinating facts about the character.

Voilà! I believe I can now send you on your way to learn Chinese characters. Have fun!

Characters and Their Building Blocks

1 丨 3rd

DEFINITION

† Communication from top to bottom.

(The symbol † indicates that this definition is ancient and obsolete)

PRONUNCIATION

gǔn

SOUND WORD

Goon skirmish
(The sound word counts more than two syllables, with the sound part at the beginning, to represent a third tone)

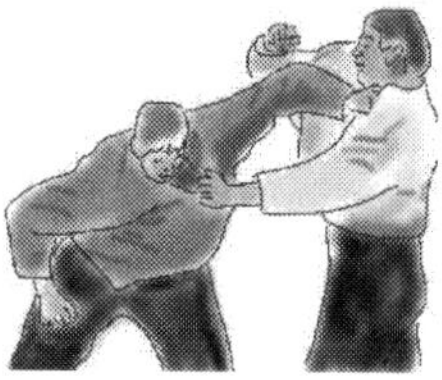

MNEMONICS

- *Stick*, *walking stick*, *pole*, because of its shape.
  (The values *stick*, *walking stick* and *pole* are underscored with a dotted line, to indicate that these are fictitious meanings that will be carried over when this character is used as a building block)
- Think of a **goon skirmish** with *sticks*.

WANT A LITTLE MORE?

- When people want to refer to this building block as the vertical calligraphic stroke used for writing characters, they call it shù.
- This is the 2nd of the 214 Kangxi radicals.

2 亅 2nd

DEFINITION

† Hook.

PRONUNCIATION

jué

SOUND WORD

<u>Due</u>lliste /dyɛlist/
French word for one who fights in a duel. (See 'Special Sound Mnemonics,' page 487)
(The sound word counts two 'pronounced' syllables, with the sound part at the beginning, to represent a second tone)

MNEMONICS

- It is also given the fictitious meaning of *stick* because of its similitude to the other 丨 STICK[1] building block.
- Think of a **duelliste** using a *stick* equipped with a hook to grapple his opponent.

WANT A LITTLE MORE?

- This building block is one of the few basic strokes used for writing Chinese characters.
- This is the 6th of the 214 Kangxi radicals.

3 丶 ˇ3rd

DEFINITION

1. *Drop* (liquid or solid).
2. *Dot, point.*

(*Drop* and *dot* are underlined to indicate that these real definitions will be used as building block values)

PRONUNCIATION

zhǔ

SOUND WORD

Judeo-Christian
Term used to represent the common beliefs of Christianity and Judaism.

MNEMONICS

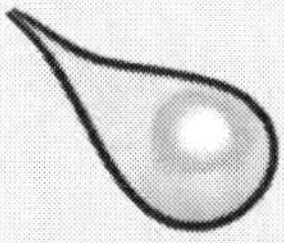

- Think of *drops* of holy water being sprinkled by a **Judeo-Christian** priest.
- Based on the context of the story, this character may mean a variety of fictitious *small things*.

WANT A LITTLE MORE?

- It may also be written slanting to the right.
- It may appear slightly stretched out (more like a short line than a dot) when used as a building block.
- When people want to refer to this building block as the dot stroke used for writing characters, they call it diǎn.
- This is the 3rd of the 214 Kangxi radicals.

4 丿 3rd

DEFINITION

Left-falling stroke in Chinese calligraphy.

PRONUNCIATION

piě

SOUND WORD

Pie de firma /pje ðe firma/ Spanish expression for a signature footer.

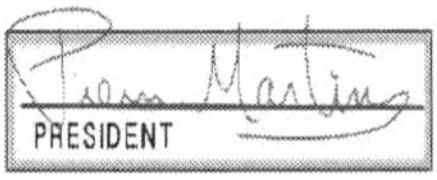

MNEMONICS

- Think of a man wearing a French *beret* or a marine *beret* (because of the way a beret is worn) and whose signature, displayed in a **pie de firma**, has a *left-falling stroke* at the end, not unlike his mustache.
- This building block is also given two other fictitious meanings due to its visual appearance:
  - *Dog collar*, because if you look at a dog wearing a collar from the side and remove the dog, this is what you are left with.
  - *Slide* for children, or the verb to *slide*.

WANT A LITTLE MORE?

- It can also appear reversed, *sliding* to the right. In that case, it represents a *right-falling stroke* in Chinese calligraphy and is pronounced nà.
- The slope of the stroke is not always as pronounced, sometimes appearing almost horizontal when used as a building block.
- This character and the preceding one for 丶 DROP are often interchangeable in the formation of characters because of their similar shapes.
- This is the 4th of the 214 Kangxi radicals.

5 乛 2nd

DEFINITION

Turning stroke in Chinese calligraphy.

PRONUNCIATION

zhé

SOUND WORD

Jelly

MNEMONICS

- *Flat cap* (hat), because of its look when seen from the side.
- Imagine a little brat putting **jelly** in your *flat cap* while you're asleep.

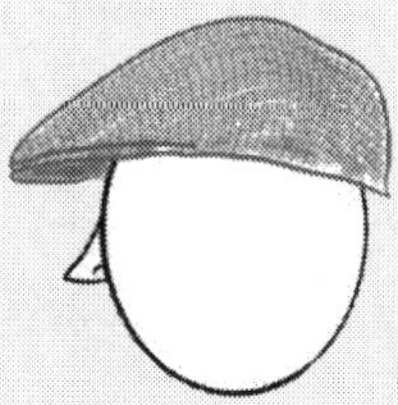

6 乚

Definition

Non-character used only as a building block.

Pronunciation

Not applicable

Sound word

Not applicable

Mnemonics

It has the shape of a *corner*.

7 亅

Definition

Non-character used only as a building block.

Pronunciation

Not applicable

Sound word

Not applicable

Mnemonics

It looks like a *coat hook*.

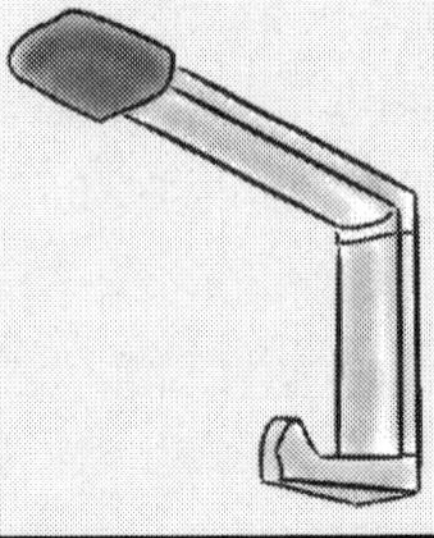

8 𠂉

DEFINITION

Non-character used only as a building block.

PRONUNCIATION

Not applicable

SOUND WORD

Not applicable

MNEMONICS

Rifle, because it looks like a man aiming with a *rifle*.

9 𠆢

DEFINITION

Non-character used only as a building block.

PRONUNCIATION

Not applicable

SOUND WORD

Not applicable

MNEMONICS

Tent, *parasol*, *umbrella*, because of its shape.

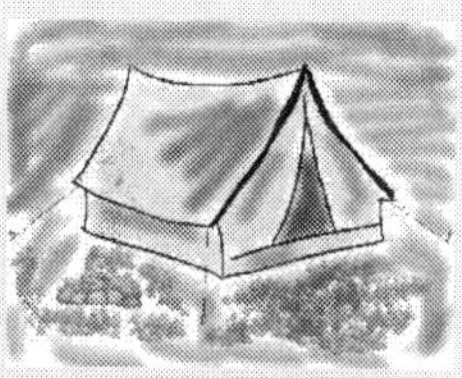

10 **厶** $\overline{1}^{st}$

DEFINITION

† *Private*, selfish.

(Although the definition of *private* is obsolete, it will still be used as a building block value)

PRONUNCIATION

sī

SOUND WORD

Ssssss
The sound of a rattle snake or of a person hissing.
(The sound word counts one syllable, to represent a first tone)

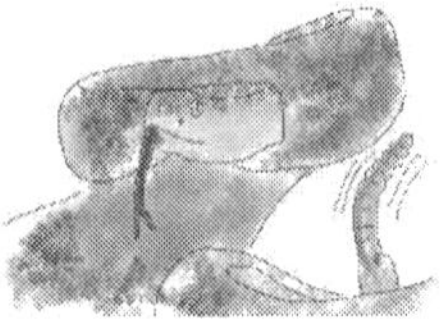

MNEMONICS

- *Nose*.
  View the character as a *nose* seen sideways, and remember that *private* is the contrary of 'nosy.'
- *Elbow*.
  Picture the character as a bent *elbow*, doing curls with a dumbbell. The repeated motion excites a rattle snake (**sssssss**) nearby.
- It can also appear reversed, like this: ㇇, when used as a building block. This is a good type of curls for the triceps…

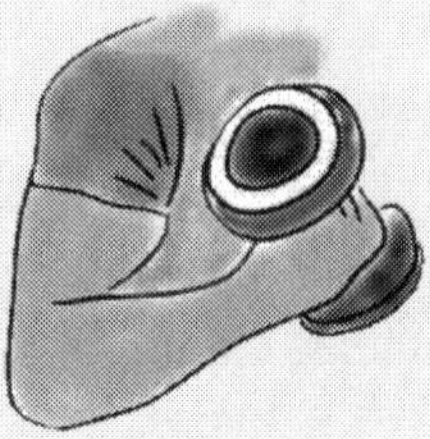

WANT A LITTLE MORE?

This is the 28th of the 214 Kangxi radicals.

11 冖 4th

DEFINITION

Cover, *top cover*; to *cover*.

PRONUNCIATION

mì

SOUND WORD

Mummy
(The sound part is at the end of the sound word, to represent a fourth tone)

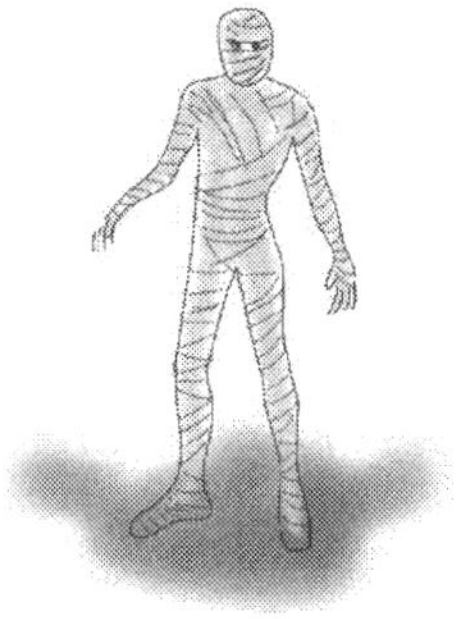

MNEMONICS

- *Hat*, *crown*; *tablecloth*, *cloth roof*, *lid*.
  This building block *covers* only the top or a small portion of a character to which it belongs, hence the meaning of *top cover*.
  - Something that covers only the top of the head, like a *hat* or a *crown*.
  - Something that covers the top of an object, like a *tablecloth*, a *cloth roof*, a *lid*.
- Picture a **mummy** wearing a *crown* (King Tut?).

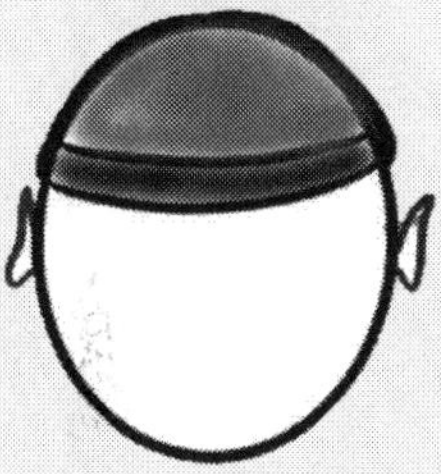

WANT A LITTLE MORE?

This is the 14th of the 214 Kangxi radicals.

12

冂

1st

DEFINITION

<u>*Cover*</u>, <u>*long cover*</u>; to <u>*cover*</u>.

† Outermost suburbs, uninhabited areas far outside the city.

PRONUNCIATION

jiōng

SOUND WORD

^{j}<u>The ONG</u>
The OverNight Guest, pronounced as one syllable.
(Note the superscript 'j' at the beginning of the sound word and see 'Special Sound Mnemonics,' page 485)

MNEMONICS

Mask, hood; shelter, cage, glass bell.

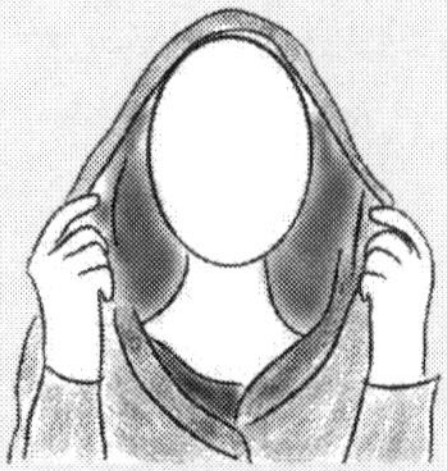

Like the building block 冖, this one also means to *cover*. However, because it *covers* the building blocks of a character all the way to the bottom, it has the meaning of *long cover*.

- Something which conceals the whole head or face of a person, like a *mask* or the *hood* of a coat.
- All sorts of long covers of various sizes that reach the ground, like a *shelter*, a *cage*, a *glass bell*.

STORY

"Dirty as he was, there was no way I would allow **the ONG** to sleep here, under my bed *covers*. I recommended that he sleeps under a bus *shelter*, far outside the city."

WANT A LITTLE MORE?

This is the 13th of the 214 Kangxi radicals.

13 乙 3rd

DEFINITION

Second.

† Fish gut.

PRONUNCIATION

yǐ

SOUND WORD

Hippopotame /ipɔpɔtam/
French word for 'hippopotamus.'
The 'h' is silent.

MNEMONICS

- To better remember its actual meaning of *second*, view it as a stylized number 2.
- *Hook, fishhook;* to be *hooked*.

  When used as a building block, all the variants of this character (㇄ and ㇾ) look like a *hook* or a *fishhook*. It also carries the fictitious meaning of 'to be *hooked*' by extension.

STORY

Fishing in an African river, my *second* catch was a **hippopotame**, found dangling at the end of my *fishhook*…

EXAMPLES

乙等 (yǐ děng) Second grade. 乙肝 (yǐ gān) Hepatitis B.

WANT A LITTLE MORE?

- This is the 5th of the 214 Kangxi radicals and the *2nd* heavenly stem (See Appendix 4: Heavenly Stems & Earthly Branches on page 503.)
- Usage frequency: Top third.

14

乞

3rd

DEFINITION

To *beg, plead for.*

PRONUNCIATION

qǐ

SOUND WORD

Chihuahua
The smallest dog.

COMPONENTS

𠂉 RIFLE[8] + 乙 HOOK[13] SECOND

(RIFLE and HOOK are underscored with a dotted line because they both are fictitious meanings. Rifle has no real value associated with it while hook's real value is SECOND, written as a superscript next to its sequence number)

MNEMONICS

- Here is your very first composite Chinese character made up of two building blocks, that you were *begging* for!
- The ancient form, , looks like a hand *begging* for food or money.

STORY

Today, I saw a man sitting in the street with a **Chihuahua** in his lap, a HOOK in place of his left hand, *begging* for money. When he asked me to spare some change, I refused, until he pulled out a RIFLE and his **Chihuahua** started growling!

EXAMPLES

乞求(qǐ qiú) To beg. 乞粮(qǐ liáng) To beg for food. 乞丐(qǐ gài) Beggar.

WANT A LITTLE MORE?

Usage frequency: Middle third.

15 一 1st

Definition

1. *One.*
2. *Whole, all, unity, together.*
3. *Briefly; once.*

Pronunciation

yī

Sound word

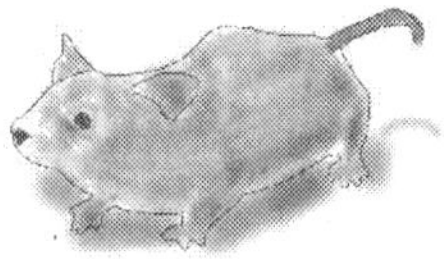

Yiiii!
A shriek at the sight of a mouse or the squeaking sound of a mouse.

Mnemonics

- This character can be viewed as an overworked number *one* lying down.
- As a building block, it provides for different meanings based on its appearance:
  - *Ceiling* if it appears towards the top of a character.
  - *Floor* if it appears towards the bottom of a character.
  - *Ground level* or *horizon* if the action of the story is outside.
  - A *slit* (narrow cut).

Story

"**Yiiii**! There is a mouse on the *floor* of our bedroom!"
"So what? Are you scared of just *one* little, tiny mouse?"

Examples

1. 一个人 (yī gè rén) One person. 一边 (yī biān) One side.
2. 一同 (yī tóng) Along, together. 一身汗 (yī shēn hàn) Sweating all over.
3. 看一看 (kàn yī kàn) Take a look.

Want a little more?

- It is pronounced with the first tone when standing alone. Its tone changes in other situations: when followed by a character in the fourth tone, it is pronounced in the second tone. In all other circumstances, it is pronounced in the fourth tone.
- This is the second most used Chinese character and the first of the 214 Kangxi radicals.

16 二 4th

DEFINITION

Two.

PRONUNCIATION

èr

SOUND WORD

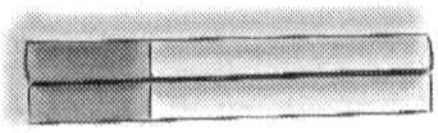

Cigarettes
(The sound part is anywhere but at the beginning of the sound word, to represent a fourth tone)

COMPONENTS

2 x 一 ONE[15]

(ONE is underscored with a solid line, because this is a real meaning)

MNEMONICS

Two times ONE.

STORY

"Give me ONE **cigarette** and then, another ONE, please!"
"You mean, *two* **cigarettes**?"

EXAMPLES

二月 (èr yuè) February. 二等 (èr děng) Second-class.

WANT A LITTLE MORE?

- Note that the bottom stroke is longer than the top one.
- This is the 7th of the 214 Kangxi radicals.
- Usage frequency: Top 500.

17 **三** $\overline{1^{st}}$

DEFINITION

Three.

PRONUNCIATION

sān

SOUND WORD

San /san/
Spanish word for 'Saint.'

COMPONENTS

3 x 一 ONE[15]

MNEMONICS

- *Three* times ONE.
- The sound word **San** counts *three* letters.

STORY

"Here are depicted the *three* American saints (starting from the North on a map): the top ONE is **San** Francisco, the middle ONE is **San** Andreas and the bottom ONE is **San** Antonio."

EXAMPLES

三角 (sān jiǎo) Triangle. 三十 (sān shí) 30.

WANT A LITTLE MORE?

- Note that the middle stroke is the shortest line of the *three*.
- This character was also interpreted as a symbol representing heaven, earth and man, with man in the middle.
- *Three* often means 'a lot' in Chinese. For instance, when a character is composed of the same building block repeated *three* times, it usually means 'a lot of' that element.
- Usage frequency: Top 500.

18A

卜

3rd

Definition

1. To *predict, practice divination, tell fortunes.*
2. To *choose* (literary).

Pronunciation

bǔ

Sound word

Booby trap

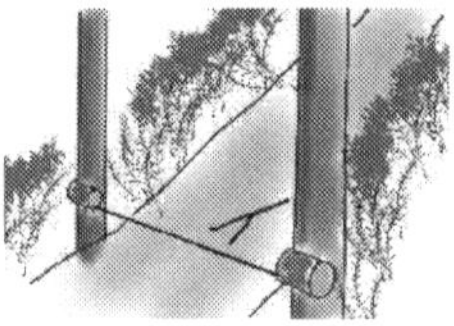

Components

丨 STICK[1] + 丶 DROP[3]

Mnemonics

A *divining rod*, as those used to *predict* where subterranean water is located. Let's pretend it *tells fortune*s as well.

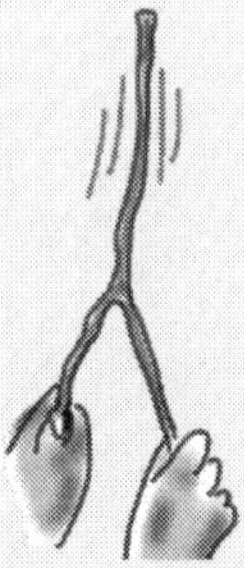

Story

A soldier comes upon something that looks like a STICK made of gold with an appendage at one extremity that seems to be spraying DROPS of some sort of liquid (a holy-water sprinkler or a *divining rod*?). He's about to pick it up when his comrade shouts, "Don't touch it! Our chief *predicted* we would come across **booby traps**!"

Examples

1. 占卜 (zhān bǔ) To practice divination. 胜败可卜 (shèng bài kě bǔ) Victory or defeat can be predicted.
2. 卜宅 (bǔ zhái) To choose a house. 卜居 (bǔ jū) To choose a dwelling place.

WANT A LITTLE MORE?

- As a building block, the second stroke is sometimes written perpendicular to the first.
- This character in fact represents a crack in a bone or a tortoise shell that was produced by heating it in a fire. The resulting cracks were interpreted and used for divination in ancient China.
- This is the 25th of the 214 Kangxi radicals.
- Usage frequency: Top third.

18B 卜

DEFINITION

Edible roots: carrots, turnips and *radishes.*

PRONUNCIATION

bo

SOUND WORD

Hobo

A person who has no place to live and no money and who travels to many different places.

(This character, with this definition, is pronounced in the neutral tone. Neutral tone characters use fourth-tone sound words)

COMPONENTS

卜 DIVINING ROD[18A] to PREDICT

STORY

A **hobo** is hungry and uses a DIVINING ROD at night to detect the presence of *edible roots* in various house gardens of the city.

EXAMPLES

萝卜 (luó bo) Radish, turnip. 红萝卜 (hóng luó bo) Carrot.

WANT A LITTLE MORE?

Usage frequency: Bottom third.

19

王

2nd

Definition

1. *King*.
2. *Surname*.

Pronunciation

wáng

Sound word

Wangler
As in Wrangler jeans, but pronounced by someone with a strong Asian accent.

Mnemonics

- This character is a pictogram of a *king*, with the three strokes representing the heaven, the humanity and the earth, joined by a vertical stroke. Hence, the *king*, who connects heaven, earth and man.
- *Zipper*.
  Let's add a memorable meaning and sometimes take this as the picture of a *zipper*.

Story

In the old days, the *king* was the only person allowed to wear **Wangler** jeans. Here, we have the proof: the *zipper* of a decomposed pair of jeans discovered lately in the tomb of an old *king*…

Examples

1. 王国 (wáng guó) Kingdom. 王室 (wáng shì) Royalty.

Want a little more?

- This is the most frequent Chinese surname (王先生: Mr. Wang).
- Usage frequency: Top 500.

20 # 主 3rd

DEFINITION

1. *Master*, *owner*, *lord*, *God*.
2. *Main*, *principal*.

PRONUNCIATION

zhǔ

SOUND WORD

Judeo-Christian
Term used to represent the common beliefs of Christianity and Judaism.

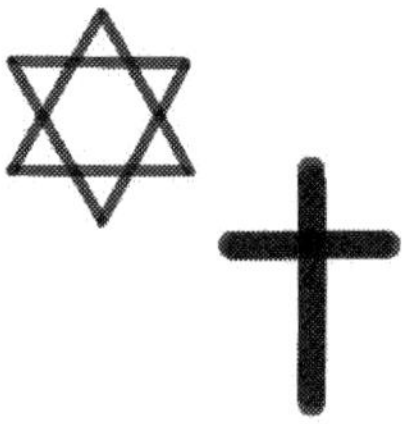

COMPONENTS

丶 DROP[3] + 王 KING[19]

MNEMONICS

The ancient form, , depicted a candle with flames rising above it, not unlike a *lord* rising above his subjects.

STORY

A momentous event in the history of France is when the first French KING, Clovis, was baptized on Christmas Day of the year 496 by having DROPS of water poured on his head to join the ranks of **Judeo-Christians** and believe, from that point on, in only one *master*, one *lord*, one *God*.

EXAMPLES

1. 主任(zhǔ rèn) Director, master, host. 主权(zhǔ quán) Sovereignty. 天主(tiān zhǔ) God (Catholicism).
2. 主旨 (zhǔ zhǐ) Main point.

WANT A LITTLE MORE?

Usage frequency: Top 100.

21

玉

4th

DEFINITION

Jade.

PRONUNCIATION

yù

SOUND WORD

Bahut /ba-y/
French word for 'sideboard', 'buffet'.

COMPONENTS

王 ZIPPER[19] KING + 丶 DROP[3]

MNEMONICS

The KING is so rich that he can afford to wear a precious *jade* on his ZIPPER.

STORY

During special ceremonies, the KING used to wear a special pair of pants with a ZIPPER equipped with a pull tab (the DROP) made of *jade*. When not in use, the pants were securely stowed away in the royal **bahut**.

EXAMPLES

宝玉(bǎo yù) Precious jade. 玉器(yù qì) Jadeware. 玉米(yù mǐ) Maize, corn (literally 'jade rice').

WANT A LITTLE MORE?

- This is the 96th of the 214 Kangxi radicals.
- Usage frequency: Top third.

22 入 4th

DEFINITION

1. To *enter*, *join*.
2. To *receive*; *income*.
3. To *conform with*, *agree with*.

PRONUNCIATION

rù

SOUND WORD

Kangaroo

MNEMONICS

This is the picture of a man extending his right leg to *enter* an area.

STORY

"Look at this funny guy, trying to *enter* the pouch of a **kangaroo**!"
"Yes, but I think he is about to *receive* a punch in the face from the marsupial!"
"I *agree with* you!"

EXAMPLES

1. 进入(jìn rù) To enter, get into.
2. 收入(shōu rù) Income.
3. 入时(rù shí) Fashionable.

WANT A LITTLE MORE?

- This is the 11th of the 214 Kangxi radicals.
- Usage frequency: Top 500.

23

人

2nd

DEFINITION

Person, *man*, *people*.

PRONUNCIATION

rén

SOUND WORD

Rent me

MNEMONICS

- This is the picture of a walking *person*. The ancient form, , looks like the letter R, which may help you remember its pronunciation.
- *Handyman*.
  To avoid confusion with all the *persons* appearing in the stories, it may help to imagine a special somebody who stands for that character. In the stories, such a *man* comes handy at times, someone who is willing to rent his services: a *handyman*. You may think of someone you know, like a *man* who is always there when you expect him the least, a know-it-all, a boastful, overzealous individual who sometimes gets on your nerves or who is bound to do stupid things, like the *handyman* here. Then, think of him when a *person* or a *man* of that nature is called for in the story.
- In most cases, it is written as 亻 on the left side of a character.

STORY

The *handyman* is so eager to help other *persons* that he walks in the streets wearing a sign around his neck that says, '**Rent me**!'

EXAMPLES

男人(nán rén) Man. 女人(nǔ rén) Woman. 个人(gè rén) Individual person. 人民(rén mín) The people.

WANT A LITTLE MORE?

- It is used as a building block in some 340 characters.
- Learn to distinguish it from 入 ENTER[22], where the right stroke is longer than the left.
- This is the 9th of the 214 Kangxi radicals.
- It is one of the top ten characters in frequency of use.

24 内[內] 4th

DEFINITION

Interior; *inside*, *inner*, *internal*, *within*.

PRONUNCIATION

nèi

SOUND WORD

Prigione /pridʒone/
Italian word for 'prison.'

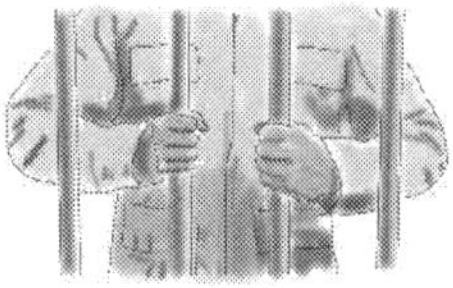

SIMPLIFIED COMPONENTS

人 MAN23 + 冂 CAGE12 LONG COVER

TRADITIONAL COMPONENTS

[入 to ENTER22 + CAGE]

MNEMONICS

A MAN *inside* or ENTERING a CAGE.

STORY

In an Italian family, the father says to his children, "My dear children, for the next two years, for a trifle matter, your papa will live *inside* and stay in the *interior* of a big CAGE with other MEN."

[His wife interrupts him. "Stop beating around the bush!" Turning towards her children, she says, "Your dad will ENTER a state **prigione** today!"]

EXAMPLES

内部(nèi bù) Inside, internal, interior. 内战(nèi zhàn) Civil war.
内脏(nèi zàng) Internal organs.

WANT A LITTLE MORE?

- Note the subtle difference between the simplified and the traditional character.
- Usage frequency: Top 500.

25

丙

3rd

DEFINITION

Third in sequence.

† Fish tail.

PRONUNCIATION

bǐng

SOUND WORD

Bingo night
An evening of bingo!

COMPONENTS

一 CEILING[15] ONE + 内 INTERIOR[24]

MNEMONICS

It looks like a flower pot hanging from the CEILING.

STORY

For the *third* **bingo night** in a row, the *third* prize is an INTERIOR flower pot designed to be hung at the CEILING.

EXAMPLES

丙等 (bǐng děng) Third rank. 丙级 (bǐng jí) Third grade.

WANT A LITTLE MORE?

- This is the 3rd heavenly stem.
- Usage frequency: Middle third.

26 **女** 3rd

DEFINITION

Woman.

PRONUNCIATION

nǚ

SOUND WORD

Nudité /nydite/
French word for 'nudity.'

MNEMONICS

- The ancient form, , depicted a person with breasts.
- View the modern form of this character as a *woman* standing with arms akimbo and legs crossed.

STORY

In the paintings of the Renaissance depicting *women*, there was a lot of **nudité**.

EXAMPLES

女人 (nǚ rén) Woman. 女儿(nǚ ér) Daughter, girl.

WANT A LITTLE MORE?

- This is the 38th of the 214 Kangxi radicals.
- Usage frequency: Top 500.

27 # 大 4th

DEFINITION

1. *Big, large, great.*
2. *Heavy, strong.*
3. *Loud.*
4. *Main, major, on a large scale.*

PRONUNCIATION

dà

SOUND WORD

Canada

MNEMONICS

- This is the picture of a 人 MAN[23] with his two arms stretched sideways to appear *big*.
- *Great Dane*.
  One of the Chinese characters for DOG[29], 犬, contains, in *large* part, this building block (plus an extra DOT[3]). To create a better mnemonic, the stories where this building block appears sometimes use the additional meaning of a *big, great* dog: A *Great Dane*. For some of you, it may help to picture a famous *Great Dane* like the cartoon character Scooby-Doo.
- As another visual aid for the connection with dog, if you look at the map of **Canada**, the right part (the province of Quebec) looks like the head of a dog seen sideways and facing East.

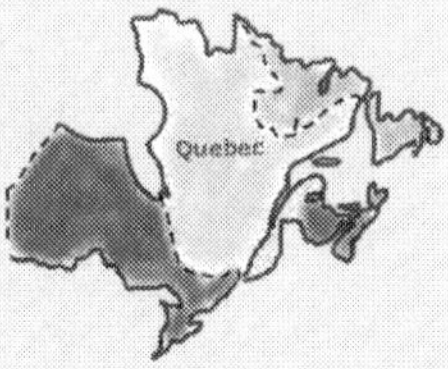

STORY

Canada is a *big* country!

EXAMPLES

1. 大人(dà rén) Adult. 大学(dà xué) University.
2. 大雨(dà yǔ) Heavy rain. 大风(dà fēng) Strong wind.
3. 大声 (dà shēng) Loud voice.
4. 大马路(dà mǎ lù) Main street. 大家(dà jiā) Everyone.

WANT A LITTLE MORE?

- This is the 37th of the 214 Kangxi radicals.
- Usage frequency: Top 100.

28 丈 4th

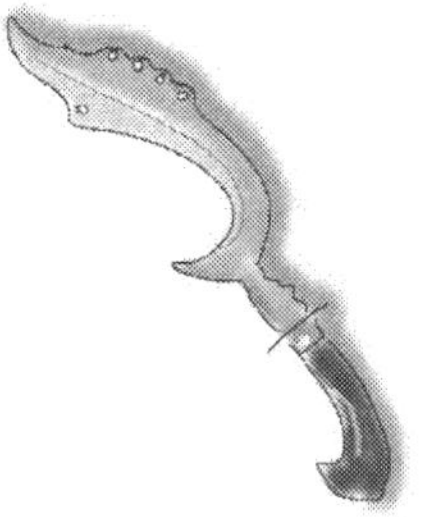

DEFINITION

1. *Elderly, old man; husband.*
2. *Unit of length of about ten feet* (3 1/3 meters); to *measure land.*

PRONUNCIATION

zhàng

SOUND WORD

Kujang
A weapon that originated in Western Java.

MNEMONICS

Limping man.

It looks like a 大 BIG[27] *old man* whose hips have given out, hence a *limping man.* This fictitious meaning will help you differentiate this character from all the other Chinese characters that mean *elderly* or *old.*

STORY

An *elderly, limping man* goes see a doctor.
"Doctor, my hips make me suffer!"
"OK, take off your pants."
"Alright, but I first need to remove the **kujang** attached to my belt."
He then pulls out a *ten-foot*-long **kujang**.
The doctor says, "No wonder your hips have given out!"

EXAMPLES

1. 丈人(zhàng rén) Respectful address for an elderly man.
   丈夫(zhàng fu) Husband. (The dotted line under fū indicates that while normally in the first tone, it is pronounced in the neutral tone in this word)
2. 丈量(zhàng liáng) To measure land.

WANT A LITTLE MORE?

- A long time ago (around 200 BC), this character used to be written , showing a hand holding a cross (nowadays, a cross symbol still represents number 10). Hence, a measurement of 10 Chinese feet.
- Usage frequency: Top third.

29 # 犬 3rd

DEFINITION

Dog.

PRONUNCIATION

quǎn

SOUND WORD

Tuant /tyɑ̃/
French verb for 'killing,' by aiming horizontally. (See 'Special Sound Mnemonics,' page 490)

COMPONENTS

大 BIG[27] + 丶 BULLET[3] DROP

MNEMONICS

- *Pit bull, wild dog.*
  For this book, let's consider the *pit bull* like some sort of ferocious *wild dog* (even though the jury is still out on whether *pit bulls* are dangerous dogs). Therefore, the BIG building block here does not stand for a gentle Great Dane but rather for a BIG bad *dog.*
- In the story, the DROP building block stands for a BULLET, a very small thing indeed. It will help you tell the difference between a gentle *dog* and a fierce *dog.*
- This character is often written 犭 when used as a building block.

STORY

A BIG *pit bull* just attacked a man who was armed. The man pulled out his gun, aimed horizontally and shot a BULLET in the *dog*'s head, **tuant** doggie instantly.

EXAMPLES

獒犬 (áo quǎn) Fierce dog. 警犬 (jǐng quǎn) Police dog.

WANT A LITTLE MORE?

- This is the 94th of the 214 Kangxi radicals.
- Usage frequency: Middle third.

30 太 4th

DEFINITION

1. *Excessively, extremely, too.*
2. *Married woman, wife.*

PRONUNCIATION

tài

SOUND WORD

Entaille /ɑ̃taj/
French word for 'notch,' 'gash' made in an object, or a 'tap hole' in a maple tree to gather the maple water.

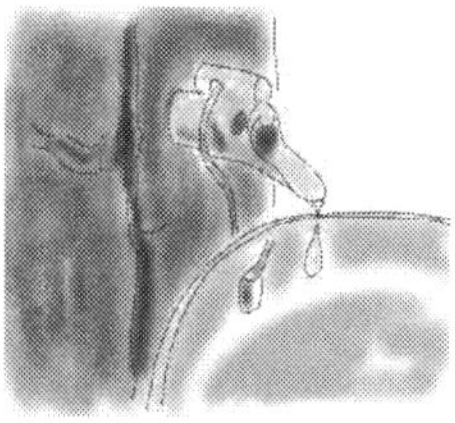

COMPONENTS

大 GREAT DANE[27] BIG + 丶 GASH[3] DROP

MNEMONICS

- You take the 大 BIG[27] character, to which you add a stroke below its left leg, making it *excessively* big.
- In the story, GREAT DANE substitutes for BIG[27] and GASH (another small thing) substitutes for DROP[3]. The position of the DROP building block in the character may remind someone of a GASH made in a pair of pants.

STORY

"Your *wife*'s GREAT DANE is *excessively* excited and the last time I saw him, he jumped on me and left a big GASH, an **entaille** in my pants!"

EXAMPLES

1. 太大了 (tài dà le) Too big. 太多了 (tài duō le) Too much. 太阳 (tài yáng) Sun.
2. 太太 (tài tài) Wife, Mrs.

WANT A LITTLE MORE?

- Not to be confused with the character for 犬 DOG[29]. The position of the DROP building block makes a world of difference.
- Usage frequency: Top 500.

31

天

1st

DEFINITION

1. *Heaven*, *sky*; *heavenly*.
2. *Day*.
3. *Weather*.

PRONUNCIATION

tiān

SOUND WORD

Tienne /tjɛn/
French word for 'yours,' feminine gender: 'la tienne.'

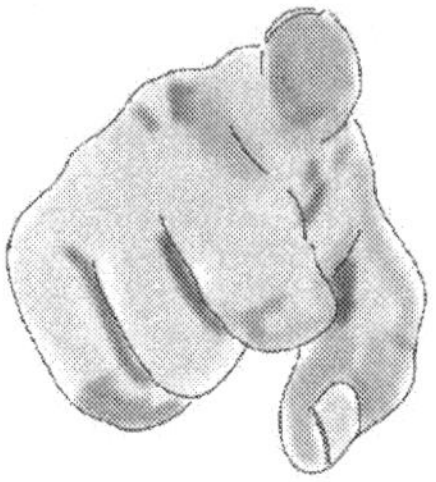

COMPONENTS

一 ONE[15] + 大 BIG[27]

MNEMONICS

This character depicts a BIG man living under the *sky* (the top horizontal stroke). Ancient form: .

STORY

ONE *day*, the *sky* opens up and I hear ONE BIG *heavenly* voice that says, "Your end is near and you'll soon come meet me in *heaven*!"
I ask, "God, whose life are you talking about exactly?"
"Pardon my French, but la **tienne**!" replies God.

EXAMPLES

1. 天文 (tiān wén) Astronomy.
2. 今天 (jīn tiān) Today.
3. 天气(tiān qì) Weather.

WANT A LITTLE MORE?

Usage frequency: Top 100.

32 夭 1st

DEFINITION

1. To <u>*die young*</u>, *prematurely.*
2. *Tender, young; graceful, supple.*

PRONUNCIATION

yāo

SOUND WORD

<u>Yao</u>urt/jauʁt/
French word for 'yogourt,' pronounced as one syllable.

COMPONENTS

丿 DOG COLLAR[4] left-falling stroke + 大 GREAT DANE[27] BIG

MNEMONICS

- Around 200 BC, this character was written , showing a man bowing his head, lacking energy.
- In the story, the left-falling stroke stands for a DOG COLLAR.

STORY

My GREAT DANE puppy enjoyed eating **yaourt** so much that when he tried to reach the fridge while I was away, he broke his *tender* neck with his DOG COLLAR and *died young.*

EXAMPLES

1. 夭亡 (yāo wáng) To die young.
2. 夭矫 (yāo jiǎo) Lithe, graceful, supple.

WANT A LITTLE MORE?

- Not to be confused with the character for 天 HEAVEN[31]. While the top building block for heaven is a horizontal line drawn from left to right, the first stroke here is slanting and drawn from right to left.
- Usage frequency: Middle third.

33

夫

1st

DEFINITION

Husband, *man*.

PRONUNCIATION

fū

SOUND WORD

Fool

COMPONENTS

一 ONE[15] + 大 BIG[27]

MNEMONICS

This is the picture of a grown *man*. In ancient China, grown *men* and officials used to wear their hair held up by a pin (ancient form: ), which is represented by the first stroke, the ONE building block in this character.

STORY

Her *husband* had just been promoted to a management position in a Chinese company. The following morning, she saw him leave for work with ONE BIG pin in his hair.

"Where are you going with your hair like that?"
"I am a *man* of power now. I need to show my employees who's the boss!"
After a moment, she said, "Please, don't make a **fool** of yourself!"

EXAMPLES

丈夫 (zhàng fū) Husband. 大夫 (dà fū) Senior official.

WANT A LITTLE MORE?

- This character is formed with the same components as the character 天 HEAVEN[31]. However, the ONE building block is not at the top of BIG but slightly lower, traversing its top part.
- Usage frequency: Top 500.

34 丰

DEFINITION

Non-character used only as a building block.

PRONUNCIATION

Not applicable

SOUND WORD

Not applicable

MNEMONICS

Telephone pole.

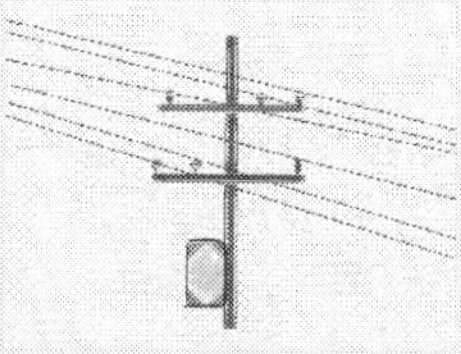

A variant of this building block is written 丰, with an extra hook on the left. In that case, it represents either the transformer (the cylinder shown on the drawing) or something/somebody hanging from the *telephone pole* in the stories.

35 牛 2nd

DEFINITION

1. *Cow, ox, bull.*
2. *Awesome* (slang).

PRONUNCIATION

niú

SOUND WORD

Neopharm
A fictitious corporation doing genetic research on farm animals.

MNEMONICS

- This is a pictogram of a *cow*, with a spine in the middle and horns on top. Ancient form: .
- Although it is probably better to learn the character as a whole, some of you may prefer to decompose it into 丶 DROP[3] + 𠂉 TELEPHONE POLE[34] and then picture a *cow* (the DROP) not wanting to be milked and trying to escape by climbing a TELEPHONE POLE…
- This character is written ⺧ or 牜 when used as a building block.

STORY

"The **Neopharm** corporation is doing genetic research on *cows* to improve their daily milk production."
"But, this is *awesome*!"

EXAMPLES

1. 牛奶(niú nǎi) Cow's milk. 放牛(fàng niú) To herd cattle.
2. 你真牛(nǐ zhēn niú) You're awesome!

WANT A LITTLE MORE?

- Learn to distinguish from the variant for 𠂉 TELEPHONE POLE[34]. The hook is not located on the same horizontal line.
- This is the 93rd of the 214 Kangxi radicals.
- Usage frequency: Top third.

36

马[馬]

3rd

DEFINITION

1. *Horse.*
2. *Surname.*

PRONUNCIATION

mǎ

SOUND WORD

Marathon
It is about horse marathons in this book…

MNEMONICS

This is the picture of a *horse*. Ancient form: .

STORY

At the end of the Boston *Horse* **Marathon** this year, the winner of the race fell from his *horse* and laid on the ground, extenuated and panting, while his *horse* looked at him with a strange look that seemed to say, “Yeah right, you’re the one doing the hard work around here!”

EXAMPLES

1. 骑马 (qí mǎ) To ride a horse. 马上 (mǎ shàng) At once, right away. 马路 (mǎ lù) Road, street. 马车 (mǎ chē) Horse-drawn cart.

WANT A LITTLE MORE?

- It ranks amongst the top 100 Chinese surnames.
- This is the 187th of the 214 Kangxi radicals.
- Usage frequency: Top 500.

37 # 羊 2nd

DEFINITION

1. *Sheep*.
2. *Surname*.

PRONUNCIATION

yáng

SOUND WORD

Yankee
Let's picture an American farmer from the North.

MNEMONICS

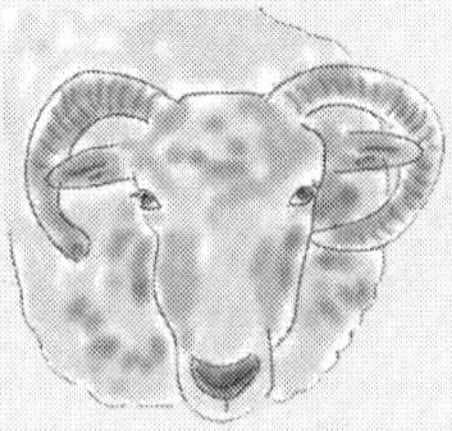

- This is a picture of a *sheep* head, with the horns at the top. Ancient form: 羊.
- *Running sheep, jumping sheep*.
  This character may also appear bent sideways, like this: ⺶ when used as a building block. In that case, it will mean a *sheep* in motion, i.e. a *running sheep* or a *jumping sheep*.
- The tail may also be missing when this character is used as a building block, appearing like this: ⺷.

STORY

"Look at this **Yankee**! He calls himself a cowboy but he raises only *sheep*!"

EXAMPLES

1. 放羊(fàng yáng) To herd sheep. 羊毛(yáng máo) Wool.

WANT A LITTLE MORE?

- This is the 123rd of the 214 Kangxi radicals.
- Usage frequency: Top third.

38

豕

3rd

DEFINITION

Boar, pig, sow, hog, swine.

PRONUNCIATION

shǐ

SOUND WORD

Shish kebab
Pieces of meat and vegetables pushed on a skewer and cooked on a grill.

MNEMONICS

This is a pictogram of a *boar*. Ancient form: .

STORY

"For me, *boar* or *pig* meat makes the best **shish kebabs**."

EXAMPLES

豕牢 (shǐ láo) Pigsty, pigpen. 夜豕 (yě shǐ) Wild boar.

WANT A LITTLE MORE?

- This is the 152nd of the 214 Kangxi radicals.
- Usage frequency: Bottom third.

39 彐 4th

DEFINITION

† Pig snout.

PRONUNCIATION

jì

SOUND WORD

Fiji
The **Fiji** Islands. A paradise which comprises an archipelago of small islands northeast of New Zealand.

MNEMONICS

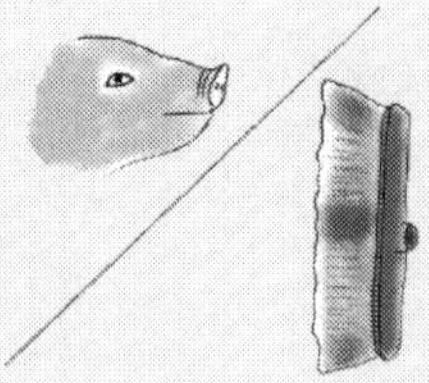

- This character looks like a *pig snout*, seen from the side. Although the meaning of *pig snout* is obsolete, it is still used in this book when this character serves as a building block.
- *Broom head, hand broom.*
  It may also represent the head of a regular broom. Therefore, a *broom head* or a *hand broom*, made with the bristles of a *pig snout*.
- The variant 彑 is also seen in some traditional characters.

STORY

In **Fiji**, they still make *broom heads* with the bristles of *pig snouts*.

WANT A LITTLE MORE?

This is the 58th of the 214 Kangxi radicals.

40	屮	4th

DEFINITION

Blade of grass, sprout.

PRONUNCIATION

chè

SOUND WORD

Satchel
A small bag with a strap that is carried over the shoulder.

MNEMONICS

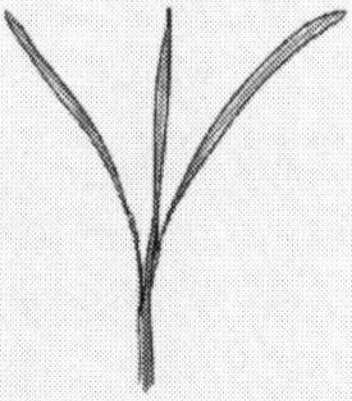

- This is a pictogram of a *blade of grass*, of a *sprout*.
- *Pitchfork*.
  It also stands for a *pitchfork* in this book because of its shape and its function as a tool to pick up dried *blades of grass* or hay.
- This character sometimes appears sideways, like this: . Not to be confused with 彐 PIG SNOUT[39].
  Also, the bottom stem of this character may appear bent to the left or to the right, like this: .

STORY

"I was picking up *blades of grass* with a *pitchfork* when I discovered under the pile a **satchel** full of hay (money)!"

WANT A LITTLE MORE?

This is the 45th of the 214 Kangxi radicals.

41

口

3rd

Definition

1. *Mouth*.
2. All sorts of *openings* or *orifices*, like a *window*, a door or an empty space that you can go through.
3. Measure word for *people*, for *objects with an opening*, for *mouthfuls*.

Pronunciation

kǒu

Sound word

Coca-Cola

Mnemonics

This character looks the part, i.e. like an open *mouth*.

Story

A young guy pours the content of a **Coca-Cola** bottle in his *mouth*.

Examples

1. 开口 (kāi kǒu) To open one's mouth. 可口可乐 (kě kǒu kě lè) Coca-Cola.
2. 瓶口 (píng kǒu) Mouth, orifice of a bottle. 门口 (mén kǒu) Doorway. 山口 (shān kǒu) Mountain pass.
3. 四口人 (sì kǒu rén) Four persons.

Want a little more?

- This is the 30th of the 214 Kangxi radicals.
- Usage frequency: Top 500.

42 囗 2nd

DEFINITION

Enclosure; to *confine*, *frame*, *encircle*, *surround*, *enclose*.

PRONUNCIATION

wéi

SOUND WORD

Weight bar

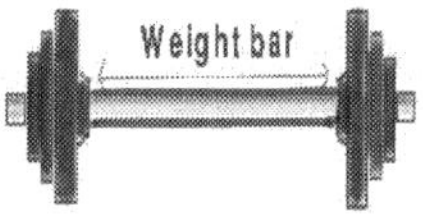

MNEMONICS

- This represents a big frame that *encircles* or contains other building blocks.
- A **weight bar** is always *framed* by weights at both extremities.
- You can also view this character as the transversal cut of a square **weight bar**.

WANT A LITTLE MORE?

- An important difference with the similar-looking character 口 for MOUTH[41] is that this character can contain or *encircle* other building blocks while the character for mouth does not.
- This is the 31st of the 214 Kangxi radicals.

43 日 4th

DEFINITION

Sun; *day*.

PRONUNCIATION

rì

SOUND WORD

Lavage /lavaʒ/
French word for the action of washing, namely clothes.

MNEMONICS

- Pictogram of the *sun*, with the middle line representing the concentrated energy in the center of the *sun*. Its ancient form was more rounded and written θ.
- By extension, it also means *day* because the sun appears during the *day*.

STORY

"Today is Sunday and the *sun* is shining. I'm going to do the **lavage** as it is a good *day* for washing clothes."

EXAMPLES

日光 (rì guāng) Sunlight. 日本(rì běn) Japan (literally 'origin of the sun,' i.e. East of China, where the sun is rising). 生日 (shēng rì) Birthday.

WANT A LITTLE MORE?

- As a building block, this character often appears squished vertically and looks like the next character 曰.
- This is the 72nd of the 214 Kangxi radicals.
- Usage frequency: Top 500.

44

曰

1st

DEFINITION

To *speak*, *say*, *talk* (literary).

PRONUNCIATION

yuē

SOUND WORD

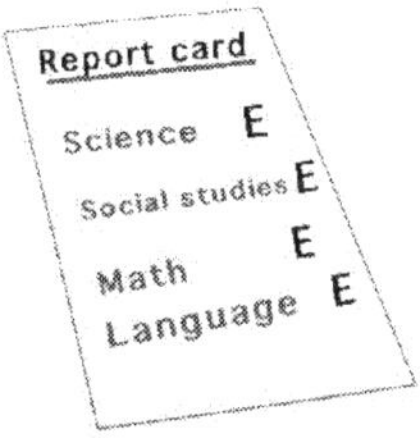

Eu E /y ə/
French expression, as in 'Il a **eu E**': 'He's got an E' on his report card, pronounced as one syllable. (See 'Special Sound Mnemonics,' page 493)

MNEMONICS

Speaking mouth, because it looks like a tongue wiggling in the 口 MOUTH[41].

STORY

"Because he let loose his *speaking mouth* and never stopped *talking* in class, his report card shows that 'il a **eu E**' for French and he's got an E for behavior."

EXAMPLES

子曰 (zǐ yuē) Confucius says… 故曰 (gù yuē) This is why we say…

WANT A LITTLE MORE?

- This character is easily confused with the character 日 for SUN or DAY[43]. When both characters appear on their own, this one here is wider and less tall.
- This is the 73rd of the 214 Kangxi radicals.
- Usage frequency: Top third.

45 白 2nd

DEFINITION

1. *White*.
2. *Easy to understand, clear, plain, obvious.*
3. *In vain, for nothing; free of charge.*

PRONUNCIATION

bái

SOUND WORD

Buyer

COMPONENTS

丶 DROP[3] + 日 SUN[43]

MNEMONICS

Picture the little dot at the top of the character as a *white* DROP of SUN. It will make it *easy to understand.*

STORY

An original new ad for detergent **buyers** says, "This new detergent, 'A DROP of SUN', will make your clothes whiter than *white*. The difference will be *obvious* to you when you look at the results. Now offered in a new package, with 25% more detergent, *free of charge*."

EXAMPLES

1. 雪白 (xuě bái) Snowy white. 白面 (bái miàn) White flour. 白天 (bái tiān) Daytime.
2. 白话 (bái huà) Vernacular language, colloquial speech.
3. 白送 (bái sòng) To be given free of charge.

WANT A LITTLE MORE?

- It ranks amongst the top 100 Chinese surnames.
- Here is an example where the SUN building block appears squished vertically.
- This is the 106th of the 214 Kangxi radicals.
- Usage frequency: Top 500.

46

臼

4th

DEFINITION

<u>*Mortar*</u>; <u>*mortar-shaped*</u>.

PRONUNCIATION

jiù

SOUND WORD

<u>Villaggio</u> /villaddʒɔ/
Italian word for 'village.' Think of an old Italian **villaggio**.

MNEMONICS

Ashtray.
This character can represent any *mortar-shaped* thing. Why not an *ashtray*? Just replace the pestle with a cigarette…

STORY

After crushing grains in his *mortar* all day, the old Italian baker, who lived all his life in the **villaggio**, smokes a cigarette at the front of his bakery and crushes his cigarette butt in a *mortar-shaped ashtray*.

EXAMPLES

杵臼 (chǔ jiù) Mortar and pestle. 石臼 (shí jiù) Stone mortar. 臼齿 (jiù chǐ) Molar (mortar-shaped tooth).

WANT A LITTLE MORE?

- This depicts a *mortar* to crush something in, not mortar used in masonry or mortar used as a weapon.
- This is the 134th of the 214 Kangxi radicals.
- Usage frequency: Bottom third.

47 # 月 4th

DEFINITION

Month; *moon*.

PRONUNCIATION

yuè

SOUND WORD

Feuillu-e /fœjy/
French word for 'leafy, deciduous.' Just add an extra French 'e' sound (ə) in your mind at the end of the sound word. (See 'Special Sound Mnemonics,' page 493)

MNEMONICS

- This is a stylized pictogram of the crescent moon, which has evolved from its ancient form: .
- It is also written  when used as a building block.

STORY

"Look at the spring *moon*. By the end of the *month*, all the leaves should have grown back and the tree in our backyard will be **feuillu-e** again!"

EXAMPLES

月亮 (yuè liàng) Moon. 二月 (èr yuè) February. 上个月 (shàng ge yuè) Last month.

WANT A LITTLE MORE?

- This is the 74th of the 214 Kangxi radicals.
- Usage frequency: Top 500.

48 **肉** 4th

Definition

Meat, flesh, muscle.

Pronunciation

ròu

Sound word

Death row

Components

冂 CAGE[12] LONG COVER + 2 x 人 PERSON[23]

Mnemonics

- *Body part.*
  The original meaning is extended to *body part* for more colorful stories…
- When you're on **death row**, you're dead *meat*…
- The character can also be seen as a rib CAGE.
- It is often written exactly like the MOON[47] character, 月 or ⺼, when used as a building block.

Story

"News flash! The two PERSONS on **death row** escaped from their 'CAGES' and ran into the jungle, but they finished as dead *meat* inside the rib CAGE of a tiger…"

Examples

鸡肉 (jī ròu) Chicken meat. 肌肉 (jī ròu) Muscle.

Want a little more?

- This is the 130th of the 214 Kangxi radicals.
- Usage frequency: Top third.

49	亠	2nd

DEFINITION

† Lid.

PRONUNCIATION

tóu

SOUND WORD

Toro /toro/
Spanish word for 'fighting bull.'

MNEMONICS

- *Cowboy hat, witch hat*, because of its shape.
- Imagine a man wearing a *cowboy hat* and riding a **toro** during a rodeo.

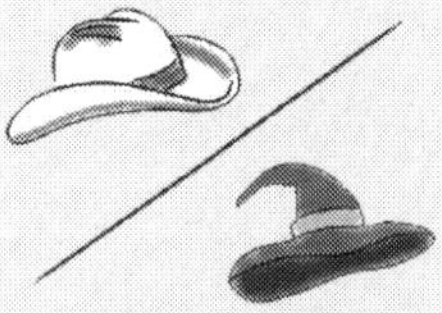

WANT A LITTLE MORE?

This is the 8th of the 214 Kangxi radicals.

50 宀 2nd

DEFINITION

House, *roof*.

PRONUNCIATION

mián

SOUND WORD

Mi-aine slip /miɛn slip/

A made-up French expression for a woman's underwear that ends at the groin. (See 'Special Sound Mnemonics,' page 487)

MNEMONICS

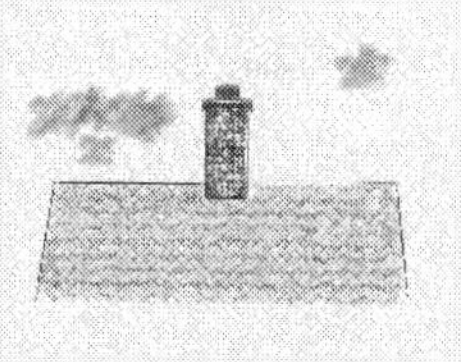

Pictogram of a *roof* 冖 COVER[11] and a chimney (the 丶 DROP[3] building block) at the top. Its ancient form, 宀, really looked the part.

STORY

Only in our own *house*, under our own *roof* are we usually willing to walk in our **mi-aine slip**.

WANT A LITTLE MORE?

This is the 40th of the 214 Kangxi radicals.

51 **亡** 2nd

DEFINITION

1. To *die*, *perish*; *deceased*.
2. To *flee*.
3. To *lose*.

PRONUNCIATION

wáng

SOUND WORD

Wangler
As in Wrangler jeans, but pronounced by someone with a strong Asian accent.

COMPONENTS

亠 COWBOY HAT[49] + ㄴ CORNER[6]

STORY

A COWBOY HAT hanging on a hook in a CORNER, above a pair of **Wangler** jeans, right where the *deceased* left it the day he *died* after *fleeing* the ward and getting *lost* in the woods, reminds us of him and his dirty pants.

EXAMPLES

1. 死亡 (sǐ wáng) To die; death. 存亡 (cún wáng) To survive or perish.
2. 出亡 (chū wáng) To flee one's country.
3. 亡失 (wáng shī) To lose, be missing.

WANT A LITTLE MORE?

Usage frequency: Top third.

52

儿[兒]

2nd

Definition

1. *Child, son, daughter, youngster.*
2. *Noun suffix* (Beijing dialect).

Pronunciation

ér

Sound word

Army

Traditional components

[臼 MORTAR-SHAPED[46] + *walking legs*]

Mnemonics

- *Walking legs, human legs.*
  The simplified character represents the legs of a *child* making his first steps, hence *walking legs* or *human legs.*
- The traditional character can be viewed as a MORTAR-SHAPED head with the fontanels not yet closed on top of *walking legs*. This is a very close representation of its ancient form: 兒.

Story

A minister says to his king, "Our enemy seems to be running out of men. They are sending an **army** of *children* and *youngsters* to attack our castle. All we can see are their *walking legs* under an oversized coat of mail.

["Some of them are very young too and are not wearing a helmet. We can still see their MORTAR-SHAPED heads (with fontanels not yet closed) on top of their *human legs*!"]

Examples

1. 儿子 (ér zǐ) Son. 女儿 (nǚ ér) Daughter.
2. 这儿(zhè ér) Here. 一点儿(yì diǎn ér) A little.

Want a little more?

- This is the 10th of the 214 Kangxi radicals.
- Usage frequency: Top 500.

53

四

4th

DEFINITION

Four.

PRONUNCIATION

sì

SOUND WORD

Confessor
A priest who listens to a person's confession in a confessional.

COMPONENTS

口 ENCLOSURE42 + 儿 HUMAN LEGS52 child

MNEMONICS

A pair of HUMAN LEGS sticking out from under the curtain inside the ENCLOSURE of a confessional equipped with *four* booths. See story.

STORY

This **confessor** is quite speedy and can tackle *four* penitents at the same time. So, they built him a confessional with *four* booths instead of two. You can see the HUMAN LEGS of the penitents in the ENCLOSURE of each bay, appearing under the curtain.

EXAMPLES

四肢 (sì zhī) Four limbs. 四月 (sì yuè) April.

WANT A LITTLE MORE?

- Because this character sounds like the character for death, 死(sǐ), Chinese people try to avoid this number at all costs. In fact, many buildings in China do not have a fourth floor. And if your phone number happens to be 444-4444, well, we wish you good luck!
- Usage frequency: Top 500.

54 五 3rd

DEFINITION

Five.

PRONUNCIATION

wǔ

SOUND WORD

Woolahoop
A special flexible hoop (made of wool) that you twirl around the waist. A variant of the Hula hoop.

MNEMONICS

The character looks like a person under a ceiling, standing on two legs in the center of a **woolahoop** lying on the floor, ready to pick it up and start twirling.

STORY

"This person is a star of the **woolahoop**! She can twirl non-stop for *five* hours straight! That's got to be a world record!"

EXAMPLES

五金 (wǔ jīn) Five principal metals (gold, silver, copper, tin, iron). 五行 (wǔ xíng) Five primary elements. 五角 (wǔ jiǎo) Pentagon. 五月 (wǔ yuè) May.

WANT A LITTLE MORE?

- The ancient character  showed the interconnection between heaven and earth (the two horizontal lines). The X in the middle represented the *five* primary elements composing the physical universe according to the ancients, that is, metal, wood, water, fire and earth.
- Usage frequency: Top 500.

55

八

1st

DEFINITION

1. *Eight*.
2. *All around*, *abundance*.

† To *separate*, *divide in half*.

PRONUNCIATION

bā

SOUND WORD

Bas /ba/
French word for 'sock.'

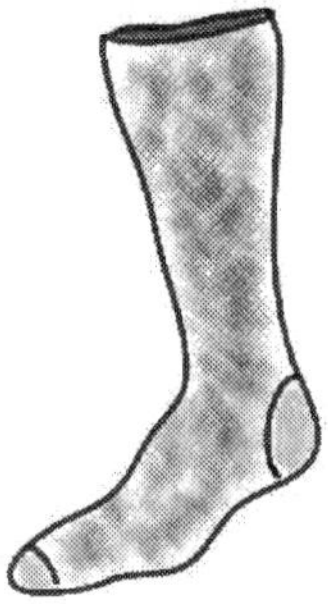

MNEMONICS

- This character's ancient definition was to *separate*, to *divide in half*. Ancient form:)(. This meaning is often apparent in other characters and will be used as one of its building block values.
- *Octopus*.
  We give it the concrete meaning of *octopus* in some of the stories because an *octopus* has *eight* limbs or legs. As a matter of fact, in Chinese, *octopus* is written with this character (see example).
- As a building block, it often appears written as two short legs, like this: 丿丶.
- *Horns*, *horny*, *devilish*.

  As a building block, it is also written 丷 and appears as such at the top of a character. In that case, it may also mean *horns*, *horny* or *devilish* because of its resemblance to a pair of *horns*.

STORY

The *octopus*'s budget for **bas** is way too high. It needs an *abundance* of money because it needs to buy *eight* socks every time.

EXAMPLES

1. 八带鱼 (bā dài yú) Octopus. 八月 (bā yuè) August.
2. 八方 (bā fāng) Eight points of the compass, all directions.
   七嘴八舌 (qī zuǐ bā shé) To talk all at the same time (an abundance of speakers).

WANT A LITTLE MORE?

- Apart from representing the number 8, this character also has the connotation of *all around*, all sides, all-encompassing. Therefore, it is often associated with *abundance* and is considered a lucky number by the Chinese. The opening ceremony of the Summer Olympics Games in Beijing was held on August 8, 2008 (08/8/8), at 8:08 pm!
- This is the 12th of the 214 Kangxi radicals.
- Usage frequency: Top 500.

56

六

4th

DEFINITION

Six.

PRONUNCIATION

liù

SOUND WORD

Bagaglio /bagalio/
Italian word for 'luggage.'

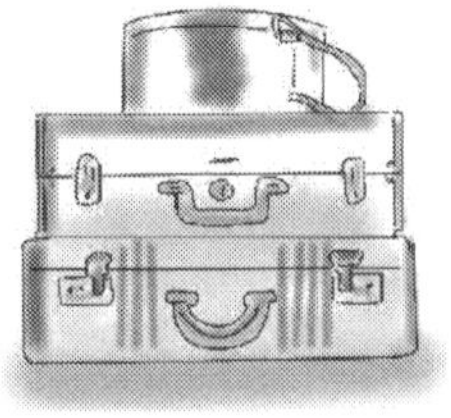

COMPONENTS

亠 COWBOY HAT[49] + 八 OCTOPUS[55] EIGHT

MNEMONICS

Picture a circus performer wearing a COWBOY HAT and walking with *six* suitcases in his extended arms. The ancient form, , even looks like a person carrying stuff.

STORY

This circus performer always carries with him *six* pieces of **bagaglio** on the road. In the big **bagaglio**, he keeps an OCTOPUS and in a small one, a COWBOY HAT. During his act, he makes the OCTOPUS dance on *six* legs and hold the COWBOY HAT over its head with the other two legs while singing, 'Hello, Dolly!'

EXAMPLES

六陈 (liù chén) The six types of grains (rice, wheat, barley, small bean, sesame, soybean). 六月 (liù yuè) June.

WANT A LITTLE MORE?

Usage frequency: Top 500.

57 七 1st

DEFINITION

Seven.

† To *chop*, *cut*.

PRONUNCIATION

qī

SOUND WORD

Cheek

MNEMONICS

- View it as an upside-down number 7 (with a transverse line as some of us write it).
- The original meaning of this character was to *cut* or *chop*, clearly shown by the first stroke *cutting* through the second.

STORY

"My young son went to visit his aunt. She pinched his **cheek** so hard that she *cut* his skin and he needed *seven* stitches!"

EXAMPLES

七月 (qī yuè) July. 七上八下 (qī shàng bā xià) To feel worried.

WANT A LITTLE MORE?

Usage frequency: Top third.

58

九

3rd

DEFINITION

Nine.

PRONUNCIATION

jiǔ

SOUND WORD

The old lady
Let's picture a very old lady here. (See 'Special Sound Mnemonics,' page 485)

MNEMONICS

- *Baseball*.
  We give it the meaning of *baseball* in some of the stories because a *baseball* team has 9 players on the field and a regular game counts 9 innings.
- Its ancient shape, , looks like a man getting ready to throw a ball.
- You can also view the character as a fancy letter 'n', for *nine*.

STORY

The old lady, a bit senile, insists to be part of a young *baseball* team. "I'm a *nine*-year-old girl! Why can't I play?" she asks.

EXAMPLES

九月 (jiǔ yuè) September. 明天九点 (míng tiān jiǔ diǎn) At 9 o'clock tomorrow.

WANT A LITTLE MORE?

Usage frequency: Top 500.

59 十 2nd

DEFINITION

1. *Ten.*
2. *Complete; perfect.*

PRONUNCIATION

shí

SOUND WORD

Sherpa
An ethnic group living in the Himalayas. They are often used as guides and porters during climbing expeditions.

MNEMONICS

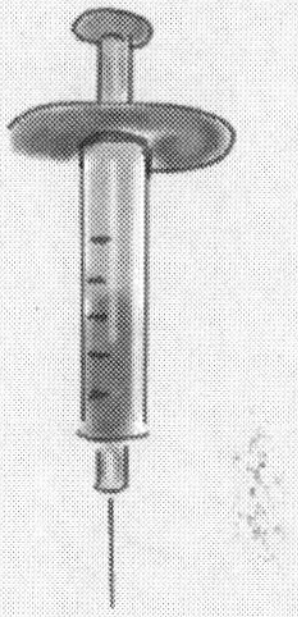

- *Cross*, because of its appearance.
- *Needle*, because of its resemblance with a syringe.
- You can also picture this as the letter 't,' for *ten*.
- Its ancient form, 十, looks identical to the modern form: a *complete, perfect ten*.

STORY

Once the first part of the climb is *complete*, the **Sherpa** and his *ten* aspiring climbers all mark a pause at the base of the big *cross*.

EXAMPLES

1. 十个人(shí ge rén) Ten people.
2. 十分(shí fēn) Fully, completely, entirely.

WANT A LITTLE MORE?

- This is the 24th of the 214 Kangxi radicals.
- Usage frequency: Top 500.

60 廿 4th

DEFINITION

Twenty.

PRONUNCIATION

niàn

SOUND WORD

Non-Darwinian

Let's picture a person whose intelligence defies the theories of evolution and the survival of the fittest…

COMPONENTS

2 x ~十 TEN[59]

MNEMONICS

It is basically two TEN merged together, with a line below for the result. TEN + TEN = 20. This is an old way of representing the number 20, now predominantly written 二十.

STORY

A *twenty*-year-old **non-Darwinian** person has just found out that TEN + TEN equals *twenty*!

EXAMPLES

廿四史 (niàn sì shǐ) The twenty-four official stories of China.

WANT A LITTLE MORE?

Usage frequency: Middle third.

61 廿

Definition

Non-character used only as a building block.

Pronunciation

Not applicable

Sound word

Not applicable

Mnemonics

Picket fence; grazing cows.
A *picket fence*, so often seen in the countryside. Behind the *picket fence*, some *grazing cows.*

62 # 卅 4th

DEFINITION

Thirty.

PRONUNCIATION

sà

SOUND WORD

Grasa /grasa/
Spanish word for 'fat,' as in 'animal fat' or fat content in food, butter, milk…

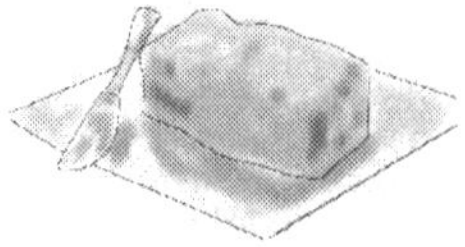

COMPONENTS

3 x 十 TEN[59]

MNEMONICS

Pictogram of three 十 TEN joined together, equivalent to modern 三十 for *thirty*, which is seen much more often.

STORY

"This baby is just *thirty* (3 x TEN) months old and he is already so fat!"
"He eats too much **grasa**, that's why!"

EXAMPLES

五卅事件 (wǔ sà shì jiàn) The anti-imperialist movement in China that occurred on May 30, 1925.

WANT A LITTLE MORE?

Usage frequency: Bottom third.

63 世 4th

Definition

1. *Generation*, *age*.
2. *World*.

Pronunciation

shì

Sound word

Amish

Components

~十 TEN[59] + 廿 TWENTY[60]

Mnemonics

TEN + TWENTY = 30 years, amounting to about a *generation*. You can view the bottom horizontal stroke as a line for the result.

Story

The young **Amish**, between the *age* of TEN and TWENTY, must learn the **Amish** lifestyle that hasn't changed for *generations*.

Examples

1. 世代(shì dài) Generation. 世纪(shì jì) Century.
2. 世界(shì jiè) World.

Want a little more?

Usage frequency: Top 500.

64 **百** 3rd

DEFINITION

Hundred.

PRONUNCIATION

bǎi

SOUND WORD

Bystanders

COMPONENTS

一 ONE[15] + 白 WHITE[45]

MNEMONICS

If you turn the character 90 degrees to the left, placing it on its left side, it looks like 100.

STORY

"There is ONE street performer, all dressed in WHITE, being watched by a *hundred* **bystanders**."

EXAMPLES

一百人(yì bǎi rén) 100 people. 百货(bǎi huò) General goods. 百姓 (bǎi xìng) Common people.

WANT A LITTLE MORE?

Usage frequency: Top 500.

65 千 1st

DEFINITION

Thousand.

PRONUNCIATION

qiān

SOUND WORD

tChienne /t'ʃjɛn/
French word for 'female dog.' Think 'Nothing but **chiennes**.' (See 'Special Sound Mnemonics,' page 488)

COMPONENTS

丿 DOG COLLAR4 left-falling stroke + 十 CROSS59 TEN

STORY

I am in Normandy, at a cemetery built in memory of the dogs who served during the war, looking at rows of a *thousand* CROSSES, each one having a DOG COLLAR placed at an angle at the top. I ask the cemetery guard about the proportion of male and female dogs amongst the *thousand* dogs that are buried there. He says, "Non, non, monsieur. There is nothing bu**t chiennes** here."

EXAMPLES

千瓦 (qiān wǎ) Kilowatt. 千里(qiān lǐ) A long distance.

WANT A LITTLE MORE?

Usage frequency: Top third.

66 匕 3rd

DEFINITION

An ancient type of *spoon*.

PRONUNCIATION

bǐ

SOUND WORD

Beat the rhythm

MNEMONICS

Spoon guy.
The character looks like a child sitting on the floor and raising one arm in front of him. Consequently, we may think of the young bald kid in the movie 'The Matrix' who sits on the ground and bends a *spoon* with his mind. We call him the *spoon guy* in the stories.

STORY

During breakfast, my young son always **beats the rhythm** with his *spoon* on the table. This morning, my oldest son, tired of this racket, decided to **beat the rhythm** on his brother's head with his own *spoon* as a riposte!

EXAMPLES

匕首 (bǐ shǒu) Dagger with a spoon-shaped handle.

WANT A LITTLE MORE?

- This is the 21st of the 214 Kangxi radicals.
- Usage frequency: Bottom third.

67

勹

1st

DEFINITION

To wrap, tie up.

PRONUNCIATION

bāo

SOUND WORD

Bar

A building where alcoholic drinks and food are served.

MNEMONICS

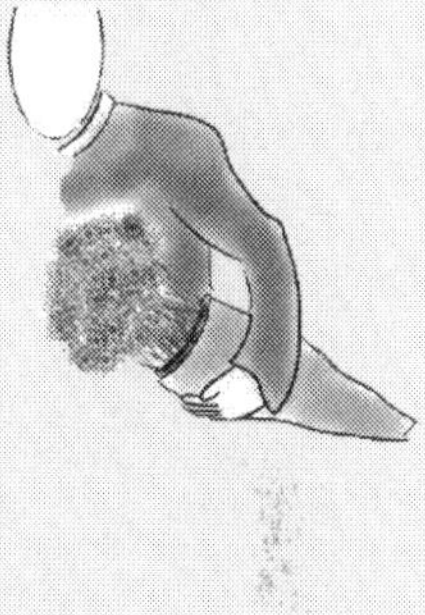

- A *bunch*.

  A *bunch* of something. Its old shape, , really looks like something *tied up* in a *bunch*.

- It is often shortened to ⺈ and written at the top of a character when used as a building block.

STORY

I am with my girlfriend one evening in a **bar** when a flower salesman enters the place, carrying a *bunch* of roses *wrapped* individually and he tries to force me to buy a rose for my girlfriend.

WANT A LITTLE MORE?

This is the 20th of the 214 Kangxi radicals.

68 勺 2nd

Definition

Ladle, spoon.

Pronunciation

sháo

Sound word

Shawnee
Algonquian-speaking people native to North America.

Components

勹 to WRAP[67] + 丶 DROP[3]

Mnemonics

Measuring spoon.
Since a *ladle* can be used to measure a volume of liquid, we also call this character a *measuring spoon.*

Story

The **Shawnee** needed no *ladle* to eat his soup. He just WRAPPED every DROP with his fingers.

Examples

勺子(sháo zǐ) Scoop, ladle. 茶勺儿(chá sháo ér) Teaspoon.

Want a little more?

Usage frequency: Bottom third.

69A 的

DEFINITION

Of.

PRONUNCIATION

de

SOUND WORD

Well, duh!
Expression to show that something just said is already known or is obvious.

COMPONENTS

白 WHITE[45] + 勺 MEASURING SPOON[68] LADLE

MNEMONICS

- This character has many grammatical functions and one of its important roles is to be used as a possessive article. Just think of the French 'de' used to mark possession. The Chinese 'de' works basically the same. For example, 王的书 means 'Wang's book' or 'The book *of* Wang.' In French, it is written 'Le livre **de** Wang.' The same **de** is found here and it sounds almost the same too!

STORY

"Excuse me, this WHITE plastic MEASURING SPOON belongs to whom?"
"Oh, I guess this is the MEASURING SPOON *of* me, because I hold it in my hand."
"**Well, duh!**"

EXAMPLES

我的书 (wō de shū) My book. 什么的 (shén me de) And whatnot.

WANT A LITTLE MORE?

This is the most frequent Chinese character and you will see it everywhere.

69B 的 2nd

DEFINITION

In reality.

PRONUNCIATION

dí

SOUND WORD

Deejay
Disc jockey.

COMPONENTS

白 WHITE45 + 勺 MEASURING SPOON68 LADLE

STORY

"This **deejay** has not had an easy life. He's always been poor. He certainly wasn't born with a silver spoon in his mouth…"
"*In reality*, I heard he was born with a WHITE MEASURING SPOON in his mouth, that was used to give him his medication. As a baby, he was always sick!"

EXAMPLES

的确 (dí què) Certainly, surely.

WANT A LITTLE MORE?

- This character carries the above meaning and pronunciation almost exclusively in the expression 的确 given in the example.
- Usage frequency: Top third.

69C **的** 4th

DEFINITION

Target, aim, bull's eye.

PRONUNCIATION

dì

SOUND WORD

Caddie
A person who carries clubs for a golfer on the golf course.

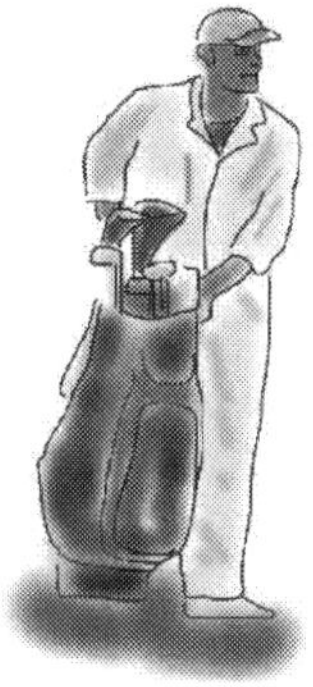

COMPONENTS

白 WHITE[45] + 勺 MEASURING SPOON[68] LADLE

STORY

A **caddie** says to his client, who is a newbie at the game, before a match, "I just want to test your level of chipping before the game. I have placed on the fairway a little WHITE MEASURING SPOON measuring 4.25 inches in length at a distance of 20 yards, to be used as a sort of *bull's eye*, and I'd like you to get as close as possible to that *target* with your wedge."
"But this is way too small!" says the golfer.
"How big do you think a golf hole is?" replies the **caddie**.

EXAMPLES

目的 (mù dì) Purpose, aim, objective.

WANT A LITTLE MORE?

Usage frequency: Top third.

70 ナ

DEFINITION

† *Left hand*.

Now a non-character used only as a building block.

PRONUNCIATION

Not applicable

SOUND WORD

Not applicable

MNEMONICS

This building block used to depict a *left hand*. Try to view a resemblance with the image on the right.

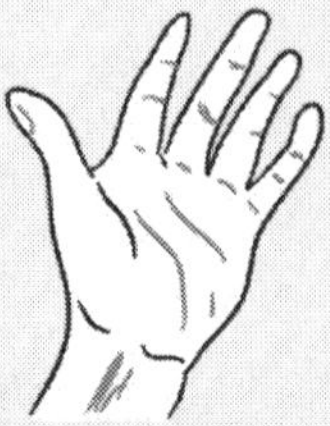

71

又

4th

DEFINITION

Again; *also, additionally.*

† *Right hand.*

PRONUNCIATION

yòu

SOUND WORD

Embryo

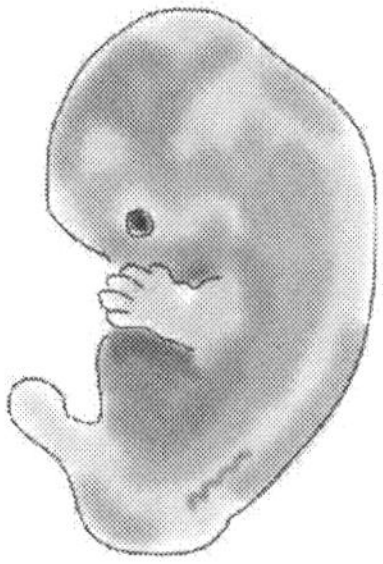

MNEMONICS

This building block used to depict a *right hand.* Ancient form: .

STORY

The **embryo** hits the inside of the uterus with his *right hand*, *again* and *again*…

EXAMPLES

复又 (fù yòu) Again, repeatedly. 又是你！(yòu shì nǐ) It's you again!

而又 (ér yòu) And yet.

WANT A LITTLE MORE?

- This is the 29th of the 214 Kangxi radicals.
- Usage frequency: Top 500.

72 乂

DEFINITION

† A right hand holding a tool.

Now a non-character used only as a building block.

PRONUNCIATION

Not applicable

SOUND WORD

Not applicable

MNEMONICS

To *hold a pen in hand*.

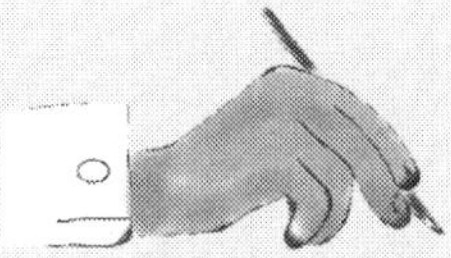

This building block looks like a deformed 又 RIGHT HAND[71]. Since the ancient meaning was a right hand holding a tool, we make that tool a pen in this book.

73

手

3rd

DEFINITION

Hand.

PRONUNCIATION

shǒu

SOUND WORD

Showstopper

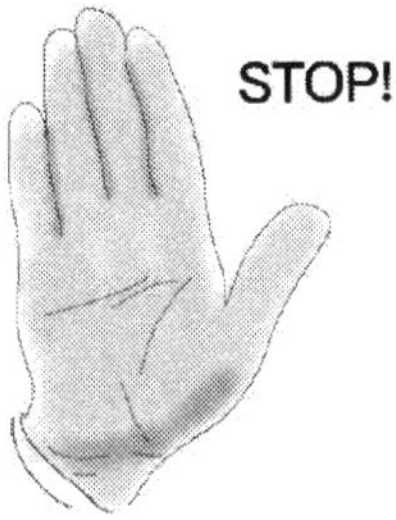

MNEMONICS

- This is a stylistic picture of a *hand* (ancient form: ). You can view this character as the lines on the palm of one *hand*.
- When used as a building block, it is most often written 扌 on the left side of a character.

STORY

My friends and I are all excited, waiting in line to enter the stadium for a free concert given by our favorite rock band. The queue is long and we progress slowly. When it's our turn to enter, the security agent puts his *hand* in our face and says, "Sorry, the stadium is full. No one else can enter."
My friend yells, "What a **showstopper** this guy is!"

EXAMPLES

动手(dòng shǒu) To act. 手指(shǒu zhǐ) finger. 握手(wò shǒu) To shake hands. 洗手(xǐ shǒu) To wash one's hands.

WANT A LITTLE MORE?

- Most characters built with the *hand* building block have something to do with movement and action.
- This is the 64th of the 214 Kangxi radicals.
- Usage frequency: Top 500.

74

廾

3rd

DEFINITION

Two hands.

PRONUNCIATION

gǒng

SOUND WORD

Gongoozler
Someone who observes things idly, like the passage or unloading of boats.

MNEMONICS

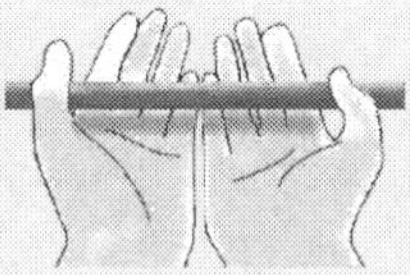

- A picture of two joined hands held up to present something. Ancient form: .
- Imagine a **gongoozler** of Italian descent who joins and holds up his *two hands* in front of his chest to explain to the captain that he is not unloading his cargo the proper way.

WANT A LITTLE MORE?

This is the 55th of the 214 Kangxi radicals.

75 止 3rd

DEFINITION

To *stop*.

† *Footprint*.

PRONUNCIATION

zhǐ

SOUND WORD

Jerrycan

MNEMONICS

- This character originally depicted a left *footprint* (), with the heel at the bottom and the toes sticking out at the top. It came to mean 'to *stop*, halt.'
- It may help, as a mnemonic, to see the new form as a policeman putting his hand out to *stop* the traffic (the right side of the character) so that a child can cross the road (the shorter vertical line on the left). See story.
- It may also be written 龰 when used as a building block.

STORY

A traffic policeman walks quickly to meet a child wanting to cross the street when his left foot is *stopped* by the collision with a full **jerrycan** he did not see resting on the ground, making him fall hard. After picking himself up, he kicks the **jerrycan** with anger with his left foot, leaving a big *footprint* on it.

EXAMPLES

停止(tíng zhǐ) To stop. 不止(bù zhǐ) Not be limited to. 止境(zhǐ jìng) Limit.

WANT A LITTLE MORE?

- This is the 77th of the 214 Kangxi radicals.
- Usage frequency: Top third.

76A 正 4th

Definition

Upright; *correct*; *straight*; *just right*.

Pronunciation

zhèng

Sound word

Tarzan, king of the jungle

Components

一 ONE[15] + 止 FOOTPRINT[75]

Mnemonics

To *straighten*.
A variant of this character, when used as a building block, is written 𤴓.
When this is the case, we give it the meaning of 'to *straighten*.' Just imagine trying to *straighten* the curved line at the bottom to make it *straight*.

Story

Tarzan, king of the jungle, is in a squatting position, looking at ONE FOOTPRINT on the ground. He finally stands *upright* (the only creature that can do that in the jungle) and says, "I was *correct*! Jane stopped here!"

Examples

正好 (zhèng hǎo) Just right. 正确 (zhèng què) Correct, right.

Want a little more?

Usage frequency: Top 500.

76B 正 1st

DEFINITION

First month of the lunar year.

PRONUNCIATION

zhēng

SOUND WORD

Jungle

The sound **zheng** is always approximated by the word 'jungle'. Although this is a two-syllable word used to represent a first tone, this exception should not lead to confusion because there are no Chinese characters pronounced zhéng (second tone).

COMPONENTS

一 ONE[15] + 止 to STOP[75]

STORY

During the *first month of the lunar year*, all the people living in the **jungle** STOP what they are doing for ONE big fiesta.

EXAMPLES

正月 (zhēng yuè) First month of the lunar year.

WANT A LITTLE MORE?

Usage frequency: Middle third.

77 疋 3rd

DEFINITION

Bolt of cloth.

PRONUNCIATION

pǐ

SOUND WORD

Pinocchio

COMPONENTS

~ 疋 to STRAIGHTEN[76A] CORRECT

MNEMONICS

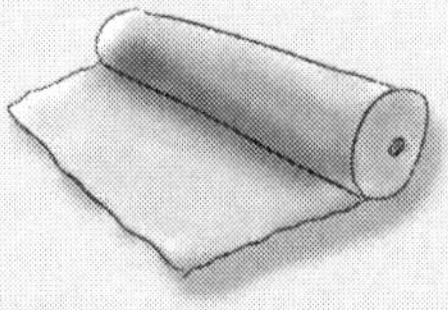

This character looks very similar to 疋 STRAIGHTEN – it only has an extra hook at the top right corner (this is why 疋 is preceded by a ~ tilde in the components section above). Think of **Pinocchio** telling a lie when he says he can carry a heavy *bolt of cloth* on his shoulder all by himself and watch his nose (the hook) STRAIGHTEN as it gets longer. Isn't that a good memory 'hook'!

WANT A LITTLE MORE?

This is the 103rd of the 214 Kangxi radicals.

78 是 4th

DEFINITION

1. To *be*.
2. *Yes.*

PRONUNCIATION

shì

SOUND WORD

Amish

COMPONENTS

日 SUN & DAY[43] + 疋 to STRAIGHTEN[76A] CORRECT

STORY

During a guided tour of an **Amish** county in Pennsylvania, an uninformed tourist pulls down a window in the bus and shouts to an **Amish** man repairing his horse carriage outside,
"Spending your DAYS STRAIGHTENING out twisted cart axles or crooked hoes under the SUN, using only your hands, is this the person you aspire to *be*?"
The **Amish** shouts back, "*Yes*!"

EXAMPLES

1. 可是(kě shì) But, however (could it be that…).
2. 是的(shì de) Yes, that's so. 就是(jiù shì) That is, namely; precisely.

WANT A LITTLE MORE?

This is the third most used Chinese character.

79 **不** 4th

不

DEFINITION

Not, *no*; negative prefix.

PRONUNCIATION

bù

SOUND WORD

Peekaboo!
A game played with babies.

MNEMONICS

This is a pictogram of a flying bird (ancient form: ) trying to reach the sky, only to be stopped by a ceiling (the horizontal stroke). Therefore, it is *not* possible for the bird to escape.

STORY

I bought for my 2-year-old boy a plush toy representing a bird. He's *not* in a good mood, so I try to make him smile by hiding and showing the bird, saying **Peekaboo**! On my last try, my son grabs the bird in his hand, looks at me in the eyes and yells a definite *no*!

EXAMPLES

不同 (bù tóng) Different. 不过 (bù guò) But, however. 不少 (bù shǎo) A lot.

WANT A LITTLE MORE?

- It is one of the top ten characters in frequency of use.
- This character is pronounced in the second tone when followed by a character in the fourth tone.

80 非 1st

DEFINITION

1. *<u>Not</u>, non-, un-.*
2. *Africa.*

PRONUNCIATION

fēi

SOUND WORD

<u>Fée</u> /fe/
French word for 'fairy,' like Disney's Tinker Bell.

MNEMONICS

It visually looks like a fairy spreading her wings, as if to say, 'you are *not* passing through!' The ancient form, , looks more like a monster you're *not* willing to challenge!

STORY

Peter Pan flew himself to *Africa* (just because he can) and he is about to enter a tavern when a **fée**, Tinker Bell, appears, spreads her wings and says, "You are *not* passing through!"

EXAMPLES

1. 是非 (shì fēi) Right and wrong. 非礼 (fēi lǐ) To be impolite. 非常 (fēi cháng) Extraordinary.
2. 南非 (nán fēi) South Africa.

WANT A LITTLE MORE?

- This is the 175th of the 214 Kangxi radicals.
- Usage frequency: Top 500.

81 **勿** 4th

DEFINITION

Not, do not.

PRONUNCIATION

wù

SOUND WORD

Steel wool

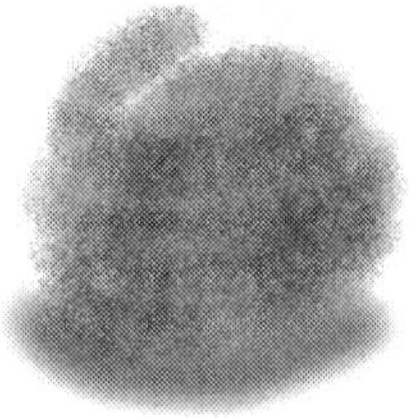

COMPONENTS

勹 BUNCH[67] to WRAP + 2 x 丿 SLIDE[4] left-falling stroke

MNEMONICS

Think of a BUNCH of **steel wool**, *not* to be used on a delicate surface because it will leave streaks. You can also interpret the two lines under the BUNCH building block as those streaks.

STORY

The amusement park owner, with an angry voice, asks his employee, "Have you cleaned the two SLIDES with a BUNCH of extra coarse **steel wool** again? I had already told you *not* to do it, because it leaves streaks on the surface!"

EXAMPLES

请勿 (qǐng wù) Please don't. 切勿 (qiè wù) Be sure not to.

WANT A LITTLE MORE?

- You now know, along with 不 NOT[79] and 非 NOT[80], the three main negation characters in Chinese.
- Usage frequency: Middle third.

82 # 子 3rd

Definition

1. *Child, son.*
2. *Seed, kernel.*
3. *Noun suffix.*
4. *Title of ancient philosophers.*

Pronunciation

zǐ

Sound word

Zerbino /dzerbino/
Italian word for 'doormat.'

Mnemonics

This is a pictogram depicting a *child* wrapped in swaddling clothes with head and arms sticking out (ancient form: ).

Story

"This morning, I opened the door of my Italian villa and guess what I found on our **zerbino**: A basket holding a newborn *child*!"

Examples

1. 子道 (zǐ dào) Filial duties. 孩子 (hái zi) Child, children.
2. 原子 (yuán zǐ) Atom.
3. 帽子 (mào zi) Hat, cap. 杯子 (bēi zi) Cup.
4. 孔子 (kǒng zǐ) Confucius.

Want a little more?

- This character is usually pronounced in the neutral tone when used as a noun suffix.
- This is the 39th of the 214 Kangxi radicals and the first earthly branch (see Appendix 4: Heavenly Stems & Earthly Branches, page 503.)
- Usage frequency: Top 100.

83A 了

DEFINITION

Did it! Marker for a completed action or a new status.

PRONUNCIATION

le

SOUND WORD

Doll killer
A sick person who likes to dismember dolls.

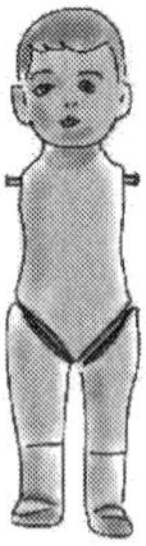

MNEMONICS

Armless child.

The character looks like a 子 CHILD[82] with no arms (ancient form: ).

STORY

The **doll killer** was finally arrested. When the police arrived at his house, they had to face a horrible scene: lots of dolls with their arms chopped off! The chief, with incomprehension, said, "He really *did it*!"

EXAMPLES

啊，你来了！(ā nǐ lái le!) Ah, you have come! 我吃了 (wǒ chī le) I ate. 太好了 (tài hǎo le) Super, great!

WANT A LITTLE MORE?

- This character, with this meaning, is always pronounced in the neutral tone.
- It is one of the top ten characters in frequency of use.

83B 了 3rd

DEFINITION

1. To *understand*.
2. Used to indicate *possibilities*.
3. To *finish*.

PRONUNCIATION

liǎo

SOUND WORD

Lia Olive oil
An olive oil producer whose family name is Lia.

MNEMONICS

The character looks like a 子 CHILD[82] with no arms. See story.

STORY

"The current generation of olive oil producers from the **Lia olive oil** family is the last one," said my father the other day.
"Why is that?" I asked.
"You need strong arms to press the olives, and all their children have been born with no arms! There is just no *possibility* to go on. They are *finished*."
"Oh… I *understand*…"

EXAMPLES

1. 了解(liǎo jiě) To understand.
2. 了不起(liǎo bu qǐ) Amazing. 到不了 (dào bù liǎo) Can't reach a place. 那件事我干不了 (nà jiàn shì wǒ gàn bù liǎo) I can't do that job.
3. 我的心事了了 (wǒ de xīn shì liǎo le) My worries are over.

WANT A LITTLE MORE?

Usage frequency: Top third.

84

才

2nd

DEFINITION

1. <u>Talent</u>, *ability, endowment.*
2. *Only then, only if, just now, not until.*

PRONUNCIATION

cái

SOUND WORD

<u>Zei</u>tung /tsaɪtʊŋ/
German word for 'newspaper.'

MNEMONICS

- *Tightrope walker.*
  The character looks like a *tightrope walker*, an activity that requires a lot of *talent*.
- As a building block, it is sometimes written 扌 at the left of a character.

STORY

"Have you read the **zeitung** this morning?"
"I'm reading it *just now.*"
"Did you read the story on the world-famous *tightrope walker*?"
"Yes. It takes a lot of *talent* and *ability* to do what he did all his life, but what happened *just now* is terrible! *Not* a single accident *until* yesterday."
"Yes, he had almost reached the other end of the rope, and *only then* did he fall!"

EXAMPLES

1. 才能 (cái néng) Ability, talent. 有才 (yǒu cái) Talented. 天才 (tiān cái) Talent; genius.
2. 刚才 (gāng cái) Just now. 他才来 (tā cái lái) He's just arrived.

WANT A LITTLE MORE?

Usage frequency: Top 500.

85 土 3rd

DEFINITION

Soil, earth, dirt, ground.

PRONUNCIATION

tǔ

SOUND WORD

Tourniquet /tuʁnikɛ/
French word for a 'roundabout.'

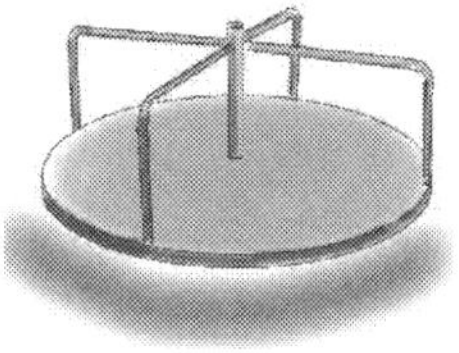

MNEMONICS

- This character, which looks essentially like its ancient form, 土, used to depict vegetation coming out of the *soil.*
- The character looks like a roundabout seen from the side: a platform suspended over the *ground* that revolves around a vertical axis.

STORY

Before the **tourniquet** can be used, it needs to be anchored firmly into the *soil.* If not, you may hit the *ground* hard and eat some *dirt*…

EXAMPLES

土地 (tǔ dì) Land, soil. 泥土(ní tǔ) Earth, soil. 土人(tǔ rén) A native.

WANT A LITTLE MORE?

- This is the 32nd of the 214 Kangxi radicals.
- Usage frequency: Top third.

86 **在** 4th

DEFINITION

1. To be located *at*, *in*, *on*.
2. To *exist*, *live*.

PRONUNCIATION

zài

SOUND WORD

Banzai!
Japanese shout during last, desperate military charges or attacks.

COMPONENTS

𠂇 TIGHTROPE WALKER[84] TALENT + 土 GROUND[85]

STORY

At the scene of an accident, a TIGHTROPE WALKER is lying *on* the GROUND and an inspector is asking questions to a witness.
"First, does he still *live*?"
"Yes, for now."
"OK. What happened?"
"He was *at* the top of the wire when he started shouting **Banzai** and running *on* the rope. That is when he slipped and fell."
"Yeah, typical of some of these guys, believing *at* one point in their life to be good enough to become tightrope runners!"

EXAMPLES

1. 现在(xiàn zài) Now, at present. 我住在北京(wǒ zhù zài běi jīng) I live in Beijing.
2. 存在(cún zài) To exist, be.

WANT A LITTLE MORE?

It is one of the top ten characters in frequency of use.

87 **有** 3rd

Definition

To <u>*have*</u>, *possess*; *there is*, *there are*.

Pronunciation

yǒu

Sound word

Yolanda
A fictional new girlfriend.

Components

ナ LEFT HAND[70] + 月 FLESH[48]

Mnemonics

For the ancient man to survive, the most important thing was to *have* 月 FLESH (meat) on hand. Ancient form: .

Story

My friend tells me, "Since **Yolanda** allowed me to put my LEFT HAND on the FLESH of her behind yesterday, I can officially say that I now *have* a new girlfriend!"

Examples

没有 (méi yǒu) Not have, there is not. 你有空吗？(nǐ yǒu kòng ma) Do you have time? 有的 (yǒu de) Some, there are some.

Want a little more?

It is one of the top ten characters in frequency of use.

88 矢 3rd

DEFINITION

1. *Dart, arrow.*
2. To *swear, vow.*

PRONUNCIATION

shǐ

SOUND WORD

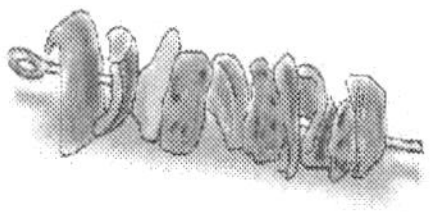

Shish kebab
Pieces of meat and vegetables pushed on a skewer and cooked on a grill.

COMPONENTS

丶 DOT[3] + 天 SKY[31]

MNEMONICS

This is a picture of an *arrow* or *dart* flying upwards (old form: ), until it becomes just a little DOT in the SKY.

STORY

"This javelin thrower is amazing! I saw him one day throw a **shish kebab** stick towards the SKY, as if it was a *dart*, until it became very small and looked like a DOT. When it fell back down, there were four birds skewered on the stick, **shish kebab** ready! I *swear*!"

EXAMPLES

1. 镝矢 (dí shǐ) Arrowhead. 放矢 (fàng shǐ) To shoot an arrow.
2. 矢言 (shǐ yán) Oath; to swear, make a vow.

WANT A LITTLE MORE?

- This is the 111th of the 214 Kangxi radicals.
- Usage frequency: Middle third.

89

弋

4th

DEFINITION

Arrow; to *shoot.*

PRONUNCIATION

yì

SOUND WORD

Abbaye /abei/
French word for 'abbey,' a Catholic monastery administered by an abbot.

MNEMONICS

- Pictogram of an *arrow* attached to a string for hunting. Ancient form: .
- You can also see it as an *arrow* being shot from a bow, with a drop of blood at the tip.

STORY

All the monks at the **abbaye** learn to *shoot arrows* at a young age, for defense purposes.

EXAMPLES

弋猎 (yì liè) To hunt. 巡弋飞弹 (xún yì fēi dàn) Cruise missile.

WANT A LITTLE MORE?

- This is another character that means ARROW, like character 矢 ARROW[88].
- This is the 56th of the 214 Kangxi radicals.
- Usage frequency: Bottom third.

90 | 戈 | 1st

戈

DEFINITION

Dagger ax.

PRONUNCIATION

gē

SOUND WORD

Ghe…
Let's take this for the sound uttered by a moronic guy. Think 'Dumb & Dumber.'

MNEMONICS

Sword.
This is a picture of a *dagger ax* or halberd (ancient form: ), an old Chinese weapon. It consists of a dagger-shaped blade mounted on a perpendicular wooden shaft with a spear point. For a better mental image, it also means *sword* in this book.

STORY

You tell your moronic friend, "Hey moron, don't play with my *dagger ax*, you'll hurt yourself!"
"**Ghe**! I won't hurt myself," he replies, just before dropping it on his head.

EXAMPLES

干戈 (gān gē) Weapons of war. 兵戈 (bīng gē) Weapons; war.

WANT A LITTLE MORE?

- This is the 62nd of the 214 Kangxi radicals.
- Usage frequency: Top third.

91

我

3rd

DEFINITION

I; *me*.

PRONUNCIATION

wǒ

SOUND WORD

Workaholic
A person addicted to work, who works excessively hard.

COMPONENTS

手 HAND[73] + 戈 SWORD[90] DAGGER AX

MNEMONICS

Think of Descartes' famous expression "*I* think, therefore *I* am" and transpose it to ancient times: "*I* fight, therefore *I* am."

STORY

With a SWORD in my HAND, *I* am fighting and chopping down my enemies one after another. *I* keep going for hours, despite my companions in arms pleading with *me* to stop, because the enemy is running away. *I* tell them, "*I* can't stop. *I* am a **workaholic**!"

EXAMPLES

我们(wǒ men) We. 我爱你(wǒ ài nǐ) I love you. 敌我(dí wǒ) The enemy and me.

WANT A LITTLE MORE?

It is one of the top ten characters in frequency of use.

92 找 3rd

DEFINITION

To *try to find*, to *search for*, *look for*, *seek*.

PRONUNCIATION

zhǎo

SOUND WORD

Jargonaut
An annoying person who uses an excessive number of jargon terms when speaking or writing.

COMPONENTS

扌 HAND[73] + 戈 SWORD[90] DAGGER AX

MNEMONICS

Learn to distinguish this character from 我 I[91]. Here, 扌 and 戈 are not touching and the 手 HAND character is abbreviated to the shape it often takes when used as a building block. Therefore, you do not have your SWORD in HAND as you are *trying to find* it.

STORY

"It's time that we became uber-efficient with our millennial third-generation paradigm shifts."
The king, puzzled, puts down the report on the table and asks, "Who wrote this gobbledygook?"
"The **jargonaut** did, Sir."
The king stands up, *searches for* his SWORD, grabs it with his HAND and says, "If somebody *tries to find me*, just say I am *looking for* the **jargonaut** and I will soon be back."

EXAMPLES

查找(chá zhǎo) To search for. 寻找(xún zhǎo) To seek, look for. 找工作(zhǎo gōng zuò) To look for a job.

WANT A LITTLE MORE?

Usage frequency: Top 500.

93 # 或 4th

DEFINITION

Or, perhaps, maybe, possibly.

PRONUNCIATION

huò

SOUND WORD

Porte-rouleau /pɔʁt ʁulo/
A toilet paper holder, or simply the little thingy with a spring in the middle that you insert in the center of the paper roll. (See 'Special Sound Mnemonics,' page 484)

COMPONENTS

口 MOUTH[41] + 一 FLOOR[15] ONE + 戈 DAGGER AX[90]

STORY

A guard was told to take care of the holy **porte-rouleau** *or* else! Well, it got stolen. *Perhaps* he was not conscientious enough? For his punishment, he had to put his MOUTH on the FLOOR and his behind was chopped off with a DAGGER AX!

EXAMPLES

或者(huò zhě) Perhaps; either ... or ... (in a statement, not a question).

或是(huò shì) Or, perhaps.

WANT A LITTLE MORE?

- This character used to represent a nation, a state, whose people, represented by mouths to feed (口), were defended by a wall (一) and weapons (戈).
- Usage frequency: Top 500.

94 也 3rd

Definition

Also.

† Ewer pitcher used for libation purposes.
† Woman's genitals.
† Coiling snake.

Pronunciation

yě

Sound word

Yellow snake

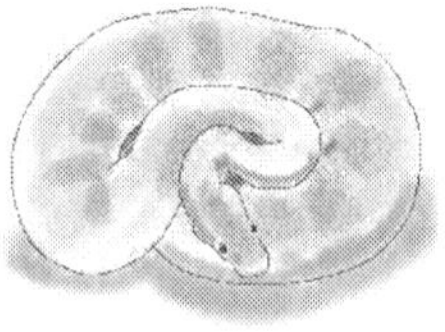

Mnemonics

Python.
Of the three ancient meanings, we keep the coiling snake as a mnemonic, more precisely the *python*, one of the largest snakes in the world, often yellow in color, a snake that can eat large mammals! Ancient form: .

Story

The owner of a pet store says, "We sell all sorts of animals. We *also* sell big **yellow snakes** like *pythons*!"

Examples

也读(yě dú) Also read as… (for a character or word). 我也是(wǒ yě shì) Me also. 也许(yě xǔ) Perhaps, maybe. 也就是说(yě jiù shì shuō) In other words.

Want a little more?

- In classical Chinese, it is also used at the end of a sentence to convey a strong affirmation (do not eat me, snake!)
- Usage frequency: Top 100.

他

DEFINITION

He; him.

PRONUNCIATION

tā

SOUND WORD

Tas /tɑ/
A French word for 'pile,' 'heap,' 'stack,' 'mass,' 'mound,' 'mountain of stuff or persons.'

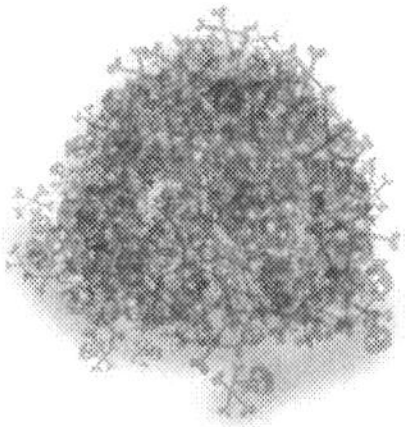

COMPONENTS

亻 MAN[23] + 也 PYTHON[94] ALSO

STORY

Two French explorers are in Burma. One of them says, "Look! What is this?" "I have no idea. It looks like a **tas** of bones and hair," replies the other.

An imposing MAN arrives on the scene from nowhere, wearing a big, dead PYTHON around his neck. While the two explorers look at *him*, *he* says, "These are the remains of a MAN. *He* was eaten by this PYTHON. When a prey is too big, the PYTHON usually spews up what it cannot digest."
"And how do you know this heap is a '*he*'?" asks an explorer.
"Easy. Look at the width of the sacrum and pelvic ring. This pelvis would obviously never permit the passage of a newborn."
"Of course!" replies an explorer, trying to appear knowledgeable.

EXAMPLES

他们(tā men) They (male). 其他(qí tā) Others. 他人很好(tā rén hěn hǎo) He is a nice person.

WANT A LITTLE MORE?

It is one of the top ten characters in frequency of use.

96 她 1st

DEFINITION

She; her.

PRONUNCIATION

tā

SOUND WORD

Tas /tɑ/
A French word for 'pile,' 'heap,' 'stack,' 'mass,' 'mound,' 'mountain of stuff or persons.'

COMPONENTS

女 WOMAN[26] + 也 PYTHON[94] ALSO

STORY

"Oh no! Look at the **tas** of regurgitated bones and hair!"
"What is it?"
"I think the WOMAN you married has been eaten by a PYTHON."
"How can you tell?"
"Is it not the wedding ring you offered *her*? *She* was wearing it all the time!"
"Ah yes! Oh well…"

EXAMPLES

她们 (tā men) They (female). 她家 (tā jiā) Her family.

WANT A LITTLE MORE?

Usage frequency: Top 100.

97

牠

1st

DEFINITION

It.

PRONUNCIATION

tā

SOUND WORD

Tas /tɑ/
A French word for 'pile,' 'heap,' 'stack,' 'mass,' 'mound,' 'mountain of stuff or persons.'

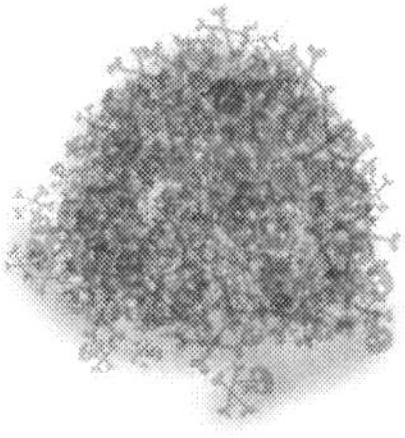

COMPONENTS

牜 COW[35] + 也 PYTHON[94] ALSO

STORY

"Well, looks like the PYTHON ate *it.*"
"Ate what?"
"The COW, of course!"
"How can you be so sure?"
"Look at the **tas** of bones, horns and fur *it* regurgitated!"

EXAMPLES

牠们 (tā men) They (animals).

WANT A LITTLE MORE?

- This character is used mostly for animals.
- Usage frequency: Top third.

98 **它** 1st

DEFINITION

It.

PRONUNCIATION

tā

SOUND WORD

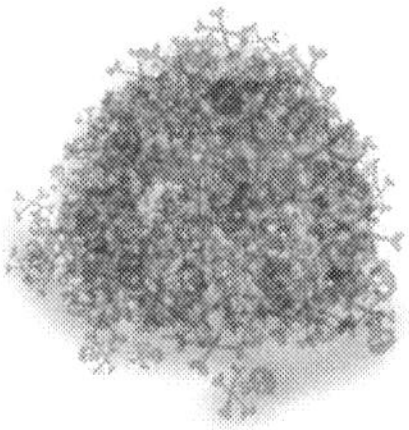

Tas /tɑ/
A French word for 'pile,' 'heap,' 'stack,' 'mass,' 'mound,' 'mountain of stuff or persons.'

COMPONENTS

宀 HOUSE[50] + 匕 SPOON[66]

STORY

My neighbor always lets his dog poop in my driveway, even after I repeatedly asked him not to. One day, I decided to have my revenge. While he was in his backyard, I entered his HOUSE silently, dropped a **tas** of dog excrement in his kitchen and planted a SPOON in *it* along with a sign that read, "Eat *it*!"
My driveway has been clean ever since.

EXAMPLES

它们 (tā men) They (inanimate objects).

WANT A LITTLE MORE?

- This is a variant of the previous 牠 character and is used more for inanimate objects.
- Usage frequency: Top 500.

99

乂

4th

DEFINITION

† To administer, govern.
† Person of stature.
† To cut grass.

PRONUNCIATION

yì

SOUND WORD

Abbaye /abei/
French word for 'abbey,' a Catholic monastery administered by an abbot.

MNEMONICS

- *Scissors, shears.*
  Pair of *scissors, shears*, because of its shape.
- A symbol indicating *danger, dangerous*. Think of the symbol ☠ for *danger*.

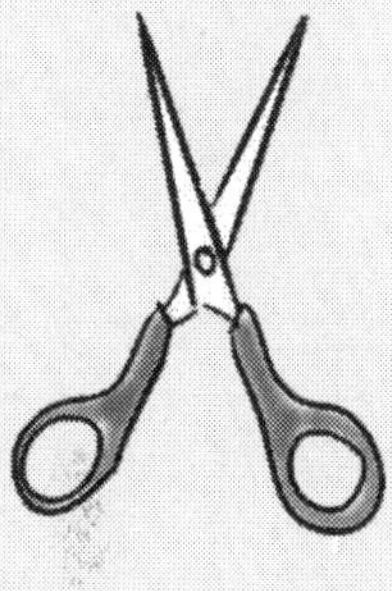

STORY

The abbot, a person of stature who governs the **abbaye**, reminds the monks that it is *dangerous* to run with a pair of *scissors* in their hands when cutting grass.

100 **爻** 2nd

DEFINITION

Lines that form the eight Chinese trigrams.

PRONUNCIATION

yáo

SOUND WORD

Yardstick
A measuring tool one yard long or a standard used for comparison.

MNEMONICS

Mesh, lace.
Let's take this as the picture of an interlaced fabric. It also looks like shoe*laces* criss-crossing at the front of a shoe. Ancient form: 爻.

STORY

Using a **yardstick**, a tailor measures a length of *mesh* composed of criss-crossing orange and black *lines* to make a Halloween costume.

EXAMPLES

阳爻 (yáng yáo) Unbroken line of a trigram. 爻象 (yáo xiàng) Diagrams used for divination.

WANT A LITTLE MORE?

- Trigrams are used in Daoist cosmology to represent the fundamental principles of reality.
- This is the 89th of the 214 Kangxi radicals.
- Usage frequency: Bottom third.

101 文 2nd

DEFINITION

1. *Language, literature; writing; literary.*
2. *Culture; refined.*
3. *Surname.*

PRONUNCIATION

wén

SOUND WORD

Wenches
Plural of wench, a young peasant girl with not much education.

COMPONENTS

亠 COWBOY HAT[49] + 乂 SHEARS[99]

MNEMONICS

Visually, you could also view this character as a *literary* person (only his head, 丶, is showing) in the process of *writing* while sitting behind a desk (一), with his legs crossed (乂) under it.

STORY

You may think that these **wenches** wearing a COWBOY HAT and cutting crop in the field with SHEARS have no *culture*, but you'd be wrong. They belong to a book club and they meet every night to talk about *literature* and other *literary* works, written in various *languages* too!

EXAMPLES

1. 语文 (yǔ wén) Spoken and written language; language and literature. 文艺 (wén yì) Literature and art. 文字 (wén zì) Characters, writing, script. 文言 (wén yán) Classical Chinese (literary language).
2. 文化 (wén huà) Culture, civilization. 斯文 (sī wén) Refined; men of letters.

WANT A LITTLE MORE?

- This is the 67th of the 214 Kangxi radicals.
- Usage frequency: Top 500.

102 言 2nd

DEFINITION

Word, *speech*; to *speak*, *say*, *talk*.

PRONUNCIATION

yán

SOUND WORD

Yenta
A woman who is meddlesome or gossipy.

COMPONENTS

亠 COWBOY HAT[49] + 二 TWO[16] + 口 MOUTH[41]

MNEMONICS

- Another way of looking at this character is seeing sound waves (the TWO horizontal lines) being emitted by a MOUTH.
- It is written 讠 when it appears as a building block on the left side of simplified characters. Think of the 讠 symbol used for Tourist information you see in many countries, where you go when you need to *speak* with guides or travel agents.

STORY

No wonder this **yenta** *speaks* so many *words*! The other day, a strong wind blew her COWBOY HAT away, revealing a MOUTH on her forehead. She has TWO MOUTHS!

EXAMPLES

言语 (yán yǔ) Words, speech, spoken language. 方言 (fāng yán) Dialect. 发言 (fā yán) To make a speech.

WANT A LITTLE MORE?

- This is the 149th of the 214 Kangxi radicals.
- Usage frequency: Top 500.

103

彡

1st

DEFINITION

† Decorative lines, *stripes*.
† *Hair* (on the head).

PRONUNCIATION

shān

SOUND WORD

Channe /ʃan/
French word for a pitcher or jug used to serve wine or water, usually made from tin.

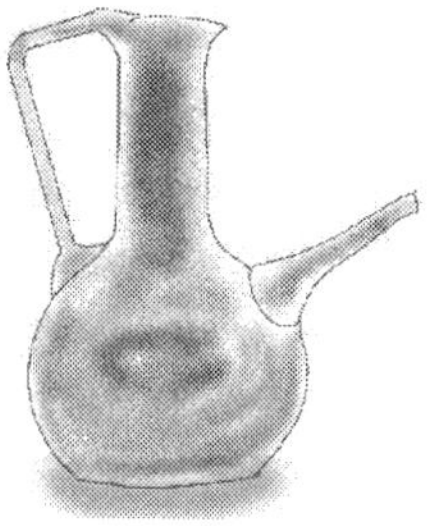

MNEMONICS

- The ancient definitions of *stripes* and *hair* are still used as actual meanings in this book. Ancient form: .
- *Wasp* (because of the *stripes*).

STORY

You're having a picnic outside and *wasps* keep buzzing around your **channe** of wine and your *hair*.

WANT A LITTLE MORE?

This is the 59th of the 214 Kangxi radicals.

104 辶[辵] 4th

DEFINITION

† To go hesitantly, moving forward and being halted.

PRONUNCIATION

chuò

SOUND WORD

Chanchullo /ʧaɲʧuʌo/
Spanish word for 'scam,' 'racket,' 'dirty tricks.' Just ignore the 'll' sound when pronouncing it.

TRADITIONAL COMPONENTS

[彡 HAIR[103] + 止 FOOTPRINT[75]]

MNEMONICS

Road.
Notice how the simplified character looks like a winding *road.*

STORY

[See yourself walking barefoot along a sandy *road* in South America, leaving FOOTPRINTS in the sand, your HAIR floating in a warm breeze, when you are halted by a peddler who wants to sell you stuff. You decide to keep moving forward, being certain this is a **chanchullo**.]

WANT A LITTLE MORE?

This is the 162nd of the 214 Kangxi radicals.

105 台

DEFINITION

† Small mound; to pile up.

Now a non-character used only as a building block.

PRONUNCIATION

Not applicable

SOUND WORD

Not applicable

MNEMONICS

Podium.
You can clearly see the step leading to the platform on which the speaker stands, with the lectern and the mike (the DROP[3]) on top. The DROP may be missing when used as a building block.

106 皁 4th

DEFINITION

1. *Mound.*
2. *Abundance.*

PRONUNCIATION

fù

SOUND WORD

Garde-fou /gaʁdəfu/
French expression for 'crash barrier,' 'guardrail,' 'railing.'

COMPONENTS

𠂤 PODIUM[105] + 十 TEN & CROSS[59]

MNEMONICS

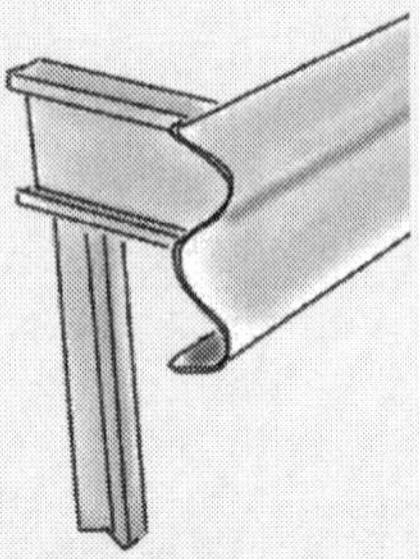

- As a building block, it is written 阝 and always appears on the left side of a character. It then looks like a **garde-fou** seen from the side.
- You can also picture a Big *mound* protected on the left side by a **garde-fou**.

STORY

A high priest stands on a PODIUM behind a **garde-fou** and next to a CROSS at the top of a big *mound*, Mount Sinai, in front of an *abundance* of spectators. He says, "This CROSS indicates the place where Moses received the TEN Commandments."

EXAMPLES

1. 阜陵(fù líng) Mound. 沙阜(shā fù) Sand hill.
2. 阜财(fù cái) To enrich.

WANT A LITTLE MORE?

- This is the 170th of the 214 Kangxi radicals.
- Usage frequency: Middle third.

107 阝 4th

DEFINITION

† City, *city wall*.

PRONUNCIATION

yì

SOUND WORD

Abbaye /abei/
French word for 'abbey,' a Catholic monastery administered by an abbot.

MNEMONICS

Just think of the hubbuB heard behind a *city wall*, compared to the quietness of an **abbaye**.

WANT A LITTLE MORE?

- Not to be confused with the building block version of 阝 MOUND[106]. Although the *city wall* building block looks the same, it is always written on the right side of a character instead of on the left.
- Its full, literary form is written 邑 and represents the 163rd of the 214 Kangxi radicals.

108

力

4th

DEFINITION

PRONUNCIATION

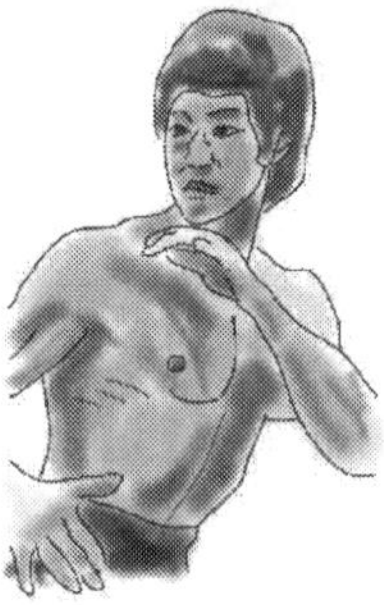

Power, force, strength. lì

SOUND WORD

Bruce Lee
The famous actor and martial artist.

MNEMONICS

- It looks like the crane pose, featured in the Karate Kid movie.
- The ancient form, , depicted a plow, something that needs *power* to be moved.

STORY

Picture **Bruce Lee** in the crane pose, standing in equilibrium on his left leg, with his right leg raised. This is the perfect image of *power* and *strength.*

EXAMPLES

力量 (lì liàng) Physical strength, power. 电力 (diàn lì) Electric power. 人力 (rén lì) Manpower.

WANT A LITTLE MORE?

- This is the 19th of the 214 Kangxi radicals.
- Usage frequency: Top 500.

109

刀

1st

DEFINITION

Knife.

PRONUNCIATION

dāo

SOUND WORD

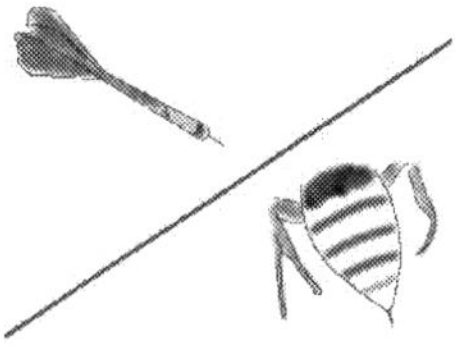

Dard /daʁ/
French word for 'dart' (game of darts), 'insect stinger' or 'dagger.'

MNEMONICS

- This is the pictogram of a *knife*. Ancient form:  .
- It is most often written 刂 when used as a building block.

STORY

During a *knife*-throwing competition, somebody played unfair and threw a **dard** instead. Too easy. He was disqualified.

EXAMPLES

刀子 (dāo zi) Small knife, dagger. 大刀 (dà dāo) Big knife.

WANT A LITTLE MORE?

- This is the 18th of the 214 Kangxi radicals.
- Usage frequency: Top third.

110 | 刃 | 4th

DEFINITION

Blade.

PRONUNCIATION

rèn

SOUND WORD

Siren
Police **siren** or fire alarm.

COMPONENTS

、 DROP[3] + 刀 KNIFE[109]

MNEMONICS

Basically, it shows the edge of a KNIFE *blade* with a DROP of blood on it.

Ancient form:  .

STORY

"We heard a police **siren** outside. Curious, we went to see what was going on. On the ground laid a woman, and next to her, a KNIFE with a DROP of blood on the *blade*…"

EXAMPLES

刀刃 (dāo rèn) Knife edge. 利刃 (lì rèn) Sharp knife.

WANT A LITTLE MORE?

Usage frequency: Middle third.

111 𦉫

Definition

Non-character used only as a building block.

Pronunciation

Not applicable

Sound word

Not applicable

Mnemonics

Barbed wire.

It looks like a 刀 KNIFE[109] with 'barbs' (the two horizontal lines on the left). Just think of 'barbs' that cut like a KNIFE. Hence, *barbed wire*.

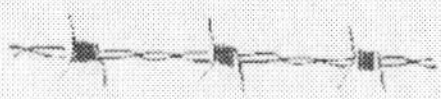

112 立 4th

DEFINITION

1. To <u>*stand*</u>.
2. To *set up*.

PRONUNCIATION

lì

SOUND WORD

Bruce <u>Lee</u>
The famous actor and martial artist.

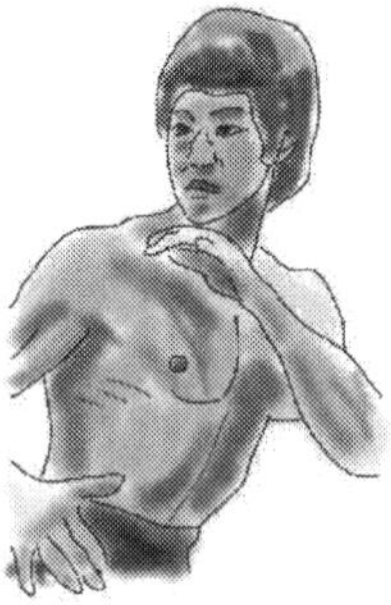

MNEMONICS

It looks like a man *standing* firmly on the ground. Ancient form: .

STORY

Just picture **Bruce Lee** *standing* firmly on the ground before moving into action.

EXAMPLES

1. 独立(dú lì) To stand alone.
2. 建立(jiàn lì) To establish, set up.

WANT A LITTLE MORE?

- This is the 117th of the 214 Kangxi radicals.
- Usage frequency: Top 500.

113 这[這] 4th

DEFINITION

This, these.

PRONUNCIATION

zhè

SOUND WORD

Gadget

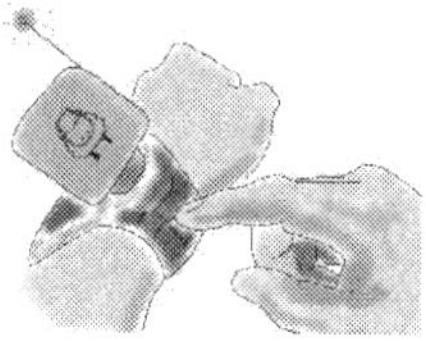

SIMPLIFIED COMPONENTS

⻍ ROAD[104] + 亠 COWBOY HAT[49] + 乂 SCISSORS[99]

TRADITIONAL COMPONENTS

[ROAD + 言 WORD[102]]

MNEMONICS

- You can also decompose the character differently and tell yourself, while studying *this* book, "*This* is the ROAD to a new 文 LANGUAGE[101] and [*these* are the WORDS I need to learn.]"
- It is also pronounced **zhèi** (think '**blue jay**') when followed by a measure word (see first example). This is the only Chinese character with that pronunciation.

STORY

My doorbell rings. I answer the door and there stands a ROAD salesman wearing a COWBOY HAT who sells SCISSORS. "Good day, sir," he says. "*This* **gadget** here can cut through anything!"

["Cut it out!" I say.
"But let me show you…"
"See? *This* **gadget** does not work because it didn't even cut your voice, which proves that *these* WORDS of yours are lies. Hit the ROAD, liar!"]

EXAMPLES

这个(zhè gè) or (zhèi gè) This one. 这里(zhè lǐ) Here.

WANT A LITTLE MORE?

Usage frequency: Top 100.

114 那 4th

DEFINITION

That, those.

PRONUNCIATION

nà

SOUND WORD

Sauna

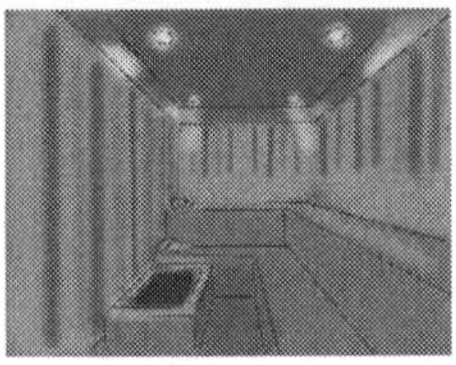

COMPONENTS

⺼ BARBED WIRE[111] + 阝 CITY WALL[107]

MNEMONICS

This character may also be pronounced **nèi** (think of the Italian sound word **prigione** for 'prison') when followed by a measure word, with the same meaning (see fourth example).

STORY

An Italian **sauna** salesman says to potential customers,

"We have mainly two models of **saunas**: This regular one here, and *that* one over there, surrounded by CITY WALLS with BARBED WIRES on top that looks like a **prigione**, designed mostly for *those* movie stars who want to keep the paparazzi at bay…"

EXAMPLES

那么 (nà me) Like that. 那里 (nà lǐ) That place, over there. 那边 (nà biān) That side. 那个 (nèi ge) That one.

WANT A LITTLE MORE?

Usage frequency: Top 100.

115 # 哪 3rd

DEFINITION

Which? Where? Who? What? How?

PRONUNCIATION

nǎ

SOUND WORD

Natural gas

COMPONENTS

口 ORIFICE[41] + 那 THAT[114]

MNEMONICS

This character may also be pronounced něi (think **neigh**borhood), with the same meaning (see first example).

STORY

"Doctor, one of my ORIFICES produces a lot of **natural gas**, scaring away the **neighborhood**."
"*Where? Which* ORIFICE?"
Showing his behind, "THAT ORIFICE!"

EXAMPLES

哪个 (něi ge) Which? 哪里 (nǎ lǐ) Where? 哪些 (nǎ xiē) Which? Who? What?

WANT A LITTLE MORE?

Usage frequency: Top third.

116 古 3rd

DEFINITION

Ancient.

PRONUNCIATION

gǔ

SOUND WORD

Goudronner /gudʁɔne/
French verb meaning 'to apply tar,' 'to cover with tar.'

COMPONENTS

十 CROSS[59] TEN + 口 OPENING[41]

MNEMONICS

Its *ancient* interpretation is that it depicts "what has been transmitted by the 口 MOUTHS of 十 TEN generations of scholars," in other words, very *ancient* teachings.

STORY

The *ancient* always gets lost and forgets where he lives. So, his French neighbors have decided to **goudronner** (write with tar) a big CROSS above the OPENING of his cave to help him find his way (oh yeah, he lives in a cave. He's that old).

EXAMPLES

古代 (gǔ dài) Antiquity. 古典(gǔ diǎn) Classical. 古老 (gǔ lǎo) Ancient.

WANT A LITTLE MORE?

Usage frequency: Top third.

117

固

4th

DEFINITION

1. *Solid, hard, strong.*
2. *Of course.*

PRONUNCIATION

gù

SOUND WORD

Ragout
Seasoned stew of meat and vegetables.

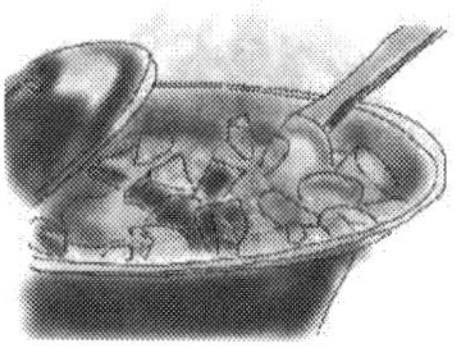

COMPONENTS

囗 to CONFINE[42] + 古 ANCIENT[116]

STORY

On an excavation site, archeologists have found a petrified ANCIENT **ragout**, as *solid* as a rock, CONFINED within the four walls of a square vessel and prepared at least 5000 years ago. *Of course*, they couldn't resist licking the *hard* concoction.

EXAMPLES

1. 巩固 (gǒng gù) To strengthen, solidify. 坚固 (jiān gù) Solid, sturdy.
2. 固然 (gù rán) Of course.

WANT A LITTLE MORE?

Usage frequency: Top third.

118 个[個] 4th

Definition

1. An *individual.*
2. Measure word for *persons* and *things.*

Pronunciation

gè

Sound word

Tree hugger
A person who loves and hugs trees.

Simplified components

人 TENT[9] + 丨 POLE[1]

Traditional components

[亻 MAN[23] + 固 SOLID[117]]

Story

An *individual* is in his TENT and when the wind starts to blow, it looks like the TENT is about to take off. The guy stands up and holds the POLE with all his might. He looks like a goddamned **tree hugger**!

[Another MAN arrives just in time to secure his setup and make it more SOLID.]

Examples

1. 个人(gè rén) An individual (person).
2. 三个人(sān gè rén) Three persons.

Want a little more?

- This is the most frequent measure word of the Chinese language.
- Usage frequency: Top 100.

119

门[門]

2nd

Definition

1. <u>*Gate*</u>, *door*, *gateway*, *doorway*.
2. *Category*, *division*, *department*.
3. Measure word for *courses of study*.

Pronunciation

mén

Sound word

<u>Men</u>u

Mnemonics

This is the picture of a *door* or *gate*. Ancient form: .

Story

You can find a **menu** behind glass at the *gate* or *door* of many restaurants, especially those belonging to the expensive *category*.

Examples

1. 门口 (mén kǒu) Entrance, doorway. 开门 (kāi mén) To open the door. 出门 (chū mén) To go out.
2. 部门 (bù mén) Department, branch.
3. 一门必修课 (yī mén bì xiū kē) A compulsory course.

Want a little more?

- This is the 169th of the 214 Kangxi radicals.
- Usage frequency: Top 500.

120

们[們]

DEFINITION

Plural marker for pronouns and a few animate nouns.

PRONUNCIATION

men

SOUND WORD

Milk<u>men</u>
Persons who sell or deliver milk and milk products.

COMPONENTS

亻 MAN[23] + 门[門] GATE[119]

STORY

A MAN arrives home from work. He opens his GATE and goes directly to his bedroom. There, he finds his wife in bed with the milkman. "What? You're cheating with the milkman?"

Another MAN pops his head out and says, "Wrong. **Milk*men***!"

EXAMPLES

我们(wǒ men) We. **人们**(rén men) People. **孩子们**(hái zǐ men) Children.

WANT A LITTLE MORE?

Usage frequency: Top 100.

121 中 1st

DEFINITION

Middle, center, in, amongst, amidst.

PRONUNCIATION

zhōng

SOUND WORD

Junk
Any kind of **junk**, including **junk** food.

COMPONENTS

丨 STICK[1] + 口 MOUTH[41]

MNEMONICS

A fried cheese STICK down the *middle* of a MOUTH.

STORY

No wonder this young guy is fat and has an expanding *middle*! Look at all the fried cheese STICKS, *amongst* other **junk** food, he puts *in* his MOUTH!

EXAMPLES

中国 (zhōng guó) China. 中午 (zhōng wǔ) Noon. 群众中 (qún zhòng zhōng) Amidst the crowd, the masses.

WANT A LITTLE MORE?

Usage frequency: Top 100.

122 上 4th

DEFINITION

1. *Above*, *up*, *over*.
2. *Previous*, *last*.
3. To *go upwards*, *go to*, *go aboard* (a vehicle).

PRONUNCIATION

shàng

SOUND WORD

Broom shank
The wooden handle of a broom. Just picture a witch broom, with magical power.

MNEMONICS

This is a very visual pictogram: a line *above* the 一 FLOOR[15] ONE.

STORY

The **broom shank** levitates by itself and floats *above* the FLOOR when it's called by the witch.

EXAMPLES

1. 上面 (shàng miàn) Above.
2. 上个月 (shàng ge yuè) Last month.
3. 上楼(shàng lóu) To go upstairs. 上班(shàng bàn) To go to work. 上船(shàng chuán) To board a ship.

WANT A LITTLE MORE?

- For the Chinese, the past is located above and the future below on a vertical timescale. Therefore, 上 stands for previous or last (time) and the next character 下 for next (time).
- Usage frequency: Top 100.

123 下 4th

DEFINITION

1. *Below*, *down*, *under*.
2. *Next*.
3. To *go down*, *descend*; *get off work*.

PRONUNCIATION

xià

SOUND WORD

Acacia /akasja/
A type of tree, pronounced in Spanish.

MNEMONICS

This is a very visual pictogram: a line *below* the 一 CEILING[15] ONE.

STORY

He fell hard when he *went down* an **acacia** tree. He is now 6 feet *below* ground.

EXAMPLES

1. 地下(dì xià) Below ground. 下午 (xià wǔ) Afternoon.
2. 下个星期 (xià ge xīng qī) Next week.
3. 下去(xià qù) To go down, descend. 下班(xià bàn) To get off work.

WANT A LITTLE MORE?

Usage frequency: Top 100.

124 金 1st

Definition

1. *Gold, metal; metallic.*
2. *Surname.*

Pronunciation

jīn

Sound word

Gin
The well-known spirit.

Components

人 TENT[9] + 王 KING[19] + 2 x 丶 FLAKE[3] DROP

Mnemonics

- Many interpretations exist for this character, from showing *metal* buried underground to showing *metal* in fusion. Ancient form: .
- It is written as 钅 (simple form) or 釒 (traditional) when used as a building block.
- In the story, the DROP[3] building block stands for FLAKES.

Story

During a military campaign, the KING is sitting in his TENT, calmly drinking **gin** from a bottle with *gold* FLAKES in it while the *metallic* sound of clashing swords and armors can be heard outside.

Examples

1. 金牌 (jīn pái) Gold Medal. 金属 (jīn shǔ) Metals in general.

Want a little more?

- It ranks amongst the top 100 Chinese surnames.
- This is the first of the five primary elements (metal, wood, water, fire, earth) said by the ancients to compose the physical universe.
- This is the 167th of the 214 Kangxi radicals.
- Usage frequency: Top 500.

125

木

4th

DEFINITION

1. *Tree*, *wood*; *wooden*.
2. *Numb.*

PRONUNCIATION

mù

SOUND WORD

Shamu
This is the name often given to a killer whale in a SeaWorld show. Lots of fun ahead!

MNEMONICS

- This is the picture of a *tree* with its roots and branches. Ancient form: .
- It may appear as 朩 when used as a building block.

STORY

Shamu was found to have a high level of cholesterol in its blood because of all the fatty fish it is being rewarded with. It now needs to follow a vegetarian diet with lots of fibers and is now being fed with whole *trees*!

EXAMPLES

1. 木头(mù tóu) Wood, timber. 木工(mù gōng) Woodwork; carpenter.
2. 冻木(dòng mù) To be numb with cold.

WANT A LITTLE MORE?

- This is the second of the five primary elements (metal, wood, water, fire, earth) said by the ancients to compose the physical universe.
- This is the 75th of the 214 Kangxi radicals.
- Usage frequency: Top third.

126

水

3rd

DEFINITION

Water, watery.

PRONUNCIATION

shuǐ

SOUND WORD

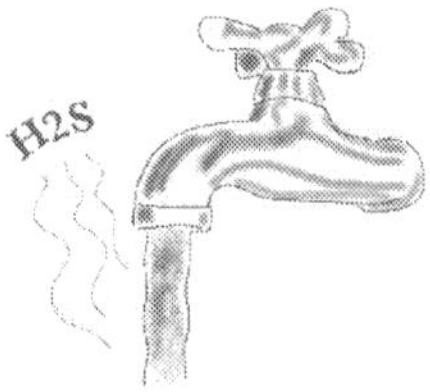

Schwefelig /ʃveːfəlɪç/
German word for 'sulfurous.' Just replace the 'v' sound of the German 'w' letter by an English 'w' for a better approximation.

MNEMONICS

- It looks like *water* flowing from a tap, splashing around. Ancient form: .
- When used as a building block, it can be written 水, 氺 or 氵 (as three dots on the left side of a character). You will see it a lot.

STORY

My German friend is at my place and I offer him a glass of tap *water*.
"Pouah! Your *water* is too **schwefelig**!"
"Come again?"
"It has too much sulfur in it!"

EXAMPLES

一杯水 (yì bēi shuǐ) A glass of water. 洪水 (hóng shuǐ) Flood.

水口 (shuǐ kǒu) Mouth of a stream.

WANT A LITTLE MORE?

- This is the third of the five primary elements (metal, wood, water, fire, earth) said by the ancients to compose the physical universe.
- This is the 85th of the 214 Kangxi radicals.
- Usage frequency: Top 500.

127 火 3rd

DEFINITION

Fire, flame.

PRONUNCIATION

huǒ

SOUND WORD

Rouleau compresseur /ʁulo kɔ̃pʁɛsœʁ/
French expression for 'steamroller.' Omit the 'l' when you pronounce it. (See 'Special Sound Mnemonics,' page 484)

MNEMONICS

- Stylized pictogram of *flames*, of *fire*. Ancient form: 火.
- It looks like a 人 MAN[23] on *fire*.
- It is sometimes written as 灬 at the bottom of a character when used as a building block.

STORY

"Look! A **rouleau compresseur** caught *fire* and there is a man on *fire* running from the *flames*!"

EXAMPLES

火车 (huǒ chē) Train. 火山 (huǒ shān) Volcano. 火力 (huǒ lì) Firepower.

WANT A LITTLE MORE?

- This is the fourth of the five primary elements (metal, wood, water, fire, earth) said by the ancients to compose the physical universe.
- This is the 86th of the 214 Kangxi radicals.
- Usage frequency: Top 500.

128A **地** 4th

DEFINITION

Earth, ground, field, place, land.

PRONUNCIATION

dì

SOUND WORD

Caddie
A person who carries clubs for a golfer on the golf course.

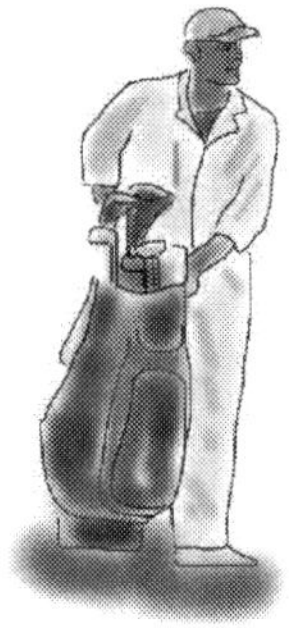

COMPONENTS

土 SOIL[85] + 也 PYTHON[94] ALSO

STORY

At a **caddies** meeting preceding a big company tournament, the organizer says, "Dear **caddies**, today, many top managers of various companies will participate in a tournament on our *grounds*. We ask you to watch closely the player you will be assigned to and the *places* he goes on the *field* at all times. As you know, the SOIL of this *land* shelters a lot of PYTHONS and we have already lost too many golfers…"

EXAMPLES

地方(dì fāng) Place, territory. 土地(tǔ dì) Land, territory. 地球(dì qiú) The earth (our planet).

WANT A LITTLE MORE?

- This is the fifth of the five primary elements (metal, wood, water, fire, earth) said by the ancients to compose the physical universe.
- Usage frequency: Top 100.

128B

地

DEFINITION

Adverbial particle, equivalent to *–ly* in English.

PRONUNCIATION

de

SOUND WORD

Well, duh!
Expression to show that something just said is already known or is obvious.

COMPONENTS

土 SOIL[85] + 也 ALSO[94]

STORY

A potential house buyer is visiting a property and the real-estate agent says, "Here is the house and here is the backyard."
The buyer asks, "This is nice, but will I ALSO own the SOIL of the property?"
The agent, losing his sense of decorum, says, "**Well, duh**! Obvious-*ly*!"

EXAMPLES

他慢慢**地**把门开开了 (ta màn màn de ba mén kāi kāi le) He slowly opened the door.

WANT A LITTLE MORE?

- This character serves to describe the way an action is performed by the subject and it precedes the action in the sentence.
- Usage frequency: Top 100.

129 **冰** 1st

DEFINITION

Ice; *icy*.

PRONUNCIATION

bīng

SOUND WORD

Bing
As in singer and actor **Bing** Crosby (1903-1977).

COMPONENTS

冫 *Ice* + 水 WATER[126]

MNEMONICS

- This is the full character for *ice*. When used as a building block, only the left part, 冫, appears on the left side of a character.
- Picture the building block 冫 as a broken icicle.
- When the *ice* building block is written under a character, it appears as two drops: ⺀.

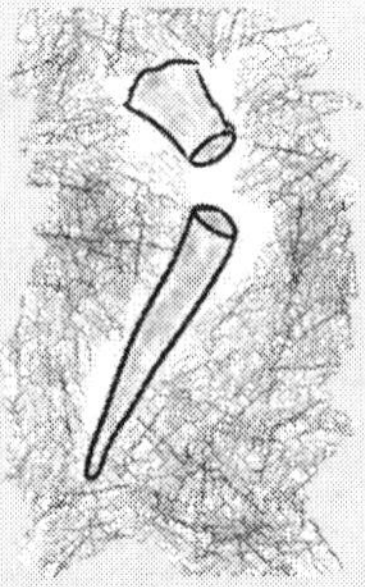

STORY

There is a rumor circulating that **Bing** was cryogenically frozen, with the hope that his resuscitation may be possible in the future. He was put in a reservoir filled with WATER that was progressively cooled down until it became a solid block of *ICE*. He was basically put on *ICE*. (Note that ice is both a COMPONENT and a *definition*, hence it is written with both *FORMATS*.)

EXAMPLES

冰水(bīng shuǐ) Iced water. 滑冰(huá bīng) To skate.

WANT A LITTLE MORE?

- The building block version of this character, 冫, is the 15th of the 214 Kangxi radicals.
- Usage frequency: Top third.

130 早 3rd

DEFINITION

Early.

† Sun rising in the morning.

PRONUNCIATION

zǎo

SOUND WORD

dSarcoma

A type of cancer. Think 'Goddamne**d sarcoma**.' (See 'Special Sound Mnemonics,' page 494)

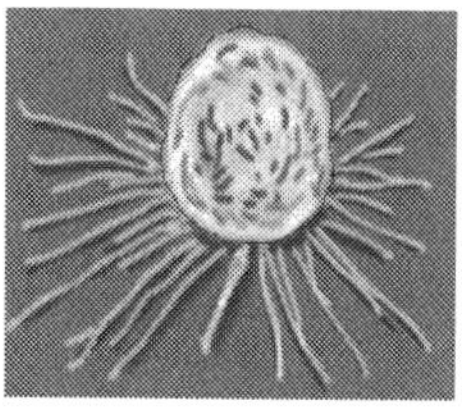

COMPONENTS

日 SUN[43] + 十 TEN[59]

MNEMONICS

Sunflower.

The fictitious meaning of *sunflower* comes from the fact that the character looks like a 'SUN' flower on a stem with two leaves.

STORY

"Since an *early* age, he exposed himself to the SUN every day, from *early* morning at around TEN, when the SUN starts to be way up in the sky, till the end of the day. I heard he developed a bad case of cancer, a goddamne**d sarcoma**."

EXAMPLES

早饭(zǎo fàn) Breakfast. 早上(zǎo shàng) Morning. 早晚(zǎo wǎn) Sooner or later.

WANT A LITTLE MORE?

Usage frequency: Top 500.

131 草 3rd

DEFINITION

1. *Grass, herb.*
2. *Draft* (document); *hasty, rough.*

PRONUNCIATION

cǎo

SOUND WORD

Tsar Bomba
Nickname for the largest hydrogen bomb ever detonated, built by the Soviet Union in the 60s.

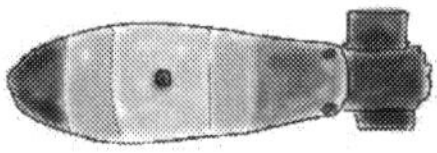

COMPONENTS

艹 *Grass* + 早 SUNFLOWER[130] EARLY

MNEMONICS

- This is the full character for *grass*. When used as a building block, only the top part, 艹, appears at the top of a character. It is the abbreviated form of an old character for *grass*, written 艸, representing two 屮 BLADES OF GRASS[40].
- Picture the building block 艹 as *grass* with its roots below ground.

- As a building block, it is also written 䒑.
- In some stories, *grass* will be a euphemism for 'marijuana'.
- *Flower.*
  We also give this character the meaning of *flower*, a beautiful type of *grass*. Just remind yourself that the **Tsar Bomba** was detonated in the 60s, during the *flower* power years.

STORY

On the morning of October 30th, 1961, the Soviet Union detonated the **Tsar Bomba**, a nuclear bomb, in northern Russia. According to a (fictitious) *draft* document, it was so powerful and the fireball so brilliant that it looked more like a giant SUNFLOWER than a mushroom cloud, rising at a height equivalent to seven times the height of Mount Everest. After the explosion, not a single patch of *GRASS* survived and no *GRASS* grew back for many years afterwards.

EXAMPLES

1. 草地(cǎo dì) Grassland.
2. 草案(cǎo àn) Draft (of a document, plan, etc.). 潦草(liáo cǎo) Hasty, careless; illegible writing.

WANT A LITTLE MORE?

- Make sure to distinguish 艹 from the character 廾 TWO HANDS[74], which has longer vertical strokes.
- The building block version of this character, 艹, is the 140th of the 214 Kangxi radicals.
- Usage frequency: Top third.

132 卓

Definition

† Sun rising through trees.

Now a non-character used only as a building block.

Pronunciation

Not applicable

Sound word

Not applicable

Components

十 TEN[59] + 日 SUN[43] + 十 TEN

Mnemonics

Timex time, 10:10; wristwatch.

The SUN framed by two 'TENS,' like in the Timex ads, where you see the Timex logo framed by the hands of a watch set at TEN past TEN, to set out the brand. Therefore, we use this precise time in the morning, *10:10 (Timex time)*, when the SUN is up, as a mnemonic. It also means a *wristwatch* by extension, because the character looks like a watch, with a band attached on both sides.

133A 干 1st

DEFINITION

1. To *offend*.
2. *Heavenly stems.*
3. To *have to do with.*
4. An army *shield.*

PRONUNCIATION

gān

SOUND WORD

Gans /gans/
German word for 'goose': the domestic goose or the wild Canada goose, known for its bad temper!

MNEMONICS

- In ancient times, this character used to depict a type of *shield*, something that you need for protection when you *offend* someone. It is still used in that sense in a few expressions.
- To *turn the soil over*.

  Since the character looks like 土 SOIL[85] turned upside down, the meaning of 'to *turn the soil over*' is sometimes used in some of the stories.

STORY

"I walked close to a wild Canadian **Gans** this morning and I somehow *offended* it, because it started attacking me. I had no *shield* to protect myself. Look at my face!"
"Yes, you should never *have anything to do with* these creatures. They're vicious."

EXAMPLES

1. 干犯(gān fàn) To offend.
2. 天干(tiān gān) The Ten Heavenly Stems.
3. 相干(xiāng gān) To have to do with.
4. 干戈(gān gē) Weapons of war (shields and swords).

WANT A LITTLE MORE?

Usage frequency: Top third.

133B

干[乾]

1st

DEFINITION

Dry.

PRONUNCIATION

gān

SOUND WORD

Gans /gans/
German word for 'goose': the domestic goose or the wild Canada goose, known for its bad temper!

SIMPLIFIED COMPONENTS

干 to TURN THE SOIL OVER133A to OFFEND

TRADITIONAL COMPONENTS

[卓 10:10132 + 乞 to BEG14]

STORY

My boss sent me on a wild **Gans** chase, to try to find the golden eggs of the golden goose. Can you believe it? Anyways, I had to TURN THE SOIL OVER during a heat wave, looking for the eggs, and everything was parched *dry*.

[It was only 10:10 in the morning on my wristwatch and I was already extenuated and dehydrated, my body totally *dry*, BEGGING for liquids.]

EXAMPLES

干燥(gān zào) Dry, arid. 太干了(tài gān le) Too dry. 擦干(cā gān) To wipe dry. 干杯(gān bēi) To make a toast; cheers! (Literally, to drink the cup dry.)

WANT A LITTLE MORE?

- The simplified character, when used in the sense of 'dry,' is the 51st of the 214 Kangxi radicals.
- Usage frequency: Top third.

133C 干[幹] 4th

DEFINITION

1. *Trunk* (tree, body).
2. To *work*, *do*, *manage* (colloquial); to *fuck* (vulgar).

PRONUNCIATION

gàn

SOUND WORD

Organes /ɔʁgan/
French for 'organs,' parts of the body that have a particular function. The final 'es' is not pronounced in French.

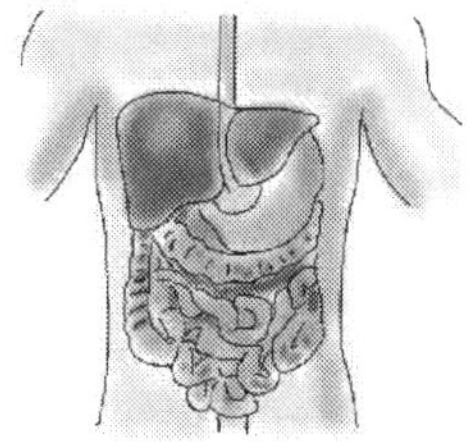

SIMPLIFIED COMPONENTS

干 to TURN THE SOIL OVER[133A] to OFFEND

TRADITIONAL COMPONENTS

[卓 10:10[132] + 人 TENT[9] + 干 to OFFEND[133A]]

STORY

This morning, I started to TURN THE SOIL OVER in my garden. It is tiring and you have to *work* hard! So much so that my *trunk* and internal **organes** were hurting all over when I left for work.

[I arrived at the office at 10:10, just in time for the Summer conference my boss was holding in a TENT outside. I was in a bad mood, because of all the manual tasks I had *managed to do* in the morning. It was OFFENDING to think that all these people were chatting peacefully under a TENT while I was inflicting so much pain on my **organes**! *F*…!]

EXAMPLES

1. 躯干 (qū gàn) Trunk, torso.
2. 干活 (gàn huó) To work on a job. 你在干什么 (nǐ zài gàn shén me) What are you doing?

WANT A LITTLE MORE?

- Note that the simplified character is the same as in the two previous entries.
- Usage frequency: Top third.

134 **幸** 4th

DEFINITION

Good fortune, *luck*.

PRONUNCIATION

xìng

SOUND WORD

Kissing

COMPONENTS

土 SOIL[85] + 丷 ABUNDANCE[55] + 干 DRY[133B]

STORY

There was a big flood of biblical proportions in the region. The only survivor in the area was a man who was living on a high mountain. After the flood, you could see him **kissing** the ground because he had the *good fortune* of owning an ABUNDANCE of DRY SOIL.

EXAMPLES

幸福(xìng fú) Happiness. 幸亏(xìng kuī) Fortunately. 幸运(xìng yùn) Good luck; lucky.

WANT A LITTLE MORE?

Usage frequency: Top third.

135 辛 1st

DEFINITION

1. <u>*Hardship*</u>, *suffering, working hard.*
2. *Hot, spicy, bitter.*

PRONUNCIATION

xīn

SOUND WORD

<u>Sin</u>
A wrong action per religious or moral law.

COMPONENTS

立 to <u>STAND</u>[112] + 十 <u>TEN</u>[59]

MNEMONICS

Hot pepper:
Let's give a concrete meaning to the adjectives *hot* and *spicy*: *hot pepper*.

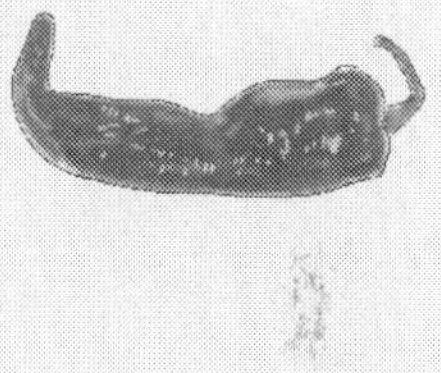

STORY

"I hate to see so much *hardship* and *suffering*. These poor children must <u>STAND</u> on their legs <u>TEN</u> hours straight each day, harvesting *hot peppers* for the market. It's a **sin** to force young children to work that hard."

EXAMPLES

1. 辛酸(xīn suān) Hardship. 辛劳(xīn láo) To toil.
2. 辛辣(xīn là) Pungent, hot, bitter.

WANT A LITTLE MORE?

- Learn to distinguish from 幸 <u>GOOD FORTUNE</u>[134]. Two very similar-looking characters with two opposite meanings.
- This is the 160th of the 214 Kangxi radicals and the 8th heavenly stem.
- Usage frequency: Top third.

136 # 禾 2nd

Definition

Grain, *standing grain*, like rice in a paddy field.

Pronunciation

hé

Sound word

Herder
It means here an American cowboy, a 'cattle **herder**,' featured in so many Western movies.

Components

丿 SLIDE[4] left-falling stroke + 木 TREE[125]

Mnemonics

This is the picture of a stalk of *grain* standing in the field, with a sagging head of *grain* at the top. Ancient form: .

Story

One morning, a **herder** surveys the *grain* field that he grows for his cattle when he sees his young boy install a SLIDE against a TREE located smack in the middle of his field. He runs to him and says, "No, no, no! You and your friends will crush and flatten my *grain* when you land at the bottom of the SLIDE!"

Examples

禾苗 (hé miáo) Grain seedling. 禾秆 (hé gǎn) Stalk of a rice plant.

Want a little more?

- This is the 115th of the 214 Kangxi radicals.
- Usage frequency: Middle third.

137 米 3rd

DEFINITION

1. *Rice*.
2. *Meter* (unit of length).

PRONUNCIATION

mǐ

SOUND WORD

Meat-and-potatoes
Often used to refer to something basic, ordinary but fundamental.

MNEMONICS

This is the pictogram of a stalk of *rice*, shaped like a star. Ancient form: . It is easier to remember it in one piece. Think 'star' and see story.

STORY

Rice is the **meat-and-potatoes**, the 'star' food of Asian countries. Each person consumes at least a cubic *meter* of the stuff per year.

EXAMPLES

1. 米饭(mǐ fàn) Cooked rice.
2. 立方米(lì fāng mǐ) Cubic meter.

WANT A LITTLE MORE?

- This is the 119th of the 214 Kangxi radicals.
- Usage frequency: Top third.

138A 爪 3rd

DEFINITION

Claw.

† To *grip* with the hand.

PRONUNCIATION

zhǎo

SOUND WORD

Jargonaut
An annoying person who uses an excessive number of jargon terms when speaking or writing.

MNEMONICS

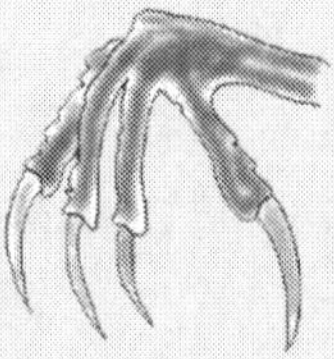

- This is the picture of the *claw* or talon of a bird, animal, monster or machine, or the nails of a human... Ancient form: .
- When used as a building block, it is written as 爫 at the top of a character or as  and its mirror image  on the sides of the character.

STORY

The **jargonaut** is outside watching a bald eagle in flight and explains to a bored audience its characteristics, "Flying above us is a Haliaeetus leucocephalus, what you people call a 'bald eagle,' plummeting towards its quarry. As it gets closer, you can tell that this avian prototype is sexually dimorphic by observing the color of the cere around its nostrils. It is so close now that you can even tell it does not suffer from Aspergillosis…Arrghhh!"

The giant eagle *grips* the **jargonaut** in its *claw* and carries him away, accompanied by big cheers from the crowd.

EXAMPLES

爪牙 (zhǎo yá) Talons and fangs. 凤爪 (fèng zhǎo) Chicken feet (popular Chinese food). 爪印 (zhǎo yìn) Paw print.

WANT A LITTLE MORE?

- This character has two pronunciations for the same meaning.
- This is the 87th of the 214 Kangxi radicals.
- Usage frequency: Middle third.

138B

爪

3rd

DEFINITION

<u>*Claw*</u>.

† To <u>*grip*</u> with the hand.

PRONUNCIATION

zhuǎ

SOUND WORD

d<u>Joua</u>bilité /dʒwabilite/
Think 'gran**de jouabilité**,' a French expression meaning 'great playability.' (See 'Special Sound Mnemonics,' page 495)

MNEMONICS

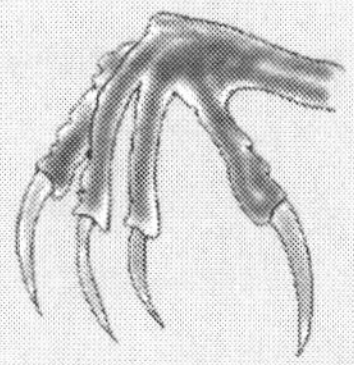

- This is the picture of the *claw* or talon of a bird, animal, monster or machine, or the nails of a human... Ancient form: .
- When used as a building block, it is written as  at the top of a character or as  and its mirror image  on the sides of the character.

STORY

A *claw* crane is a type of game commonly found in arcades, where you try to *grip* a toy with a mechanical *claw*. That type of game offers a gran**de jouabilité** for kids who like to play, which explains its popularity.

EXAMPLES

爪子 (zhuǎ zi) Claw, paw, talon. 鸡爪子 (jī zhuǎ zi) Chicken feet.

WANT A LITTLE MORE?

- This character has two pronunciations for the same meaning.
- This is the 87th of the 214 Kangxi radicals.
- Usage frequency: Middle third.

139 瓜 1st

DEFINITION

Melon, squash.

PRONUNCIATION

guā

SOUND WORD

Gouache
Opaque water paint.

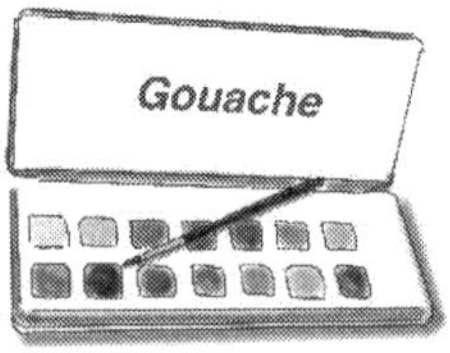

COMPONENTS

爪 CLAW[138A] + 厶 ELBOW[10] PRIVATE

MNEMONICS

- This character looks like the fusion of CLAW and ELBOW.
- Note the similarity between the sounds of **gouache** and '*squash.*'

STORY

This tribe has a special way of making **gouache**. One person holds a *melon* in his CLAWS and another uses his ELBOW to '*squash*' it with force. They then collect the juice, thicken it by evaporation, add some gum and there's your **gouache**!

EXAMPLES

西瓜(xī guā) Watermelon. 笋瓜(sǔn guā) Winter squash. 南瓜(nán guā) Pumpkin. 黄瓜(huáng guā) Cucumber.

WANT A LITTLE MORE?

- This is the 97th of the 214 Kangxi radicals.
- Usage frequency: Top third.

140 𠫓

DEFINITION	PRONUNCIATION
Non-character used only as a building block.	Not applicable

SOUND WORD

Not applicable

COMPONENTS

十 CROSS[59] TEN + 亠 TOP COVER[11]

MNEMONICS

Church.

A CROSS over a TOP COVER (roof) represents a *church*.

141 ⺌

Definition

Non-character used only as a building block.

Pronunciation

Not applicable

Sound word

Not applicable

Components

冖 HAT[11] TOP COVER + 'spikes'

Mnemonics

Jester hat.
This building block looks like a HAT with three spikes on top.

142 𭕄 [𦥯]

DEFINITION

Non-character used only as a building block.

PRONUNCIATION

Not applicable

SOUND WORD

Not applicable

SIMPLIFIED COMPONENTS

'hand' + 冖 HAT[11] TOP COVER

TRADITIONAL COMPONENTS

[臼 CLAWS[138A] + 爻 MESH[100 lines] + HAT]

MNEMONICS

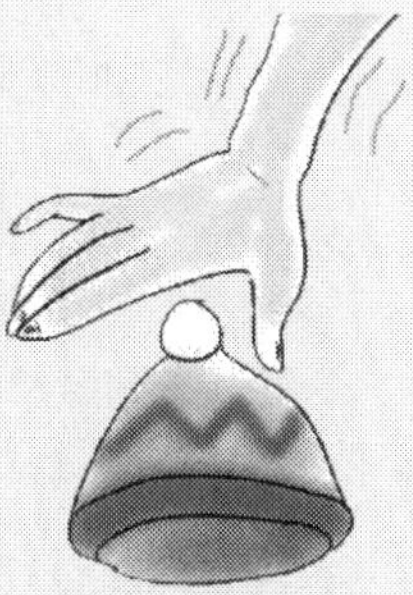

- To *uncover*, to *haul up*.
  Imagine the simplified character as the picture of a 'hand' (the three dots) reaching down to take the cover off something, i.e. to *uncover* and *haul up* something. The traditional building block on the right shows the *uncovering* of an object made with MESH, accomplished with two hands or CLAWS (one on each side). Just think of a winter HAT as the object at the center of the story below.
- In a few occasions, this building block will appear as 龸 instead, the 冖 HAT being replaced by a straight line.

STORY

"The teacher reaches down with his 'hand' to take off, once again, the HAT of the student sitting in class.
"How many times do I have to tell you to *uncover* your head before class?"

[Using his CLAWS, he stretches out the MESH of the HAT.
"There! You won't put this one on anymore, that's for sure!"]

WANT A LITTLE MORE?

Note the slight difference between the simplified version of this building block and the previous one for 𰀁 JESTER HAT[141].

143A

采[採]

3rd

DEFINITION

1. To *pick*, *pluck*, *collect*, *choose*, *gather*.
2. To *fell a tree*.

PRONUNCIATION

cǎi

SOUND WORD

Zeichnungen /tsaɪçnʊŋən/
German word for 'drawings (plural)'.

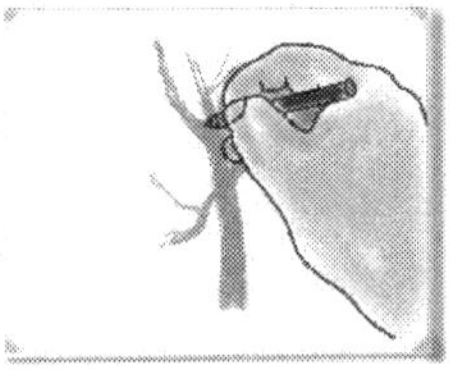

SIMPLIFIED COMPONENTS

爫 CLAW[138A] + 木 TREE[125]

TRADITIONAL COMPONENTS

[扌 HAND[73] + CLAW + TREE]

STORY

In a drawing class (**Zeichnungen**), a teacher says, "Today, we will learn how to draw nature. Let us *choose* a model."
Pointing at a TREE outside, he says, "*Pick* this TREE."
Hearing that, a burly guy stands up and goes outside, jumps into a crane nearby and starts lowering the CLAW of the machine over the TREE when the teacher runs outside and shouts,

["Not with a machine, you moron! You need to draw it with your HANDS! Your HANDS! …???... No! No!! Do not try to *pluck* it from the ground with your HANDS! Leave the TREE alone and come inside right now!"]

EXAMPLES

1. 采摘(cǎi zhāi) To pick. 采用(cǎi yòng) To select for use.
2. 采伐(cǎi fá) To fell a tree.

WANT A LITTLE MORE?

Usage frequency: Top third.

143B 采[採] 4th

DEFINITION

Fief; allotment to a feudal noble.

PRONUNCIATION

cài

SOUND WORD

Poli<u>zei</u> /politsaɪ/
German word for 'police.'

SIMPLIFIED COMPONENTS

爫 CLAW[138A] + 木 TREE[125]

TRADITIONAL COMPONENTS

[土 SOIL[85] + CLAW + TREE]

MNEMONICS

The SOIL building block in the traditional character helps you distinguish this entry from the previous one.

STORY

The **Polizei** just arrested a crazy man dressed in a medieval costume who was pulling out TREES with a mechanical CLAW on a property. At the time of the arrest, he said, "This is my *fief*, awarded by the king himself! I want to build a castle and these TREES are in the way.

["I need to protect my *fief*, my SOIL!!"]

EXAMPLES

采地(cài dì) Fief. 采邑(cài yì) Fief.

WANT A LITTLE MORE?

Usage frequency: Bottom third.

144 采 4th

Definition

† To sift.
† To distinguish.

Pronunciation

biàn

Sound word

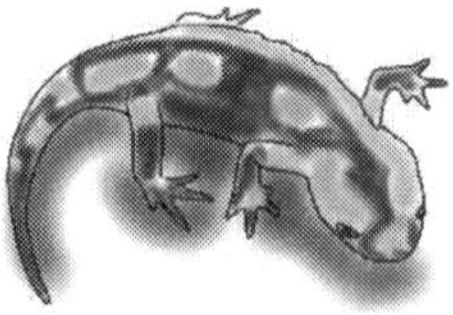

Amphibian
An animal (like a frog, a toad or a salamander) that can live both on land and in water.

Components

丿 to SLIDE[4] left-falling stroke + 米 RICE[137]

Mnemonics

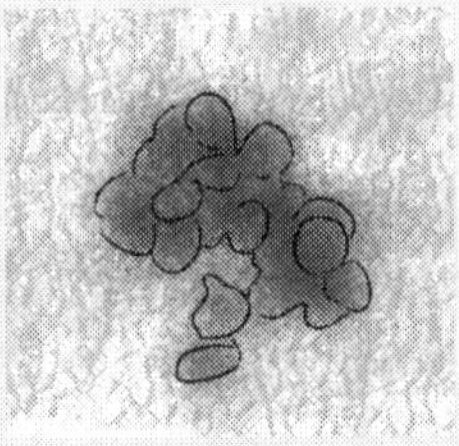

Manure.

Think of non-digested grains of RICE SLIDING out the bottom of farm animals that you recuperate by sifting. Gross, but effective mnemonic.

Story

"What do you do for a living?"
"Originally, I used to study how easily RICE SLIDES down the bottom of farm animals. Nowadays, I do research on the feeding habit of frogs. I sift *manure* from **amphibians**, like the bullfrog."
"Bullshit!"

Want a little more?

- This character differs from 采 to PICK[143A]. Here, we have a SLIDE building block at the top instead of a 爫 CLAW[138A].
- This is the 165th of the 214 Kangxi radicals.

145 来[來] 2nd

DEFINITION

To *come*, *arrive*.

PRONUNCIATION

lái

SOUND WORD

Light meal

SIMPLIFIED COMPONENTS

一 ONE[15] + 米 RICE[137]

TRADITIONAL COMPONENTS

[木 TREE[125] + 2 x 人 PERSON[23]]

STORY

There was once a period of famine in our country and as I was walking down the street, I heard someone call me.
"Pssst! Do you want to share a **light meal** with me? You look so meager. *Come*!"
When I *arrived* at his hovel, he said, "I have ONE grain of RICE. Let's share it."

[So, we, two PERSONS in all, *came* together, sat in the shade of a TREE and gobbled this **light meal**…]

EXAMPLES

下来(xià lái) To come down. 回来(huí lái) To return, come back.
来宾(lái bīn) Guest.

WANT A LITTLE MORE?

Usage frequency: Top 100.

146A

为[為]

2nd

DEFINITION

To *act*, *act as*, *accomplish*, *be*, *become*.

PRONUNCIATION

wéi

SOUND WORD

Weight bar

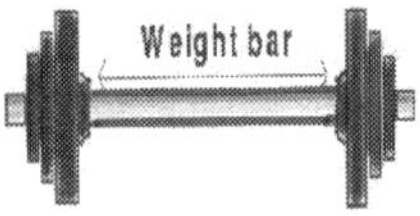

SIMPLIFIED COMPONENTS

2 x 丶 DROP[3] + 力 POWER[108]

TRADITIONAL COMPONENTS

[DROP + 'belly fat' + 灬 FIRE[127]]

MNEMONICS

- For the traditional character, it is easier to look at it as 'belly fat' that you need to burn (FIRE and DROP of sweat) to *become* fit and lean.
- The ancient form, , depicted an elephant (some etymologists say it is a monkey) trained to do hard work.

STORY

When you want to *become* fit, you need to *act*, start exerting POWER and sweat profusely (at least two DROPS). The best way to do this is to use a **weight bar**.

[The **weight bar** will allow you to sweat (just one DROP) and activate your internal FIRE that will help you burn your 'belly fat' and *accomplish* your goal.]

EXAMPLES

作为 (zuò wéi) Action; to accomplish. 成为 (chéng wéi) To become, turn into.

WANT A LITTLE MORE?

Usage frequency: Top 100.

146B 为[為] 4th

DEFINITION

Because of, for, for the sake of, on behalf of.

PRONUNCIATION

wèi

SOUND WORD

K-Way
The famous waterproof jacket.

SIMPLIFIED COMPONENTS

2 x 丶 DROP[3] + 力 POWER[108]

TRADITIONAL COMPONENTS

[DROP + 'belly fat' + 灬 FIRE[127]]

MNEMONICS

The same visual hook of 'belly fat' explained in the previous entry is used here.

STORY

"Why is this boxer exercising while wearing a **K-Way**? He's all covered with DROPS of sweat. What is it *for*?"
"He's doing it *because of* boxing rules. He needs to make weight before his next fight. So, he is exerting POWER in a **K-Way** to sweat abundantly *for the sake of* losing the excess weight.

["The **K-Way** is like a furnace, keeping the heat of his internal FIRE inside, allowing him to sweat (DROP) abundantly and burn his 'belly fat' at the same time."]

EXAMPLES

因为 (yīn wèi) Because, for. 为了 (wèi le) For the sake of. 为什么 (wèi shén me) Why?

WANT A LITTLE MORE?

Usage frequency: Top 100.

147 办[辦] 4th

DEFINITION

To *manage*, *handle*, *deal with*.

PRONUNCIATION

bàn

SOUND WORD

Taliban
An Islamic fundamentalist political movement in Afghanistan.

SIMPLIFIED COMPONENTS

2 x 丶 DROP[3] + 力 POWER[108]

TRADITIONAL COMPONENTS

[2 x 辛 HARDSHIP[135] + POWER]

STORY

"The American soldiers have to expend a lot of POWER and expel a lot of sweat (the two DROPS of water) just trying to *manage* the situation with the **Taliban**."

["Yes, the **Taliban** is tough and can inflict a lot of HARDSHIP with much less military POWER!"]

EXAMPLES

办法(bàn fǎ) Way, means. 办公(bàn gōng) To handle business.
惩办(chéng bàn) To punish.

WANT A LITTLE MORE?

- Note that the simplified character uses the same components as the previous character 为, but the placement of the DROPS is different.
- Usage frequency: Top 500.

148A # 和 **2nd**

DEFINITION

1. *Harmony; with, and.*
2. *Gentle, mild.*

PRONUNCIATION

hé

SOUND WORD

Herder
It means here an American cowboy, a 'cattle **herder**,' featured in so many Western movies.

COMPONENTS

禾 GRAIN136 + 口 MOUTH41

MNEMONICS

If you live in *harmony with* people, you are willing to share your GRAIN and let them put it in their MOUTHS. Ancient form: .

STORY

Two gunshots are heard, followed by the sound of two men falling from a balcony. Through the mist appears a **herder**, chewing on a stalk of GRAIN inserted at the corner of his MOUTH. He says to the gangsters, "I am usually *gentle and mild* and I like *harmony*. If you want to live *with* me *and* the people of this town, you'd better change your ways!" He spits, slowly turns around, then leaves.

EXAMPLES

1. 和平(hé píng) Peace. 你和他(nǐ hé tā) You and him.
2. 温和(wēn hé) Temperate, mild. 和蔼(hé ǎi) Affable.

WANT A LITTLE MORE?

- Get ready. This character has four different pronunciations associated with various meanings.
- Usage frequency: Top 100.

148B

和

4th

DEFINITION

To *join in the singing.*

PRONUNCIATION

hè

SOUND WORD

Fernseher /fɛʁnzeːɐ/
German word for 'television.'

COMPONENTS

禾 GRAIN136 + 口 MOUTH41

STORY

"Last night, the **Fernseher** (television) broadcast a bunch of call-and-response songs. The whole family *joined in the singing*, even my baby brother who was eating and whose MOUTH was full of GRAINS. The television screen was covered with GRAINS after his performance."

EXAMPLES

附和(fù hè) To chime in with. 唱和(chàng hè) To sing a song with others.

WANT A LITTLE MORE?

Usage frequency: Bottom third.

148C

和

2nd

DEFINITION

To *mix with water*; to *knead*.

PRONUNCIATION

huó

SOUND WORD

Rouleau pâte /ʁulo pɑt/
Rolling pin. The exact French expression is 'rouleau à pâte,' but we drop the 'l' of 'rouleau' and the middle 'à.' (See 'Special Sound Mnemonics,' page 484)

COMPONENTS

禾 GRAIN[136] + 口 MOUTH[41]

STORY

To make bread, you first need to crush GRAINS to produce flour that you *mix with water* and *knead* for a while, using a **rouleau pâte**. After that, you bake it in the oven. Only then can you put it in your MOUTH.

EXAMPLES

和泥 (huó ní) To mix and stir mortar. 和面 (huó miàn) To knead flour.

WANT A LITTLE MORE?

Usage frequency: Bottom third.

148D **和** 4th

DEFINITION

To *mix*, *blend*, *stir*, to *make trouble.*

PRONUNCIATION

huò

SOUND WORD

Porte-rouleau /pɔʁt ʁulo/
A toilet paper holder, or simply the little thingy with a spring in the middle that you insert in the center of the paper roll. (See 'Special Sound Mnemonics,' page 484)

COMPONENTS

禾 STANDING GRAIN[136] + 口 MOUTH[41]

STORY

One morning, the coffee shop was out of stir sticks. Not wanting to *make trouble*, I went outside with my coffee, plucked a strand of STANDING GRAIN, *stirred* my coffee with it and wiped it clean with my MOUTH afterwards. I didn't want to do like the guy before me, who went into the bathroom, *mixed* his coffee with the **porte-rouleau** and licked it after that!

EXAMPLES

和药 (huò yào) To mix medicinal herbs. 和了 (huò le) To stir coffee; to make trouble.

WANT A LITTLE MORE?

Usage frequency: Bottom third.

149 国[國] 2nd

DEFINITION

Country, nation.

PRONUNCIATION

guó

SOUND WORD

Growth rate

(The sound **guo** is approximated with English words beginning with the syllable 'gro.')

SIMPLIFIED COMPONENTS

口 to CONFINE[42] + 玉 JADE[21]

TRADITIONAL COMPONENTS

[口 to ENCIRCLE[42] + 或 PERHAPS[93]]

STORY

The economic **growth rate** of this *country* is phenomenal. All the JADE they've accumulated is CONFINED within its borders for now.

[PERHAPS they will not be able to keep it all for themselves, because other *nations* are already beginning to ENCIRCLE them to lay a siege…]

EXAMPLES

国家(guó jiā) Country, nation. 帝国(dì guó) Empire. 中国(zhōng guó) China.

WANT A LITTLE MORE?

- The underlying logic behind the construction of this character is that a *nation* has wealth (玉) within its border (口), with the traditional character also showing mouths (口) that it needs to feed and weapons (戈) for defense.
- Usage frequency: Top 100.

150 **至** 4th

DEFINITION

1. *Until, till, up to.*
2. *Extremely, most.*

PRONUNCIATION

zhì

SOUND WORD

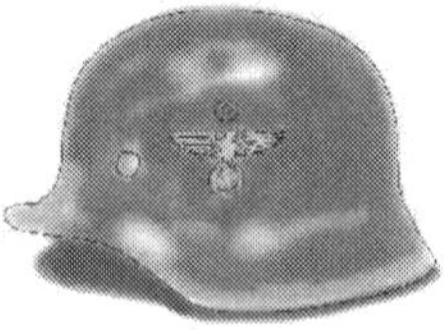

Soldier
For this sound, let's think of the proud, disciplined, tough German **soldier** of World War II.

COMPONENTS

一 ONE[15] + 厶 ELBOW[10] PRIVATE + 土 GROUND[85]

MNEMONICS

The ancient form, , shows a bird diving towards its target *until* it reaches the ground.

STORY

Lying on his belly and supporting his rifle with ONE ELBOW on the GROUND, the German **soldier** fired *until* all his ammunition was expended. He was *extremely* resilient *till* the end.

EXAMPLES

1. 直至(zhí zhì) Until, up to. 至今(zhì jīn) Until now. 甚至(shèn zhì) Even to the point of.
2. 至爱(zhì ài) Most beloved. 北至(běi zhì) Summer solstice.

WANT A LITTLE MORE?

- This is the 133rd of the 214 Kangxi radicals.
- Usage frequency: Top 500.

151 **到** 4th

Definition

1. To *arrive, reach a place, go to.*
2. *Up to.*
3. Indicates the *completion of a verbal action.*

Pronunciation

dào

Sound word

To **endow**, to be **endowed**.

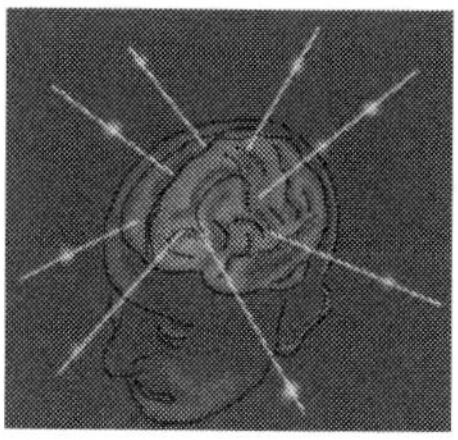

Components

至 UNTIL[150] + 刂 KNIFE[109]

Story

The chief of a special mission waits for his main man to *arrive* and says to him, "I have selected you because you are **endowed** with singular… err… convincing abilities. You see the guard at the door of this complex? You walk *up to* him and hit him with your KNIFE UNTIL he opens the door."

Examples

1. 来到 (lái dào) To arrive.
2. 直到 (zhí dào) Up to, until.
3. 得到 (dé dào) To obtain. 做得到 (zuò de dào) It can be done.

Want a little more?

Usage frequency: Top 100.

152 以 3rd

DEFINITION

1. *Using, by means of; because of; so that, in order to.*
2. *From a point on.*

PRONUNCIATION

yǐ

SOUND WORD

Hippopotame /ipɔpɔtam/
French word for 'hippopotamus.'
The 'h' is silent.

COMPONENTS

乚 HOOK[13] SECOND + 丶 DROP[3] + 人 MAN[23]

MNEMONICS

The ancient form, , depicts a man (on the right) *using* a plow (left side of the character).

STORY

A MAN is dragging a dead **hippopotame** *using* a HOOK, *from point* A to point B. He must work hard *in order to* move it, as the DROP of sweat testifies.

EXAMPLES

1. 以教书为生(yǐ jiāo shū wèi shēng) To make a living by means of teaching. 所以(suǒ yǐ) So, therefore. 可以(kě yǐ) Can. 以为 (yǐ wéi) To suppose, think incorrectly; to consider something as.
2. 以及(yǐ jí) As well as. 以后(yǐ hòu) After, afterwards. 以下(yǐ xià) Below, under.

WANT A LITTLE MORE?

- In modern Chinese, this character is often viewed as an empty prefix or suffix, not carrying any specific meaning of its own (see last three entries of Example 1).
- Usage frequency: Top 100.

153

丁

1st

DEFINITION

1. *Male, man.*
2. *Occupation.*
3. *Cubes of food.*
4. *Fourth in a series.*
5. *Surname.*

† This character used to depict a nail.

PRONUNCIATION

dīng

SOUND WORD

DINK
Acronym for 'Double Income, No Kids.'

MNEMONICS

Nail; to *nail*; *T-shaped*.
Based on its ancient meaning and shape, these three related meanings will appear in the stories when the character is used as a building block.

STORY

This well-dressed, rich *male* **DINK** belongs to the *fourth* generation of a family owning a *nail* manufacturing company. His *occupation* does not allow him to have babies, let alone prepare *cubes of food* for them.

EXAMPLES

1. 成丁 (chéng dīng) Adult male.
2. 园丁 (yuán dīng) Gardener.
3. 肉丁 (ròu dīng) Diced meat.
4. 丁等 (dīng děng) Fourth grade.

WANT A LITTLE MORE?

- It ranks amongst the top 100 Chinese surnames.
- This is the 4th heavenly stem.
- Usage frequency: Top third.

154A 钉[釘] 1st

DEFINITION

Nail.

PRONUNCIATION

dīng

SOUND WORD

DINK
Acronym for 'Double Income, No Kids.'

COMPONENTS

钅 [金] GOLD[124] + 丁 NAIL[153 male]

STORY

This **DINK** has a lot of money to spend. So, he bought himself GOLD *NAILS*. Whenever he tries to hammer the *NAILS*, they keep bending out of shape, because they are too soft! A rich person's problem…

EXAMPLES

钉子 (dīng zǐ) Nail. 螺钉 (luó dīng) Screw.

WANT A LITTLE MORE?

- This is the modern character for *nail*, complete with the METAL (or GOLD) building block.
- Usage frequency: Middle third.

154B 钉[釘] 4th

DEFINITION

To *nail*; to *sew on.*

PRONUNCIATION

dìng

SOUND WORD

Building

COMPONENTS

钅[金] METAL124 + 丁 NAIL153 male

STORY

One day, I saw METAL NAILS sticking out on each façade of a **building**. I asked the guard at the door the reasons for that. He said, "The **building** was about to crumble. We had to *nail* those little thingies to keep it together."

Suddenly, I felt the urge to walk away very quickly…

EXAMPLES

钉入(dìng rù) To nail into. 钉钮扣(dìng niǔ kòu) To sew on buttons.

WANT A LITTLE MORE?

Usage frequency: Middle third.

155 可 3rd

DEFINITION

1. <u>*Can*</u>, <u>*could*</u>, to *be permitted.*
2. *But, however.*

PRONUNCIATION

kě

SOUND WORD

<u>Kö</u>lnischwasser /kœlnɪʃvasɐ/ German word for 'eau de Cologne,' a perfume made of essential oils and alcohol.

COMPONENTS

口 MOUTH[41] + 丁 T-SHAPED[153] male

MNEMONICS

Some etymologists view the origin of this character as a consenting MOUTH exhaling breath. Ancient form: .

STORY

My husband *can* open anything with his teeth. Lately, I found an old bottle of **Kölnischwasser** that used to belong to my grandfather, *but* it was impossible to open. I asked my husband if he *could* try. He just put the T-SHAPED cap in his MOUTH, pulled and said, "There. Anything else?"

EXAMPLES

1. 可以(kě yǐ) Can. 可能(kě néng) To be possible; possibility.
   可爱(kě ài) Lovable (literally 'can be loved'), cute.
2. 可是(kě shì) But, however.

WANT A LITTLE MORE?

Usage frequency: Top 100.

156 **哥** 1st

DEFINITION

<u>*Older brother*</u>.

PRONUNCIATION

gē

SOUND WORD

<u>Ghe</u>!
Let's take this for the sound uttered by a moronic guy. Think 'Dumb & Dumber.'

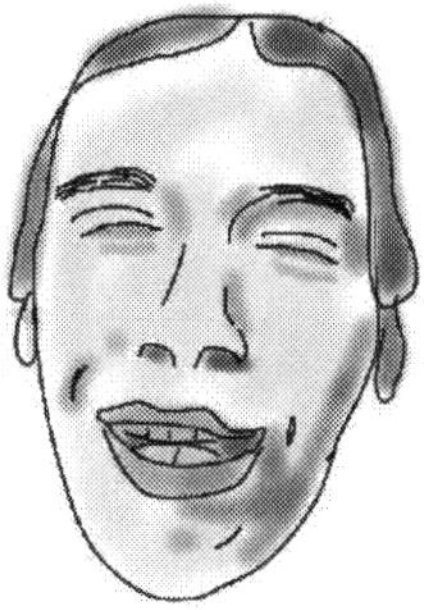

COMPONENTS

2 x 可 <u>CAN</u>155

MNEMONICS

Just assume that you have an *older brother* who thinks he <u>CAN</u> do anything twice as good as you. We all know this is not possible…

STORY

"Look at my moronic (**Ghe**!) *older brother*, who thinks he <u>CAN</u> do anything twice as good as me. There he is, dressed in a miniskirt and thinking he <u>CAN</u> dance the French <u>CAN</u>-<u>CAN</u>!"

EXAMPLES

哥哥(gē gē) Older brother. 哥儿(gē ér) Brothers, boys.

WANT A LITTLE MORE?

Usage frequency: Top third.

157

兄

1st

DEFINITION

Elder brother.

PRONUNCIATION

xiōng

SOUND WORD

Sion /sjɔ̃/
As in French 'Prieuré de **Sion**' (Priory of **Sion**), pronounced 'see-ɔ̃,' an old Order. For this book, let's create its counterpart, a satanic sect called the 'Purgatory of **Sion**.'

COMPONENTS

口 MOUTH[41] + 儿 HUMAN LEGS[52] child

MNEMONICS

Just view this character as a big MOUTH on HUMAN LEGS, running after you.

Ancient form: .

STORY

"I always knew my *elder brother*, with his gangly HUMAN LEGS and his big MOUTH, would not amount to much. He's just joined the Purgatory of **Sion**…"

EXAMPLES

兄长 (xiōng zhǎng) Elder brother. 兄弟 (xiōng dì) Brothers.

WANT A LITTLE MORE?

- This is a second character with the meaning of older brother (see previous character 哥). Using the meaning of *elder brother* for this character in the stories will help tell both characters apart.
- Usage frequency: Top third.

158 兑[兌] 4th

DEFINITION

To *cash*; to *convert*, *exchange* (money).

PRONUNCIATION

duì

SOUND WORD

Postgraduate
A student who continues to study for an advanced degree after earning a bachelor's degree.

SIMPLIFIED COMPONENTS

丷 DEVILISH[55] EIGHT +

兄 ELDER BROTHER[157]

TRADITIONAL COMPONENTS

[八 OCTOPUS[55] EIGHT + ELDER BROTHER]

MNEMONICS

You can view this character as your ELDER BROTHER expelling words (the two dots at the top of the simplified character) as he barters with his mouth.

Ancient form: 兑.

STORY

"My ELDER BROTHER is a **postgraduate** in finance and business, but he often uses a lot of DEVILISH tactics when he barters to make money. Last year he *cashed* in a lot.

[""By selling what? you may ask. By selling OCTOPUSES, of all things!"]

EXAMPLES

兑现(duì xiàn) To cash a check. 兑换(duì huàn) To exchange, convert (money).

WANT A LITTLE MORE?

Usage frequency: Middle third.

159A

说[說]

1st

DEFINITION

To *speak*, *say*.

PRONUNCIATION

shuō

SOUND WORD

Shoo off
To expel, chase away.

COMPONENTS

讠[言] SPEECH[102] + 兑[兌] to CASH[158]

STORY

This fraudulent preacher is trying to CASH in big by giving SPEECHES. More often than not, however, they **shoo off** the guy from the stage, not allowing him to *speak*.

EXAMPLES

说中文(shuō zhōng wén) To speak Chinese. 小说(xiǎo shuō) Fiction, novel.

WANT A LITTLE MORE?

Usage frequency: Top 100.

159B 说[說] 4th

DEFINITION

To *persuade*, *win over*.

PRONUNCIATION

shuì

SOUND WORD

Échoué /eʃwe/
French verb, synonymous of 'failed,' as in a failed exam, test, action…

COMPONENTS

讠[言] WORD[102] + 兑[兌] to CASH[158]

STORY

The members of a lobby group tried to CASH in on the gullibility of the French prime minister by using enticing WORDS to *persuade* the government to reduce tariffs on their industry, but they did not *win* him *over*. In the end, 'ils ont **échoué**', it was a big failure…

EXAMPLES

游说(yóu shuì) To go lobbying. 游说团 (yóu shuì tuán) Lobby group.

WANT A LITTLE MORE?

Usage frequency: Bottom third.

160 寸 4th

Definition

1. *Inch, Chinese inch* (1.3 American inch).
2. *Little, small.*

Pronunciation

cùn

Sound word

Datsun
The **Datsun** car.

Mnemonics

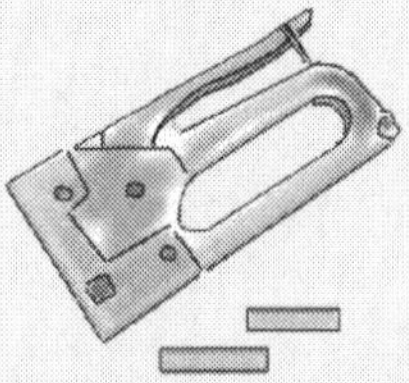

- This character used to depict a hand, with the dot indicating the pulse an *inch* down the wrist. Ancient form: ⺕.
- *Staple*; *staple gun*; to *staple*.
  A more concrete meaning is used for this character, something that can be visualized, based on its shape: one-*inch staples* that you apply with a *staple gun*. The little 丶 DROP[3] (of blood) on the left combined with the building block that looks like a 丁 NAIL[153], help us make the connection with a *staple gun*. The meaning extends to the verb to *staple* and figuratively to the expression '*staple* food.'

Story

"My *little* **Datsun** is pretty beat up. I had to make it hold in one piece using lots of one-*inch staples*!"

Examples

1. 英寸 (yīng cùn) English inch. Also written 吋.
2. 寸步 (cùn bù) Small step.

Want a little more?

- You will sometimes see it written 吋, with an extra mouth on the left. In that case, it means English *inch*.
- This is the 41st of the 214 Kangxi radicals.
- Usage frequency: Top third.

161 寺 4th

Definition

Buddhist temple; *mosque.*

Pronunciation

sì

Sound word

Confessor
A priest who listens to a person's confession in a confessional.

Components

土 SOIL[85] + 寸 STAPLE[160] INCH

Story

Before you can visit the **confessor** at this *Buddhist temple*, you need to prove you're worthy and a real believer. You need to walk barefoot on STAPLES strewn on the SOIL at the entrance of the temple.

Examples

禅寺 (chán sì) Buddhist temple. 礼拜寺 (lǐ bài sì) Mosque.

Want a little more?

Usage frequency: Top third.

162

时[時]

2nd

DEFINITION

Time, period.

PRONUNCIATION

shí

SOUND WORD

Sherpa
An ethnic group living in the Himalayas. They are often used as guides and porters during climbing expeditions.

SIMPLIFIED COMPONENTS

日 SUN43 + 寸 STAPLE160 INCH

TRADITIONAL COMPONENTS

[日 DAY43 + 寺 BUDDHIST TEMPLE161]

STORY

To be able to tell the *time*, the **Sherpa** built himself a sundial by planting just the tips of a big STAPLE into the ground and reading the shadow line produced by the SUN.

[Otherwise, the **Sherpa** needs to climb for a *period* of one DAY to the closest BUDDHIST TEMPLE and read the clock on the tower there. Not worth it, because it takes way too much *time*!]

EXAMPLES

时间 (shí jiān) Time, duration. 小时 (xiǎo shí) Hour.
什么时候？(shén me shí hòu) When.

WANT A LITTLE MORE?

Usage frequency: Top 100.

163 襾 4th

DEFINITION

Cork.

PRONUNCIATION

yà

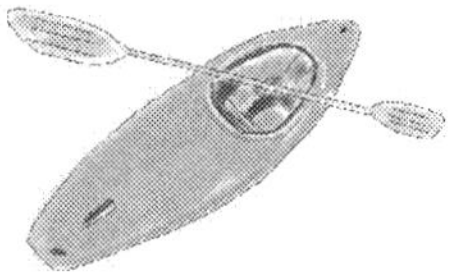

SOUND WORD

Kayak

MNEMONICS

To *uncork*.

This is the modern variant of the old 襾 character, which looks like a *cork* plugged into a bottle. The meaning to *uncork* is used by extension.

STORY

A man notices that his **kayak** is leaking and he plugs the hole with a *cork*.

164

西

1st

DEFINITION

West; *occidental, western.*

PRONUNCIATION

xī

SOUND WORD

Scie /si/
French word for 'saw.' Just think of a 'seesaw.'

COMPONENTS

一 ONE[15] + ~四 FOUR[53]

MNEMONICS

- *West* is ONE of the FOUR directions on a wind vane.
- It appears as 覀 when used as a building block, i.e. it has the same shape as the CORK[163] character. In that case, it can be used either as *West* or as CORK in the stories. To imprint this association in your mind, just remember that many people living in *western* countries like to pop the CORKS to celebrate.

STORY

West is ONE of the FOUR directions on a wind vane, unless you cut it out with a **scie**!

EXAMPLES

西方 (xī fāng) The West, the Occident. 西北(xī běi) Northwest.

WANT A LITTLE MORE?

- This is the 146th of the 214 Kangxi radicals.
- Usage frequency: Top 500.

165A 要 4th

DEFINITION

1. To *want*.
2. *Shall, will; must; important, vital.*

PRONUNCIATION

yào

SOUND WORD

Rail yard
A series of railroad tracks for storing, sorting, or loading and unloading railroad cars.

COMPONENTS

西 WEST[164] + 女 WOMAN[26]

STORY

A long time ago, a friend told me, "Have you seen the movie 'Once upon a time in the WEST'? If not, you *must*. When I saw the actress Claudia Cardinale appear in the **rail yard** scene, I said to myself, 'Wow, I *want* that WOMAN!'"

EXAMPLES

1. 需要(xū yào) To want, require. 不要(bú yào) Don't want; don't need to do something.
2. 将要(jiāng yào) To be going to, will. 重要(zhòng yào) Important. 要紧(yào jǐn) Important, vital.

WANT A LITTLE MORE?

Usage frequency: Top 100.

165B 要 1st

DEFINITION

To *demand*, *request*, *coerce*.

PRONUNCIATION

yāo

SOUND WORD

Yaourt /jauʁt/
French word for 'yogourt.'

COMPONENTS

覀 WEST[164] + 女 WOMAN[26]

STORY

A difficult Asian WOMAN says to her husband, "On your way back from your business trip to the WEST, I *demand* that you bring me some of that Danone stuff."
"You mean **yaourt**?"
"Yes, and you'd better not forget it!"
"Are you *coercing* me?"
"Yes, I am. Any problem with that?"
"No. That's fine. Thank you, darling."

EXAMPLES

要求 (yāo qiú) To demand, request. 要挟 (yāo xié) To coerce.

WANT A LITTLE MORE?

Usage frequency: Bottom third.

166 **向** 4th

Definition

1. *Towards*; *direction.*
2. *Surname.*

Pronunciation

xiàng

Sound word

Négo<u>ciant</u> /negɔsjɑ̃/
French word for 'merchant,' 'wholesaler.'

Components

丶 DROP[3] + 冂 MASK[12] LONG COVER + 口 MOUTH[41]

Mnemonics

Originally, this character depicted a house with a window and a chimney on top (Ancient form: ). The *direction* the window was facing was important for the ancestors.

Story

I go see the **négociant** and I notice that he wears a surgical MASK over his MOUTH. As soon as he sees me, he turns around and looks *towards* the back of his store. I ask him what's the matter.
He says, "The flu virus is highly contagious this winter and I do not want to get sick. It suffices that somebody coughs in your *direction* and that you inhale one single DROP of that breath and you're in bed for a couple of months. I can't afford to lose all these sales!"

Examples

1. 方向 (fāng xiàng) Orientation. 向来 (xiàng lái) Always, all along, up to now.

Want a little more?

- It ranks amongst the top 100 Chinese surnames.
- Usage frequency: Top 500.

167

小

3rd

DEFINITION

Small.

PRONUNCIATION

xiǎo

SOUND WORD

She awoke early…

MNEMONICS

- The character looks like a person with arms down and no head.
- It is also written ⺌ at the top part of other characters.

STORY

She awoke early, in the wee *small* hours of the morning, detecting a *small* change in her body. She was not feeling her head!

EXAMPLES

小学 (xiǎo xué) Primary school. 从小 (cóng xiǎo) Since childhood.
大小 (dà xiǎo) Size. 小时 (xiǎo shí) Hour.

WANT A LITTLE MORE?

- This is the 42nd of the 214 Kangxi radicals.
- Usage frequency: Top 100.

168 **尚** 4th

DEFINITION

1. To *esteem*, to *value*.
2. *Still, yet* (formal).

PRONUNCIATION

shàng

SOUND WORD

Broom shank
The wooden handle of a broom. Just picture a witch broom, with magical power.

COMPONENTS

⺌ SMALL[167] + 冂 SHELTER[12] LONG COVER + 口 WINDOW[41]

STORY

She was living a simple life, sleeping in a SMALL SHELTER with a single WINDOW. She was scary too, wearing a funny hat and living alone with her **broom shank**. *Still*, everybody *esteemed* this woman so much, lest they be transformed into a mouse…

EXAMPLES

1. 高尚(gāo shàng) Noble, lofty. 崇尚(chóng shàng) To uphold, respect.
2. 为时尚早(wéi shí shàng zǎo) It is still too early.

WANT A LITTLE MORE?

Usage frequency: Top third.

169

㕣

DEFINITION

Non-character used only as a building block.

PRONUNCIATION

Not applicable

SOUND WORD

Not applicable

COMPONENTS

亠 COWBOY HAT[49] + 口 MOUTH[41]

MNEMONICS

Tall.
The man wearing a COWBOY HAT is so *tall* that people keep looking at him with their MOUTH wide open.

170 亠口冖

DEFINITION

Non-character used only as a building block.

PRONUNCIATION

Not applicable

SOUND WORD

Not applicable

COMPONENTS

亠口 TALL[169] + 冖 TOP COVER[11]

MNEMONICS

- A *dome*, at the top of a building or structure, i.e. a TALL TOP COVER.
- The TOP COVER part of this character may sometimes appear elongated, like this: 亠口冂, looking even more like a real *dome*.

171	高	1st

DEFINITION

1. *High, tall.*
2. *Surname.*

PRONUNCIATION

gāo

SOUND WORD

Gawk
To stare at someone or something, speechless.

COMPONENTS

亠 DOME[170] + 口 OPENING[41]

MNEMONICS

Eiffel Tower.
This is the picture of a *high* DOME with an OPENING below. Why, but this is the *Eiffel Tower*!

STORY

This is the same story every year. You see a bunch of tourists go into the OPENING under the *high* DOME of the *Eiffel Tower*, look upwards and **gawk**.

EXAMPLES

1. 高大(gāo dà) Tall and big. 我比他高(wǒ bǐ tā gāo) I'm taller than him. 高兴(gāo xìng) Happy.

WANT A LITTLE MORE?

- It ranks amongst the top 100 Chinese surnames.
- This is the 189th of the 214 Kangxi radicals.
- Usage frequency: Top 500.

172 # 京 1st

DEFINITION

Capital (of a country).

PRONUNCIATION

jīng

SOUND WORD

Jink
A **jink** maneuver is an air combat technique where you make a quick, evasive turn.

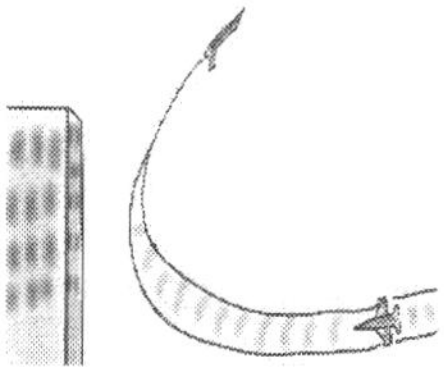

COMPONENTS

亠 TALL[169] + 小 SMALL[167]

MNEMONICS

The character derives from its ancient form , a tower or an imposing house on a hill representing an important building in the *capital.*

STORY

A fighter pilot needs to do an emergency landing because of a malfunction of his aircraft. He makes a **jink** maneuver to avoid the TALL capitol building in the *capital*, but he cannot avoid trouncing a SMALL crowd of people in the street!

EXAMPLES

北京(běi jīng) Beijing (literally 'northern capital'). 京城(jīng chéng) Capital of a country.

WANT A LITTLE MORE?

Usage frequency: Top third.

173 **尢** 1st

DEFINITION

† Lame.

PRONUNCIATION

wāng

SOUND WORD

Wang

As in **Wang** Laboratories, a computer company which was at its peak in the 1980s and ceased to exist in 1992. It built its first minicomputer in 1973, the **Wang** 2200. Let's associate this sound with a very old computer.

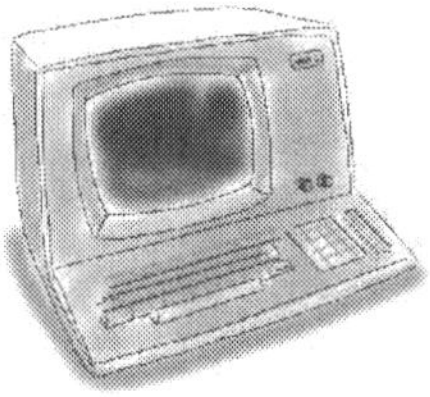

COMPONENTS

一 ONE[15] + 儿 WALKING LEGS[52] child

MNEMONICS

- This is a pictogram of a lame person with a broken leg.
- *Crutches.*
  Just picture a lame **Wang** computer, equipped with ONE pair of WALKING LEGS. It is so old and obsolete now that it needs *crutches.*

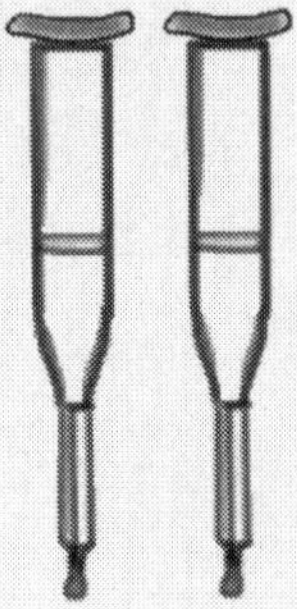

WANT A LITTLE MORE?

This is the 43rd of the 214 Kangxi radicals.

174 尤 2nd

Definition

1. <u>*Outstanding*</u>; *particularly*, *especially*.
2. *Fault*, *mistake*; to *blame*.
3. *Surname*.

Pronunciation

yóu

Sound word

<u>Yo</u>-yo

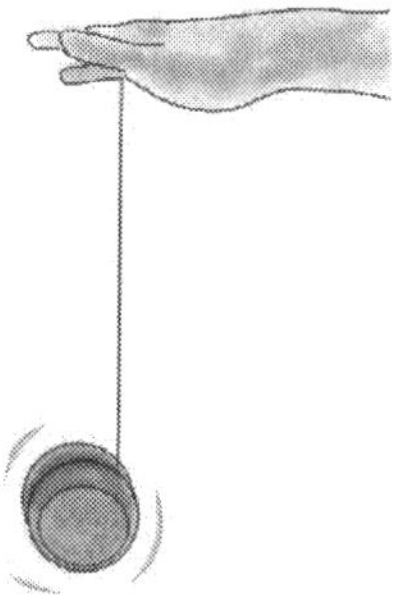

Components

尢 CRUTCHES[173] + 丶 SMALL THING[3] DROP

Mnemonics

- The DROP building block stands for a SMALL THING, a tiny **yo-yo** in the story.
- A lame person on CRUTCHES who plays **yo-yo** will stand out (*out-standing*).

Story

"You should have seen the winner of the World **yo-yo** competition this year! Standing on CRUTCHES and holding a very SMALL THING (a tiny, tiny **yo-yo**, really), he made it do things I had never yet seen and without a single *mistake*! It was an *outstanding* performance, *especially* if you consider the smallness of his toy and his handicap."

Examples

1. 拔尤 (bá yóu) To promote those of outstanding ability. 尤其 (yóu qí) Especially.
2. 效尤 (xiào yóu) To follow a bad example. 尤人 (yóu rén) To blame others.

Want a little more?

Usage frequency: Top third.

175 **就** 4th

DEFINITION

1. *Right away*, *at once*, *immediately*; *just*, *merely*; *exactly*, *precisely*, *indeed*.
2. To *undertake*.

PRONUNCIATION

jiù

SOUND WORD

Villaggio /villaddʒɔ/
Italian word for 'village.' Think of an old Italian **villaggio**.

COMPONENTS

京 CAPITAL[172] + 尤 OUTSTANDING[174]

STORY

I am in the republic of San Marino, located in the Apennine Mountains of the Italian peninsula. I *undertake* a long climb, moving towards the CAPITAL, expecting to discover an OUTSTANDING city, but I *just* find a small **villaggio** at the end of the road. I ask one of the locals if this is *indeed* the CAPITAL, and he replies *right away*, "*Exactly*!"

EXAMPLES

1. 就是(jiù shì) Exactly, precisely; just; simply. 你去我就去(nǐ qù wǒ jiù qù) If you go, then I'll go.
2. 成就(chéng jiù) Achievement, accomplishment.

WANT A LITTLE MORE?

Usage frequency: Top 100.

176

山

1st

DEFINITION

Mountain.

PRONUNCIATION

shān

SOUND WORD

Channe /ʃan/
French word for a pitcher or jug used to serve wine or water, usually made from tin. This word is spoken mostly in the French part of Switzerland, the 'mountain' country.

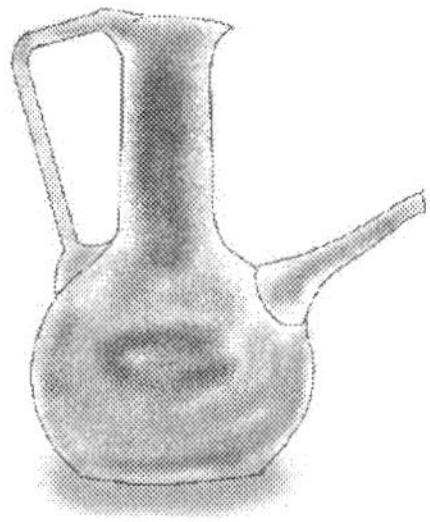

MNEMONICS

This is a pictogram of a *mountain*, with three peaks. Ancient form: .

STORY

Some people living in the *mountains* of Switzerland still make use of a **channe** to pour wine from the Valais in their glass.

EXAMPLES

山峰(shān fēng) Mountain peak. 山水(shān shuǐ) Landscape.

WANT A LITTLE MORE?

- This is the 46th of the 214 Kangxi radicals.
- Usage frequency: Top 500.

177

出

1st

Definition

1. To <u>*exit*</u>, *go out*, *come out*, *put out*, *produce*.
2. To *occur*, *happen*.
3. To *exceed*, *go beyond*.
4. A measure word for *dramas*, *plays*, or *operas*.

Pronunciation

chū

Sound word

<u>**Chew**</u>
A big **chew** of tobacco.

Components

2 x 山 <u>MOUNTAIN</u>176

Mnemonics

Although this character is built as one <u>MOUNTAIN</u> on top of another, its initial meaning has more to do with sprouting leaves *coming out* of the soil. Let's picture a tobacco plant *exiting* from the ground, something you can **chew** on.

Story

"I went to a spitting competition the other day. Contestants were sitting next to a tobacco plant and at the signal, had to put a few leaves in their mouth to obtain a sizable **chew** and then let it *exit* with force while aiming at a target. Sometimes, the spit *went beyond* the intended target and hit the <u>MOUNTAIN</u> of spectators standing behind, which created *some drama*. But you must accept that these things are bound to *happen*."

Examples

1. 出来(chū lái) To exit. 出国(chū guó) To go abroad. 出钱(chū qián) To pay out money.
2. 出事(chū shì) Something happened.
3. 超出(chāo chū) To go beyond, exceed.
4. 一出京剧(yī chū jīng jù) A Beijing opera play.

Want a little more?

Usage frequency: Top 100.

178 亼

DEFINITION

Non-character used only as a building block.

PRONUNCIATION

Not applicable

SOUND WORD

Not applicable

COMPONENTS

人 TENT[9] + 一 ONE[15]

MNEMONICS

Gathering.
A *gathering* of people around ONE table under a big TENT.

179

雨

3rd

DEFINITION

Rain; to rain.

PRONUNCIATION

yǔ

SOUND WORD

Humanité /ymanite/
French word for 'Humanity.' Remember that the letter 'H' is always silent in French. Let's imagine a beauty contest, such as Miss Universe, but instead of being for the whole universe, with aliens and all, this one is restricted to participants from earth and is called 'Miss **Humanité**.'

COMPONENTS

一 CEILING[15] ONE + 冂 SHELTER[12] LONG COVER + 丨 STICK[1] + 4 x 丶 DROP[3]

STORY

During the Miss **Humanité** pageant, the CEILING started to leak and DROPS of water fell on the contestants. The volume of water became so important that it felt like pouring *rain*. Using his STICK, the host guided the participants towards the closest SHELTER and the show was canceled. It was later reported that aliens were at the origin of this incident, not happy to be left out of the pageant...

EXAMPLES

暴雨 (bào yǔ) Torrential rain. 雨水 (yǔ shuǐ) Rainwater. 雨衣 (yǔ yī) Raincoat.

WANT A LITTLE MORE?

- It appears vertically compressed when used as a building block.
- This is the 173rd of the 214 Kangxi radicals.
- Usage frequency: Top third.

180A 云[雲] 2nd

DEFINITION

Cloud, cloudy.

PRONUNCIATION

yún

SOUND WORD

Union /ynjɔ̃/
French word for 'union,' as in marriage.

SIMPLIFIED COMPONENTS

二 TWO16 + 厶 PRIVATE10

TRADITIONAL COMPONENTS

[雨 RAIN179 + TWO + PRIVATE]

STORY

The TWO of them had decided to celebrate their **union** in PRIVATE and they were on *cloud* nine.

[Until RAIN started falling on their wedding suit and dress...]

EXAMPLES

云彩 (yún cǎi) Clouds. 白云 (bái yún) White cloud. 多云的 (duō yún de) Cloudy.

WANT A LITTLE MORE?

Usage frequency: Top third.

180B	云	2nd

DEFINITION

To *say*, *state* in classical literature.

PRONUNCIATION

yún

SOUND WORD

Union /ynjɔ̃/
French word for 'union,' as in marriage.

COMPONENTS

二 TWO[16] + 厶 ELBOW[10] PRIVATE

STORY

After the celebration of their **union**, they walk down the aisle with their TWO ELBOWS interlocked when the new husband *says*, "Now that we are officially married under the equal-sharing rules, I have to *state* that this **union** is based on lies. I do not really like you. I just wanted your money."
"*Say* again?" replies the wife.

EXAMPLES

人云亦云 (rén yún yì yún) To parrot others' words.

WANT A LITTLE MORE?

Usage frequency: Bottom third.

181A 曾 2nd

DEFINITION

In the past, formerly, referring to something that happened previously.

PRONUNCIATION

céng

SOUND WORD

tSunken

A grea**t sunken** treasure; a grea**t sunken** depression.

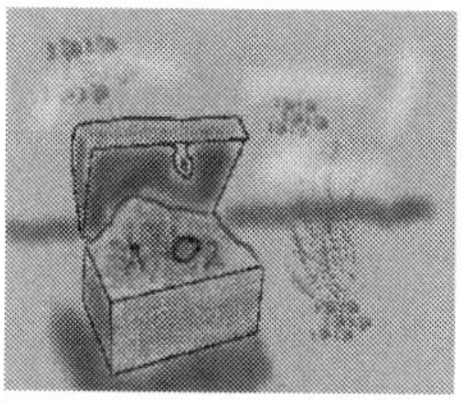

MNEMONICS

Terracotta warrior.

This character is easier to remember visually. It looks like the head of a *terracotta warrior*, built *in the past*, a long time ago during the reign of the first Chinese emperor. You can see his eyes on top, under some sort of hat, and his mouth below.

STORY

(True story) There once was a tyrannical Chinese emperor who lived *in the past* and declared himself the first emperor. Before he died in 210 BC, he ordered that a vast mausoleum be built in his honor to protect him in the afterlife. This grea**t sunken** treasure was discovered in 1974 to the east of Xi'an in Shaanxi province by farmers digging a water well. Thousands of life-sized *terracotta warriors* have been unearthed so far.

EXAMPLES

曾经 (céng jīng) Once before. 不曾 (bù céng) Never.

WANT A LITTLE MORE?

Usage frequency: Top 500.

181B 曾 1st

Definition

1. *Great-grandfather, great-grandson* (separated by two generations).
2. *Surname.*

Pronunciation

zēng

Sound word

Zeng /dseng/

Zen, meaning 'to be in a calm, meditative state of mind,' pronounced in Italian, with an added 'g.' When you are in that state of mind, it is easy to mentally add a 'g' at the end of this word…

Components

曾 TERRACOTTA WARRIOR 181A IN THE PAST

Story

"I saw an old picture of my *great-grandfather* of Asian descent. He was sitting in a **Zen** posture and his face looked imperturbable, like the one displayed by the TERRACOTTA WARRIORS."

Examples

1. 曾孙 (zēng sūn) Great-grandson. 曾祖 (zēng zǔ) Great-grandfather.

Want a little more?

- It ranks amongst the top 100 Chinese surnames.
- Usage frequency: Bottom third.

182A 会[會] 4th

DEFINITION

1. To *be able to*, *can*, *know how to.*
2. To *assemble*, *meet*, *gather*; *union*, *group*, *association*, *meeting.*

PRONUNCIATION

huì

SOUND WORD

Trouer /tʁue/
French verb meaning 'to make a hole (trou)', or 'to have a hole in something.' The image often associated with this verb in the stories is a power drill.

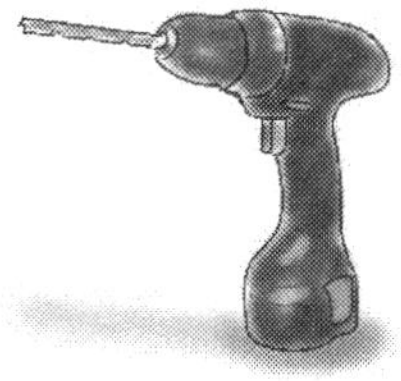

SIMPLIFIED COMPONENTS

人 TENT9 + 云 CLOUD180A

TRADITIONAL COMPONENTS

[亼 GATHERING178 + ~曾 TERRACOTTA WARRIOR181A IN THE PAST]

STORY

Overseeing the excavation site of the first Chinese emperor tomb, I must remain vigilant with my personnel. The other day, I was walking towards the big TENT where we usually hold our *group meetings* when I saw a CLOUD of dust coming out of it and heard a power drill.

[I went inside and saw a GATHERING of archeologists who were in the process of **trouer** a TERRACOTTA WARRIOR's head with a drill (hint: they had already damaged the head; the 'horns' at the top of the character had disappeared).
"What do you think you are doing?" I shouted.
"We wanted to *be able to* say with certainty if the head is full or just an empty shell," one of them replied.
"Do you have any idea of the value of these things? Do you really think you *can* do these sorts of things without consulting me first?"] (To be followed…)

EXAMPLES

1. 你会说中文吗? (nǐ huì shuō zhōng wén ma?) Do you speak Chinese?
2. 会议(huì yì) Meeting, conference. 开会(kāi huì) To hold a meeting.

WANT A LITTLE MORE?

Usage frequency: Top 100.

182B

会[會]

3rd

DEFINITION

Moment; a *brief period.*

PRONUNCIATION

huǐ

SOUND WORD

<u>Rouer</u> de coups /ʁwe də ku/ French expression meaning 'to beat somebody black and blue.'

COMPONENTS

会[會] to <u>BE ABLE TO</u>182A

STORY

(This is the sequel of the story for character 182A.)

"Do you really think you can do these sorts of things without consulting me first?" I asked. There was a *brief period* of silence. I then took the broken head (which turned out to be full) and I used it to **rouer de coups** all the archeologists, screaming all the while, "Are you <u>ABLE TO</u> say if it's full or empty now?" Within *moments*, they were all on the ground.

EXAMPLES

会儿(huǐ ér) Moment. 过一会儿(guò yī huǐ ér) Later.

WANT A LITTLE MORE?

Usage frequency: Middle third.

182C 会 [會] 4th

Definition

Accounting; accountant.

Pronunciation

kuài

Sound word

Bulkwise
In terms of bulk.

Components

会 [會] to BE ABLE TO[182A]

Story

A carpenter says to his work fellows, "Have you seen the new guy? **Bulkwise**, he is no bigger than my wife. I don't think he will BE ABLE TO lift a single plank of wood."
"He won't have too. He's the new *accountant* of our firm."

Examples

财会 (cái kuài) Finance and accounting. 会计 (kuài jì) Bookkeeper, accountant.

Want a little more?

Usage frequency: Bottom third.

183 尔[爾] 3rd

DEFINITION

1. *Thou* (archaic you).
2. *Thus, so, like that.*
3. Used for its sound.

PRONUNCIATION

ěr

SOUND WORD

Auricular
Relating to the ear or hearing.

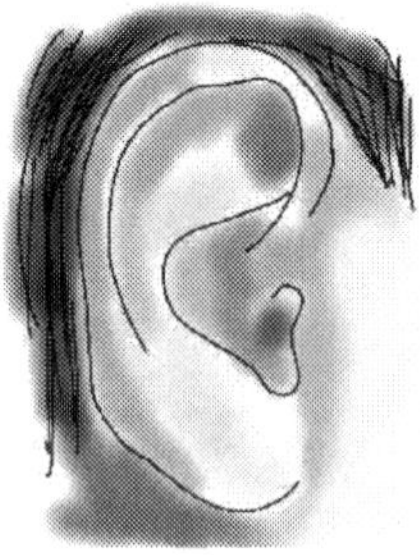

SIMPLIFIED COMPONENTS

⺈ to WRAP[67] + 小 SMALL[167]

MNEMONICS

Standing hanger.
The traditional character is taken as a whole and given the fictitious meaning of *standing hanger* because of its resemblance to it. The X's represent a lattice of some sort suspended on the hanger, like a coat of mail…

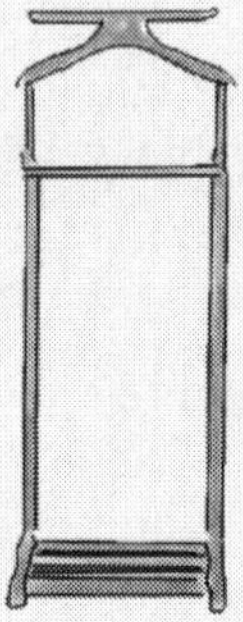

STORY

A group of medieval knights discuss in a castle when Borin appears with an **auricular** bandage, tightly WRAPPED around his right ear, making it appear very SMALL. "Hey Borin! Why do *thou* show up *like that*?"

["Last night," says Borin, "I got up to relieve myself and crashed into my *standing hanger*. My ear got stuck in a ring of my coat of mail suspended on the hanger, tearing half of it off."
"If *standing hangers* give *thou* trouble, what will *thou* do with Saracens? *Thou* will surely end up with more than an **auricular** lesion!" And the whole room burst into laughter.]

Examples

1. 尔等(ěr děng) You all. 菲尔之讨(fēi ěr zhī tǎo) It is not your fault.
2. 不尔(bù ěr) Not so.
3. 爱尔兰(ài ěr lán) Ireland.

Want a little more?

- It is mostly used nowadays for its sound in foreign words.
- Usage frequency: Top 500.

184 **你** 3rd

DEFINITION

You.

PRONUNCIATION

nǐ

SOUND WORD

Nearsighted
Short-sighted.

COMPONENTS

亻 HANDYMAN[23] MAN + 尔 THOU[183]

STORY

The HANDYMAN sees a fuzzy shape approaching, and only when his friend is at two feet from his face, says, "Oh, it's THOU! Since I am **nearsighted**, I did not recognize THOU at first."
His friend says, "OK. Cut that crap. I know *you* like to show off, but we do not say THOU anymore since Shakespeare is dead. *You* is the word now. *YOU*!"
"Wow, THOU are in a bad mood!" says the HANDYMAN.

EXAMPLES

你的 (nǐ de) Your, yours. 你们 (nǐ men) You (plural). 你好 (nǐ hǎo) Hello; How are you?

WANT A LITTLE MORE?

Usage frequency: Top 100.

185

业[業]

4th

DEFINITION

Industry, *profession*, *business*, *occupation*, *trade*.

PRONUNCIATION

yè

SOUND WORD

Embouteillait /ɑ̃buteje/
From the French verb 'embouteiller' (to bottle or put in a bottle), conjugated in the imperfect tense, translating to 'he/she was bottling…'

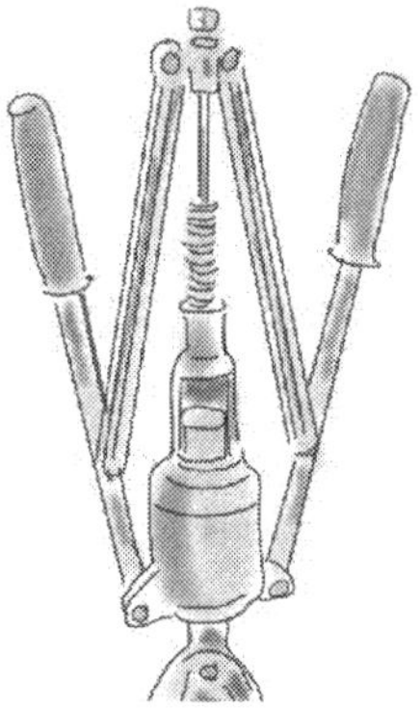

SIMPLIFIED COMPONENTS

'Bottling apparatus'

TRADITIONAL COMPONENTS

[丵 WINERY[186] + 木 WOODEN[125]]

MNEMONICS

Note how the simplified character looks very much like the bottling apparatus shown above for the sound word!

STORY

Every fall, as was customary in the wine *industry*, the French producer, using a 'bottling apparatus,' **emboutaillait** his wine…

[… in the WOODEN shack of his WINERY.]

EXAMPLES

工业(gōng yè) Industry. 农业(nóng yè) Agriculture, farming.

WANT A LITTLE MORE?

- The traditional version of this character depends on the 丵 WINERY building block introduced next, which in turn depends on this INDUSTRY building block, creating a circular relation. This is enough to make your head spin, just like when you drink too much wine!
- Usage frequency: Top 500.

186 丵 2nd

Definition

† Thick grass, bush.

Pronunciation

zhuó

Sound word

Jeweler
A seller of fine jewelry.

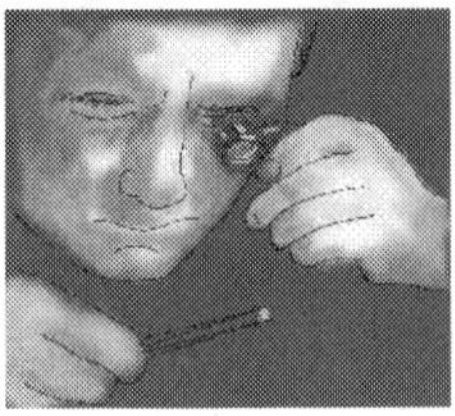

Components

业 INDUSTRY[185] + 丷 ABUNDANCE[55] + 干 DRY[133B]

Mnemonics

Winery.
An INDUSTRY which produces an ABUNDANCE of DRY wines. Another way of looking at it: a type of INDUSTRY not found in a 'DRY' country, like in Saudi Arabia, famous however for its jewelry and where this **jeweler** resides.

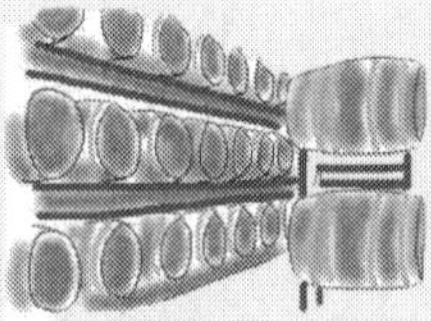

Want a little more?

Note the circular relation between this building block and the traditional version of the 業 INDUSTRY[185] character.

187 对[對] 4th

DEFINITION

1. *That's right!*
2. Measure word for a *couple*, a *pair*.
3. To *be opposite*, *oppose*, *face*.
4. To *answer*, *reply*.

PRONUNCIATION

duì

SOUND WORD

Postgraduate
A student who continues to study for an advanced degree after earning a bachelor's degree.

SIMPLIFIED COMPONENTS

又 RIGHT HAND[71] +
寸 STAPLE GUN[160] INCH

TRADITIONAL COMPONENTS

[丵 WINERY[186] + 一 ONE[15] +
寸 STAPLE[160] INCH]

STORY

"You did what? You nailed the guy's RIGHT HAND with your STAPLE GUN?" "*That's right!* Here's why...

["This presumed **postgraduate** in oenology owns the WINERY *opposite* my house. I had asked him many times not to park his delivery truck in front of my driveway, because it blocks my exit. He was always *opposed* to that idea and never *replied*. So, when I saw him park his truck at the same place once again, I ran out and nailed him to the dashboard, using only ONE STAPLE. Or maybe *a couple*…"]

EXAMPLES

1. 对了 (duì le) That's correct, right.
2. 一对夫妻 (yī duì fū qī) A married couple.
3. 反对 (fǎn duì) To oppose, be against. 对面 (duì miàn) Across from.
4. 对答 (duì dá) To answer.

WANT A LITTLE MORE?

Usage frequency: Top 100.

188

生

1st

DEFINITION

1. To *give birth*, to *be born*; *life*.
2. *Unfamiliar*, *new*.
3. *Raw; unripe, green.*

PRONUNCIATION

shēng

SOUND WORD

J'saigne de la tête
'I bleed from the head'. (See 'Special Sound Mnemonics,' page 491)

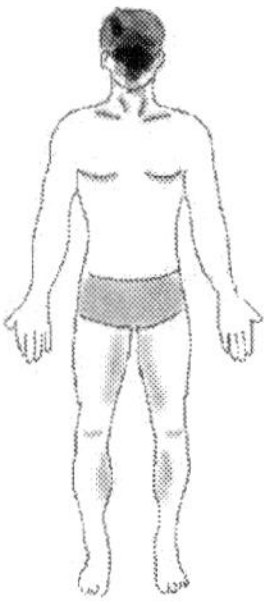

COMPONENTS

牛 COW[35] + 土 SOIL[85]

MNEMONICS

The character originally showed a 屮 SPROUT[65] coming out of the 土 GROUND[85], meaning *birth*. Ancient form: . We prefer the better graphical representation of COW and SOIL, since the character looks like the merging of these two building blocks. See story.

STORY

A COW *gives birth* to a calf that falls on the SOIL, bleeding from the head (**j'saigne** de la tête). It may be difficult to watch for a person *unfamiliar* with it.

EXAMPLES

1. 生活 (shēng huó) Life. 先生 (xiān shēng) Sir, Mr. (born first). 生日 (shēng rì) Birthday.
2. 生字 (shēng zì) New character (to learn).
3. 生菜 (shēng cài) Raw vegetable salad, romaine lettuce.

WANT A LITTLE MORE?

- This is the 100th of the 214 Kangxi radicals.
- Usage frequency: Top 100.

189 **能** 2nd

DEFINITION

To *be capable, able*; *can do*; *ability*, *capability*.

† A bear.

PRONUNCIATION

néng

SOUND WORD

[n]**English**
Think of a**n English** man from London.

COMPONENTS

厶 ELBOW[10] PRIVATE + 月 FLESH[48] + 2 x 匕 SPOON[66]

MNEMONICS

This character used to depict a bear, the left side of the character representing its body and head and the right side its claws. Ancient form: . The bear is a very *capable* animal…

STORY

Hard to believe, but what this impeccably-dressed person, a**n English** man from London, is *capable* of doing is nothing short of extraordinary. He is *able* to hold a live bear by the neck with his bent ELBOW and play the SPOONS on the FLESH of the bear's belly with his other hand. It takes a lot of *ability*!

EXAMPLES

能够 (néng gòu) Can, be able to. 能力 (néng lì) Ability, capacity.
不可能 (bù kě néng) Impossible.

WANT A LITTLE MORE?

Usage frequency: Top 100.

190 熊 2nd

DEFINITION

1. *Bear.*
2. *Surname.*

PRONUNCIATION

xióng

SOUND WORD

Si on gagne /si ɔ̃ gaɲ/
French expression that means 'If we win.'

COMPONENTS

能 CAPABLE[189] + 灬 FIRE[127]

STORY

A French king organized a contest. Whoever is CAPABLE of holding a live grizzly *bear* over a cooking FIRE for a minute wins the hand of his daughter and all the riches that come with it. My friend tells me, "Wow! Let's try it. Can you imagine, **si on gagne**?
"Well, can you imagine if we don't?" I ask back.

EXAMPLES

1. 北极熊(běi jí xióng) Polar bear. 熊猫(xióng māo) Panda. 灰熊(huī xióng) Grizzly bear.

WANT A LITTLE MORE?

- It ranks amongst the top 100 Chinese surnames.
- Usage frequency: Top third.

191

而

2nd

DEFINITION

And, *as well as*, *yet*, *but* (shows causal relation, change of state or contrast).

† A beard.

PRONUNCIATION

ér

SOUND WORD

Army

MNEMONICS

Shovel.

Because of a striking resemblance, a *shovel* is used as the mnemonic for this character.

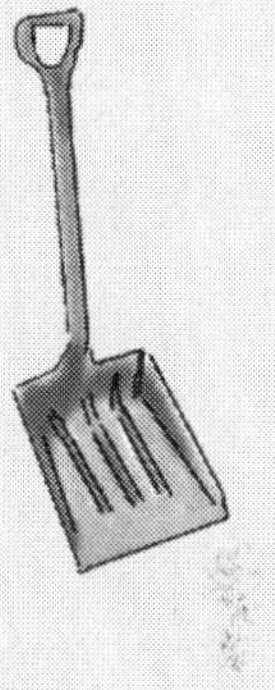

STORY

A minister says to his king, "There is a revolt brewing. There is now an **army** of peasants at the gate of your castle. Not to worry though, because from what I see, they are only equipped with *shovels*. *But*, wait… *and* catapults!!"

EXAMPLES

美丽而善良 (měi lì ér shàn liáng) Beautiful and kindhearted. 而且 (ér qiě) Furthermore. 反而 (fǎn ér) On the contrary.

WANT A LITTLE MORE?

- This is the 126th of the 214 Kangxi radicals.
- Usage frequency: Top 100.

192 彳 4th ㇏

DEFINITION

To *step forward*, to *progress*, to *make progress*.

† To step with the left foot.

PRONUNCIATION

chì

SOUND WORD

Body snatcher
A person who steals corpses and limbs from graves to sell or dissect them.

COMPONENTS

丿 to SLIDE[4] left-falling stroke + 亻 MAN[23]

MNEMONICS

This character used to indicate movement on foot, more precisely stepping with the left foot.

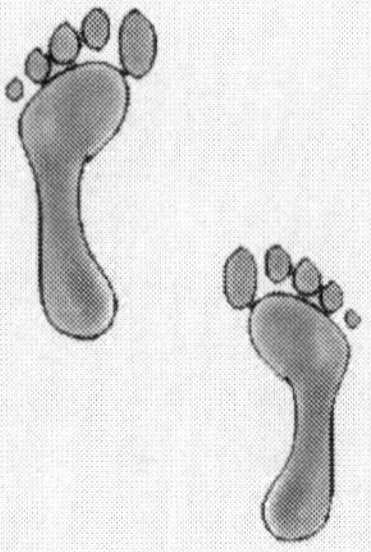

STORY

A ski racer is at the gate and at the signal, the MAN *steps forward* and *makes* good *progress* by SLIDING down the mountain faster than his opponents. Unfortunately, he falls and dies, to the great pleasure of the **body snatcher**. Top quality body parts!

WANT A LITTLE MORE?

This is the 60th of the 214 Kangxi radicals.

193 旦 4th

Definition

Daybreak, *dawn*.

Pronunciation

dàn

Sound word

Ramadan
The ninth month of the Muslim year, during which fasting is observed from sunrise to sunset.

Components

日 SUN[43] + 一 HORIZON[15] ONE

Mnemonics

The SUN over the HORIZON. Ancient form: .

Story

During the **Ramadan**, from *daybreak*, i.e. when the SUN appears over the HORIZON, until sunset, you are not allowed to eat or drink.

Examples

元旦 (yuán dàn) New Year's Day. 旦夕 (dàn xī) A short while.

Want a little more?

Usage frequency: Top third.

194A 得

DEFINITION

1. *Sentence particle* used after a verb to show *possibility* or describe *how the action is performed.*
2. *Verb suffix* with no special meaning.

PRONUNCIATION

de

SOUND WORD

Well, duh!
Expression to show that something just said is already known or is obvious.

COMPONENTS

彳 to STEP FORWARD & PROGRESS[192] + 旦 DAYBREAK[193] +
寸 STAPLE GUN[160] INCH

STORY

At DAYBREAK, a drill sergeant does a demonstration in front of his soldiers. "Private Jones, please STEP FORWARD!" After Private Jones executes the order, the drill sergeant takes out his STAPLE GUN, nails the outer rim of the Private's shoes *firmly* to the ground and yells again, "Private Jones, please STEP FORWARD!"
"Sir, I *can't* move!"
"And why, Private?"
"**Well, duh**!"
"Exactly! Remember this important lesson, soldiers: Enemies nailed in place cannot PROGRESS!"

EXAMPLES

1. 来得及(lái de jí) To be able to do something. 说得快(shuō de kuài) To speak quickly.
2. 认得(rèn de) To recognize, know. 懂得(dǒng de) To comprehend.

WANT A LITTLE MORE?

Usage frequency: Top 100.

194B 得 2nd

Definition

To *obtain, get, gain.*

Pronunciation

dé

Sound word

De Gaulle /də gol/
A French general who led the Free French Forces during World War II. His statement below has been greatly modified for this book.

Components

彳 to STEP FORWARD[192] + 旦 DAYBREAK[193] + 寸 STAPLE GUN[160] INCH

Story

De Gaulle was the first French leader to STEP FORWARD and to exhort the French population to form the French resistance after the fall of France during World War II. The appeal that he wrote at DAYBREAK the previous day and broadcast from London on June 18, 1940, is well-known. "Do not give up the fight. Use any means at your disposal, even if your only weapon is a STAPLE GUN. We will *obtain* the support of the British Empire and the United States of America and we will assuredly *gain* victory at the end!"

Examples

得到 (dé dào) To succeed in obtaining. 取得 (qǔ dé) To gain, acquire.
得了 (dé le) Enough! Done, finished.

Want a little more?

Usage frequency: Top third.

194C

得

3rd

Definition

Must; to *have to*, *ought to*, *need to*.

Pronunciation

děi

Sound word

Daily dozen
Physical exercises you 'must' do every day, especially in the morning.

Components

彳 to STEP FORWARD[192] + 旦 DAYBREAK[193] + 寸 STAPLE GUN[160] INCH

Story

Every day at DAYBREAK, my neighbor living in the apartment just above mine does his **daily dozen**. I am woken up by the sound of his tape: "STEP FORWARD, step backward, jump! STEP FORWARD…" For 45 minutes, my apartment is shaking every time he hits the floor. I realized I *had to do* something about this. So, this morning, I took my STAPLE GUN and knocked on his door. When he answered, I stapled his two feet to the ground before he had the chance to react. I then said, "You *must* stop doing your **daily dozen** at DAYBREAK!"

Examples

总得(zǒng děi) Must, to have to. 我得走了 (wǒ děi zǒu le) I must go.

Want a little more?

Usage frequency: Top third.

195 田 2nd

DEFINITION

1. *Field* (an area of land).
2. *Surname.*

PRONUNCIATION

tián

SOUND WORD

Tienda /tjenda/
Spanish word for 'grocery store,' 'shop.'

MNEMONICS

- It represents a cultivated *field* with irrigation ditches, separated in four plots, seen from above. Ancient form: .
- *Tennis court.*
  In some stories, it can also represent a *tennis court.*

STORY

When the produce reaches maturity in the *field*, it is shipped to a **tienda**.

EXAMPLES

1. 油田 (yóu tián) Oil field. 水田 (shuǐ tián) Irrigated field.

WANT A LITTLE MORE?

- It ranks amongst the top 100 Chinese surnames.
- This is the 102nd of the 214 Kangxi radicals.
- Usage frequency: Top third.

196 **肉** 2nd

DEFINITION

† *Rump*, an animal's hind legs and tail.
† Animal footprint.

PRONUNCIATION

róu

SOUND WORD

Rodent
Rats, squirrels, gophers…etc.

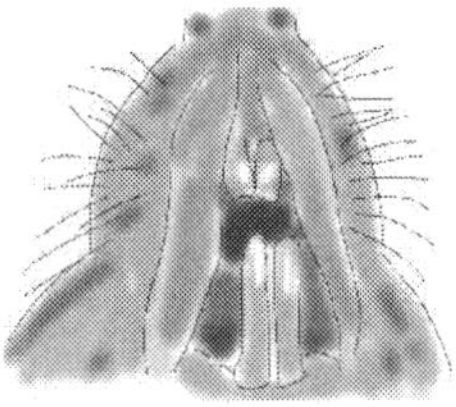

MNEMONICS

This is a pictogram of an animal's *rump*, with its butt and tail.

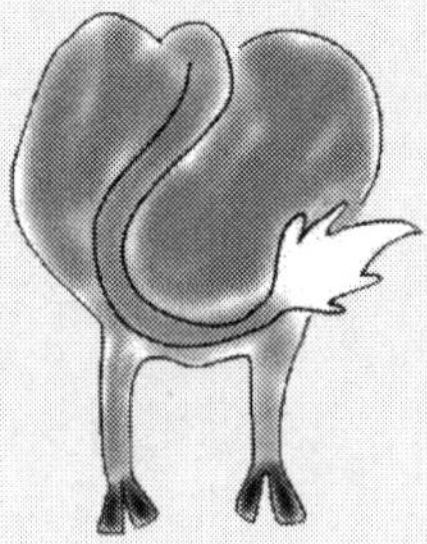

STORY

"Are you sure it was a **rodent**, sweetie?"
"Yes… I saw its *rump* when it ran away!"

WANT A LITTLE MORE?

- This is the 114th of the 214 Kangxi radicals.

197 万[萬] 4th

DEFINITION

1. *Ten thousand*; *a great number.*
2. *Surname.*

† *Scorpion.*

PRONUNCIATION

wàn

SOUND WORD

Okinawan
People living on the island of Okinawa, close to Japan, or something related to Okinawa. Site of an important battle during World War II.

SIMPLIFIED COMPONENTS

一 ONE[15] + ~勹 BUNCH[67] to WRAP

TRADITIONAL COMPONENTS

[艹 GRASS[131] + 田 FIELD[195] + 禸 RUMP[196]]

MNEMONICS

The traditional character is a pictogram of a *scorpion*. Ancient form: .

STORY

During the battle of Okinawa, the Japanese and the **Okinawans** were coming out in *great numbers*, ONE BUNCH of *ten thousand* after another.

[When taken prisoners, they were forced to sit, by putting their RUMP on a GRASS FIELD infested with *scorpions*.]

EXAMPLES

1. 百万 (bǎi wàn) One million. 万一 (wàn yī) A very small percentage or chance; if by any chance.

WANT A LITTLE MORE?

- It ranks amongst the top 100 Chinese surnames.
- Usage frequency: Top 500.

198 方 1st

DEFINITION

1. *Direction; side.*
2. *Place.*
3. *Aspect.*
4. *Square* (shape).
5. *Surname.*

PRONUNCIATION

fāng

SOUND WORD

Fang
A long, sharp tooth on a snake, a tiger, a bat…

MNEMONICS

To *run away*.
This character is easier to remember visually. It looks like a man, seen from the *side*, *running away* (from 万 SCORPIONS[197]?) in the opposite *direction*.

STORY

I was sitting by the *side*, in the central *place* of a village in India, in a '*square*' if you will, when I saw a man coming in my *direction*, *running away* from a tiger showing its **fangs**!

EXAMPLES

1. 方向 (fāng xiàng) Direction. 东方 (dōng fāng) The East.
2. 地方 (dì fāng) Place.
3. 方面 (fāng miàn) Aspect.
4. 立方 (lì fāng) Cube.

WANT A LITTLE MORE?

- It ranks amongst the top 100 Chinese surnames.
- This is the 70th of the 214 Kangxi radicals.
- Usage frequency: Top 100.

199

于[於]

2nd

DEFINITION

1. *In, at, to, towards, from, by, out of.*
2. *Surname.*

PRONUNCIATION

yú

SOUND WORD

Ulysse /ylis/
The French name for Ulysses, the main character in the two famous (and oldest) novels written by the Greek poet Homer: 'The Iliad' and 'The Odyssey.'

TRADITIONAL COMPONENTS

[方 to RUN AWAY198 DIRECTION + 人 MAN23 + ⺀ ICE129]

MNEMONICS

- *Boat anchor.*
  The simplified version of this character resembles a *boat anchor* and is the meaning it will carry when used as a building block.
- This character is a preposition with many directional meanings.

STORY

One day, **Ulysse** got lost and found himself surrounded by icebergs *in* all directions. "Where *to* go?" he wondered. He tried to throw his *boat anchor in* the water, but it stayed *at* the surface of the frozen sea.

[He then saw ICE MEN coming *towards* him *from* all directions, but it was too late *by* then to RUN AWAY *from* them! (Homer had forgotten that part in the Odyssey…)]

Examples

1. 位于 (wèi yú) To be located at/in. 对于 (duì yú) In regard to, towards. 生于北京 (shēng yú běi jīng) To be born in Beijing.

Want a little more?

- The simplified version 于 ranks amongst the top 100 Chinese surnames.
- The traditional character is also used as a surname, but it is pronounced in the first tone in that case.
- Usage frequency: Top 100.

200 目 4th

DEFINITION

Eye.

PRONUNCIATION

mù

SOUND WORD

Sha<u>mu</u>
This is the name often given to a killer whale in a SeaWorld show. Lots of fun ahead!

MNEMONICS

- This is a pictogram of an *eye*, with the iris in the middle. Ancient form: .
- This character is sometimes written on its side, like this: 罒, when used as a building block.

STORY

Shamu jumped high in the air and splashed down hard, spraying lots of salty water in the spectator's *eyes*.

EXAMPLES

目前 (mù qián) At present (in front of one's eyes). 盲目 (máng mù) Blind.

WANT A LITTLE MORE?

- This is the 109th of the 214 Kangxi radicals.
- Usage frequency: Top 500.

201 自 4th

Definition

1. *Myself, himself, herself, oneself, itself.*
2. *Nature, naturally.*
3. *From.*

† A *nose*.

Pronunciation

zì

Sound word

Against all odds

Components

丶 DROP[3] + 目 EYE[200]

Mnemonics

This is a primitive pictogram of a *nose*. In China, a person points to his or her *nose* when talking about *himself/herself*. Ancient form:  .

Story

Against all odds, the man with no arms and legs has been able to put DROPS in his EYES, all by *himself*!

Examples

1. 自己 (zì jǐ) Oneself. 自动 (zì dòng) Automatic (move by itself).
   自行车 (zì xíng chē) Bicycle (a vehicle that I move myself).
2. 自然 (zì rán) Nature, natural world.
3. 自左而右 (zì zuǒ ér yòu) From left to right.

Want a little more?

- This is the 132nd of the 214 Kangxi radicals.
- Usage frequency: Top 100.

202

老

3rd

Definition

1. *Old man*; *experienced.*
2. A prefix used before the surname of a person to *indicate affection* or *familiarity.*

Pronunciation

lǎo

Sound word

Laryngitis
A medical condition in which the throat and larynx become sore.

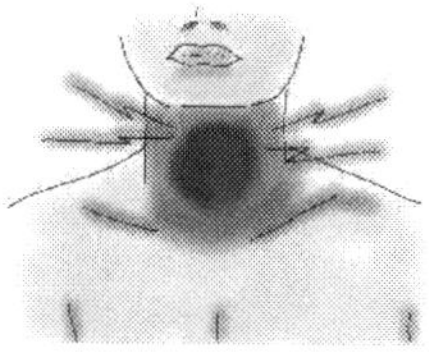

Components

土 DIRT[85] + ノ to SLIDE[4] left-falling stroke + 匕 SPOON[66]

Mnemonics

- This is the pictogram of an *old man* with long hair leaning on a stick. Ancient form: .
- As a building block, it is written simply as 耂 at the top of a character, dropping the 匕 SPOON.

Story

"Aging is no fun. I am an *old man* now, hardly staying on my feet, SLIDING often and hitting the DIRT, breaking my hips... I cannot eat solid food, having to be SPOON fed. And I am often sick, getting one **laryngitis** after another…"

Examples

1. 老人(lǎo rén) Old man, woman. 老头子(lǎo tóu zǐ) Old man. 老师(lǎo shī) Teacher.
2. 老王(lǎo wáng) Dear old Wang! 老乡 (lǎo xiāng) Fellow villager.

Want a little more?

- This is the 125th of the 214 Kangxi radicals.
- Usage frequency: Top 500.

203 **者** 3rd

DEFINITION

A *person who does something*, a doer, a maker.

PRONUNCIATION

zhě

SOUND WORD

Jacuzzi

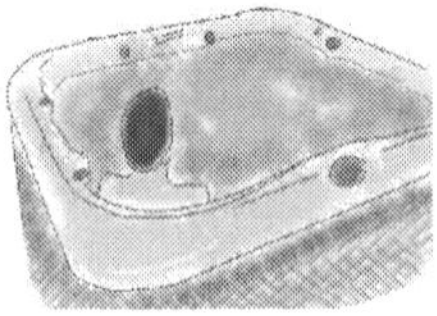

COMPONENTS

耂 OLD MAN[202] + 日 SUN & DAY[43]

MNEMONICS

To *drudge*; a *drudge*.
The meaning of this character is extended to the verb to *drudge* or its noun equivalent, meaning to work all day, doing hard, menial or monotonous work.

STORY

This OLD MAN is a real *doer*. He *drudges* all DAY under the SUN in his backyard while his neighbor spends all his time in a **Jacuzzi**…

EXAMPLES

读者 (dú zhě) Reader. 作者 (zuò zhě) Author, writer. 新闻记者 (xīn wén jì zhě) Journalist.

WANT A LITTLE MORE?

- This character is equivalent to the –ist or –er suffixes in English (see examples).
- Usage frequency: Top 500.

204

著

4th

Definition

1. To *write books*.
2. *Famous*, *prominent*, *outstanding*.

Pronunciation

zhù

Sound word

Laggiù /laddʒu/
Italian adverb meaning 'down there,' 'under,' 'below,' 'over there.'

Components

艹 GRASS[131] + 者 to DRUDGE[203] DOER

Mnemonics

This character originally depicted the action of *writing* words on bamboo scrolls. Ancient form: .

Story

Writing books is a tough job. You often need to DRUDGE looking for interesting words and expressions while working **laggiù**, in your basement or in the hole you call your office. You sometimes need 'external help.' No wonder that some *outstanding* writers were also *famous* for being good GRASS smokers…

Examples

1. 著作 (zhù zuò) To write; book, writings.
2. 著名 (zhù míng) Famous. 显著 (xiǎn zhù) Notable, remarkable, outstanding.

Want a little more?

Usage frequency: Top third.

205A 着[著]

DEFINITION

1. It indicates an *action in progress*, equivalent to the -ing suffix in English.
2. It indicates an *accompanying action or event.*

PRONUNCIATION

zhe

SOUND WORD

Gadget

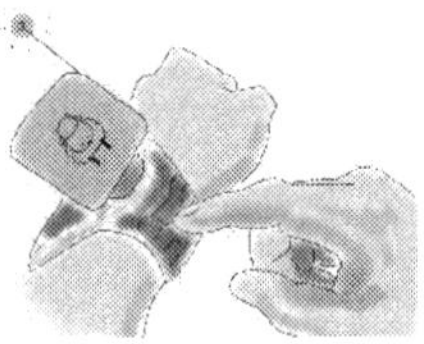

SIMPLIFIED COMPONENTS | TRADITIONAL COMPONENTS

⺷ RUNNING SHEEP[37] SHEEP + 目 EYE[200] [艹 GRASS[131] + 者 to DRUDGE[203] DOER]

MNEMONICS

Shepherd.
This character is one of the most difficult to understand and remember because of all its meanings and different pronunciations (4 in all). For this reason, let's try to simplify it. All the stories related to this character involve a *shepherd*. Why? Because a *shepherd* must 'keep an EYE on his RUNNING SHEEP while [DRUDGING through the GRASS]."

STORY

The *shepherd* was tired of keep*ing* an EYE on his RUNNING SHEEP all day, so he bought himself a **gadget**.

[This **gadget** allows him to monitor his sheep from a distance. He can now be watch*ing* TV, runn*ing* errands, read*ing* books or sleep*ing* while the sheep are the only ones that need to DRUDGE through the GRASS!]

EXAMPLES

1. 他睡着呢(tā shuì zhe ne) He is sleeping.
2. 她说着看了我一眼(tā shuō zhe kàn le wǒ yī yǎn) She looked at me while speaking.

Want a little more?

- Although the traditional version 著 is sometimes encountered in old text with this meaning, nowadays it is mainly used for 'to write books,' as described in the preceding entry.
- Usage frequency: Top 100.

205B 着[著] 1st

DEFINITION	PRONUNCIATION
Tricks, *ideas*, *techniques*, *moves* (in chess or elsewhere).	zhāo
	SOUND WORD
	Jar

COMPONENTS

着[著] SHEPHERD[205A] action in progress

STORY

One day, the SHEPHERD got an *idea* while watching his ewes. He poured sheep milk in a **jar**, added in a culture and waited. Thanks to this novel *technique*, we can now consume feta cheese from Greece, Roquefort cheese from France and Ricotta cheese from Italy, all originating from this *idea*! It was a clever *move*!

EXAMPLES

妙着 (miào zhāo) Clever move. 着儿(zhāo ér) A move (in chess); an idea, a plan, a trick.

WANT A LITTLE MORE?

Usage frequency: Middle third.

205C 着[著] 2nd

DEFINITION

1. To *touch*, *come in contact with* (most often with water or the ground).
2. To *feel*, *be affected by*.
3. To *catch fire*, *burn*, *be lit*.
4. To *fall asleep*.
5. Indicates the *successful result of a verb*.

PRONUNCIATION

zháo

SOUND WORD

Jarring
To undergo severe vibration or a physical jolt. To have a harsh or unpleasant effect on someone or something.

COMPONENTS

着[著] SHEPHERD205A action in progress

STORY

With no rain during the preceding month, the grass was very dry. The SHEPHERD lit a cigarette and threw the match over his shoulder. As soon as the match *came into contact* with the grass, it *caught fire*, engulfing all the sheep nearby in flames. It was **jarring** to see how the SHEPHERD was really *affected* by this incident afterwards. He was unable to *fall asleep*, even though he was continuously counting in his head the sheep he lost that day. A **jarring** experience altogether.

Examples

1. 我脚疼的不能着地(wǒ jiǎo téng de bù néng zháo dì) My foot hurts so much that I cannot put it on the ground.
2. 着急(zháo jí) To feel anxious.
3. 木炭着了 (mù tàn zháo le) The charcoal is lit. 灯点着了 (dēng diǎn zháo le) The lamp is lit.
4. 睡着 (shuì zháo) To fall asleep.
5. 我的书找着了 (wǒ de shū zhǎo zháo le) I have found my book. 他猜着了 (tā cāi zháo le) He guessed right.

Want a little more?

Usage frequency: Top third.

205D

着[著]

2nd

DEFINITION

1. To *wear clothes.*
2. To *touch, contact.*
3. To *apply, attach, use.*
4. To *send.*

PRONUNCIATION

zhuó

SOUND WORD

Jeweler
A seller of fine jewelry.

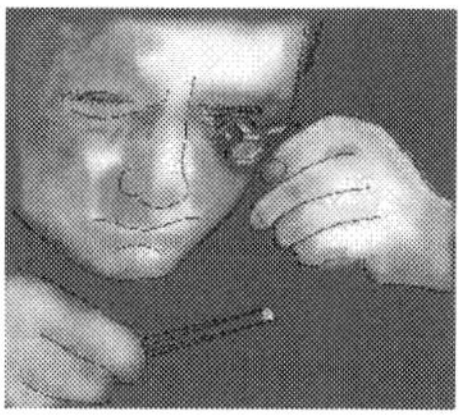

COMPONENTS

着[著] SHEPHERD[205A] action in progress

STORY

The SHEPHERD thinks to himself, "To *wear clothes* made from sheep wool is fine, but how about other products, like wool jewelry?" He decides to make a few samples, *using* and *applying* glue to different parts to make them stick together. He then *sends* the wool thing to the **jeweler** to have it appraised.

EXAMPLES

1. 衣着(yī zhuó) Clothing. 着装(zhuó zhuāng) To wear clothes.
2. 附着(fù zhuó) To touch, come into contact with.
3. 着墨(zhuó mò) To apply ink to paper (to write).
4. 着人去办(zhuó rén qù bàn) To send somebody to do it.

WANT A LITTLE MORE?

Usage frequency: Bottom third.

206 之 1st

Definition

1. *Of*, a possessive marker in classical Chinese, equivalent to modern 的 OF[69A].
2. *Him*, *her*, *it*, *this*, *that* in classical Chinese, when replacing an objective noun or pronoun.

Pronunciation

zhī

Sound word

Jerk
Just imagine an ignorant, cocky person who is inconsiderate and does stupid things. It may help to think of a person you know.

Mnemonics

Zzzz… or *Zorro*.
Think of *Zorro*, making a Z sign with his saber or the universal symbol for sleeping: *zzzz*…, with a nasal 丶 DROP[3] at the top to prevent snoring.

Story

I was sleeping (*zzzz*…) last night when my friend erupted in my room and said, "Look! I got myself a *Zorro* costume for the Halloween party. It even has an authentic saber!" He then made the sign *of Zorro* on my chest, swish… swish… swish, leaving a big Z tear on my Burberry pajama. I looked at *him* and said, "You're a **jerk**, you know that, don't you?"

Examples

1. 原因之一(yuán yīn zhī yī) One of the reasons. 之后 (zhī hòu) Later, afterwards. 三天之内 (sān tiān zhī nèi) Inside of three days. 百分之百 (bǎi fēn zhī bǎi) A hundred percent.
2. 诺之(nuò zhī) Promise it, her, him.

Want a little more?

- This character is now mostly seen in certain set phrases and expressions.
- Usage frequency: Top 100.

207 年 2nd

DEFINITION

Year; age.

PRONUNCIATION

nián

SOUND WORD

Niente /njɛnte/
Italian word for 'nothing,' 'nil,' 'zero,' as in 'far **niente**,' doing nothing.

COMPONENTS

𠂉 RIFLE[8] + ⺧ TELEPHONE POLE[34]

MNEMONICS

- The ancient form, , depicts a man harvesting grain, a task done once a *year*.
- The extra hook on the left of the ⺧ TELEPHONE POLE building block stands for the transformer in the story.

STORY

An Italian man of a certain *age* was caught firing at a TELEPHONE POLE transformer with his RIFLE, damaging it. He said, "I was tired of doing **niente**, so, I thought, what the heck!"
He got one *year* in prison.

EXAMPLES

今年(jīn nián) This year. 明年(míng nián) Next year. 青年(qīng nián) Youth, young people.

WANT A LITTLE MORE?

Usage frequency: Top 100.

208 冎 3rd

Definition

† *Skeleton*.
† To cut flesh from bones.

Pronunciation

guǎ

Sound word

Guacamole /gwakamole/
An avocado-based dip.

Mnemonics

This is supposed to depict a skull and a vertebra, hence a *skeleton*.

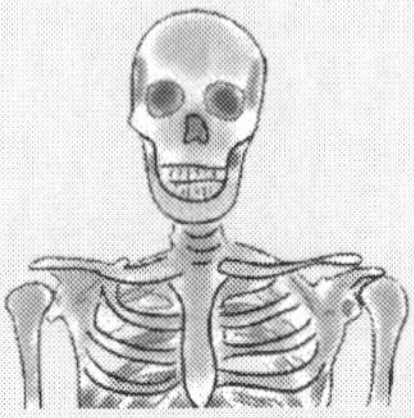

Story

"The *skeleton* found near Roswell, New Mexico, is believed to belong to an alien. It was as green as **guacamole**."

209 骨 3rd

DEFINITION

Bone.

PRONUNCIATION

gǔ

SOUND WORD

Goudronné
/gudʁɔne/
French verb meaning 'covered with tar.'

COMPONENTS

冎 SKELETON208 + 月 FLESH48

MNEMONICS

If you strip off the FLESH from the *bones*, you end up with a 冎 SKELETON.

STORY

The chief curator of a Paris museum says to his assistants, "To obtain a SKELETON that will not deteriorate with time, make sure to strip all the FLESH from the *bones* beforehand. After that, the *bones* need to be **goudronnés**."

EXAMPLES

骨头 (gǔ tóu) Bone. 骨灰 (gǔ huī) Bone ash.

WANT A LITTLE MORE?

- This is the 188th of the 214 Kangxi radicals.
- Usage frequency: Top third.

210 **咼[咼]** 1st

DEFINITION

Surname.

† *Jaw, jawbone.*

PRONUNCIATION

guō

SOUND WORD

Groan
A deep sound due to pain, despair, etc.

SIMPLIFIED COMPONENTS

口 MOUTH[41] + 内 INTERIOR[24]

TRADITIONAL COMPONENTS

[冎 SKELETON[208] + MOUTH]

MNEMONICS

- To see the INTERIOR of your MOUTH, you need to open your *jaw*.
- [The part of the SKELETON forming your MOUTH is the *jawbone*.]

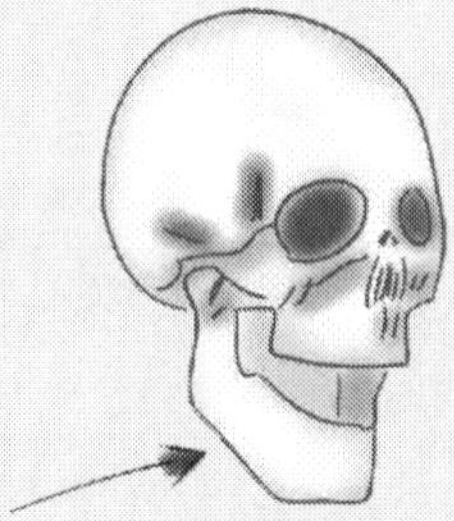

STORY

In a dentist's waiting room, a patient asks,

"Why all the grunts we're hearing in the next room?"
"One of our patients, Mr. *Guo*, **groans** because the dentist tries to forcefully open his *jaw* to see the INTERIOR of his MOUTH."

["His MOUTH must hold a shameful secret."
"Yes, he must have a SKELETON in his closed *jaw*."]

WANT A LITTLE MORE?

Now only used as a surname.

211

过[過]

4th

DEFINITION

1. To *cross, go over, pass* (time), *celebrate* (a holiday).
2. Marker of an *experience* (completed or past action).
3. *Surname.*

PRONUNCIATION

guò

SOUND WORD

Hombre antiguo /ombre antiɣwo/
Spanish expression for an 'old man.'

SIMPLIFIED COMPONENTS

辶 ROAD[104] + 寸 STAPLES[160] INCH

TRADITIONAL COMPONENTS

[ROAD + 咼 JAW[210]]

STORY

An **hombre antiguo**, deaf and blind, wants to *cross* the ROAD. Just to *pass the time* and have some fun, a group of youngsters close by decide to nail his two shoes to the ground with STAPLES while he's waiting for the light. When his guide dog hears the beeping signal, the man just can't move!

[The dog pulls harder and the **hombre antiguo** ends up falling face first on the ROAD, breaking his JAW. An *experience* he'll never forget.]

EXAMPLES

1. 经过(jīng guò) To go through, undergo. 过来(guò lái) To come over. 过年(guò nián) To celebrate the New Year. 不过(bù guò) However, but, only, no more than.
2. 你去过中国吗? (nǐ qù guò zhōng guó ma) Have you ever been to China?

WANT A LITTLE MORE?

Usage frequency: Top 100.

212 友 3rd

DEFINITION

Friend.

PRONUNCIATION

yǒu

SOUND WORD

Yolanda
A fictional new girlfriend.

COMPONENTS

𠂇 LEFT HAND[70] + 又 RIGHT HAND[71]

MNEMONICS

Two *friends*, holding hands. Ancient form: .

STORY

"**Yolanda** and I are real *friends* now. She insists that I hold her LEFT HAND with my RIGHT HAND when we walk."

EXAMPLES

朋友(péng yǒu) Friend, boyfriend, girlfriend. 女友(nǚ yǒu) Girlfriend.

WANT A LITTLE MORE?

Usage frequency: Top third.

213 友 2nd

DEFINITION

† A running dog with hind leg tied.

PRONUNCIATION

bá

SOUND WORD

Bath mat
A small mat for standing on before or after taking a shower, to prevent slipping.

COMPONENTS

友 FRIEND[212] + 丶 DROP[3]

MNEMONICS

To *take a shower*.
DROPS of water falling on my FRIEND.

STORY

My FRIEND is at my place, *taking a shower*. DROPS of water are falling on her head. I make sure the **bath mat** is in place.

214 癶 1st

DEFINITION

† Two legs stretched in order to climb inside a chariot or straddle something.

PRONUNCIATION

bō

SOUND WORD

Boat

MNEMONICS

Standing with legs spread apart.
This definition is not only a good visual representation of the character but also close to its ancient meaning.

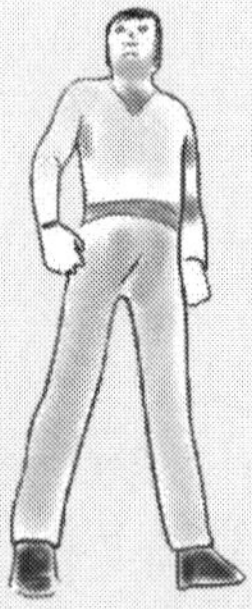

STORY

The captain is *standing with his legs spread apart* at the bow of his **boat**. He looks like the king of the world!

WANT A LITTLE MORE?

This is the 105th of the 214 Kangxi radicals.

215 **弓** 1st

DEFINITION

<u>*Bow*</u> (of a weapon or of a stringed instrument; anything *bow-shaped*).

PRONUNCIATION

gōng

SOUND WORD

<u>**Gong**</u>

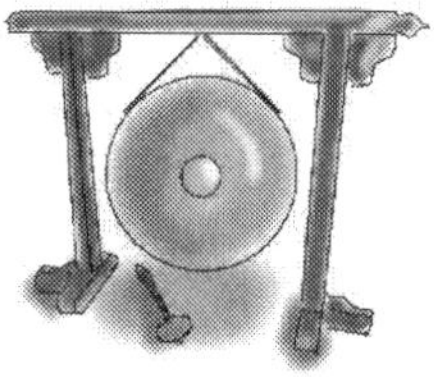

MNEMONICS

This is the picture of a *bow* to shoot arrows.

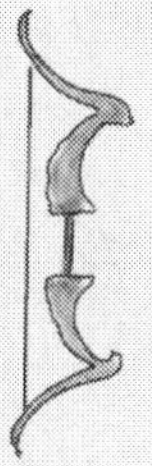

STORY

An orchestra conductor tells the first violin, "Please hit the **gong** with your *bow* to signal the start of the piece." The first violin takes out a *bow* weapon from a cello case and shoots the **gong** with it.

EXAMPLES

弓箭 (gōng jiàn) Bow and arrow. 弓子 (gōng zǐ) Bow of a stringed instrument; anything that is bow-shaped.

WANT A LITTLE MORE?

- This is the 57th of the 214 Kangxi radicals.
- Usage frequency: Middle third.

216 从[從] 2nd

DEFINITION

1. To *follow*; *follower*.
2. *From*, *since*.

PRONUNCIATION

cóng

SOUND WORD

tSong-dance
Think 'Hit **song-dance**,' a dance you do on a hit song. Let's picture line dancing for this one.

SIMPLIFIED COMPONENTS

2 x 人 PERSON[23]

TRADITIONAL COMPONENTS

[彳 to STEP FORWARD[192] + 2 x PERSON + 止 FOOTPRINT[75]]

MNEMONICS

The simplified character looks like one PERSON *following* another, *from* point A to point B.

STORY

Two PERSONS are doing a hit **song-dance** by line dancing. They *follow* each other's steps.

[I see them STEP FORWARD and back, trying to walk in the same FOOTPRINTS. And I hear them flirting with each other: "*Since* when do you come here? Where are you *from*?"]

EXAMPLES

1. 跟从(gēn cóng) To follow.
2. 自从(zì cóng) Since. 从前(cóng qián) In the past.
   从一到三(cóng yī dào sān) From one to three.

WANT A LITTLE MORE?

Usage frequency: Top 100.

217 由 2nd

Definition

From; cause, reason; owing to; through, via.

† It represents the germination of a grain, hence a *sprout* or to *sprout*.

Pronunciation

yóu

Sound word

Yo-yo

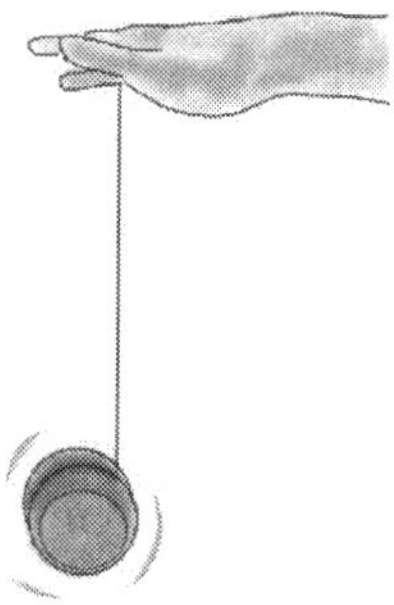

Components

丨 WALKING STICK[1] + 田 FIELD[195]

Mnemonics

The character looks like a **yo-yo** dangling at the end of a cord.

Story

A grower of Brussels *sprouts* wants to show us his facilities. He arrives with a WALKING STICK in one hand and a **yo-yo** in the other and he asks us to follow him. While playing **yo-yo** and doing all sorts of moves like the 'Around the world' trick, he takes us *from* his house *through* his FIELD.
"For what *reason* do you play with a **yo-yo**?" I ask.
"Oh, this is to keep the mosquitoes away *from* me," he says.

Examples

由此(yóu cǐ) From this. 来由 (lái yóu) Reason, cause. 由于(yóu yú) Owing to. 经由 (jīng yóu) Via, by way of.

Want a little more?

- This is another character that means 'from,' like 从 FROM[216].
- Usage frequency: Top 500.

218 黄[黃] 2nd

Definition

1. *Yellow.*
2. *Surname.*

Pronunciation

huáng

Sound word

Roue en grès /ʁuɑ̃ɡʁɛ/
French expression for 'sandstone wheel.' Let's imagine prehistoric wheels like those seen in the cartoon The Flintstones.

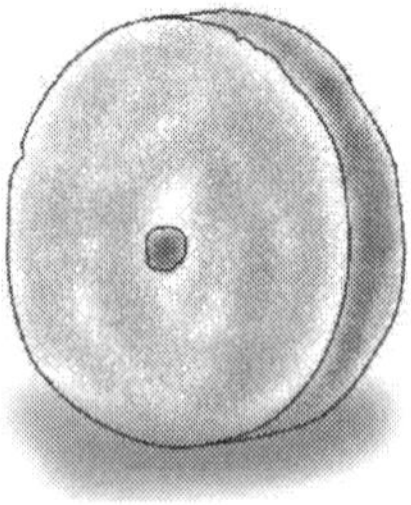

Simplified components

廿 GRAZING COWS[61] +
由 to SPROUT[217] + 八 OCTOPUS[55] EIGHT

Traditional components

[廿 TWENTY[60] + 一 ONE[15] +
to SPROUT + OCTOPUS]

Mnemonics

Its ancient form, , used to depict a flaming arrow, from which *yellow* derives.

Story

GRAZING COWS are eating peacefully when a giant *yellow* OCTOPUS SPROUTS from under an old **roue en grès** that was left in the field, grabs a cow with its tentacles and carries it under, in its hiding place.

[Over the month, not ONE, but TWENTY cows disappeared that way! With this terrifying SPROUTING OCTOPUS, no wonder the cows now have a *yellow* streak down their back!]

Examples

1. 黄色(huáng sè) Yellow. 黄油(huáng yóu) Butter. 蛋黄(dàn huáng) Yolk.

Want a little more?

- It ranks amongst the top 100 Chinese surnames.
- This is the 201st of the 214 Kangxi radicals.
- Usage frequency: Top third.

219

夊

3rd

DEFINITION

† To *walk slowly*.

PRONUNCIATION

zhǐ

SOUND WORD

Jerrycan

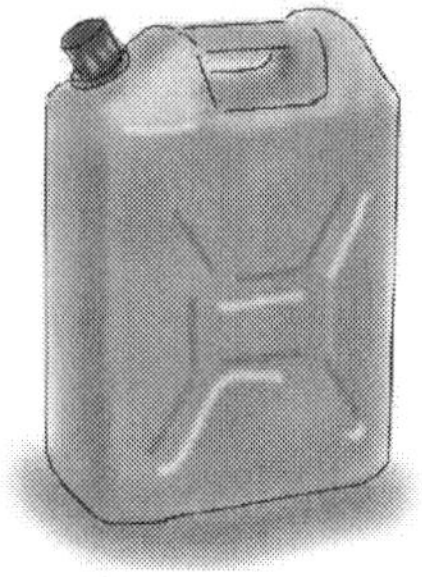

MNEMONICS

Picture an old man who trips over a **Jerrycan** and falls hard. After he lifts himself up, he is holding his back (the top left stroke) while *walking slowly*.

WANT A LITTLE MORE?

- It can also be pronounced suī.
- This is the 34th and 35th of the 214 Kangxi radicals (radical 34 and radical 35 used to be different, but nowadays they are both written the same and most Chinese fonts don't make the distinction anymore.)

220

攵

1st

DEFINITION

† To *hit*, *strike*.

PRONUNCIATION

pū

SOUND WORD

Pou or **poux** /pu/
French word for 'louse' or 'lice.'

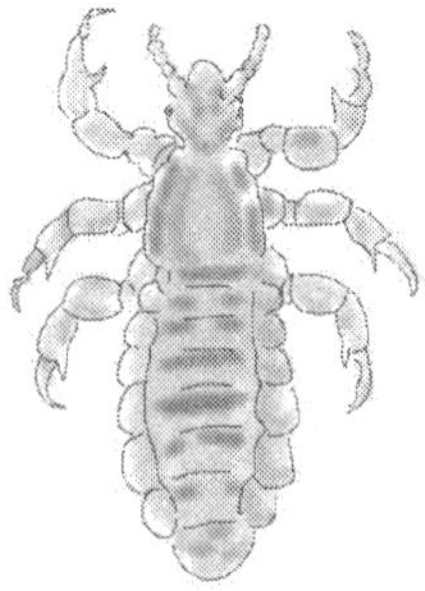

MNEMONICS

This character is also written 攴, which looks more like its ancient form: . You can clearly see a hammer on top *hitting* a 又 RIGHT HAND[71] below. Just picture yourself *hitting* your hand while trying to crush a louse (**pou**) with a hammer.

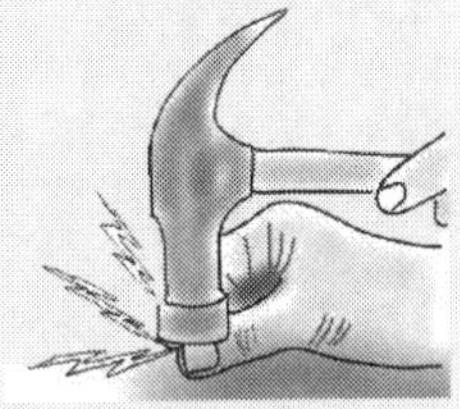

WANT A LITTLE MORE?

- Learn to distinguish from 夂 to WALK SLOWLY[219].
- This is the 66th of the 214 Kangxi radicals.

221

敞

3rd

DEFINITION

1. *<u>Spacious</u>, roomy.*
2. *Openly, uncovered.*

PRONUNCIATION

chǎng

SOUND WORD

<u>Chang</u>uito /ʧaŋgito/
American Spanish word for 'shopping cart.'

COMPONENTS

尚 to <u>ESTEEM</u>168 + 攵 to <u>HIT</u>220

STORY

A manager spends much of his days riding his **changuito** in the *spacious* aisles of his supermarket, making noise by <u>HITTING</u> the shelves with a metal stick as he races by. This is great fun for him, even though doing this *openly* in front of the customers is a bit disconcerting. His employees <u>ESTEEM</u> him so much, though, that they do not dare say a word.

EXAMPLES

1. 宽敞 (kuān chǎng) Roomy.
2. 门敞着 (mén chǎng zhe) The door is open.

WANT A LITTLE MORE?

Usage frequency: Middle third.

222

厂 [廠]

3rd

DEFINITION

1. *Factory, plant.*
2. *Yard, depot.*

† *Cliff.*

PRONUNCIATION

chǎng

SOUND WORD

Changuito /ʧaŋgito/
American Spanish word for 'shopping cart.'

TRADITIONAL COMPONENTS

[广 CASTLE[223] EXTENSIVE + 敞 SPACIOUS[221]]

MNEMONICS

The simplified version was an ancient character meaning *cliff* and it looks the part too.

STORY

One day, the employees of a *factory* decide to have some fun during a lunch break and, sitting in **changuitos** belonging to the company, start racing against each other down a *cliff*.

[The *factory* owner is in his SPACIOUS CASTLE next door and when he sees what's going on, he goes outside immediately and, walking at a furious pace, goes to meet the employees. As soon as he arrives, he jumps in a **changuito** and starts racing too!]

EXAMPLES

1. 厂家 (chǎng jiā) Factory. 厂长 (chǎng zhǎng) Factory director.
2. 基地工厂 (jī dì gōng chǎng) Depot.

WANT A LITTLE MORE?

- Another circular relation where the traditional version of this character depends on the 广 CASTLE building block introduced next, which in turn depends on the simplified character for FACTORY.
- This is the 27th of the 214 Kangxi radicals.
- Usage frequency: Top third.

223 广 [廣] 3rd

DEFINITION

Extensive, *wide*; *numerous*.

† *Shelter*.

PRONUNCIATION

guǎng

SOUND WORD

Guangtanamera
Just picture a group of Mexican mariachis singing 'Guantanamera' (with an extra 'g'). They adapted the title for the Chinese music market.

SIMPLIFIED COMPONENTS

丶 DROP[3] + 厂 CLIFF[222]

TRADITIONAL COMPONENTS

[DROP + CLIFF + 黃 YELLOW[218]]

MNEMONICS

- It originally meant a shed or a *shelter*, perhaps to protect from the rain, which would explain the DROP of water at the top.
- *Castle*.
  What brings to mind the combination of *extensive*, *numerous* (rooms) and *shelter*? A *castle*, of course. Just picture a *castle* atop a CLIFF.

STORY

A group of mariachis is at the top of a CLIFF. One of them hears a DROP of rain falling on his hat.
"It's starting to rain. We'd better take *shelter* in that *castle* over there. Andale!"
Once inside, they start singing **Guangtanamera** in the *extensive* hall.

[The owner, hearing that, is not happy. He turns YELLOW with anger (he suffers from hepatitis) and has them kicked out and rolled down the CLIFF.]

EXAMPLES

广大 (guǎng dà) Vast, large scale, numerous. 广告 (guǎng gào) Advertisement (wide-ranging message).

WANT A LITTLE MORE?

- This is the 53rd of the 214 Kangxi radicals.
- Usage frequency: Top 500.

224 戊 4th

DEFINITION

Fifth (of the 10 heavenly stems).

† This character used to depict some sort of weapon.

PRONUNCIATION

wù

SOUND WORD

Steel wool

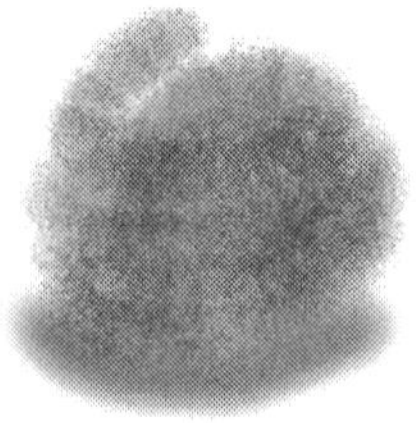

COMPONENTS

厂 CLIFF222 + 戈 DAGGER AX90

MNEMONICS

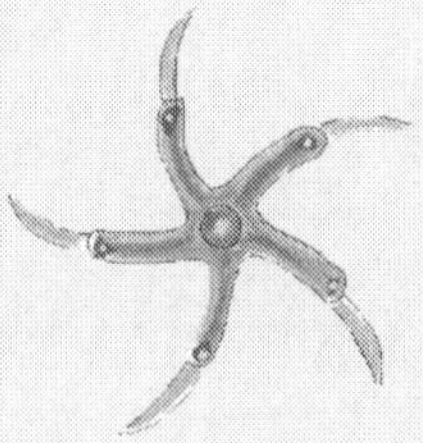

Throwing star.
Let's take this for a star-shaped weapon (because the character represents the ordinal number *fifth*, hence a weapon with five branches), like the *throwing star* of the ninjas.

STORY

On his *fifth* attempt, a man finally reaches the top of a CLIFF. There, armed with only **steel wool**, he needs to fight against a guy equipped with *throwing stars* and wielding a DAGGER AX!!!

EXAMPLES

戊辰(wù chén) Fifth year of the sexagenary cycle.

WANT A LITTLE MORE?

- This is the 5th heavenly stem.
- Usage frequency: Middle third.

225 **戌** 1st

DEFINITION

7-9 p.m.

† To *destroy*.

PRONUNCIATION

xū

SOUND WORD

Su /sy/
Past participle of the French verb 'savoir': 'to know.' For example, the expression 'Si seulement j'avais **su**' means 'If only I had known.' This is the turn of phrase we use for this sound.

COMPONENTS

戊 THROWING STAR[224] fifth + 一 ONE[15]

STORY

With only ONE THROWING STAR, he was able to *destroy* the whole French army! It took place around *8 p.m.*… If only the army had known (**su**) in advance the time of the attack!

EXAMPLES

戌时 (xū shí) 7-9 p.m.

WANT A LITTLE MORE?

- This is the 11th earthly branch.
- Usage frequency: Middle third.

226 戍 4th

DEFINITION

To *defend*; *garrison*.

PRONUNCIATION

shù

SOUND WORD

Cashew

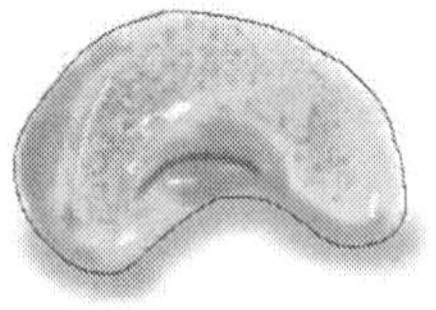

COMPONENTS

丶 NUT[3] DROP + 戊 THROWING STAR[224] fifth

MNEMONICS

- The DROP component stands for a NUT in the story.
- Originally, the DROP component on the left was a 人 MAN[23] (ancient form: ) visible in the ancient character: . Hence, a MAN *defending* something with a weapon.

STORY

Equipped with THROWING STARS, this squirrel military unit will *garrison* and *defend* its NUTS reserve down to the last **cashew**!

EXAMPLES

戍边 (shù biān) To garrison the frontier.

WANT A LITTLE MORE?

- Learn to distinguish from 戌 DESTROY[225], where there is a horizontal stroke instead of a DROP on the left side.
- Usage frequency: Middle third.

227 # 幺 **1st**

DEFINITION

1. *Tiny*, *negligible*.
2. *Number 1* when spoken.

† A silk *cocoon*.

PRONUNCIATION

yāo

SOUND WORD

Yaourt/jauʁt/
French word for 'yogourt.'

MNEMONICS

This represents a coil of silk thread, or a silk *cocoon*. A *tiny* thing, really… Ancient form: 8 (showing two *cocoons* tied by a thread?)

STORY

Here's the flavor of the month: **yaourt** with *tiny* pieces of crunchy silk *cocoons*.

EXAMPLES

1. 幺儿(yāo ér) Youngest son.
2. 打幺幺令(dǎ yāo yāo líng) Dial 110.

WANT A LITTLE MORE?

- Number 1 being normally pronounced yī and number 7 qī, Chinese people have developed the habit of pronouncing number 1 yāo when listing telephone numbers, to avoid confusion between the two numbers.
- This is the 52nd of the 214 Kangxi radicals.
- Usage frequency: Bottom third.

228 糸 1st

DEFINITION

<u>*Thread*</u>, <u>*silk thread*</u>.

PRONUNCIATION

sī

SOUND WORD

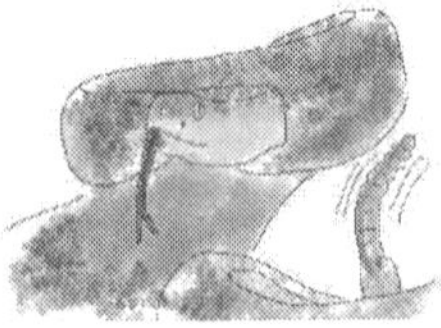

<u>Sssssss</u>
The sound of a rattle snake or of a person hissing.

COMPONENTS

幺 <u>COCOON</u>[227] + 小 <u>SMALL</u>[167]

MNEMONICS

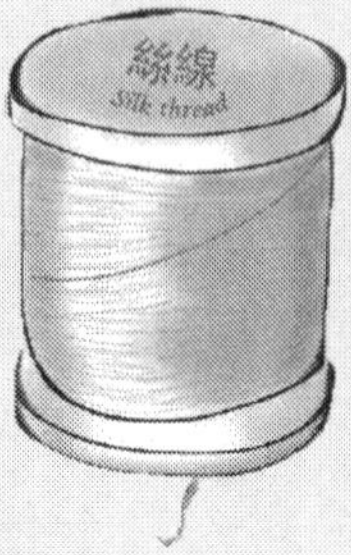

- This is a pictogram of twisted *silk threads*. Ancient form: 糸.
- A <u>SMALL</u> piece of a silk <u>COCOON</u>, hence a *thread*.
- Think of the similitude between the shape of a piece of *silk thread* lying on the ground and a rattle snake (**sssssss**).
- *Silky*.
  It is also given the extended meaning of *silky* in some of the stories.
- It is written 纟 [糹] on the left side of a character when used as a building block.
- It can also be pronounced mì. Think of a **mu<u>mmy</u>** being wrapped in *silk threads*.

WANT A LITTLE MORE?

This is the 120th of the 214 Kangxi radicals.

229A

几[幾]

1st

DEFINITION

1. *Small table, tabouret.*
2. *Almost.*

PRONUNCIATION

jī

SOUND WORD

Jeep

TRADITIONAL COMPONENTS

[2 x 幺 NEGLIGIBLE[227] + ~戍 to DEFEND[226]]

MNEMONICS

The simplified character is an image of a *small table* or *tabouret.*

STORY

A man is sitting outside on a terrace, at a *small table*, when a **Jeep** arrives from nowhere and hits him! Gee!

[Some people try to DEFEND the driver after the collision, but the number of people on his side, only two, is *almost* NEGLIGIBLE.]

EXAMPLES

1. 茶几 (chá jī) Tea table.
2. 几乎 (jī hū) Almost.

WANT A LITTLE MORE?

- The traditional character is only used for the meaning *almost*, never for a *small table.*
- Note that the traditional character uses the ancient form of the component 戍 to DEFEND, with a 人 MAN[23] instead of a 丶 DROP[3] building block at the bottom left corner.
- This is the 16th of the 214 Kangxi radicals.
- Usage frequency: Bottom third.

229B 几[幾] 3rd

Definition

How many? How much? Several, a few.

Pronunciation

jǐ

Sound word

Jigsaw puzzle

Simplified components

几 SMALL TABLE[229A]

Traditional components

[2 x 幺 COCOON[227] +
~戍 to DEFEND[226]]

Story

A few of us are about to embark on a mission and our chief describes the situation to us. A map is laid out on a SMALL TABLE.

[He says, "We're about to attack the COCOON depot and we can see from afar that it is heavily DEFENDED." He turns towards one of his officers, "*How many* are they?"
"I don't know," says the officer, "but this is going to be a real **jigsaw puzzle** trying to get into the complex!"]

Examples

几个人 (jǐ gè rén) How many people? 几时 (jǐ shí) At what time?

Want a little more?

- In practice, this character is used to form questions about numbers when the answer is expected to be a small number, usually not exceeding ten.
- Note that the traditional character uses the old form of the component 戍 to DEFEND, with a 人 MAN[23] instead of a 丶 DROP[3] building block at the bottom left corner.
- Usage frequency: Top 500.

230

虫[蟲]

2nd

DEFINITION

Insect, bug, worm.

PRONUNCIATION

chóng

SOUND WORD

Chunky
As in '**chunky** soup,' '**chunky** peanut butter.'

MNEMONICS

- This character is a pictogram of an *insect*. The traditional version repeats the building block three times to represent 'a lot of' *insects* and to help you get the message. Ancient form: .
- It may help some of you to see the simplified character as a 口 MOUTH[41] living in the ~土 SOIL[85], which is basically what a *worm* is…

STORY

Today, my soup was particularly **chunky**, until I realized I had left it on the kitchen counter since the night before and lots of *insects* and *worms* had found refuge in it! Gross!!!

EXAMPLES

虫子 (chóng zi) Insect, worm, bug. 害虫 (hài chóng) Pest, harmful insect.

WANT A LITTLE MORE?

- This is the 142nd of the 214 Kangxi radicals.
- Usage frequency: Top third.

231 风[風] 1st

DEFINITION

1. *Wind.*
2. *News, rumors.*
3. *Style, custom, manner.*

PRONUNCIATION

fēng

SOUND WORD

Feng!
As in 'What the **feng**!', a politically correct way of expressing surprise, amazement or frustration...

SIMPLIFIED COMPONENTS

几 SMALL TABLE[229A] + 乂 SHEARS[99]

TRADITIONAL COMPONENTS

[几 HOW MANY[229B] + 丶 DROPPINGS[3] DROP + 虫 INSECT[230]]

MNEMONICS

- The DROP building block stands for INSECT DROPPINGS in the story.
- The story makes use of the two different meanings for the character 几, to help you associate them.

STORY

My friend's *style* of living is unkempt, to say the least. He invited us, my wife and I, to eat at his place yesterday. Bad *news*! We were sitting at a SMALL TABLE outside when a big gust of *wind* blew the tablecloth away, revealing SHEARS with blood on the blades under the table. **Feng**!

[And all around our feet, some INSECT DROPPINGS, I could not tell HOW MANY, moving in a whirl because of the *wind* and hitting our uncovered legs. Gross! I couldn't help but yell to him, "What the **feng**, Joe!"]

EXAMPLES

1. 今天刮大风(jīn tiān guā dà fēng) It is windy today.
2. 放风(fàng fēng) To spread rumors.
3. 作风(zuò fēng) Style of work.

WANT A LITTLE MORE?

- This is the 182nd of the 214 Kangxi radicals.
- Usage frequency: Top third.

232 殳 1st

DEFINITION

† Name of an old weapon.

PRONUNCIATION

shū

SOUND WORD

Shoe

COMPONENTS

几 HOW MANY[229B] + 又 RIGHT HAND[71]

MNEMONICS

Projectile: a *sling* or to *sling*.
We give it the meaning of a *sling* because the top building block looks like the little *sling* pouch holding a *projectile* at the end of a string, that you throw with your RIGHT HAND. The ancient form, , looks like a *sling* that has just been released from the hand.

STORY

A protester is using his **shoes** as *projectiles* that he throws at a politician with his RIGHT HAND. Guess HOW MANY he threw?

WANT A LITTLE MORE?

This is the 79th of the 214 Kangxi radicals.

233 **示** 4th

DEFINITION

To *show*, *reveal*, *indicate*.

† *Altar*, *ancestor*.

PRONUNCIATION

shì

SOUND WORD

Amish

COMPONENTS

二 TWO[16] + 小 SMALL[167]

MNEMONICS

- This character used to depict a sacrificial *altar* (ancient form: 𥘅). It also stands for *ancestor*, for whom the sacrifices were made. These values, much easier to visualize, will be used when the character is a building block.
- Just picture a table supported by three heavy legs, over which a body lies (the top stroke), being *shown* to those present and to the dead *ancestors*.
- As a component, it is also written 礻 . It can be viewed as a torch (with the dot at the top being the flame and the bottom part being the hand holding it) which allows to *show* or *reveal* something.

STORY

An **Amish** preacher stands behind the *altar* and says to his people, "I will speak less clearly today because I had TWO SMALL front teeth pulled out last night, with a string attached to a door knob, of course. I would like to *reveal* them to you, but they are 'TWO SMALL' to *show* you from here..."

EXAMPLES

表示 (biǎo shì) To show, express. 提示 (tí shì) To point out.

WANT A LITTLE MORE?

- This is the 113th of the 214 Kangxi radicals.
- Usage frequency: Top 500.

234 衣 1st

DEFINITION

Clothes; *dress*, *robe*.

PRONUNCIATION

yī

SOUND WORD

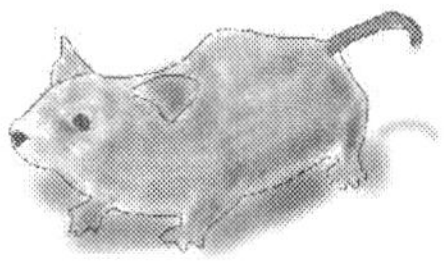

Yiiii!
A shriek at the sight of a mouse or the squeaking sound of a mouse.

MNEMONICS

- You can picture this as a full outfit, with a 亠 COWBOY HAT[49] and *clothes* floating and waving in the air. Just pretend to be in Dallas, Texas. But it is probably better to remember it in one piece. The ancient form, , shows a *robe* with long sleeves.
- As a component, it is written 衤 (not to be confused with the component form of ALTAR[233], 礻, which has one less stroke). To help you remember the difference, just view the extra dot as a belt buckle sticking out at the back of the *robe*.
- This character may be split in the middle when used as a component, with another building block occupying the space between the COWBOY HAT and the bottom part.

STORY

When I was a young boy, I enjoyed playing tricks on the girls. I would put my COWBOY HAT on and then, feeling empowered, I would put a fake mouse in their *clothes*. **Yiiii**!

EXAMPLES

衣服(yī fú) Clothing. 大衣(dà yī) Top coat.

WANT A LITTLE MORE?

- This is the 145th of the 214 Kangxi radicals.
- Usage frequency: Top third.

235 𧘇

DEFINITION

Non-character used only as a building block.

PRONUNCIATION

Not applicable

SOUND WORD

Not applicable

MNEMONICS

Gown.

It shows the bottom part of the 衣 CLOTHES[234] character, without the hat. Hence, a *gown.*

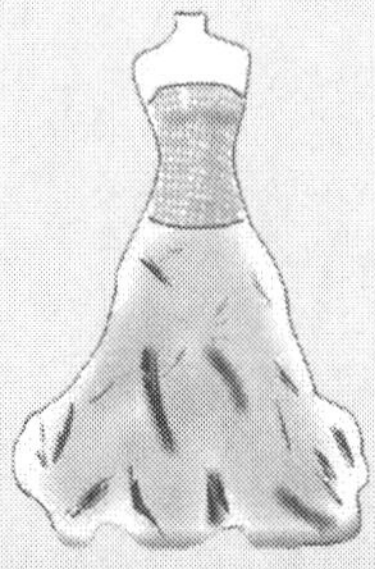

236 𧘇

DEFINITION

Non-character used only as a building block.

PRONUNCIATION

Not applicable

SOUND WORD

Not applicable

MNEMONICS

Skirt, kilt.

It shows the bottom part of a piece of 衣 CLOTHES[234], worn under a belt (the horizontal stroke at the top). Therefore, a *skirt* for a woman or a *kilt* for a man.

237A

长[長]

2nd

DEFINITION

Long; length.

PRONUNCIATION

cháng

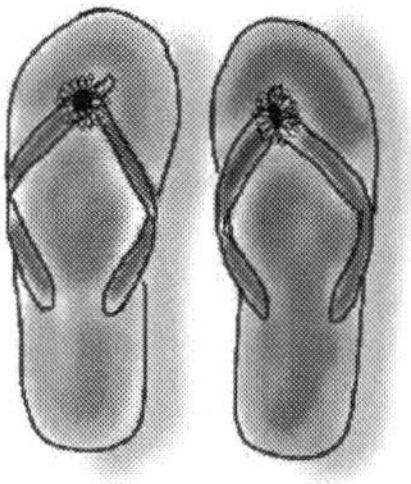

SOUND WORD

Chanclas /ʧanklas/
Spanish word for 'thong sandals,' 'flip-flop sandals.'

MNEMONICS

- This used to depict a man of power with *long* hair. Ancient form: .
- For easier recall, think rather of a woman in SKIRT[236], with *long* hair tied by a hair clip (for the simplified character, where SKIRT is slightly altered) or by a comb barrette (for the traditional character).

STORY

"Look at the woman over there, wearing a SKIRT and walking in **chanclas**, her *long*, tied hair flowing in the wind behind her. She's a natural beauty!"

EXAMPLES

长发(cháng fà) Long hair. 长期(cháng qī) Long period of time.
长度(cháng dù) Length.

WANT A LITTLE MORE?

- This is the 168th of the 214 Kangxi radicals.
- Usage frequency: Top 500.

237B 长[長] 3rd

DEFINITION

1. *Chief*, *head*, *elder*.
2. To *grow*, *develop*, *increase*.

PRONUNCIATION

zhǎng

SOUND WORD

Janglesome
Synonym of boisterous, quarrelsome.

MNEMONICS

As said in the previous entry, this is a picture of a man of power, with long, tied hair, as used to be the custom in ancient China. For this character, just picture him in a 𠘨 KILT[236].

STORY

"The oldest son of the Scottish *chief* tries to gain respect by emulating his father, showing off in his KILT and assuming a superior air, but he is too **janglesome**. I think he will *develop* into a despot!"

EXAMPLES

1. 部长 (bù zhǎng) Head of a section. 军长 (jūn zhǎng) Army commander.
2. 生长 (shēng zhǎng) To grow, develop. 长大 (zhǎng dà) To grow up.

WANT A LITTLE MORE?

Usage frequency: Top third.

238 **彪** $\bar{1}^{st}$

DEFINITION

Long hair.

PRONUNCIATION

biāo

SOUND WORD

Billard /bijaʁ/

The game of billiards or pool, pronounced in French. For this sound, we use the pool cue as the mnemonic, the long, thin wooden stick. Just picture the cue as forming the number one, to remind you that it represents the first tone.

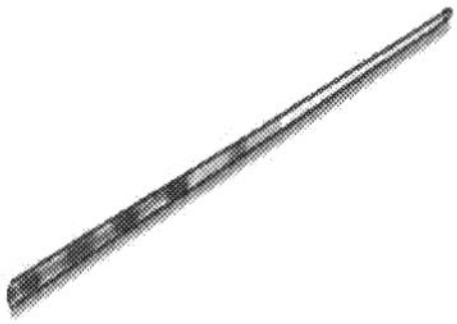

COMPONENTS

~長 LONG[237A] + 彡 HAIR[103]

MNEMONICS

This one is easy. LONG + HAIR = *long hair*!

STORY

"This gorgeous girl with *long hair* really knows how to hold her pool cue (**billard**)."

WANT A LITTLE MORE?

This is the 190th of the 214 Kangxi radicals.

239A 发[發] 1st

DEFINITION

1. To *send out*, *issue*; to *shoot*, *emit*.
2. To *develop*, *expand*.
3. To *start*, *come into existence*.
4. To *make a fortune*.

PRONUNCIATION

fā

SOUND WORD

Fax

SIMPLIFIED COMPONENTS

~友 to TAKE A SHOWER[213]

TRADITIONAL COMPONENTS

[癶 to STAND WITH LEGS SPREAD APART[214] + 弓 BOW[215] + 殳 PROJECTILE[232]]

MNEMONICS

Shampoo; to *shampoo*.
The simplified character can be viewed as the merging of the building block to TAKE A SHOWER with an extra stroke at the top left that represents the raised arm of a person putting *shampoo* on his or her *hair*.

STORY

I'm at my friend's place TAKING A SHOWER. I notice that his *shampoo* bottle is shaped like a cruise missile with the word **Fax** written on it and the fragrance is just fantastic. When I come out of the shower, I ask him where I could get that *shampoo*.

[He says, "You cannot buy it in a store. You first need to *send out* a **fax** to the **Fax** company, which stands for '**F**ast **A**rcher **X**press.' Within a few minutes, a special courier arrives. He does not come to your door. He STANDS in the street with his LEGS SPREAD APART and *shoots* a PROJECTILE, the *shampoo* bottle, with his BOW through your window. Because of its special and novel delivery service, the company has been *expanding* tremendously since it *came into existence*. They are *making a fortune*!"]

Examples

1. 发出 (fā chū) To issue, send out. 发射(fā shè) To shoot.
2. 发展(fā zhǎn) To develop, expand.
3. 出发(chū fā) To set out.
4. 发家(fā jiā) To build up the family fortune. 发财(fā cái) To get rich.

Want a little more?

Usage frequency: Top 100.

239B 发[髮] 4th

DEFINITION

Hair on the human head.

PRONUNCIATION

fà

SOUND WORD

Sofa

SIMPLIFIED COMPONENTS

发 to SHAMPOO[239A] to send out

TRADITIONAL COMPONENTS

[髟 LONG HAIR[238] +

犮 to TAKE A SHOWER[213]]

STORY

I need to SHAMPOO my **sofa**, because…

[…my girlfriend TOOK A SHOWER at my place and slept on my **sofa**. After she left, I found a lot of LONG HAIR on it.]

EXAMPLES

头发(tóu fà) Hair on the human head. 白发(bái fà) Gray hair. 理发(lǐ fà) Haircut.

WANT A LITTLE MORE?

Usage frequency: Top third.

240 ⺁

DEFINITION

Non-character used only as a building block.

PRONUNCIATION

Not applicable

SOUND WORD

Not applicable

MNEMONICS

- To *drag*.
  It looks like an arm (upper stroke) *dragging* an object behind (lower stroke).

WANT A LITTLE MORE?

Note the difference with 厂 CLIFF[222], where the top stroke is more horizontal and not sloping as much.

241 后[後] 4th

DEFINITION

1. *Behind, back, rear, after, later.*
2. *Queen, empress.*

PRONUNCIATION

hòu

SOUND WORD

Bourreau /buʁo/
French word for 'professional executioner,' 'torturer.'

SIMPLIFIED COMPONENTS

厂 to DRAG[240] + 一 ONE[15] + 口 MOUTH[41]

TRADITIONAL COMPONENTS

[彳 to STEP FORWARD[192] + 幺 TINY[227] + 夂 to WALK SLOWLY[219]]

MNEMONICS

Back in the old days, the place of the *queen* was often in the *back*, *behind* the king.

STORY

A lot of people came to see the execution of the *queen*, guilty of adultery. They see the **bourreau** DRAG the *queen behind* him by the hair. He climbs the steps of the scaffold and hooks her to ONE beam of the gallows, by the MOUTH. She looks like a big catch.

[The **bourreau** then looks *back* and sees some curious in the crowd of spectators who STEPPED FORWARD to get closer. He WALKS SLOWLY towards them and says, "*Back* up a TINY bit, you guys. You will be able to get closer *later*, *after* I'm done with her."]

EXAMPLES

1. 以后 (yǐ hòu) Afterwards. 后面 (hòu miàn) At the back, in the rear. 后天 (hòu tiān) The day after tomorrow.
2. 王后 (wáng hòu) Queen.

WANT A LITTLE MORE?

Usage frequency: Top 100.

242 故 4th

DEFINITION

1. *On purpose*; *reason, cause.*
2. *Incident.*
3. *Original, former; old friends.*

PRONUNCIATION

gù

SOUND WORD

Ragout

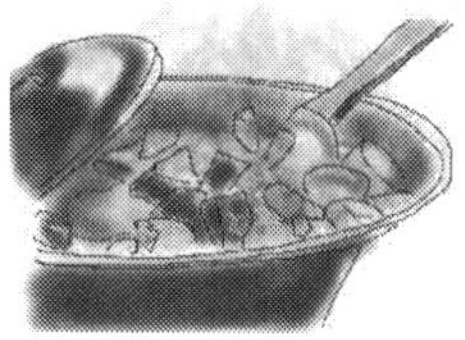

COMPONENTS

古 ANCIENT[116] + 攵 to HIT[220]

STORY

"What is the *cause* of all this clatter in the geriatric ward?"

"It's Mr. Dungworth. This obnoxious ANCIENT keeps HITTING his bowl of **ragout** with his spoon. I am sure he does it *on purpose* just to annoy his *old friends*!"

EXAMPLES

1. 故意(gù yì) Intentionally, deliberately. 缘故(yuán gù) Cause, reason.
2. 事故(shì gù) Incident.
3. 故居(gù jū) Former home. 亲故(qīn gù) Relatives and old friends.

WANT A LITTLE MORE?

Usage frequency: Top third.

243 乍 4th

Definition

1. *Suddenly*.
2. *For the first time*, *at first*.
3. To *extend*, *spread*.

Pronunciation

zhà

Sound word

Hijack
To seize an airplane or another vehicle by threat or by force, for ransom or political objectives.

Mnemonics

Backsaw, because of its appearance.

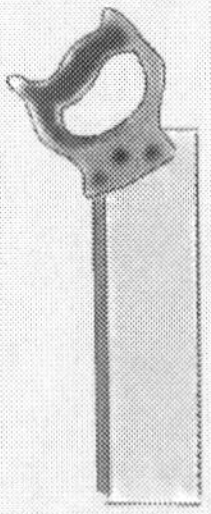

Story

Suddenly, a hijacker erupts in the cockpit, *extends* his arm forward and, pointing a *backsaw* at the pilot, says, "I **hijack** your plane and… what the hell? Not again!? I brought a *backsaw* instead of my gun!"
And the pilot says with a grin, "Ya, you did that *the first time* too!"

Examples

1. 卒乍 (cù zhà) Suddenly.
2. 乍看 (zhà kàn) At first glance.
3. 乍翅(zhà chì) To spread wings.

Want a little more?

Usage frequency: Middle third.

244 作 4th

DEFINITION

To *do*, *make*.

PRONUNCIATION

zuò

SOUND WORD

Guardswoman
Let her be a tough prison guard.

COMPONENTS

亻 HANDYMAN[23] MAN + 乍 BACKSAW[243] SUDDENLY

STORY

Because of a minor infraction, the HANDYMAN must spend a day in prison. The **guardswoman** goes see him and says, "Hey you! I need somebody to *do* some work and cut wood with a BACKSAW, and you look the type. Come!" The HANDYMAN replies, "No thanks. I'm fine. I'm just here for a day anyways…"

The **guardswoman** plants her two feet firmly on the ground and with fists on her waist says, "Am I being too 'abstract' for you? If you prefer, you can *make* me force you to *do* it. Your choice!"

EXAMPLES

工作 (gōng zuò) Work, job. 作为 (zuò wéi) Conduct, action. 名作 (míng zuò) Famous work.

WANT A LITTLE MORE?

- There is another character with the same pronunciation that means basically the same thing: 做, which is described next. Both characters are often interchangeable. However, there is a small difference: the current character is used more for *making* abstract things while 做 is used more for *making* concrete things. There is a hook in the stories to help you remember this.
- Usage frequency: Top 100.

245 **做** 4th

DEFINITION

To *do*, *make*, *produce*.

PRONUNCIATION

zuò

SOUND WORD

Guardswoman
Let her be a tough prison guard.

COMPONENTS

亻 MAN[23] + 故 ON PURPOSE[242]

STORY

The **guardswoman** hits a prisoner until he falls face first on the ground. One of her colleagues yells, "Hey! What are you *doing*?"

The **guardswoman** replies, "This MAN looked at me funny and I'm sure he did it ON PURPOSE. I just wanted to *make* him hit the 'concrete' floor!"

EXAMPLES

做法(zuò fǎ) Way of making something. 做工(zuò gōng) To do manual work. 你做什么工作？(nǐ zuò shén me gōng zuò) What is your job?

WANT A LITTLE MORE?

- This character is used more for *making* concrete things. See explanation of previous character 作.
- Usage frequency: Top 500.

246A

里

3rd

DEFINITION

1. *Village.*
2. *Half-kilometer, Chinese mile.*

PRONUNCIATION

lǐ

SOUND WORD

Little green man
Extraterrestrial or Martian.

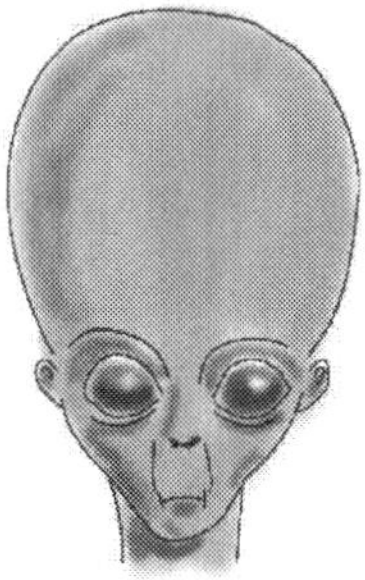

COMPONENTS

田 FIELD[195] + 土 SOIL[85]

MNEMONICS

- *Radar.*
  A *radar* is basically a big vertical structure placed on the GROUND or SOIL that detects electromagnetic FIELDS, hence the fictitious meaning. It represents all sorts of *radars*, like speed *radars* used by the police.

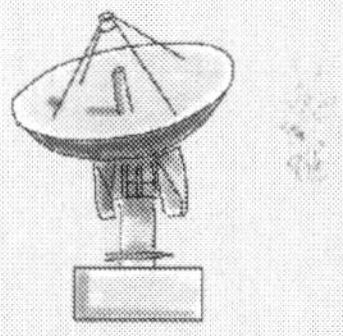

- *Computer.*
  A desktop *computer* looks almost like this character, but, unlike a *radar*, it emits electromagnetic FIELDS. The character can represent all sorts of *computers* (handheld, laptop or desktop).

STORY

"News flash! A few **little green men** have been sighted last night in a FIELD at approximately *half a kilometer* from a small *village* within the county. The SOIL has been found to be highly radioactive on site during the following investigation. NASA *radars* and *computers* had apparently detected an unidentified object in the sky a few minutes before the sighting."

Examples

1. 村里(cūn lǐ) Village, hamlet.
2. 公里(gōng lǐ) Kilometer. 华里(huá lǐ) Chinese mile. 英里(yīng lǐ) English mile.

Want a little more?

- This is the 166th of the 214 Kangxi radicals.
- Usage frequency: Top third.

246B

里[裡]

3rd

DEFINITION

Inside; *lining inside* a garment.

PRONUNCIATION

lǐ

SOUND WORD

Little green man
Extraterrestrial or Martian.

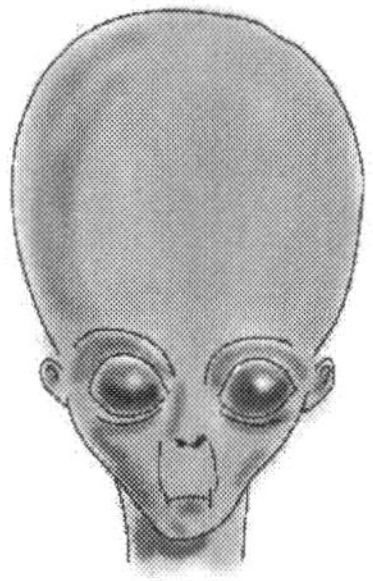

SIMPLIFIED COMPONENTS

田 FIELD[195] + 土 GROUND[85]

TRADITIONAL COMPONENTS

[衤 CLOTHES[234] + FIELD + GROUND]

STORY

The spaceship was finally found on the GROUND in a FIELD. The body of a **little green man** was discovered *inside* and was transported to area 51 for further analysis.

[It was found that the *lining inside* the alien's CLOTHES was made of a material unknown to man.]

EXAMPLES

这里(zhè lǐ) Here. 里面(lǐ miàn) Inside. 心里(xīn lǐ) In your heart/mind.

WANT A LITTLE MORE?

- The traditional character may also appear with the CLOTHES building block split in the middle, like this: 裏.
- Usage frequency: Top 100.

247 用 4th

DEFINITION

To *use*; *use* (noun).

PRONUNCIATION

yòng

SOUND WORD

Utilisation /ytilizasjɔ̃/
French word for 'utilization,' 'use.' Make sure to pronounce the 'ion' part as a French would.

COMPONENTS

冂 LONG COVER[12] + 丰 TELEPHONE POLE[34]

STORY

A president of a French telephone company says to its linesmen, "We noticed that some of you *use* a LONG COVER to protect yourselves from the atmospheric conditions when working on a TELEPHONE POLE. We repeat that the **utilisation** of a metallic LONG COVER is prohibited because of the high risks of electrocution. I expect to see you all at the funerals of our departed colleague John this afternoon."

EXAMPLES

使用 (shǐ yòng) To use, employ. 有用 (yǒu yòng) Useful. 不用 (bú yòng) Don't have to, no need to.

WANT A LITTLE MORE?

- This is the 101st of the 214 Kangxi radicals.
- Usage frequency: Top 100.

248 首 3rd

DEFINITION

1. *Chief*; *head*; *first*.
2. Measure word for *poems*, *songs*.

PRONUNCIATION

shǒu

SOUND WORD

Showstopper

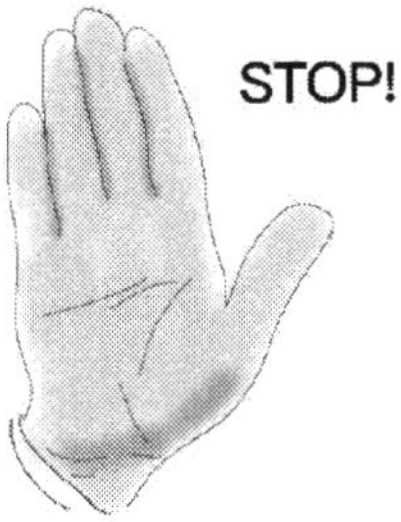

COMPONENTS

⺍ GRASS[131] + 自 MYSELF[201]

MNEMONICS

This used to depict a *head* () and it came to mean figuratively the *head* of a group, a *chief*, the one in *first* place.

STORY

I work for a lawn care company. One morning on Halloween day, I see my boss arrive with a patch of GRASS on his *head*, while humming the *song* 'Forrest lawn' by John Denver. He says, "Look, I costumed MYSELF as lawn and I did it all by MYSELF. What do you think?"
Not knowing what to say, I blurted, "Errr… Wow, this is quite a **showstopper**, *chief*!"

EXAMPLES

1. 首领(shǒu lǐng) Chief. 首都(shǒu dū) Capital of a country.
2. 唐诗三百首(táng shí sān bǎi shǒu) Three hundred poems of the Tang dynasty.

WANT A LITTLE MORE?

- This is the 185th of the 214 Kangxi radicals.
- Usage frequency: Top 500.

249 道 4th

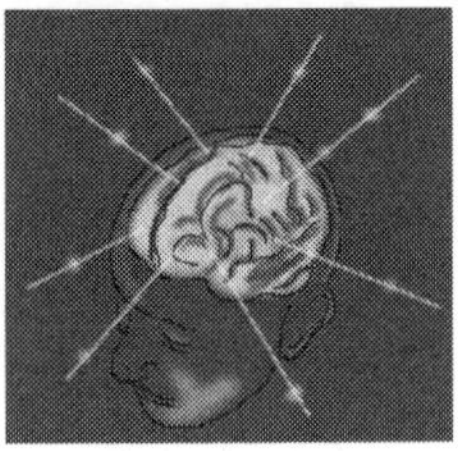

Definition

1. *Way, path; principle, reason, doctrine; Taoism.*
2. To *say, communicate.*

Pronunciation

dào

Sound word

To **endow**, to be **endowed**.

Components

辶 ROAD[104] + 首 CHIEF[248]

Story

"Our CHIEF has been **endowed** with *reason* and with the capacity to *communicate* and to find the proper *way* on the ROAD of life. Let's follow his *doctrine*."

Examples

1. 道路(dào lù) Way; path. 知道(zhī dào) To know. 道教(dào jiào) Taoism.
2. 道喜(dào xǐ) To offer congratulations on a happy occasion.

Want a little more?

Usage frequency: Top 100.

250A 行 2nd

Definition

1. *OK, alright.*
2. To *go*, *do*, *travel*, *walk*.

Pronunciation

xíng

Sound word

Signal
Road or hand **signals**. Just pronounce 'singnal' in your head.

Components

亻 to STEP FORWARD[192] + 一 ONE[15] + 丁 NAIL[153] male

Mnemonics

- This character used to depict a crossroad. Ancient form: .
- *Walkway, pavement, in the middle of my walk.*
  All these values are related to *walking*. Also, this character is usually split down the middle vertically, with another building block occupying the space between STEP FORWARD and ONE + NAIL, creating a sort of *walkway*.

Story

A male person was *walking* on the street and he failed to see the road **signal** that said, 'Men at work. Proceed with caution.' So, he accidentally STEPPED FORWARD on ONE NAIL. He cursed so loud that people from a mile around came to see what was *going* on, repeatedly asking,
"Are you *alright*? Are you *ok*?"
"Yes, yes… Please *go* now."

Examples

1. 行吗?(xíng ma) Is this okay? 不行(bù xíng) Won't do, not good.
2. 行动(xíng dòng) To move about, take action. 行人(xíng rén) Pedestrian.

Want a little more?

- This is the 144th of the 214 Kangxi radicals.
- Usage frequency: Top 100.

250B 行 2nd

DEFINITION

1. *Row*; *line* or *column of print* on a page.
2. *Profession*, *firm*, *line of business*.

PRONUNCIATION

háng

SOUND WORD

Hang tight!

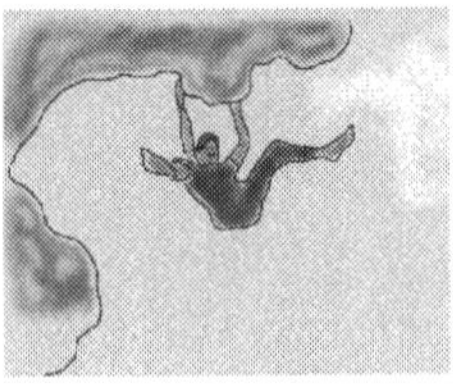

COMPONENTS

亻 to STEP FORWARD[192] + 一 ONE[15] + 丁 NAIL[153] male

STORY

In an old printing *firm*, a male typesetter was arranging the *lines of print* before sending them to press when he inadvertently STEPPED FORWARD on ONE big, rusty, 6-inches long NAIL that had been dropped by accident on the floor. The other employees of the *firm* heard him scream and rushed to see what was going on. After seeing blood pouring all over, one of them said, "**Hang tight**! We're calling an ambulance!"

EXAMPLES

1. 第一行 (dì yī háng) First row.
2. 银行 (yín háng) Bank.

WANT A LITTLE MORE?

Usage frequency: Top third.

251 夕 1st

DEFINITION

Evening, dusk.

PRONUNCIATION

xī

SOUND WORD

Scie /si/
French word for 'saw.' Just think of a 'seesaw.'

MNEMONICS

This is the pictogram of an early evening crescent moon (ancient form: ), less bright than the regular crescent moon  (modern form 夕), because there is a part missing.

STORY

In the *evening*, Pierrot took a **scie** and cut a piece of the moon for Colombine.

EXAMPLES

前夕 (qián xī) Eve. 夕阳 (xī yáng) Sunset.

WANT A LITTLE MORE?

- This is the 36th of the 214 Kangxi radicals.
- Usage frequency: Middle third.

252 **歹** 3rd

DEFINITION

Vicious, *malevolent*, *wicked*, *bad*, *evil*.

† Broken bone, *bone fragment*.

PRONUNCIATION

dǎi

SOUND WORD

Dynamite
As in a stick of **dynamite**.

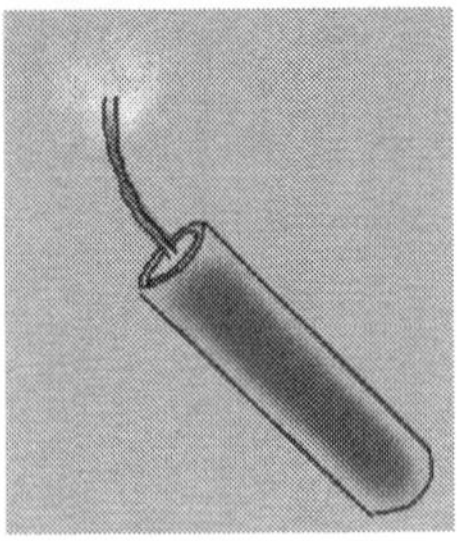

COMPONENTS

(一 CEILING[15] ONE) or (卜 DIVINING ROD[18A] to PREDICT) + 夕 EVENING[251]

MNEMONICS

- Can also be written as 歺, with a DIVINING ROD on top instead of ONE, hence identifying DIVINING ROD as a component above.
- Some etymologists believe this character used to depict a piece of broken bone, hence a *bone fragment*.

STORY

"ONE EVENING, I was in my bed when I heard a big explosion that made me jump to the CEILING. A *vicious* scoundrel had blown up the neighbor's cat with **dynamites**, and there were *bone fragments* all over the street. We had to use a DIVINING ROD to find all the pieces!"

EXAMPLES

歹毒(dǎi dú) Vicious. 歹徒(dǎi tú) Evildoer, gangster.

WANT A LITTLE MORE?

- This is the 78th of the 214 Kangxi radicals.
- Usage frequency: Middle third.

253

死

3rd

DEFINITION

1. *Dead*; to *die*.
2. *Inflexible*, *rigid*, *stiff*.

PRONUNCIATION

sǐ

SOUND WORD

Syrupy
Thick and sweet liquid.

COMPONENTS

歹 BONE FRAGMENT[252] + 匕 SPOON[66]

STORY

The poor man… He went to see a healer and was offered a SPOON of a **syrupy** liquid sprinkled with dragon BONE FRAGMENTS as a cure for his cough, but he is now *dead* and *stiff*.

EXAMPLES

1. 死亡 (sǐ wáng) To be dead, doomed. 我饿死了！(wǒ è sǐ le) I'm starving!
2. 死板 (sǐ bǎn) Stiff, inflexible.

WANT A LITTLE MORE?

Usage frequency: Top 500.

254 **尸 [屍]** 1st

DEFINITION

Corpse.

PRONUNCIATION

shī

SOUND WORD

Sure
The English adjective '**sure**' is what sounds the most like this phoneme.

TRADITIONAL COMPONENTS

[*Corpse* + 死 DEAD[253]]

MNEMONICS

- The simplified version is a pictogram of a *corpse*. Ancient form:  .
- You can view it as a dangling backbone still attached to the head.

STORY

During a criminal investigation on a crime scene, an assistant brings the *CORPSE* of a man to the coroner, and all is left are the jawbone and the spine still attached to the maxilla. Holding it by the mouth, the assistant asks, "Are you **sure** about this *CORPSE*?"

[The coroner, exasperated by the stupid questions of his assistant, replies, "Yes, I am **sure** he's DEAD!"]

EXAMPLES

尸体(shī tǐ) Corpse. 尸检(shī jiǎn) Autopsy.

WANT A LITTLE MORE?

- This is the 44th of the 214 Kangxi radicals.
- Usage frequency: Top third.

255 户 [戶] 4th

DEFINITION

Door, household, family.

PRONUNCIATION

hù

SOUND WORD

Loup-garou /lugaʁu/
French for 'werewolf,' a person who changes into a wolf when the moon is full.

COMPONENTS

丶 GASH3 DROP + 尸 CORPSE254

STORY

On a particular night when the moon is full, I hear a loud scratching noise on my *door*, and I see the moonlight suddenly shine through a big GASH in the *door*. I go open it and see the CORPSE of a man we know, who used to live in a *household* on the same street as us, hanging from our *door* knocker.
My wife asks, "Who is it?"
"Ah, nothing to worry. It's the **loup-garou** who still plays tricks on us. He's so hilarious!"

EXAMPLES

户口 (hù kǒu) Number of households. 用户 (yòng hù) Consumer.

WANT A LITTLE MORE?

- This is the 63rd of the 214 Kangxi radicals.
- Usage frequency: Top third.

256 斤 1st

DEFINITION

Catty (weight equal to 0.5 kg).

† *Ax*.

PRONUNCIATION

jīn

SOUND WORD

Gin
The well-known spirit.

MNEMONICS

- This character used to represent an *ax*, a hatchet. Ancient form:  .
- Just imagine a Barbarian 厂 DRAGGING[240] his victim by the hair with one hand and holding an *ax* in his other hand.

STORY

He drank too much **gin** and started throwing his *ax*, weighting a *catty*, at people. Cathy died…

EXAMPLES

公斤 (gōng jīn) Kilogram. 斤两 (jīn liǎng) Weight.

WANT A LITTLE MORE?

Usage frequency: Top third.

257 斥 4th

Definition

1. To *reject*, *repel*, *oust*.
2. To *blame*, *reprove*, *reprimand*.
3. To *expand*, *open up* (literary).
4. To *fund*, *spend* (literary).
5. To *reconnoiter*, *scout* (literary).

Pronunciation

chì

Sound word

Body snatcher
A person who steals corpses and limbs from graves to sell or dissect them.

Components

斤 AX[256] + 丶 GASH[3] DROP

Story

A **body snatcher** *reprimands* his trainee, "Look at all the mess you made again of the bodies and you're the only one to *blame*. You made too many GASHES on the limbs with your AX! I need to *reject* them all. Next time, I will have to show you how to do it using your own body!"

Examples

1. 排斥 (pái chì) To repel, reject.
2. 申斥 (shēn chì) To reprimand.
3. 斥地(chì dì) To expand a territory.
4. 斥资 (chì zī) To fund.
5. 斥候(chì hòu) To scout, reconnoiter the enemy.

Want a little more?

Usage frequency: Top third.

258 所 3rd

Definition

1. *Place*; *office*; measure word for *houses*, *schools*…etc.
2. *What, that which, those whom* (used before a verb as the agent of the action).
3. *Therefore.*

Pronunciation

suǒ

Sound word

Suocero /swotʃero/
Italian word for 'father-in-law.'

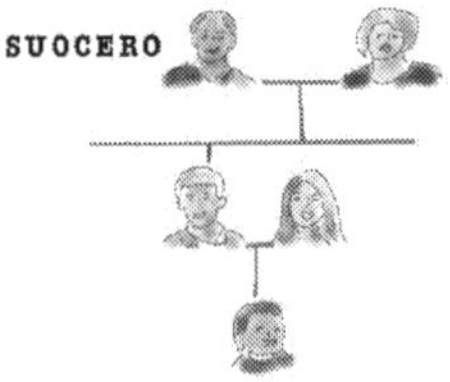

Components

~户 DOOR[255] + 斤 AX[256]

Story

Scene 1: Jim is married to the daughter of an Italian man known to have a short fuse. One day on his way to work, Jim decides to stop by his **suocero**'s *place* to say hello.
"So, how's my daughter?" inquires the **suocero**.
"She's a fine woman. Of course, we have our moments but, as we say, '*That which* does not kill us makes us stronger'" says Jim. The conversation continues for 5 minutes and Jim goes to work. The **suocero**, however, is in a bad mood and the more he thinks about it, the more he gets furious.

Scene 2: In Jim's *office*, one of his teammates suddenly yells, "There is a crazy man outside that hits our DOOR with an AX and keeps screaming, 'My daughter is not a witch!' 'My daughter is not a witch!'"

Examples

1. 研究所(yán jiū suǒ) Research institute.
2. 我所说的话(wǒ suǒ shuō de huà) What I said. 所有的(suǒ yǒu de) All.
3. 所以(suǒ yǐ) Therefore.

Want a little more?

Usage frequency: Top 100.

259

然

2nd

DEFINITION

1. *<u>However</u>, but.*
2. *Although.*
3. *Like that, thus, as it should be; of course, obviously.*
4. *Correct, right.*

† To cook, roast.

PRONUNCIATION

rán

SOUND WORD

<u>Ran</u>som

COMPONENTS

夕 <u>MEAT</u>[48] + 犬 <u>DOG</u>[29] + 灬 <u>FIRE</u>[127]

STORY

I see my neighbor cooking some <u>MEAT</u> over a <u>FIRE</u> in his backyard. I ask him what he is cooking that smells so good. He says, "A <u>DOG</u>."
"Did you say a <u>DOG</u>?"
"*Correct*!"
"*But* why?"
"I stole that <u>DOG</u> from a rich man and I demanded a **ransom**. *However*, he didn't pay on time. *Although* I liked the <u>DOG</u>, I had to keep my promises. *Thus*, I've decided to cook it."
"Just *like that*?"
"*Of course*!"

EXAMPLES

1. 然而 (rán ér) But, however.
2. 虽然 (suī rán) Although.
3. 当然 (dāng rán) Like that; certainly, of course. 不然 (bù rán) Otherwise.
4. 然否 (rán fǒu) Is that correct?

WANT A LITTLE MORE?

Usage frequency: Top 100.

260

家

1st

DEFINITION

1. *Home, family.*
2. *Suffix* to describe a person engaged in a certain art or profession (-ist/-er/-ian).

PRONUNCIATION

jiā

SOUND WORD

[i]**The arch**
It can be a structural arch or anything that has a curved shape. (See 'Special Sound Mnemonics,' page 485)

COMPONENTS

宀 HOUSE[50] + 豕 PIG[38]

MNEMONICS

When at *home*, in their own HOUSE, some people live like PIGS.

STORY

"You know the HOUSE with **the arch** on our street? Well, I heard they keep a PIG in their *home*!"
"Yeah, the guy is some sort of agronom*er*, huh, agronomi*an*?"
"Agronom*ist*!"

EXAMPLES

1. 国家(guó jiā) Country, nation. 家庭(jiā tíng) Family. 大家(dà jiā) Everyone.
2. 专家(zhuān jiā) Specialist. 文学家(wén xué jiā) Literary person. 作家(zuò jiā) Writer.

WANT A LITTLE MORE?

Usage frequency: Top 100.

261 束 4th

DEFINITION

1. *Bundle*; to *bind*, *tie*.
2. To *control*, *restrain*.

PRONUNCIATION

shù

SOUND WORD

Cashew

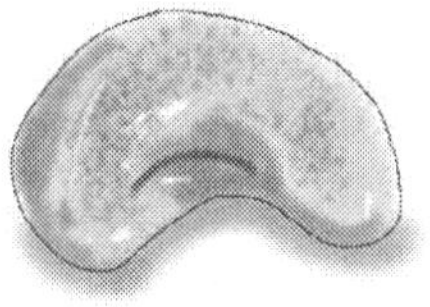

COMPONENTS

木 TREE[125] + 口 OPENING[41]

MNEMONICS

This is a pictogram depicting a *bundle* of firewood *tied* with a rope. Ancient form: .

STORY

"They know I love **cashews**, so they bought me for Christmas a **cashew** TREE *tied* in a *bundle*! They put it inside a box but they did a poor job, because you could see the roots and the top of the TREE sticking out from both OPENINGS of the box. I couldn't *control* myself and I just burst into laughter."

EXAMPLES

1. 花束(huā shù) Flower bouquet. 束紧 (shù jǐn) To bind up.
2. 管束(guǎn shù) To restrain, control.

WANT A LITTLE MORE?

Usage frequency: Top third.

262A 重 4th

Definition

1. *<u>Heavy</u>*.
2. *Important, serious.*

Pronunciation

zhòng

Sound word

Long <u>Johns</u>
Long underwear. Pronounce 'Long Jongs'.

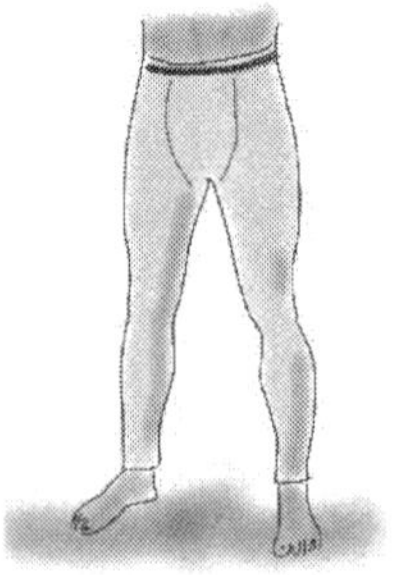

Components

千 <u>THOUSAND</u>[65] + 里 <u>INSIDE</u>[246B]

Mnemonics

This used to depict a man carrying a heavy 束 <u>BUNDLE</u>[261]. Ancient form: .

Story

The strong man arrives on stage wearing **long Johns**. His coach is backstage, shooting to him the last instructions, "Listen! This is *important*. There are one <u>THOUSAND</u> pounds <u>INSIDE</u> the metal box you are about to lift. This is *heavy*. Keep your back straight!"

Examples

1. 重量(zhòng liàng) Weight. 多重(duō zhòng) How heavy?
2. 重要(zhòng yào) Important, major.

Want a little more?

Usage frequency: Top 500.

262B **重** 2nd

DEFINITION

Again, *once more*; to *repeat*.

PRONUNCIATION

chóng

SOUND WORD

Chunky

As in '**chunky** soup,' '**chunky** peanut butter.'

COMPONENTS

千 THOUSAND[65] + 里 INSIDE[246B]

STORY

A new peanut butter ad says, 'Each jar of our **chunky** peanut butter contains a THOUSAND pieces of peanuts INSIDE. You'll like it so much that you'll want to *repeat* the experience *once more* and eat it *again* and *again*…'

EXAMPLES

重新 (chóng xīn) Once again. 重复 (chóng fù) To repeat.

WANT A LITTLE MORE?

Usage frequency: Top third.

263A 种[種] 3rd

DEFINITION

1. *Kind, type, race, breed, species.*
2. *Seed.*

PRONUNCIATION

zhǒng

SOUND WORD

Junk dealer
Let's assume a special type of **junk** dealer here: a drug dealer…

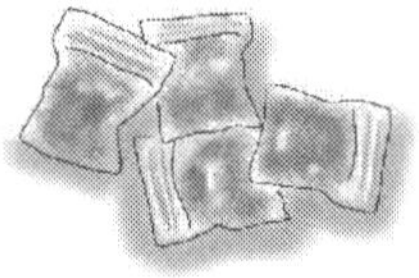

SIMPLIFIED COMPONENTS

禾 STANDING GRAIN[136] + 中 MIDDLE[121]

TRADITIONAL COMPONENTS

[STANDING GRAIN + 重 HEAVY[262A]]

STORY

A **junk dealer** tells me, "If you are looking for Marijuana *seeds*, I have the best *type* there is. However, if you're looking for something special, I have this." He takes out a little plastic bag containing a *kind* of green herb. "This is made with the MIDDLE part of a *species* of STANDING GRAIN. It provides quite a buzz!

["I'm telling you, man. This is HEAVY stuff!"]

EXAMPLES

1. 各种 (gè zhǒng) Various kinds.
2. 种子 (zhǒng zi) Seed.

WANT A LITTLE MORE?

Usage frequency: Top 100.

263B

种[種]

4th

DEFINITION

To *plant*, *cultivate*.

PRONUNCIATION

zhòng

SOUND WORD

Long Johns
Long underwear. Pronounce 'Long Jongs'.

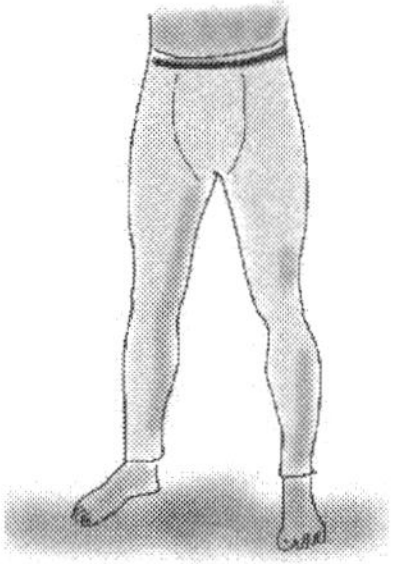

SIMPLIFIED COMPONENTS

禾 STANDING GRAIN[136] +
中 MIDDLE[121]

TRADITIONAL COMPONENTS

[STANDING GRAIN + 重 HEAVY[262A]]

STORY

My wife says, "Here we go again! The farmer next door is *planting* his new crop of STANDING GRAIN in the MIDDLE of his field, bare-chested and wearing only his **long Johns**. It doesn't provide for a good view."

["Especially on an old man as HEAVY as himself. He needs to *cultivate* his image better," I add.]

EXAMPLES

种植(zhòng zhí) To plant. 耕种(gēng zhòng) To till, cultivate.

WANT A LITTLE MORE?

Usage frequency: Top third.

264 丰 4th

DEFINITION

† *Hand holding something.*

PRONUNCIATION

niè

SOUND WORD

Tataranieto /tatara'njeto/
Spanish for 'great-great-grandson,' a son of the fourth generation. Picture a spoiled, mischievous child here.

MNEMONICS

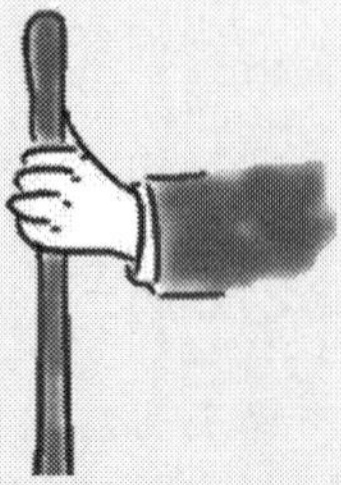

- This is a pictogram of a *hand holding something.*
- Just picture a turbulent great-great-grandson (**tataranieto**) holding a stick in his *hand*, while you wonder about the nasty plan he has in mind.

265 肀

DEFINITION

Non-character used only as a building block.

PRONUNCIATION

Not applicable

SOUND WORD

Not applicable

MNEMONICS

Field hockey stick.

Since the character looks like the 聿 HAND HOLDING[264] character, imagine a *stick* used for playing *field hockey* (because of the curved shape at its base).

266 聿 4th

DEFINITION

1. *Suddenly*; *and then* (literary).
2. Used for its sound.

† *Writing brush*.

PRONUNCIATION

yù

SOUND WORD

Bahut /bay/
French word for 'sideboard', 'buffet'.

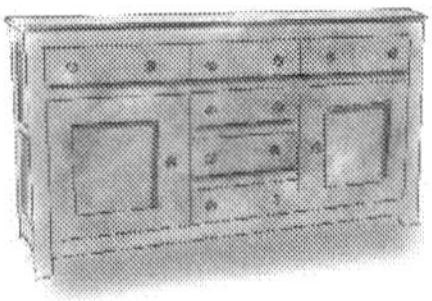

MNEMONICS

This is a pictogram showing a 肀 HAND HOLDING a *writing brush*. The *writing brush* is more apparent in the ancient form: 聿.

STORY

I ask my helper to apply varnish to the old **bahut** with a brush. I return an hour later and see him diligently applying a coat of lacquer. *And then*, I *suddenly* realize he is holding my expensive *writing brush* in his hand. I shout, "When I said with a brush, I meant a paint brush, not my *writing brush*!"

EXAMPLES

1. 聿至 (yù zhì) To arrive suddenly.
2. 聿利斯 (yù lì sī) Ulysse.

WANT A LITTLE MORE?

- This is the 129th of the 214 Kangxi radicals.
- Usage frequency: Middle third.

267 事 4th

DEFINITION

1. *Matter, thing, affair, work, job.*
2. *Incident, event.*

PRONUNCIATION

shì

SOUND WORD

Amish

COMPONENTS

十 CROSS[59] TEN + 口 MOUTH[41] + 尹 FIELD HOCKEY STICK[265]

STORY

There was an *incident* last week during a field hockey game opposing an **Amish** team and a non-**Amish** one. During the game, a non-**Amish** player hit an **Amish** player hard on the MOUTH with his FIELD HOCKEY STICK and made the sign of the CROSS while smirking. He then added, "This is what I call a 'CROSS' check. Ha ha ha!"
Everybody shouted, "Hey! What's the *matter* with you!"
This *affair* even made the news.

EXAMPLES

1. 事情 (shì qíng) Affair, matter, thing. 办事 (bàn shì) To handle affairs, work. 有事 (yǒu shì) To be busy, occupied.
2. 事件 (shì jiàn) Incident, event.

WANT A LITTLE MORE?

Usage frequency: Top 100.

268 成 2nd

DEFINITION

1. To <u>*become*</u>, <u>*turn into*</u>.
2. To *finish*, *complete*, *accomplish*, *succeed*.

PRONUNCIATION

chéng

SOUND WORD

<u>Chain</u> saw
The sound **cheng** is always approximated by the word **chain** in this book.

COMPONENTS

戊 THROWING STAR[224] fifth + 刀 KNIFE[109]

STORY

Two men are starting a fight in the street. One has a KNIFE in his hand and the other one is holding THROWING STARS. It is *becoming* intense and each man has the clear intention of cutting his opponent to pieces. Suddenly, a third man wearing a mask appears with a **chain saw** and says, while revving the engine, "If you intend to *turn* this *into* a massacre, go ahead. I'll make sure to *finish* the job!"

EXAMPLES

1. 成为 (chéng wéi) To turn into.
2. 完成(wán chéng) To complete.

WANT A LITTLE MORE?

Usage frequency: Top 100.

269 **多** 1st

DEFINITION

Many, a lot of, much.

PRONUNCIATION

duō

SOUND WORD

Duo
As in a music duet.

COMPONENTS

2 x 夕 EVENING[251]

MNEMONICS

One EVENING on top of another, that's way too *much*…

STORY

It was bound to happen. He finally broke his guitar on the head of the flutist… You must understand that this **duo** spends *a lot of* time together. And these two play *many, many* EVENINGS together. Something had to give…

EXAMPLES

差不多 (chà bu duō) Almost, about. 多少 (duō shǎo) How many? How much? 太多了 (tài duō le) Too many; too much.

WANT A LITTLE MORE?

Usage frequency: Top 100.

270 川 1st

DEFINITION

Stream, *rivulet*, *river*, *creek*.

PRONUNCIATION

chuān

SOUND WORD

Metabetchouan /Metabɛtʃuan/ This is an exception to the rule for the tone. For the first tone, think of 'On the banks of the river' and see 'Special Sound Mnemonics,' page 483.

MNEMONICS

- This character depicts a flowing *stream* of water. Ancient form: 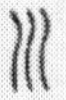.
- It is also written 巛 when used as a building block.

STORY

I am standing on the shore of the *river* **Metabetchouan**, looking at the peaceful *stream* of water flowing before me.

EXAMPLES

冰川 (bīng chuān) Glacier. 四川 (sì chuān) Sichuan province (Szechuan) in southwest China.

WANT A LITTLE MORE?

- This is the 47th of the 214 Kangxi radicals.
- Usage frequency: Top third.

271 工 $\overline{1^{st}}$

DEFINITION

Work.

PRONUNCIATION

gōng

SOUND WORD

Gong

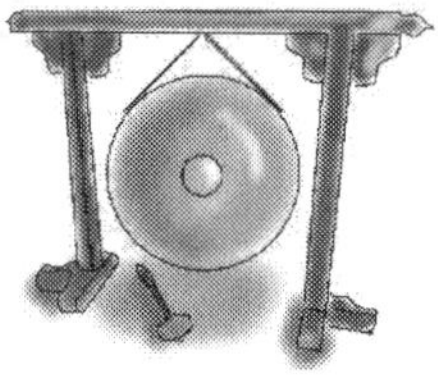

MNEMONICS

I-beam.

This used to depict a carpenter's square. We give it a more modern meaning in this book, a steel *I-beam*. Just imagine looking at an *I-beam* from one of its extremities and you'll understand why.

STORY

His sole *work* is to hit a **gong** with an *I-beam* to let the workers know when it is time to take a break.

EXAMPLES

工人(gōng rén) Worker. 手工(shǒu gōng) Handicraft.

WANT A LITTLE MORE?

- This is the 48th of the 214 Kangxi radicals.
- Usage frequency: Top 500.

272 𢀖[巠] 1st

Definition

† Underground watercourse.

Pronunciation

jīng

Sound word

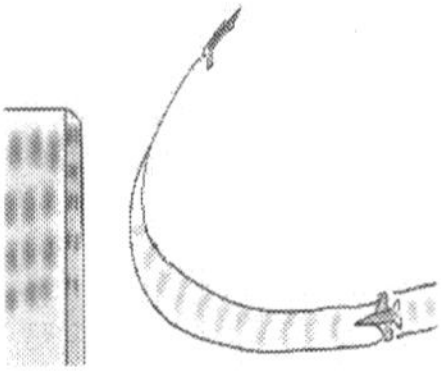

Jink
A **jink** maneuver is an air combat technique where you make a quick, evasive turn.

Traditional components

[一 ONE15 + 巛 STREAM270 + 工 I-BEAM271 WORK]

Mnemonics

- *Tower crane.*
  A big machine with a long arm that is used by builders for lifting and moving heavy objects.
  - The simplified version of the character is better remembered in one piece. It looks like a claw that grabs an I-BEAM.
  - The traditional character can be viewed as ONE STREAM of steel threads lifting an I-BEAM.

Picture a fighter pilot having to perform a **jink** maneuver to avoid hitting a *tower crane*.

273 **经[經]** 1st

DEFINITION

1. *Classics, scripture.*
2. To *pass through, undergo.*
3. To *manage.*
4. *Surname.*

PRONUNCIATION

jīng

SOUND WORD

Jink
A **jink** maneuver is an air combat technique where you make a quick, evasive turn.

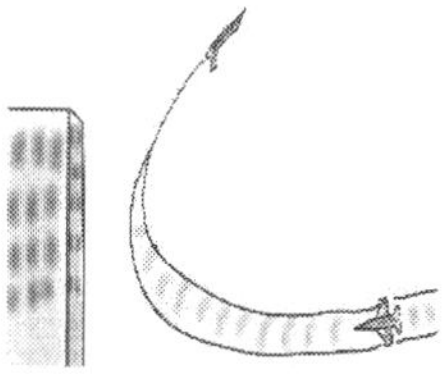

COMPONENTS

纟 [糸] THREAD228 + 圣[巠] TOWER CRANE272

STORY

Chinese *scriptures* tell us of an unidentified flying object that once appeared close to a construction site, approaching a TOWER CRANE at full speed. The 'pilot' apparently *managed* to do a **jink** maneuver at the last second and was able to *pass through* the THREADS of the TOWER CRANE…

EXAMPLES

1. 经典(jīng diǎn) Classics, scripture.
2. 经历 (jīng lì) To go through, undergo. 经常 (jīng cháng) Day-to-day, every day.
3. 经理(jīng lǐ) Manager, director.

WANT A LITTLE MORE?

Usage frequency: Top 100.

274 **其** 2nd

DEFINITION

His, *her*, *its*, *theirs*; *he*, *she*, *it*; *that*, *such* (mostly used in written Chinese).

† Winnowing basket.

PRONUNCIATION

qí

SOUND WORD

Cheetah
The fastest mammal on the planet.

MNEMONICS

- This is the picture of a winnowing basket, used to separate grain from chaff. Ancient form: .
- *Clothes hamper*.
  For a modern interpretation, since it looks more like a basket on wheels that can be used to put soiled clothes in, we call it a *clothes hamper*.

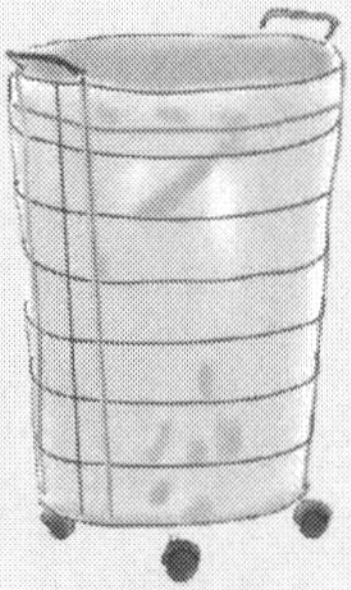

STORY

In this family, every member has *his* or *her* own *clothes hamper*, marked '*his*' and '*her*'. Even the family's **cheetah** has one (the *clothes hamper* marked '*its*').

EXAMPLES

使人各尽**其**能 (shǐ rén gè jǐn qí néng) To make everybody do his best. 正当**其**时 (zhèng dāng qí shí) Just at that moment. **其**他 (qí tā) Others. **其**中 (qí zhōng) Amongst them.

WANT A LITTLE MORE?

Usage frequency: Top 100.

275 **甚** 4th

DEFINITION

Very, *extremely*.

PRONUNCIATION

shèn

SOUND WORD

Operation

As in a medical **operation**.

COMPONENTS

其 CLOTHES HAMPER[274] his + ⺃ CORNER[6]

STORY

A surgeon talks to his assistants before a head **operation**, "This patient is *extremely* crazy. A *very* real basket case. Well, a HAMPER case, to be exact. He insists to have his CLOTHES HAMPER always placed right in the CORNER of his bedroom, with a precision of a few nanometers."

EXAMPLES

不甚(bù shèn) Not very. 甚是(shèn shì) Extremely. 甚至(shèn zhì) To the point of.

WANT A LITTLE MORE?

Usage frequency: Top third.

276A 什 2nd

DEFINITION

What?

PRONUNCIATION

shén

SOUND WORD

Chenil /ʃənil/
French word for 'kennel,' a place where dogs are kept.

COMPONENTS

亻 HANDYMAN[23] MAN + 十 TEN[59]

STORY

One day, the HANDYMAN tells me, "I think I am a TEN!"
I say, "*What?*"
He says, "Look, with the various skills I possess and the beautiful face of mine, I really think I am a TEN."
"Well, from my point of view," I say, "your dog face is better suited to be seen amongst the other residents of a **chenil**."

EXAMPLES

什么 (shén me) What? 什么时候 (shén me shí hòu) When.

WANT A LITTLE MORE?

- You may sometimes see this character being replaced by 甚 (see EXTREMELY[275]) for the same meaning of *what?*
- Usage frequency: Top 500.

276B

什

2nd

DEFINITION

1. *Assorted, various.*
2. *Ten* (used in fractions, on checks to prevent fraud, etc.).

PRONUNCIATION

shí

SOUND WORD

Sherpa
An ethnic group living in the Himalayas. They are often used as guides and porters during climbing expeditions.

COMPONENTS

亻 HANDYMAN[23] MAN + 十 TEN[59]

STORY

During a pause while climbing, the **Sherpa** tells his clients, "The HANDYMAN who is accompanying us just told me he has brought for you all a plate of *assorted* cold cuts and he is graciously offering it to you."
"Wow! Thank you, HANDYMAN!"
"Ah, it's nothing," says the HANDYMAN. He then leans towards the **Sherpa** and whispers in his ear, "You can write me a check at the end of the expedition. *TEN* dollars a pop."

EXAMPLES

1. 什菜 (shí cài) Mixed vegetables.

WANT A LITTLE MORE?

Usage frequency: Middle third.

277 **林** 2nd

DEFINITION

1. *Woods, grove; forestry.*
2. *Group, circle of people.*
3. *Surname.*

PRONUNCIATION

lín

SOUND WORD

Linen
All sorts of products made of **linen**: towels, bed **linens**, tablecloths, men's or women's wear.

COMPONENTS

2 x 木 TREE[125]

MNEMONICS

One TREE = wood. Two TREES = *woods.*

STORY

This *group* of students in *forestry* is spending a week in the *woods* as part of their curriculum. You can see, hanging between two TREES, **linen** towels and underwears left to dry.

EXAMPLES

1. 林业(lín yè) Forest industry.
2. 艺林(yì lín) Artistic circles.

WANT A LITTLE MORE?

- It ranks amongst the top 100 Chinese surnames.
- Usage frequency: Top 500.

278 **森** 1st

DEFINITION

1. *Forest, full of trees.*
2. *Gloomy.*

PRONUNCIATION

sēn

SOUND WORD

Scent
A pleasant smell produced by something.

COMPONENTS

3 x 木 TREE[125]

MNEMONICS

A multitude of TREES constitutes a *forest.*

STORY

My friend always hangs three air fresheners in the form of a TREE on his car mirror. "I like the *forest* **scent** so much!" he says.

EXAMPLES

1. 森林(sēn lín) Forest.
2. 阴森(yīn sēn) Gloomy.

WANT A LITTLE MORE?

Usage frequency: Top third.

279 # 麻 2nd

Definition

1. *Hemp* (variety of Cannabis).
2. *Tingling*; to have *pins and needles.*
3. To *bother.*
4. *Pockmarked, pitted.*
5. *Surname.*

Pronunciation

má

Sound word

Mafia

Components

广 CASTLE[223] EXTENSIVE + 林 GROVE[277]

Story

The inspector had *pins and needles* in his legs when he broke into the CASTLE of the **mafia** boss and discovered a *hemp* GROVE in the basement. However, he did nothing because he did not want to *bother* the *pockmarked*-face boss sleeping upstairs...

Examples

1. 麻醉剂 (má zuì jì) Narcotic.
2. 发麻 (fā má) To have pins and needles.
3. 麻烦 (má fán) To trouble somebody.
4. 大麻子 (dà má zǐ) Person with a pockmarked face.

Want a little more?

- This is the 200th of the 214 Kangxi radicals.
- Usage frequency: Top third.

280A 么[麼]

DEFINITION

Interrogative suffix; adverbial suffix: What? Whatever, like that.

PRONUNCIATION

me

SOUND WORD

Elbow creamer
Think of it as a special cream product that you apply to your elbow (elbow grease?).

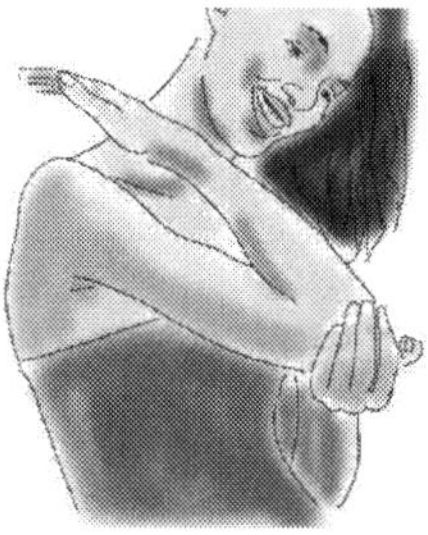

SIMPLIFIED COMPONENTS

丶 DROP[3] + 厶 ELBOW[10] PRIVATE

TRADITIONAL COMPONENTS

[麻 HEMP[279] + 幺 NEGLIGIBLE[227]]

MNEMONICS

An **elbow creamer**? *What* will they think of next? *Whatever*!

STORY

"This **elbow creamer** is quite powerful," says the salesperson. "You just need to add one DROP on your ELBOW, *like that*, to heal *whatever* ailment you may have!"
"*What*? But how?"

["It's a secret mixture. All I can tell you is that it contains a NEGLIGIBLE amount of HEMP."]

EXAMPLES

什么 (shén me) What? Whatever. 怎么 (zěn me) How. 那么 (nà me) Like that.

WANT A LITTLE MORE?

Usage frequency: Top 100.

280B 麼[麼] 2nd

DEFINITION

Tiny, petty, insignificant.

PRONUNCIATION

mó

SOUND WORD

Model /mɔdəl/
As in 'top model,' but pronounced in German, which is a better approximation than in English.

SIMPLIFIED COMPONENTS

麻 HEMP279 + 丶 DROP3 + 厶 ELBOW10 PRIVATE

TRADITIONAL COMPONENTS

[HEMP + 幺 NEGLIGIBLE227]

STORY

"You know that Nadia, our top **model**, is in detox, don't you? She was smoking too much HEMP. She'll work today nonetheless. She's using patches that contain a *tiny* amount of HEMP, a DROP, glued to her ELBOW."
"Are you sure it won't affect her walk?"

["Certain. The quantity of HEMP is NEGLIGIBLE. This is an *insignificant* amount…"]

EXAMPLES

幺麼 (yāo mó) Petty, insignificant.

WANT A LITTLE MORE?

Usage frequency: Middle third.

281 **去** 4th

DEFINITION

To go, *leave*; to *remove*.

PRONUNCIATION

qù

SOUND WORD

Dévêtu /devɛtʃy/
French verb meaning 'undressed.'
In this book, the Chinese **qu** sound is represented by the French 'tu,' preferably the French-Canadian version.

COMPONENTS

土 DIRT[85] + 厶 ELBOW[10] PRIVATE

STORY

At 1 PM, Michel comes back to the office, completely **dévêtu**, except for a pair of underwear, and with DIRT on his ELBOWS.

"Where did you *go*?" asks one of his buddies.
"I went to the beach next door during lunch hour. There was nobody there, so I *removed* my clothes down to my underwear. I rolled my pants and vest in a ball, laid on my back and fell asleep. I woke up an hour later and looked around, my ELBOWS planted in the DIRT. I wanted to *leave*, but I realized somebody had stolen my clothes…"
All his mates start laughing. "Here are your clothes!" says one.

EXAMPLES

出去(chū qù) To go out. 回去(huí qù) To go back. 上去(shàng qù) To go up. 撤去(chè qù) To remove, pull out.

WANT A LITTLE MORE?

Usage frequency: Top 100.

282

法

3rd

DEFINITION

1. *Law, rule.*
2. *Method, way.*
3. *France.*

PRONUNCIATION

fǎ

SOUND WORD

Faraday
Michael **Faraday**, English scientist and discoverer of an important law of Physics regarding electromagnetic induction, which is at the origin of our capacity to produce electricity.

COMPONENTS

氵 WATER[126] + 去 to GO[281]

STORY

Michael **Faraday** was an English scientist who was also a member of the Science Academy (Académie des Sciences) in *France*. He has made huge contributions to society.
Thanks to **Faraday**'s *Law*, man now has a *method* to produce electricity. One *way* of doing it is to allow rushing WATER to GO into giant turbines.

EXAMPLES

1. 法制 (fǎ zhì) Legal system. 语法 (yǔ fǎ) Grammar.
2. 方法 (fāng fǎ) Method, way.
3. 法国 (fǎ guó) France.

WANT A LITTLE MORE?

Usage frequency: Top 100.

283 学[學] 2nd

DEFINITION

To *learn*, *study*.

PRONUNCIATION

xué

SOUND WORD

Schüler /ʃyːlɐ/
German word for 'male learner(s),' 'student(s),' 'pupil(s).' This is a good approximation if you suppress the 'l' sound.

COMPONENTS

⺍[與] to UNCOVER[142] + 子 CHILD[82]

STORY

To commemorate the opening of a new school in Germany, the director, standing in front of the building, UNCOVERS a statue of a CHILD in the *learning* pose of 'the Thinker of Rodin,' representing a **Schüler** *studying* a book.

EXAMPLES

学生(xué shēng) Student, pupil. 学中文(xué zhōng wén) To study Chinese. 化学(huà xué) Chemistry. 大学(dà xué) University.

WANT A LITTLE MORE?

Usage frequency: Top 100.

284 **如** 2nd

DEFINITION

As if, if, such as, like.

PRONUNCIATION

rú

SOUND WORD

Rudeness

COMPONENTS

女 WOMAN[26] + 口 MOUTH[41]

STORY

With great **rudeness**, he grabbed the arm of the WOMAN and kissed her on the MOUTH, *as if* such bad behaviour would ever be acceptable!

EXAMPLES

爱国如家(ài guó rú jiā) To love one's country as if it were home. 如果(rú guǒ) If. 例如(lì rú) Such as. 如此(rú cǐ) Thus, like this.

WANT A LITTLE MORE?

Usage frequency: Top 100.

285A

都

1st

DEFINITION

All, *entirely*.

PRONUNCIATION

dōu

SOUND WORD

Dough
A mixture of flour and water to make donuts or another name for money.

COMPONENTS

者 MAKER[203] + 阝 CITY WALL[107]

STORY

A donut MAKER was forced to close his business outside the CITY WALLS. There was a sign on the door that said, '*Entirely* out of business. Thieves came and took *all* my **dough**.'

EXAMPLES

全都(quán dōu) All, without exception. 大都(dà dōu) For the most part. 不都(bù dōu) Not all.

WANT A LITTLE MORE?

Usage frequency: Top 100.

285B

都

1st

DEFINITION

1. *Metropolis*, *capital city*.
2. *Surname*.

PRONUNCIATION

dū

SOUND WORD

Dew
Moisture condensed upon the surface of cool bodies.

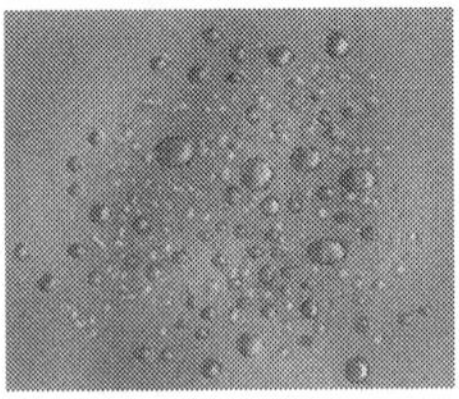

COMPONENTS

者 to DRUDGE[203] DOER + 阝 CITY WALL[107]

STORY

A well-run *metropolis* must rely on an army of workers. From early morning, when there is still **dew** on the ground, you can see them already DRUDGING within the CITY WALLS, delivering and sweeping.

EXAMPLES

1. 都市 (dū shì) City, metropolis. 首都 (shǒu dū) Capital of a country.

WANT A LITTLE MORE?

Usage frequency: Bottom third.

286A

同

2nd

DEFINITION

Same, similar, together, in common, in unison; with.

PRONUNCIATION

tóng

SOUND WORD

Tonka

An American toy company mostly known for its toy trucks.

COMPONENTS

冂 HOOD[12] LONG COVER + 一 ONE[15] + 口 MOUTH[41]

MNEMONICS

Christmas carols choir.

A group of singers wearing a HOOD and singing as if *with* ONE MOUTH, *in unison.*

STORY

All members of the *Christmas carols choir* are singing *with* ONE another, *in unison.* Covered under their HOOD, they sing *together* and the sound seems to be coming from only ONE MOUTH.

And for that great performance, they all received from their director the *same* **Tonka** truck!

EXAMPLES

不同 (bù tóng) Different. 同意 (tóng yì) To agree with. 同事 (tóng shì) Coworkers. 谁同我去？(shéi tóng wǒ qù) Who's coming with me?

WANT A LITTLE MORE?

Usage frequency: Top 100.

286B

同

4th

DEFINITION

Lane, alley.

PRONUNCIATION

tòng

SOUND WORD

Bastogne

A Belgian town, site of the Siege of **Bastogne**, an important World War II battle that was part of the larger Battle of the Bulge. The Americans had to defend the town at all costs.

COMPONENTS

冂 GLASS BELL[12] LONG COVER + 一 ONE[15] + 口 ORIFICE[41]

STORY

"Mein General, the Americans are hidden in various narrow *lanes* and *alleys* of **Bastogne** and they refuse to surrender. What should we do?"
"Alright, we will place a gigantic GLASS BELL covering the town. They will not be able to last too long without food."
"But sir, the citizens will suffocate. We should at least provide a few ORIFICES in the glass to allow them to breathe!"
"OK. ONE ORIFICE. ONE!"

EXAMPLES

胡同 (hú tòng) Lane, alley (a type of narrow streets or alleys, found prominently in Beijing).

WANT A LITTLE MORE?

Usage frequency: Bottom third.

287 贝 [貝] 4th

DEFINITION

Shellfish, *shell*, *clam*, *mussel*, *cowrie*; *money*.

PRONUNCIATION

bèi

SOUND WORD

Sick bay
A place on a ship (or a spaceship) that is used to care for sick or injured people.

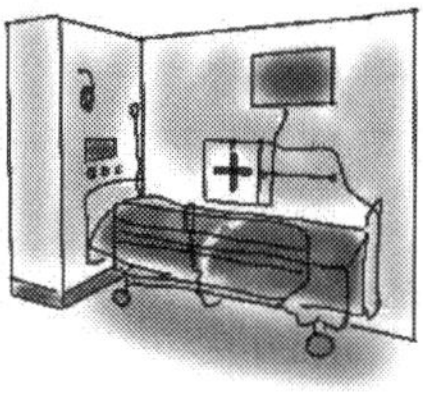

SIMPLIFIED COMPONENTS

冂 SHELTER[12] LONG COVER + 'tongue'

TRADITIONAL COMPONENTS

[目 EYE[200] + 八 OCTOPUS[55] EIGHT]

MNEMONICS

- This is a pictogram of a *cowrie*. The *cowrie* served as an early form of *money*. Ancient form: .
- The simplified character looks like a *clam* with a 'tongue' sticking out of its SHELTER.

STORY

During a cruise aboard a ship, a man accepted a challenge. To win some *money*, he ate a lot of *shellfish*, along with their *shells*, or SHELTERS if you will, to impress his friends. He is now in the **sick bay**, rolling with pain.

[The reason of his pain may have to do with the desiccated EYE of an OCTOPUS he also consumed.]

EXAMPLES

贝壳 (bèi ké) Shell. 贝类 (bèi lèi) Shellfish, mollusks. 贝币 (bèi bì) Shells used as money.

WANT A LITTLE MORE?

- This is the 154th of the 214 Kangxi radicals.
- Usage frequency: Top third.

288 见[見] 4th

DEFINITION

To *see*, *perceive*, *observe*.

PRONUNCIATION

jiàn

SOUND WORD

Hygienist
As in dental **hygienist**, in that dreaded of all places: the dentist's chair.

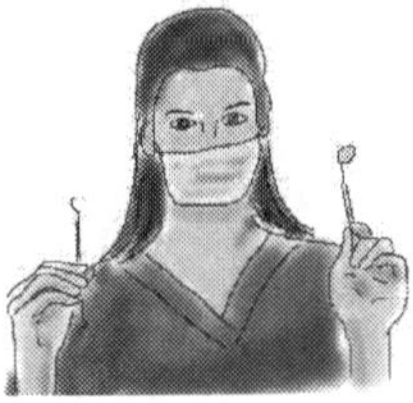

SIMPLIFIED COMPONENTS

冂 COVER[12] + 儿 HUMAN LEGS[52] child

TRADITIONAL COMPONENTS

[目 EYE[200] + HUMAN LEGS]

MNEMONICS

The traditional character shows a big EYE over HUMAN LEGS, meaning to *see*.

Ancient form: .

STORY

The **hygienist** welcomes me to the dentist office, but the only thing I want to do is look around and try to *see* where I can run for COVER with my HUMAN LEGS!

[I am now in the dentist chair (they were able to catch me) and the **hygienist** is looking at my teeth through a big magnifying glass. From my point of view, all I *see* is a big EYE sitting on top of HUMAN LEGS.]

EXAMPLES

看见 (kàn jiàn) To see. 再见 (zài jiàn) Good-bye, see you again.

WANT A LITTLE MORE?

- This is the 147th of the 214 Kangxi radicals.
- Usage frequency: Top 500.

289 **现[現]** 4th

DEFINITION

1. *Present*, *now*, *current*.
2. To *show*, *appear*, *be revealed*.

PRONUNCIATION

xiàn

SOUND WORD

Pharmacienne /faʀmasjɛn/
French word for a woman pharmacist.

COMPONENTS

王 KING[19] + 见[見] to SEE[288]

STORY

The French KING has a crush on the new **pharmacienne**. So, trying to *appear* ill, he says to his adviser, "I want to SEE the **pharmacienne** *now*!"

EXAMPLES

1. 现在(xiàn zài) Now, at present.
2. 出现(chū xiàn) To appear.

WANT A LITTLE MORE?

Usage frequency: Top 100.

290A

当[當]

1st

DEFINITION

1. To *serve as*, *be equal to.*
2. *Should, ought to.*
3. *At a given time or place.*

PRONUNCIATION

dāng

SOUND WORD

Dang

Euphemism for Damn!

SIMPLIFIED COMPONENTS

⺌ SMALL[167] +

彐 PIG SNOUT & BROOM HEAD[39]

TRADITIONAL COMPONENTS

[⺍ JESTER HAT[141] + 口 MOUTH[41] +

田 FIELD[195]]

STORY

I look outside one morning and see my whole vegetable garden wiped out. "**Dang**!" I go outside and my neighbor says over the fence, "A wild pig did it. I was there *at that time*. You see, its PIG SNOUT *serves as* a SMALL BROOM HEAD.

["It buries it in the ground and can sweep with its MOUTH a FIELD clean in no time!"
"So, what *should* I do?" I asked.
"Wear this JESTER HAT. It will scare them away."
"**Dang**! I *ought to* have thought of that!"]

EXAMPLES

1. 当老师(dāng lǎo shī) To serve as a teacher. 相当 (xiāng dāng) To be equal to.
2. 当然(dāng rán) As it should be, of course. 应当 (yīng dāng) Ought to, should.
3. 当时(dāng shí) At that time.

WANT A LITTLE MORE?

Usage frequency: Top 100.

290B 当[當] 4th

DEFINITION

1. *Suitable, adequate, appropriate.*
2. To *consider, treat as.*

PRONUNCIATION

dàng

SOUND WORD

Burundanga /burundaŋga/
Drug used to induce a trance-like state. Also called scopolamine, it has been reported as sometimes being used to incapacitate victims before attacking them.

SIMPLIFIED COMPONENTS

⺌ SMALL167 + 彐 PIG SNOUT39

TRADITIONAL COMPONENTS

[⺍ JESTER HAT141 + 口 MOUTH41 + 田 TENNIS COURT195 FIELD]

STORY

"Some top athletes make use of heavy drugs. Take the tennis top seed of the moment, Pete Hog. He's a well-known user of **burundanga**, making him do crazy things that he *considers appropriate*. He appeared yesterday at a press conference, wearing a SMALL PIG SNOUT mask and he kept repeating, 'I am a hog.' He *considered* himself a real hog and wanted to be *treated as* such!"

["Yeah, or take his main competitor, Jack Foolswing, another known **burundanga** user, who thought it was *suitable* to appear naked on the TENNIS COURT and dance with a JESTER HAT in his MOUTH…"]

EXAMPLES

1. 适当 (shì dàng) Suitable, proper.
2. 当做 (dàng zuò) To consider, treat as.

WANT A LITTLE MORE?

Usage frequency: Top third.

291A

没[沒]

2nd

DEFINITION

Not have; not (negative prefix for verbs).

PRONUNCIATION

méi

SOUND WORD

Medic

SIMPLIFIED COMPONENTS

氵 WATER[126] + 殳 SLING[232]

TRADITIONAL COMPONENTS

[WATER + ~刀 KNIFE[109] + 又 RIGHT HAND[71]]

STORY

I am in the emergency room of a hospital. Actually, I have been waiting here for 10 hours straight! The **medic** apparently "*not have* time to see me!" I've had enough of this! I open the door of his office and shoot a few WATER balloons at him with my SLING.

[He then takes his bistoury KNIFE in his RIGHT HAND and starts chasing me, but he slips on the WATER left by the exploded balloons. "Him *not* got hold of me! Hee hee!"]

EXAMPLES

没有 (méi yǒu) Not have. 没事 (méi shì) To have nothing to do; never mind; nothing wrong. 没用 (méi yòng) Useless.

WANT A LITTLE MORE?

Usage frequency: Top 100.

291B # 没[沒] **4th**

DEFINITION

To *sink*, *drown*, *inundate*, *submerge*.

PRONUNCIATION

mò

SOUND WORD

Eskimo

SIMPLIFIED COMPONENTS

氵 WATER[126] + 殳 SLING[232]

TRADITIONAL COMPONENTS

[WATER + ~刀 KNIFE[109] + 又 AGAIN[71]]

STORY

The **Eskimo** hunts the walrus when it's *submerged* in the WATER. When the walrus pops its head out of the WATER, the **Eskimo** shoots a few stones with a SLING and then waits for it to *drown*.

[Sometimes, the **Eskimo** needs to get very close and hit the walrus AGAIN and AGAIN with his KNIFE until it *sinks* in the WATER.]

EXAMPLES

沉没(chén mò) To sink. 淹没(yān mò) To inundate, drown. 浸没(jìn mò) To immerse, submerge.

WANT A LITTLE MORE?

Usage frequency: Middle third.

292 动[動] 4th

DEFINITION

To *move*, *get moving*.

PRONUNCIATION

dòng

SOUND WORD

Slam-dunk
A basketball shot that is performed when a player jumps in the air and throws the ball downward with force through the basket.

SIMPLIFIED COMPONENTS

云 CLOUD180A + 力 POWER108

TRADITIONAL COMPONENTS

[重 HEAVY262A + POWER]

STORY

This basketball player has so much POWER! Whenever he *gets moving* or jumps to **slam-dunk** the ball, he leaves a CLOUD of smoke behind!

[Not only that, he can *move* HEAVY objects too. Once, during a game, a pesky fan jumped on the court, ran to him and started shouting in his face. To *move* him out of the way, he just took the guy and **slam-dunked** him! That's POWER!]

EXAMPLES

运动(yùn dòng) To move; sports, athletics. **别动**!(bié dòng) Don't move! **动物**(dòng wù) Animal.

WANT A LITTLE MORE?

Usage frequency: Top 100.

293 主

DEFINITION

Non-character used only as a building block.

PRONUNCIATION

Not applicable

SOUND WORD

Not applicable

MNEMONICS

Plant.
This character looks like a *plant* coming out of the soil.

294 麦[麥] 4th

DEFINITION

Wheat, barley, oats.

PRONUNCIATION

mài

SOUND WORD

Oh my…
An expression of surprise or exasperation…

SIMPLIFIED COMPONENTS

龶 PLANT[293] + 夂 to WALK SLOWLY[219]

TRADITIONAL COMPONENTS

[來 to COME[145] + ~to WALK SLOWLY]

STORY

I watch the new helper I just hired to tend my field of *wheat* and *barley*. I see him WALK so SLOWLY between the PLANTS. I say to myself, "We'll never get the work done on time. **Oh my**…"

[Becoming impatient, I decide to talk to him about his speed. I say, "Hey! Please COME here!" And I watch him WALK SLOWLY towards me for the next ten minutes! **Oh my**…]

EXAMPLES

麦子 (mài zǐ) Wheat, barley. 麦片 (mài piàn) Oatmeal.

WANT A LITTLE MORE?

- This is the 199th of the 214 Kangxi radicals.
- Usage frequency: Top third.

295A	面	4th ╲

DEFINITION

Face (of a human or an object), *surface*, *top*; *aspect*, *side*; used for *location* or *direction.*

PRONUNCIATION

miàn

SOUND WORD

Bohemian
A socially unconventional person, someone who does not follow society's traditional rules of behavior.

COMPONENTS

百 HUNDRED[64] + 目 EYE[200]

MNEMONICS

Picture this character as the merging of the building blocks for HUNDRED and EYE.

STORY

A **bohemian** woman is walking naked in the street. The *surface* of her body is covered with painted flowers, giving her the *aspect* of a bouquet. Seeing HUNDREDS of EYES looking in her *direction*, she screams, "Please stop looking at my *face*!"
Somebody shouts, "We're not, I assure you!"

EXAMPLES

面前 (miàn qián) In the face of somebody. 南面 (nán miàn) Southern face. 表面 (biǎo miàn) Surface, face. 方面 (fāng miàn) Aspect, side. 里面 (lǐ miàn) Inside.

WANT A LITTLE MORE?

- This is the 176th of the 214 Kangxi radicals.
- Usage frequency: Top 100.

295B 面[麵] 4th

DEFINITION

Flour, noodles.

PRONUNCIATION

miàn

SOUND WORD

Bohemian
A socially unconventional person, someone who does not follow society's traditional rules of behavior.

SIMPLIFIED COMPONENTS

面 FACE[295A]

TRADITIONAL COMPONENTS

[麥 WHEAT[294] + FACE]

STORY

A **bohemian** artist is trying to sell a painting on the street. It depicts a plate of *noodles*. A woman stops to look at it while stuffing her FACE with a bean sprouts salad.

[The **bohemian**, wanting to make a sale, says to her, "So that you know, the *noodles* I painted are made with organic, whole-WHEAT *flour*."]

EXAMPLES

面粉 (miàn fěn) Wheat flour. 炒面 (chǎo miàn) Fried noodles.

WANT A LITTLE MORE?

- This is a separate entry from the previous one because the traditional character 麵 only means *flour, noodles*.
- Usage frequency: Top third.

296 㔾 2nd

Definition

† A seal.

Pronunciation

jié

Sound word

The aircrew
The crew of an aircraft or one member of such a crew. (See 'Special Sound Mnemonics,' page 485)

Mnemonics

Bent in half, in pain.
Picture a member of **the aircrew** *in pain* after eating food served to the passengers in economy class.

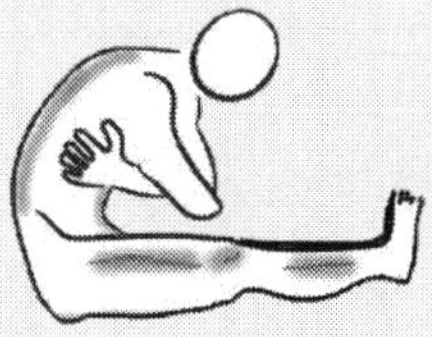

297 卩 2nd

DEFINITION

† A kneeling person in submission.

PRONUNCIATION

jié

SOUND WORD

The aircrew
The crew of an aircraft or one member of such a crew. (See 'Special Sound Mnemonics,' page 485)

MNEMONICS

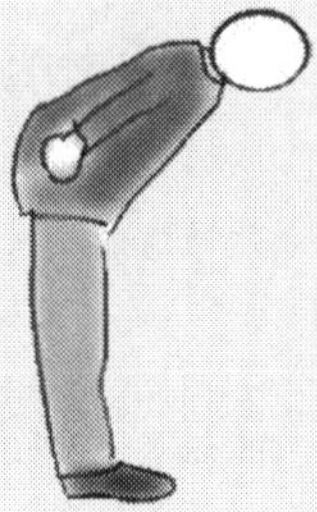

- To *bow down*.
  Although it was long believed to be equivalent to the previous character 㔾 and represent a seal for signing documents, its ancient meaning is now known to depict a kneeling person in submission. This book uses a similar meaning: to *bow down* with deference, like the Chinese or Japanese do.
- Just picture a member of **the aircrew** welcoming passengers aboard the plane by *bowing down* to the extreme, his head hitting his knees.
- This building block is sometimes written ⺋, with an extended horizontal stroke.

WANT A LITTLE MORE?

This is the 26th of the 214 Kangxi radicals.

298 己 3rd

DEFINITION

Self.

PRONUNCIATION

jǐ

SOUND WORD

Jigsaw puzzle

MNEMONICS

- Think of the letter 'S' written backwards, for the mirror image of your *Self*, your Soul.
- *Guardian angel.*
  For a concrete representation of this meaning, this character stands for your *guardian angel*, standing on your shoulder, guiding you and recording all your actions, good or bad.

STORY

A *guardian angel* says to his assigned person, "There you go again, back to your old *self*! I had already told you not to do that! I do not understand you anymore. You are like a **jigsaw puzzle** to me!"

EXAMPLES

自己 (zì jǐ) Oneself. 知己 (zhī jǐ) To know oneself.

WANT A LITTLE MORE?

- This is the 6th heavenly stem.
- This is the 49th of the 214 Kangxi radicals.
- Usage frequency: Top 500.

299 巳 4th

DEFINITION

9-11 a.m.

† Fetus.

PRONUNCIATION

sì

SOUND WORD

Confessor
A priest who listens to a person's confession in a confessional.

MNEMONICS

Some etymologists believe that this character represented the picture of a *fetus*.

STORY

She has gotten pregnant and believes she has sinned. She goes see the **confessor** and tells him about the *fetus*. He tells her, "You have to say 10 Hail Mary at *10 a.m.* every day and no one should know about our relation!"

EXAMPLES

巳时 (sì shí) 9-11 a.m.

WANT A LITTLE MORE?

- This is the 6th earthly branch.
- Usage frequency: Middle third.

300 **已** 3rd

Definition

1. *Already.*
2. To *stop*, *cease.*

Pronunciation

yǐ

Sound word

Hippopotame /ipɔpɔtam/
French word for 'hippopotamus.'
The 'h' is silent.

Mnemonics

Notice the shape of this character. It fits right between the 己 SELF[298] and the 巳 FETUS[299] characters, the curved stroke extending slightly above the horizontal line in the middle. Therefore, it could represent a FETUS whose SELF is *already* half-developed, or for a stronger mnemonic, the back of a FETUS head *already* half-eaten (see story).

Story

We arrived at the zoo in a hurry, but it was *already* too late. The **hippopotame** had crushed the pregnant lady and had *already* eaten half of her fetus! All we could do was yell, "*Stop*! *Stop*!"

Examples

1. 已经 (yǐ jīng) Already.
2. 不已 (bù yǐ) Endlessly.

Want a little more?

Usage frequency: Top 500.

301 **巴** $\overline{1}^{st}$

DEFINITION

1. *Suffix* for certain nouns.
2. Used for its sound.

† Great snake.

PRONUNCIATION

bā

SOUND WORD

Bas /ba/
French word for 'sock.'

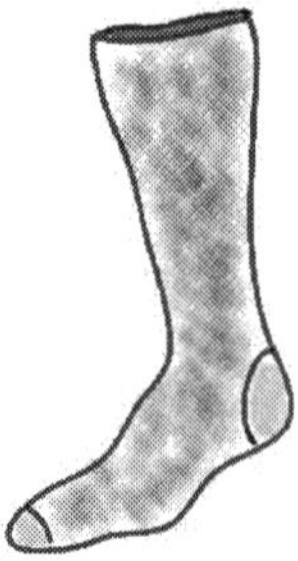

MNEMONICS

Cobra.
Although this character is more often associated with the python snake, it may be easier, mnemonically and visually, to associate it with the *cobra* snake, the 'eyeglasses snake.' Think of the eyeglass pattern on the back of a *cobra*'s head that looks like the top part of this character.

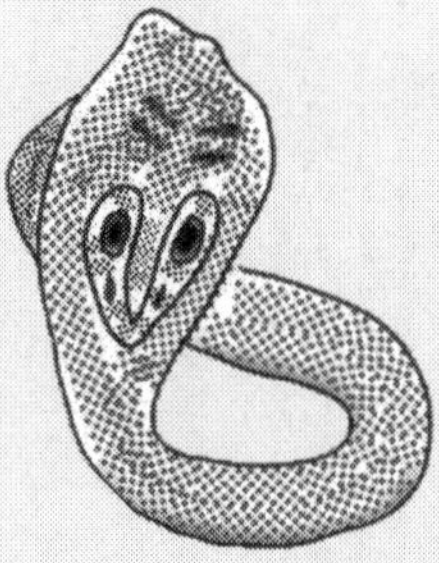

STORY

This morning, I found a *cobra* in my **bas**!

EXAMPLES

1. 尾巴 (wěi bā) Tail. 嘴巴 (zuǐ bā) Mouth.
2. 巴西 (bā xī) Brazil. 阿米巴 (ā mǐ bā) Amoeba.

WANT A LITTLE MORE?

Usage frequency: Top third.

302 走 3rd

DEFINITION

To *walk*, *go*, *move*.

PRONUNCIATION

zǒu

SOUND WORD

Zoccoli /dsɔkkoli/
Italian word for 'clog shoes,' 'sabots.'

COMPONENTS

土 SOIL[85] + 龰 to STRAIGHTEN[76A] CORRECT

MNEMONICS

The ancient form, , clearly shows a man (top part) walking with his feet (bottom part).

STORY

An Italian designer wants to organize a fashion show to promote his new collection of **zoccoli** and he has gathered a group of top models for this purpose. He wants them to *walk*, not on a catwalk, but directly on soft SOIL, to display the 'cross-country' capabilities of his shoes. *Walking* in those clogs is not an easy task for the models, who constantly fall face first on the SOIL. The designer keeps *moving* towards each of them, STRAIGHTENING their backs and whispering, "*Go* and keep your back straight when you *walk*!"

EXAMPLES

行走(xíng zǒu) To walk. 我们走吧! (wǒ men zǒu ba) Let's go!

WANT A LITTLE MORE?

- Note that the last stroke of SOIL merges into the first stroke of to STRAIGHTEN in this character.
- This is the 156th of the 214 Kangxi radicals.
- Usage frequency: Top 500.

303 起 3rd

DEFINITION

1. To *rise, raise, get up*; to *start, begin.*
2. *Together.*

PRONUNCIATION

qǐ

SOUND WORD

Chihuahua
The smallest dog.

COMPONENTS

走 to WALK[302] + 己 GUARDIAN ANGEL[298] SELF

STORY

As soon as I *got up* this morning, me and my **Chihuahua** went to WALK outside *together* and, as usual, he defecated on the sidewalk. I left it there and pursued my walk when I heard my GUARDIAN ANGEL say in my ear, "Pick it up. Pick it up!"
"Please do not *start*! You're *beginning* to get on my nerves!" I replied.

EXAMPLES

1. 起来(qǐ lái) To get up, arise. 发起(fā qǐ) To initiate, start.
2. 一起(yī qǐ) Together.

WANT A LITTLE MORE?

Usage frequency: Top 100.

304A

看

4th

DEFINITION

1. To *see*, *look at*, *watch*; *read*.
2. To *think that*, *have the view that*.

PRONUNCIATION

kàn

SOUND WORD

Alaskan
From Alaska.

COMPONENTS

手 HAND[73] + 目 EYE[200]

MNEMONICS

A HAND placed over the EYES to look at something. Note that the HAND building block is curved to the left, as it should be when you place your left HAND over your EYES.

STORY

A Russian politician, standing at the edge of the Russian coast and *watching* the Bering Strait, says to her comrade, "I *think* that if you place your HAND above your EYES like this on a clear day, you can *see* the **Alaskan** coast!"

EXAMPLES

1. 看见 (kàn jiàn) To see. 好看 (hǎo kàn) Good-looking. 看书 (kàn shū) To read.
2. 你看怎么样 (nǐ kàn zěn me yàng) What do you think of that?

WANT A LITTLE MORE?

Usage frequency: Top 100.

304B

看

1st

DEFINITION

To *look after*, *tend.*

PRONUNCIATION

kān

SOUND WORD

Can
As in a tin **can** for food.

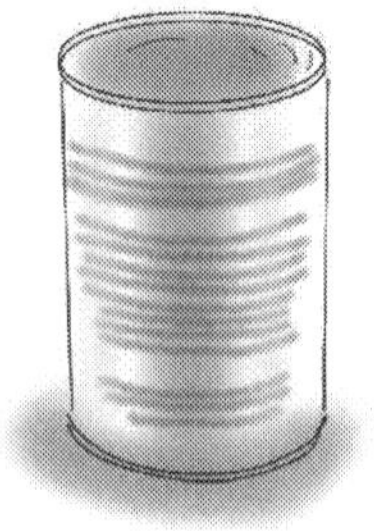

COMPONENTS

手 HAND[73] + 目 EYE[200]

STORY

In a very poor family, a mother tells her young son, "Jimmy, your mom has to leave the house for a few minutes. You are in charge of *looking after* the only **can** of food left. Put your HAND above your EYES like this and observe any potential intruders that may approach it! I will be back as soon as possible!"

EXAMPLES

看管 (kān guǎn) To look after. 看守 (kān shǒu) To watch, guard.

WANT A LITTLE MORE?

Usage frequency: Middle third.

305 定 4th

Definition

1. To *fix*, *set*; to *determine*, *decide*.
2. To *subscribe*, *order*.

Pronunciation

dìng

Sound word

Building

Components

宀 ROOF[50] + 疋 to STRAIGHTEN[76A] CORRECT

Story

A rich man reads a story in a newspaper he had just *subscribed* to about an earthquake in a foreign city in which he owns a **building**. He calls a contractor and says, "Please *determine* if the ROOF of my **building** needs to be STRAIGHTENED and if so, *fix* it!"

Examples

1. 一定 (yī dìng) Certainly, surely. 决定 (jué dìng) To decide. 定价 (dìng jià) To set a price.
2. 定报 (dìng bào) To subscribe to a newspaper.

Want a little more?

Usage frequency: Top 100.

306A

分

1st

DEFINITION

1. *Part*, *fraction*; to *divide*, *distinguish*.
2. A measure word for *units of length*, *area*, *weight*, *money*, *time* or *points*.

PRONUNCIATION

fēn

SOUND WORD

Fen
A type of wetland. It can support a rich community of plants and animals.

COMPONENTS

八 OCTOPUS[55] EIGHT + 刀 KNIFE[109]

MNEMONICS

To *divide* with a KNIFE.

STORY

A biologist *divides* an OCTOPUS in two with his KNIFE and says to his assistant, "Here's your *part*. You've got *one kilogram*'s worth of OCTOPUS meat. Enjoy!"
"Where did you get it?"
"Oh, I caught it in the **fen** over there…"

EXAMPLES

1. 部分(bù fēn) Part, section. 分裂(fēn liè) To split, divide.
   不分左右(bù fēn zuǒ yòu) Can't distinguish between left and right.
2. 分量(fēn liàng) Weight. 六点十分(liù diǎn shí fēn) Ten past six.
   一百分(yì bǎi fēn) 100 points (on a scorecard).

WANT A LITTLE MORE?

Usage frequency: Top 100.

306B 分 4th

DEFINITION

1. *Component.*
2. *Duty*; what is *within one's rights* or *obligations.*

PRONUNCIATION

fèn

SOUND WORD

Ibupro<u>fen</u>
A well-known drug used for relieving pain and helping with fever.

COMPONENTS

八 to <u>SEPARATE</u>[55] + 刀 <u>KNIFE</u>[109]

STORY

During a visit to a pharmacological lab, I ask, "What is this man doing over there?"
"He belongs to our Quality Assurance group. His sole *obligations* are to <u>SEPARATE</u> an **ibuprofen** tablet many times with a <u>KNIFE</u> and analyze its *components.*"
"Yes! This is my *duty*!" shouts the guy.

EXAMPLES

1. 成分 (chéng fèn) Component.
2. 本分 (běn fèn) One's duty.

WANT A LITTLE MORE?

Usage frequency: Bottom third.

307 罥 2nd

DEFINITION

† To stare, gaze.

PRONUNCIATION

huán

SOUND WORD

Roue en or /ʁuɑ̃n-ɔʁ/
French expression for a golden wheel or a circular object made of gold.

COMPONENTS

罒 EYE[200] + 一 ONE[15] + 口 MOUTH[41] + 𧘇 GOWN[235]

MNEMONICS

Princess.
You stare at a beautiful *princess* in a GOWN, with striking EYES and ONE smiling MOUTH, riding a cart with golden wheels (**roues en or**).
If you prefer, you can also picture the top of the character as her crown.

308A

还[還]

2nd

DEFINITION

Also, still, yet, even; in addition, still more.

PRONUNCIATION

hái

SOUND WORD

High-five
The celebratory hand gesture.

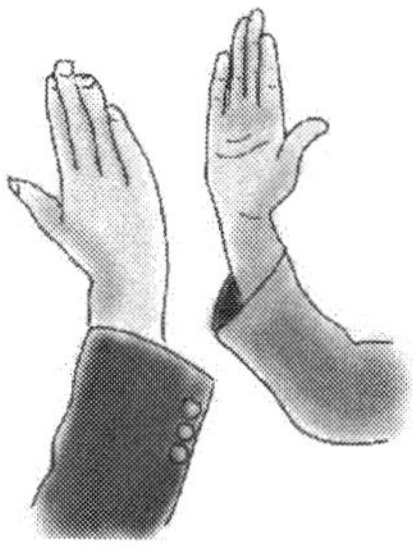

SIMPLIFIED COMPONENTS

辶 ROAD[104] + 不 NOT[79]

TRADITIONAL COMPONENTS

[ROAD + 睘 PRINCESS[307]]

STORY

It was almost midnight and Cinderella was *still* NOT on the ROAD.

[*Yet*, the PRINCESS was able to escape just in time and her scheme remained undetected by the prince. When she got home, she **high-fived** everybody, *even* the rat, and *also* the pumpkin!]

EXAMPLES

还是(hái shì) Still; after all; or. 还有 (hái yǒu) Furthermore, in addition.

WANT A LITTLE MORE?

Usage frequency: Top 100.

308B 还[還] 2nd

DEFINITION

To *return*, *come back*; to *give back*, *repay*.

PRONUNCIATION

huán

SOUND WORD

Roue en or /ʁuɑ̃n-ɔʁ/
French expression for a golden wheel or a circular object made of gold.

SIMPLIFIED COMPONENTS

辶 ROAD[104] + 不 NOT[79]

TRADITIONAL COMPONENTS

[ROAD + 睘 PRINCESS[307]]

STORY

The French fairy says, "Cinderella, you have to hit the ROAD in the golden carriage with the **roues en or** and *come back* before midnight. If NOT, the spell will be broken!"

["Ya, ya, I will," says the PRINCESS.

We know the rest of the story. The prince had to *return* and *give her back* the glass slipper….]

EXAMPLES

归还(guī huán) To return, revert. 偿还(cháng huán) To pay back.

WANT A LITTLE MORE?

Usage frequency: Middle third.

309 井 3rd

DEFINITION

A *well*.

PRONUNCIATION

jǐng

SOUND WORD

Jingle bells
When you see the name Santa in the story, think of '**jingle bells**.'

MNEMONICS

This is the picture of a *well*, or if you prefer, the grating covering its opening to prevent a fall.

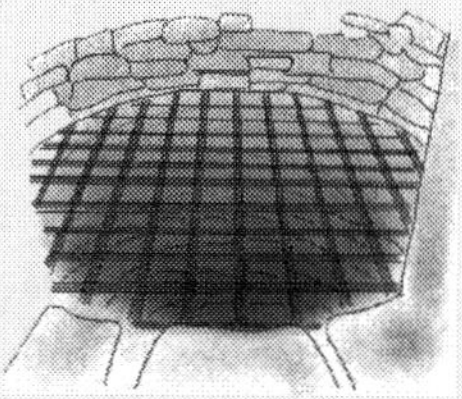

STORY

Santa Claus is getting old. He is still capable of singing **jingle bells**, but he suffers from memory lapses… There he is, trying to enter a *well* instead of a chimney...

EXAMPLES

水井 (shuǐ jǐng) Well. 油井 (yóu jǐng) Oil well.

WANT A LITTLE MORE?

Usage frequency: Top third.

310 **隹** 1st

DEFINITION

† A kind of short-tailed bird.

PRONUNCIATION

zhuī

SOUND WORD

Joey
A colloquial word meaning a unique guy, tall and handsome.

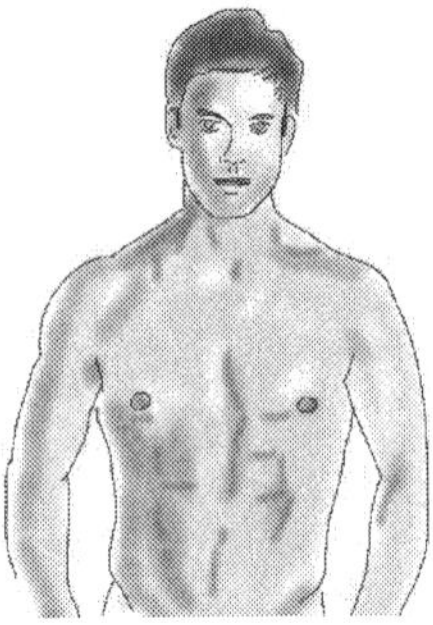

COMPONENTS

亻 PERSON[23] + ~主 OWNER[20]

MNEMONICS

Ostrich.
For a memorable image, think of a bird that is at least as tall as a PERSON, even a 'notch above' its OWNER in height (because the right building block counts an extra notch compared to 主 OWNER). What else then than the domestic *ostrich*, raised for its eggs, feathers and meat, and which can reach 2.75 m (9.0 ft) in height? It even has a short tail, short enough for our purpose! And it's beautiful too. A real **Joey**!

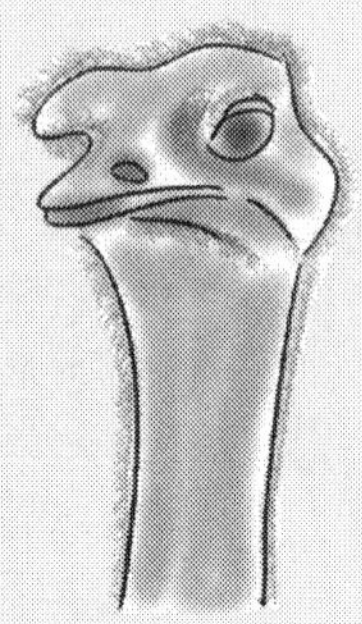

WANT A LITTLE MORE?

This is the 172nd of the 214 Kangxi radicals.

311 进[進] 4th

DEFINITION

1. To *advance, go forward, progress.*
2. To *enter.*

PRONUNCIATION

jìn

SOUND WORD

Car engine or simply **engine**.

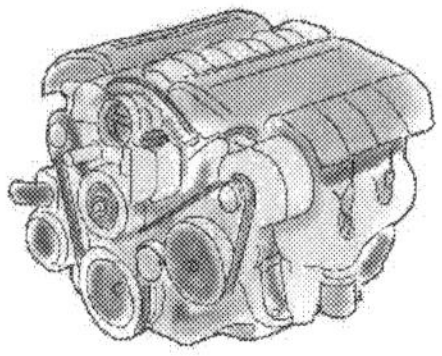

SIMPLIFIED COMPONENTS

辶 ROAD[104] + 井 WELL[309]

TRADITIONAL COMPONENTS

[ROAD + 隹 OSTRICH[310]]

STORY

A driver was *going forward* at a good pace when he was forced to swerve quickly towards the side of the ROAD. He failed to see the WELL, hitting it with force. The shock lifted up the front of his car and caused the **engine** to become detached from the frame, *enter* the opening and fall at the bottom of the WELL.

[All this to avoid an OSTRICH crossing the ROAD!]

EXAMPLES

1. 进步 (jìn bù) To progress, advance.
2. 进来 (jìn lái) To enter. 请进 (qǐng jìn) Come in! 进口 (jìn kǒu) Import; to import.

WANT A LITTLE MORE?

Usage frequency: Top 100.

312A 好 3rd

DEFINITION

Good.

PRONUNCIATION

hǎo

SOUND WORD

Howitzer
A type of heavy artillery piece.

COMPONENTS

女 WOMAN[26] + 子 CHILD[82]

MNEMONICS

A WOMAN with a CHILD suggests something *good*. Ancient form: .

STORY

This WOMAN saved the city. Holding her CHILD in one arm and manning a **Howitzer** with the other, she destroyed the opposing forces. She's that *good*!

EXAMPLES

好人(hǎo rén) Good person. 好看 (hǎo kàn) Good-looking.
太好了 (tài hǎo le) Great!

WANT A LITTLE MORE?

Usage frequency: Top 100.

312B

好

4th

DEFINITION

1. To *like*, *be fond of*; *hobby*.
2. To *be liable to*, *susceptible to*.

PRONUNCIATION

hào

SOUND WORD

Know-how
Expertise.

COMPONENTS

女 WOMAN26 + 子 CHILD82

STORY

"This WOMAN is really *fond of* CHILDREN. Looking after them is her *hobby*. However, do not hire her as a nanny for newborns because she doesn't have the **know-how**. She *is susceptible* to neglect holding their head and therefore *liable to* really hurt them."

EXAMPLES

1. 爱好(ài hào) To like, be fond of; hobby. 她好说话(tā hào shuō huà) She likes to talk.
2. 他好发脾气(tā hào fā pí qì) He is susceptible to lose his temper.

WANT A LITTLE MORE?

Usage frequency: Middle third.

313 **咅** 3rd

DEFINITION

To *vomit, spit out.*

PRONUNCIATION

pǒu

SOUND WORD

Poker face
A face on a person that shows no emotion.

COMPONENTS

立 to STAND[112] + 口 MOUTH[41]

MNEMONICS

Try to picture someone STANDING on the MOUTH of somebody else to prevent him from *vomiting.*

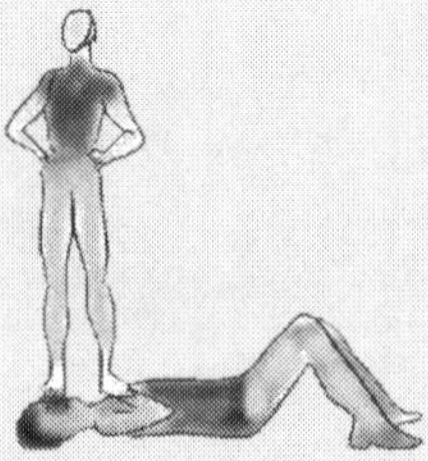

STORY

"I am a competitor in the World Poker Championship. I am so nervous I just want to *vomit*, but I still need to keep a **poker face**."

314 **音** $\bar{1}^{st}$

DEFINITION

Sound, tone, noise.

PRONUNCIATION

yīn

SOUND WORD

Inn
A place where you can eat and sleep.

COMPONENTS

立 to STAND[112] + 曰 SPEAKING MOUTH[44] to speak

STORY

I'm inside an **inn** and I see a guy speaking loudly to the clerk. I take him by the neck, throw him on the ground and STAND on his SPEAKING MOUTH, saying, "Shush! Not a *sound* now!" Muffled *noise* could still be heard coming from his SPEAKING MOUTH, though.

EXAMPLES

声音 (shēng yīn) Sound, voice. 录音 (lù yīn) To record sound. 音乐 (yīn yuè) Music.

WANT A LITTLE MORE?

- Not to be confused with the previous character 音, where the 口 MOUTH is silent, while the mouth here is speaking, making noise.
- This is the 180th of the 214 Kangxi radicals.
- Usage frequency: Top third.

315 **部** 4th

DEFINITION

1. *Ministry*, *department*, *section*, *part*, *division*; *troops*.
2. A measure word for *works of literature*, *films*, *machines*, etc.

PRONUNCIATION

bù

SOUND WORD

Peekaboo!
A game played with babies.

COMPONENTS

咅 to VOMIT[313] + 阝 CITY WALL[107]

STORY

The officer in charge of my military *division* always tries to be funny, even in the worst of circumstances. We were standing by, next to the CITY WALLS of the town we were about to attack. The *troops* were so nervous that some men in my *section* were VOMITING constantly. Our officer came behind us silently and yelled **Peekaboo**! He scared us so much that we all VOMITED on our *machines*!

EXAMPLES

1. 部分(bù fēn) Part, section. 部门(bù mén) Department, branch. 部长(bù zhǎng) Minister. 部队(bù duì) Army, troops.
2. 一部圣经(yī bù shèng jīng) A bible. 一部机器(yī bù jī qì) A machine.

WANT A LITTLE MORE?

Usage frequency: Top 100.

316 | 此 | 3rd

DEFINITION

<u>*This*</u>, <u>*these*</u> (literary).

PRONUNCIATION

cǐ

SOUND WORD

Zeugenstand /tsɔʏgənʃtant/
German word for 'witness box.'

COMPONENTS

止 to STOP[75] + 匕 SPOON[66]

STORY

The district attorney is eating a sundae while questioning the witness and keeps hitting the **Zeugenstand** with his SPOON. The judge says, "STOP *this*!"

EXAMPLES

此处 (cǐ chù) This place, here. 如此 (rú cǐ) Like this.

WANT A LITTLE MORE?

Usage frequency: Top 500.

317 # 些 1st

DEFINITION

Some, a few, several; a measure word for a *small* or *indefinite amount.*

PRONUNCIATION

xiē

SOUND WORD

Sciait /sjɛ/
Third person, imperfect tense of the French verb 'scier,' to saw. 'Il **sciait**' is equivalent to 'He was sawing.'

COMPONENTS

此 THESE[316] + 二 TWO[16]

STORY

"There was *some* noise last night; it sounded like sawing noise."
"It was our French neighbor. Il **sciait** *several* big logs with his new saw, like THESE TWO you see besides his house."

EXAMPLES

这些 (zhè xiē) These. 好些 (hǎo xiē) A good many, a great deal; a little better.

WANT A LITTLE MORE?

Usage frequency: Top 100.

318

永

3rd

DEFINITION

Forever, always, perpetual; eternity.

PRONUNCIATION

yǒng

SOUND WORD

Young Kickers
A fictional soccer team. Despite its name, let's assume this is a professional, world class team composed of adult players.

COMPONENTS

丶 DROP[3] + ~水 WATER[126]

MNEMONICS

Note the left 'hook' at the top of the WATER building block and then read the story.

STORY

The **Young Kickers** just won the World Cup by crushing the competition. For that performance alone, they will *forever* be remembered. Perhaps for the wrong reason. Can we say, 'enhanced performance'? Their coach took the habit of adding a DROP of a special something in the WATER bottles of the players and they kinda got 'hooked' on it…

EXAMPLES

永远(yǒng yuǎn) Always, forever. 永不(yǒng bù) Never. 永生(yǒng shēng) Eternal life.

WANT A LITTLE MORE?

Usage frequency: Top third.

319 # 样[樣] 4th

DEFINITION

Manner, model, pattern; appearance, shape; type, kind.

PRONUNCIATION

yàng

SOUND WORD

Bowyang
A piece of string or a strap tied around the trouser leg below the knee to prevent the bottom of the trouser from dragging. **Bowyangs** are commonly used by sheep shearers.

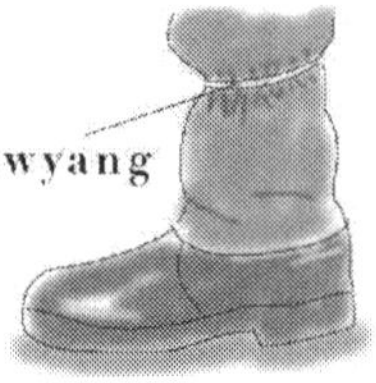

SIMPLIFIED COMPONENTS

木 TREE[125] + 羊 SHEEP[37]

TRADITIONAL COMPONENTS

[TREE + SHEEP + 永 FOREVER[318]]

STORY

I am getting ready to shear my first SHEEP. The instructor is leaning on a TREE, looking at me while I put the **bowyangs** on. I ask him, "I put them in this *manner*?"
He looks at me, incredulous. "What *kind* of fool are you? Look at the *shape* of your sleeves now, all puffed up. The **bowyang** does not go on the arms!

["If you want to keep this *appearance*, go ahead, but I guarantee you'll be remembered FOREVER, Michelin man!" He then detaches the SHEEP I was supposed to shear from the TREE and they both leave.]

EXAMPLES

这样(zhè yàng) Like this, this way. 样子(yàng zi) Appearance, shape; pattern, model.
哪样(nǎ yàng) What kind? 怎么样(zěn me yàng) How is it? How are things?

WANT A LITTLE MORE?

Usage frequency: Top 100.

320 **理** 3rd

DEFINITION

Reason, logic; logical; principle, theory, fields of knowledge.

PRONUNCIATION

lǐ

SOUND WORD

Little green man
Extraterrestrial or Martian.

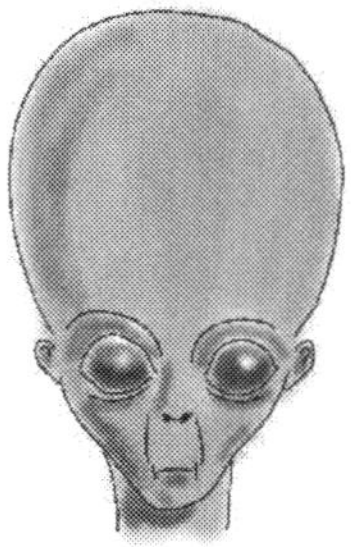

COMPONENTS

王 KING[19] + 里 HALF KILOMETER[246A]

STORY

The KING is informed that a group of men has been spotted HALF A KILOMETER from the castle. They do not appear to be his own people nor belong to a group of sworn enemies.
The KING, being a *logical* man, says, "It stands to *reason* that they must be **little green men**."

EXAMPLES

理论(lǐ lùn) Theory. 心理(xīn lǐ) Psychology. 治理(zhì lǐ) To rule, administer.

WANT A LITTLE MORE?

Usage frequency: Top 100.

321

心

1st

DEFINITION

1. *Heart*, *mind*.
2. *Center*.

PRONUNCIATION

xīn

SOUND WORD

Sin
A wrong action per religious or moral law.

MNEMONICS

- This is a picture of a *heart*, with drops of blood coming in and going out through the veins and arteries. Ancient form: .
- It is most often written 忄 or ⺗ when used as a building block.

STORY

"You intend to eat this huge sundae after all the hamburgers you consumed? Are you out of your *mind*? I consider it a **sin** to eat food that can block the arteries of your *heart*!"

EXAMPLES

1. 心脏 (xīn zàng) Heart. 心情 (xīn qíng) Mental state, mood.
2. 中心 (zhōng xīn) Center, middle, hub.

WANT A LITTLE MORE?

- This is the 61st of the 214 Kangxi radicals.
- Usage frequency: Top 100.

322 | 本 | 3rd

DEFINITION

1. *Basis*, *foundation*, *origin*; *roots* or *stems* of plants; *one's own*, *this*.
2. *Capital* (finance).
3. Measure word for *books*, *magazines*…etc.

PRONUNCIATION

běn

SOUND WORD

Benefit

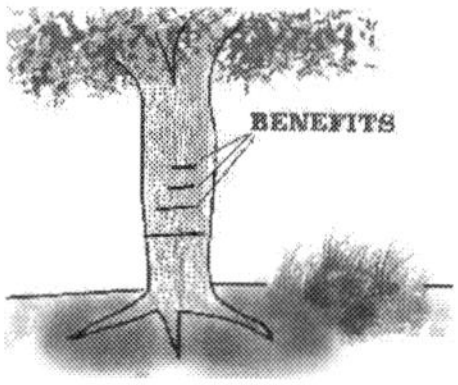

COMPONENTS

木 TREE[125] + 一 ONE[15]

MNEMONICS

The horizontal line at the bottom of the TREE historically represented its *roots*.

STORY

Before the invention of paper, a *book*keeper had to record the present *capital* by etching ONE notch on the *stem* (trunk) of a TREE, allowing him to see the current level compared to the *basis* and calculate the **benefits**. Nowadays, the *book*keeper can write it down in all sorts of *books*.

EXAMPLES

1. 根本(gēn běn) Essence, foundation. 本国(běn guó) This country, our own country. 日本(rì běn) Japan (where the sun rises or originates in the morning).
2. 资本(zī běn) Capital.
3. 本子(běn zi) Notebook. 一本书(yī běn shū) A book.

WANT A LITTLE MORE?

Usage frequency: Top 100.

323 # 刖 4th

DEFINITION

To *cut off the feet* as a form of punishment.

PRONUNCIATION

yuè

SOUND WORD

Feuillu-e /fœjy/
French word for 'leafy, deciduous.' (See 'Special Sound Mnemonics,' page 493)

COMPONENTS

月 MEAT[48] + 刂 KNIFE[109]

MNEMONICS

Butcher.
Someone who cuts MEAT with a KNIFE, like game MEAT, that is, from animals living in the wild amongst all the **feuillus-e**, the deciduous trees.

EXAMPLES

断手刖足 (duàn shǒu yuè zú) To cut off somebody's hands and feet.

WANT A LITTLE MORE?

Usage frequency: Bottom third.

324 前 2nd

DEFINITION

In front; former, previous.

PRONUNCIATION

qián

SOUND WORD

^{t}Cheyenne
You may think of the sentence, 'Nothing bu**t Cheyenne**.' (See 'Special Sound Mnemonics,' page 488)

COMPONENTS

丷 HORNS[55] EIGHT + 一 ONE[15] + 刖 BUTCHER[323] to cut off feet

STORY

In the Old West, a sheriff wants to meet with a group of Cheyenne to reach a truce. Standing before him are nothing bu**t Cheyenne** and *in front* of the group stands a man wearing ONE set of HORNS on his head. "He is probably their leader," thinks the sheriff. When the sheriff gets ready to talk, one of the men accompanying him says, "Be careful with him! He is known as the BUTCHER!"

EXAMPLES

前面 (qián miàn) Front. 前天 (qián tiān) The day before yesterday.
以前 (yǐ qián) Before, previously.

WANT A LITTLE MORE?

- This character could also be decomposed as 䒑 GRASS[131] + 刖 BUTCHER.
- Usage frequency: Top 100.

325	开[開]	1st

Definition

1. To *open*.
2. To *start*.
3. To *hold a meeting*.
4. To *drive a vehicle*.

Pronunciation

kāi

Sound word

Caille /kaj/
French word for 'quail.'

Simplified components

一 CEILING[15] ONE + 廾 TWO HANDS[74]

Traditional components

[門 GATE[119] + CEILING + TWO HANDS]

Mnemonics

The character historically depicted TWO HANDS removing the bolt on a GATE.

Ancient form: 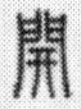.

Story

We were hearing noise in the attic. So, my husband climbed a ladder and, using his TWO HANDS, *started* to remove the bolt that held the CEILING trap in place. As soon as he *opened* it, a **caille** flew out in his face.

[The bird escaped through the GATE of the house and we saw it being hit by a neighbor *driving* his car fast, on his way to a *meeting* he was supposed to *hold*…]

Examples

1. 开门 (kāi mén) To open the door. 开明 (kāi míng) Open-minded.
2. 开始 (kāi shǐ) To begin, start.
3. 开会 (kāi huì) To hold or attend a meeting.
4. 开车 (kāi chē) To drive.

Want a little more?

Usage frequency: Top 100.

326 **但** 4th

DEFINITION

1. *But, yet, however.*
2. *Only, merely.*

PRONUNCIATION

dàn

SOUND WORD

Ramadan
The ninth month of the Muslim year, during which strict fasting is observed from sunrise to sunset.

COMPONENTS

亻 HANDYMAN[23] MAN + 旦 DAYBREAK[193]

STORY

The HANDYMAN wants to know everything. So, he decides to try the Islam religion, *merely* to know it better. *However*, he is not too serious with respect to the five pillars, including the **Ramadan**. The local imam pays him a visit.

"I heard you did not fast a single day during the **Ramadan** this year. You know this is a grave sin!"
"*But, but, but*," says the HANDYMAN, "during the whole **Ramadan** month, I went on a cruise around Antarctica. It was dark all day. I never saw a single DAYBREAK. So, technically…"

EXAMPLES

1. 但是(dàn shì) But, however.
2. 不但(bù dàn) Not only.

WANT A LITTLE MORE?

Usage frequency: Top 100.

327 **因** 1st

DEFINITION

Cause, *reason*; *because*.

PRONUNCIATION

yīn

SOUND WORD

Inn

A place where you can eat and sleep.

COMPONENTS

口 to ENCLOSE[42] + 大 BIG[27]

STORY

"Who has ENCLOSED a BIG fierce-looking guard inside my **inn**, preventing me from entering? What is the *reason* for that?" asks the owner.
The employees, picketing outside, yelled, "We are the *cause* of it. Pay us more and the guard is gone."

EXAMPLES

因为 (yīn wèi) Because. 原因 (yuán yīn) Reason.

WANT A LITTLE MORE?

Usage frequency: Top 100.

328A 只 3rd

DEFINITION

Only.

PRONUNCIATION

zhǐ

SOUND WORD

Jerrycan

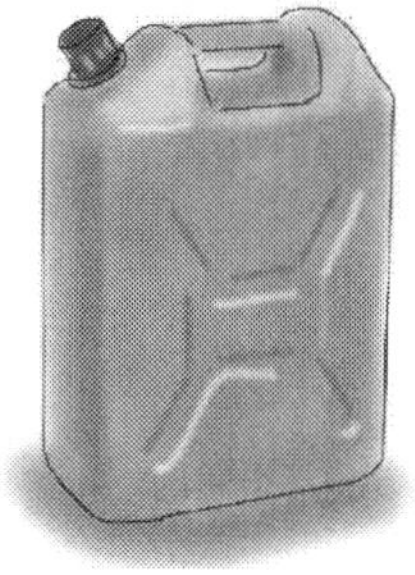

COMPONENTS

口 MOUTH[41] + 八 OCTOPUS[55] EIGHT

STORY

The aquarium director tells his employees, "When feeding the OCTOPUS, you can *only* pour into its MOUTH the equivalent of one **jerrycan** of fish sauce at a time."

EXAMPLES

只好(zhǐ hǎo) May as well, to have to, have no choice but. 只有四天 (zhǐ yǒu sì tiān) Only have 4 days.

WANT A LITTLE MORE?

Usage frequency: Top 100.

328B 只[隻] 1st

Definition

Measure word for *birds* and some *animals*, *boats*, *containers*; one *body part* or *thing that comes in pairs* (nostrils, feet, shoes… etc.).

Pronunciation

zhī

Sound word

Jerk

Just imagine an ignorant, cocky person who is inconsiderate and does stupid things.

Simplified components

口 ORIFICE[41] + 八 ABUNDANCE[55]

Traditional components

[隹 OSTRICH[310] + 又 RIGHT HAND[71]]

Mnemonics

The traditional character shows a RIGHT HAND holding a bird. Ancient form: .

Story

"This **jerk** is such a pervert! He has an ABUNDANCE of animals on his farm, and when comes time to *'measure'* their number, he does not go by a head count, but prefers to tally the number and type of ORIFICES."
"What do you mean?"

["Take for instance the OSTRICHES. For each *pair* of *birds* he owns, he likes to feel them both with his RIGHT HAND, if you know what I mean."
"Wow, what a **jerk**!"]

Examples

一只狗 (yī zhī gǒu) A dog. 一只箱子 (yī zhī xiāng zi) A case, chest. 一只鼻孔 (yī zhī bí kǒng) One nostril.

Want a little more?

Usage frequency: Top third.

329A

相

1st

DEFINITION

Each other, one another, mutually.

PRONUNCIATION

xiāng

SOUND WORD

Scie à angle /si a ɑ̃gl/
French expression for 'miter saw.' Literally 'saw with angles.' Needs to be pronounced rapidly as one syllable. The final 'le' sound is not heard when said quickly.

COMPONENTS

木 WOOD[125] + 目 EYE[200]

STORY

These two carpenters help *each other* out. One of them measures the plank of WOOD with his EYES and draws a line on it with a pencil while the other makes the cut with the **scie à angle**.

EXAMPLES

互相 (hù xiāng) Mutually. 相反 (xiāng fǎn) To be opposite.

WANT A LITTLE MORE?

Usage frequency: Top 500.

329B 相 4th

DEFINITION

1. *Looks, appearance; photograph.*
2. To *examine, appraise.*
3. *Prime minister.*

PRONUNCIATION

xiàng

SOUND WORD

Négociant /negɔsjɑ̃/
French word for 'merchant,' 'wholesaler.'

COMPONENTS

木 TREE[125] + 目 EYE[200]

STORY

"Last night, I saw with my own EYES our strange **négociant** hiding from me behind a TREE. I'm quite sure it was him, because the man had the same *look* and *appearance*. I even took a *photograph*. Here. Could you *examine* it and tell me if it's him?"
"No, this is our *prime minister*!"

EXAMPLES

1. 相貌 (xiàng mào) Appearance.
2. 相士(xiàng shì) Fortune-teller, who appraises a person's ability.
3. 首相(shǒu xiàng) Prime minister.

WANT A LITTLE MORE?

Usage frequency: Middle third.

330

想

3rd

DEFINITION

1. To *think*, *think about*, *believe*, *suppose*, *want to*, *plan to*.
2. To *miss*, *long for*.

PRONUNCIATION

xiǎng

SOUND WORD

Scientifique /sjɑ̃tifik/
French for 'scientist.'

COMPONENTS

相 EACH OTHER[329A] + 心 HEART[321]

STORY

A **scientifique** is doing research on cardiac synchronization, where a person tries to sync his or her HEART with a loved one for emotional healing. He says to his pretty, busty assistant, "I *suppose* we will have to try it ourselves. We'll put our hand on EACH OTHER's HEARTS. What do you *think*?"

EXAMPLES

1. 思想(sī xiǎng) Thought, thinking. 想象(xiǎng xiàng) To imagine. 想要(xiǎng yào) Would like to have.
2. 我想你(wǒ xiǎng nǐ) I miss you.

WANT A LITTLE MORE?

Usage frequency: Top 100.

331 页[頁] 4th

DEFINITION

Page.

† Head (human).

PRONUNCIATION

yè

SOUND WORD

Embouteillait /ɑ̃buteјɛ/
From the French verb 'embouteiller' (to bottle or put in a bottle), conjugated in the imperfect tense, translating to 'he/she was bottling…'

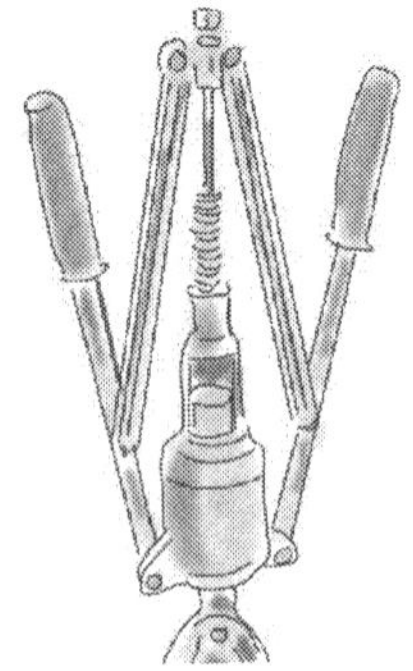

COMPONENTS

一 ONE15 + 丶 DROP3 + 贝 [貝] CLAM287

MNEMONICS

- Originally meant the *head* of a person and gradually came to represent the *page* of a book. Ancient form: .
- To make the connection easy to recall, just picture the *head* of the personality of the year on the first *page* of Time magazine. The original meaning of *head* is still used in this book, since it is easier to make memorable images with it.

STORY

The bottler of this important Italian distiller insisted to add ONE DROP of CLAM juice to each bottle whenever he was bottling (**emboutaillait**). He claimed it improved the taste. When he told his boss Vito what he was doing, Vito looked straight at him and said, "Well, I think we are not on the same *page*." His *head* was found in his horse's stall the following day…

EXAMPLES

首页 (shǒu yè) First page. 主页 (zhǔ yè) Homepage.

WANT A LITTLE MORE?

- This is the 181st of the 214 Kangxi radicals.
- Usage frequency: Top third.

332 **豆** 4th

DEFINITION

Beans; peas.

† A serving dish equipped with legs.

PRONUNCIATION

dòu

SOUND WORD

Speedo
The famous tight swimwear.

COMPONENTS

一 ONE15 + 口 MOUTH41 + 䒑 GRASS131

MNEMONICS

- This is the picture of a vessel or dish for food. Ancient form: 豆.
- If it helps, you can view it as a small can of *beans* (the MOUTH building block) being warmed up over a Bunsen burner (the GRASS building block) and releasing steam at the top (the ONE building block).

STORY

ONE swimmer was disqualified because he smoked GRASS and put a lot of *beans* in his MOUTH before the race. His **Speedo** was all puffed up when he showed up at the start, conferring him an unfair advantage, according to the judges…

EXAMPLES

豆腐 (dòu fǔ) Tofu. 土豆 (tǔ dòu) Potato.

WANT A LITTLE MORE?

- This is the 151st of the 214 Kangxi radicals.
- Usage frequency: Top third.

333 头[頭] 2nd

Definition

1. *Head, hair, beginning, first.*
2. *Nominal localizer.*
3. *Substantive suffix.*
4. Measure word for *oxen, livestock*, etc.

Pronunciation

tóu

Sound word

Toro /toro/
Spanish word for the aggressive fighting bull often used in bullfighting.

Simplified components

'Hairs' + ~大 GREAT DANE[27] BIG

Traditional components

[豆 BEANS[332] + 頁 HEAD[331]]

Mnemonics

Hairy head.
This is another character for *head*. To help us differentiate with the other ones, this one will represent a *hairy head* (the two DROPS on the left represents '*hairs*' in the simplified character), animal or human.

Story

At the sight of the **toro**, the 'hairs' on the back of the GREAT DANE's *head* stood on end, displaying a very *hairy head.*

[At that moment, a toreador arrived just in time and placed himself between the **toro** and the dog. However, when he saw the **toro** charging, the toreador lowered his *HEAD* and spilled his BEANS.]

Examples

1. 头发 (tóu fà) Hair on the human head. 起头 (qǐ tóu) At first.
2. 里头 (lǐ tóu) Inside, interior.
3. 骨头 (gǔ tóu) Bone.
4. 三头牛 (sān tóu niú) Three cows.

Want a little more?

Usage frequency: Top 500.

334

母

3rd

DEFINITION

Mother, female; breasts.

PRONUNCIATION

mǔ

SOUND WORD

Muchacha /mutʃatʃa/
Spanish word for a beautiful young woman.

MNEMONICS

- This is a pictogram of a kneeling person with *breasts*. Ancient form: .
- It may be written 毋 when used as a building block.

STORY

Two Spanish young men are walking in the street when one of them says, "Qué **muchacha**! Look at the *mother*. No! Not her *breasts*, her face!"

EXAMPLES

母亲(mǔ qīn) Mother. 母音(mǔ yīn) Vowel (the mother of all sounds).
母乳(mǔrǔ) Breast milk.

WANT A LITTLE MORE?

Usage frequency: Top third.

335 贯[貫] 4th

DEFINITION

1. To *pass through*; to *pierce*.
2. To *string together*.

PRONUNCIATION

guàn

SOUND WORD

Iguana

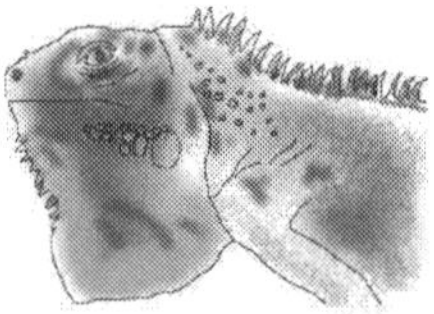

COMPONENTS

毌 BREAST[334] + 贝[貝] MONEY[287]

STORY

"MONEY is being offered for the capture of the **iguana** that *passed through* here yesterday. It bit and *pierced* the BREAST of a woman who was lying on the beach."

EXAMPLES

1. 贯穿 (guàn chuān) To run through, penetrate.
2. 联贯 (lián guàn) To link up, string together.

WANT A LITTLE MORE?

Usage frequency: Top third.

336 实 [實] 2nd

DEFINITION

Real, *true*, *really*; *solid*.

PRONUNCIATION

shí

SOUND WORD

Sherpa
An ethnic group living in the Himalayas. They are often used as guides and porters during climbing expeditions.

SIMPLIFIED COMPONENTS

宀 HOUSE[50] + 头 HAIRY HEAD[333] head

TRADITIONAL COMPONENTS

[HOUSE + 貫 to PASS THROUGH[335]]

STORY

A **Sherpa** has mounted *real* HAIRY HEADS on spikes in front of his HOUSE. They belonged to climbers who did not survive the expeditions he organized. They are used to remind would-be adventurers of the risks involved.

[You need to PASS THROUGH a row of them before entering his HOUSE. This is *really* scary!]

EXAMPLES

其实 (qí shí) As a matter of fact, actually. 实话 (shí huà) Truth. 事实 (shì shí) Fact.

WANT A LITTLE MORE?

Usage frequency: Top 100.

337

车[車]

1st

DEFINITION

Car, cart, chariot, vehicle.

PRONUNCIATION

chē

SOUND WORD

Chev'
Abbreviation for Chevrolet.

CHEV'

MNEMONICS

- The traditional character depicts a *cart* axle seen from above, with the wheels on both sides and the wooden body in the middle.

  Ancient form: 車.
- As for the simplified version, it may help you to view it as ~云 CLOUDS[180A] of smoke being released at a 十 CROSS[59] road by all the *cars* idling.

STORY

The **Chev'** brand was founded in Detroit, in November 1911, by racer Louis Chevrolet, who developed *cars* and other *vehicles* that offer performance, durability and value.

EXAMPLES

汽车 (qì chē) Motor vehicle. 开车 (kāi chē) To drive a vehicle.

WANT A LITTLE MORE?

- This is the 159th of the 214 Kangxi radicals.
- Usage frequency: Top 500.

338 军[軍] 1st

DEFINITION

Army, military.

PRONUNCIATION

jūn

SOUND WORD

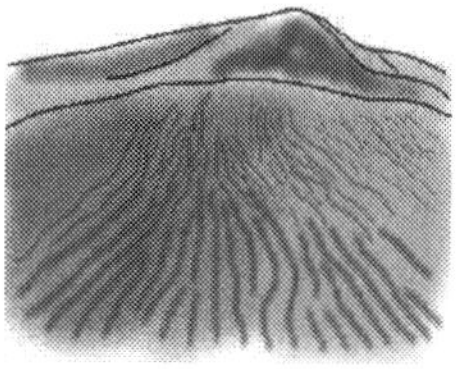

Dune /dyn/
Sand dune, but pronounced with the French 'u.' (See 'Special Sound Mnemonics,' page 487)

COMPONENTS

冖 CLOTH ROOF[11] TOP COVER + 车[車] CAR[337]

STORY

When the French *army* is in the desert, soldiers need to install a CLOTH ROOF on their *military* CARS (**dune** buggies, in fact) to protect themselves from the strong sun rays.

EXAMPLES

军队(jūn duì) Armed forces. 敌军(dí jūn) Enemy troops.

WANT A LITTLE MORE?

Usage frequency: Top 500.

339 **意** 4th

DEFINITION

1. *Idea, meaning, thought.*
2. To *wish, desire; intention.*

PRONUNCIATION

yì

SOUND WORD

Abbaye /abei/
French word for an abbey, a Catholic monastery administered by an abbot.

COMPONENTS

音 SOUND[314] + 心 HEART[321]

STORY

"A monk in an **abbaye** once told me that if you *wish* to find an *idea*, you just need to listen to the SOUND of your HEART."

EXAMPLES

1. 意见 (yì jiàn) Idea, opinion. 意思 (yì sī) Idea, thought, meaning. 意义 (yì yì) Meaning, sense.
2. 用意 (yòng yì) Intention, purpose.

WANT A LITTLE MORE?

Usage frequency: Top 500.

无[無]

2nd

DEFINITION

Nothing, none; not have, lack; un-, -less.

PRONUNCIATION

wú

SOUND WORD

Woo-hoo!
Bursting with excitement!

TRADITIONAL COMPONENTS

[𠂉 RIFLE[8] + 2 x 廿 PICKET FENCE[61] + 灬 FIRE[127]]

MNEMONICS

The simplified character looks like a happy person walking, free as a bird, having *nothing* to do.

STORY

At last, I do *not have* work to do! **Woo-hoo**! I frolic in the street, listening to the Whitney Houston song 'I have *nothing*' and singing along.

[Then an *un*-happy guy, obviously jealous of my joie de vivre and *lacking* judgment, starts firing his RIFLE at me from over his PICKET FENCE! As a riposte, I set his PICKET FENCE on FIRE! *Nothing* is left after I am done with it! **Woo-hoo**!]

EXAMPLES

无论 (wú lùn) No matter what. 无数 (wú shù) Innumerable.

WANT A LITTLE MORE?

- This is the 71st of the 214 Kangxi radicals.
- Usage frequency: Top 500.

341 㒳

Definition

Non-character used only as a building block.

Pronunciation

Not applicable

Sound word

Not applicable

Components

⺕ CLAWS[138A] + 一 ONE[15] + 八 to SEPARATE[55]

Mnemonics

Jaws of life.
The emergency rescue equipment used to open a damaged passenger vehicle, i.e. ONE set of CLAWS to SEPARATE parts of a vehicle.

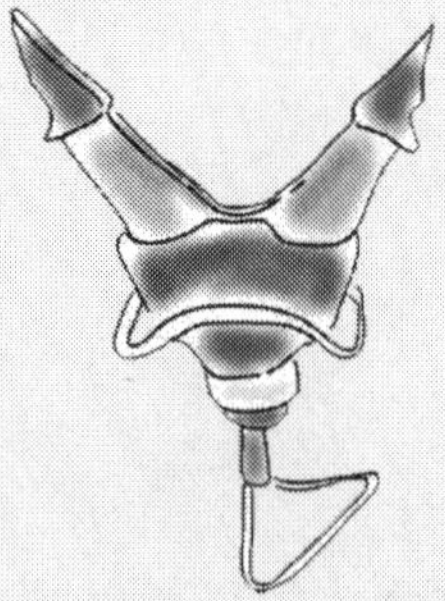

342 **与[與]** 3rd

Definition

1. To *offer, give.*
2. *And, together with.*

Pronunciation

yǔ

Sound word

Humanité /ymanite/
French word for 'Humanity.' Let's imagine a beauty contest, such as Miss Universe, but restricted to participants from earth, called 'Miss **Humanité**.'

Traditional components

[舁 JAWS OF LIFE[341] + *headless horse*]

Mnemonics

- *Headless horse.*
  - The simplified character looks indeed like a 马 HORSE[36] without a head.
  - The traditional character looks like a horse whose body is trapped in the JAWS OF LIFE, and its head gets severed. See story.
- Lastly, the rare character 舄, which used to represent a magpie (now obsolete), will also take the value of a *headless horse* when it appears as a traditional building block in the stories because of its resemblance to the 馬 HORSE character (you can easily picture a crushed head on top).

STORY

After the winner of the Miss **Humanité** contest had walked down the aisle with her crown, the host says to her, "This year, *together with* what you've already been *given*, we have something else to *offer* you. Something strong, faithful, something that will help you travel in style between the various activities you must attend… A brand-new horse!"
"Oh! Thank you so much! But, but… the horse has no head!"
"That's true. This is a *headless horse*.

["The poor beast. It used to belong to a road emergency squad and once, while on the scene of a car accident, it got too close, its head got stuck in the JAWS OF LIFE and it got severed from its body. But it is still a good horse. Anyhoo, you should never look a gift horse in the mouth, and it's guaranteed you won't."]

EXAMPLES

1. 赐与 (cì yǔ) To grant, bestow. 赠与 (zèng yǔ) To give as a present.
2. 与此同时 (yǔ cǐ tóng shí) At the same time, moreover.

WANT A LITTLE MORE?

Usage frequency: Top 500.

343A 把 3rd

Definition

1. To *hold, grasp, handle.*
2. A measure word for *things with handles.*
3. To *guard.*
4. *Used to position the object of a verb before it.*

Pronunciation

bǎ

Sound word

Balaclava
A knitted garment that covers the head and neck, with holes for the eyes and mouth.

Components

扌 HAND[73] + 巴 COBRA[301] suffix

Story

A biologist explains how to *handle* a COBRA, "Before you attempt to *grasp* a COBRA with your HAND, I recommend you wear a **balaclava** to *guard* yourself from potential attacks. This way, the COBRA will think you are one of its own species and will be less aggressive."

Examples

1. 把握(bǎ wò) To grasp firmly.
2. 把子(bǎ zi) Bundle. 火把(huǒ bǎ) Torch.
3. 把守(bǎ shǒu) To guard.
4. 把门打开(bǎ mén dǎ kāi) To open the door.

Want a little more?

Usage frequency: Top 500.

343B | **把** | **4th**

DEFINITION

Grip, handle.

PRONUNCIATION

bà

SOUND WORD

Ali Baba
Of the folk tale '**Ali Baba** and the Forty Thieves.'

COMPONENTS

扌 HAND[73] + 巴 COBRA[301] suffix

STORY

The door leading to the cave of **Ali Baba** has a *handle* in the shape of a COBRA. If you put your HAND on it without pronouncing the magic words 'Open sesame', the *handle* transforms itself into a real COBRA!

EXAMPLES

把子(bà zǐ) Handle. 门把(mén bà) Door knob, handle.

WANT A LITTLE MORE?

Usage frequency: Middle third.

344 # 机[機] 1st

DEFINITION

1. *Machine.*
2. *Opportunity.*

PRONUNCIATION

jī

SOUND WORD

Jeep

SIMPLIFIED COMPONENTS

木 TREE[125] + 几 TABOURET[229A]

TRADITIONAL COMPONENTS

[TREE + 幾 HOW MANY[229B]]

STORY

The *machine* of the year award was given last night to a portable contraption that sits on a **Jeep**; you feed TREES at one end and finished TABOURETS come out at the other end. The *machine* is driven by a belt attached to the engine of the **Jeep**.

[It is hard to tell now HOW MANY TREES the *machine* can process in a day. But it seems a good *opportunity* for the inventors to increase their market share.]

EXAMPLES

1. 机车 (jī chē) Engine. 手机(shǒu jī) Cell phone.
2. 机会 (jī huì) Opportunity.

WANT A LITTLE MORE?

Usage frequency: Top 500.

345 **氏** 4th

DEFINITION

Family name, *surname*; *clan*, *family*.

PRONUNCIATION

shì

SOUND WORD

Amish

MNEMONICS

Plow.

This character looks like a *plow*, with two moldboards or hooks.

STORY

I was driving through Lancaster County in **Amish** country with a friend when he said, "I knew that the **Amish** had *family names* like Yoder, Stoltzfus and Hershberger, but I didn't know they also had that *surname*."

"What *surname*?"

"I saw written in big letters on a *plow* drawn by horses the name of its owner, 'John Deere.'"

EXAMPLES

姓氏(xìng shì) Surname. 氏族(shì zú) Clan.

WANT A LITTLE MORE?

- This is the 83rd of the 214 Kangxi radicals.
- Usage frequency: Top third.

346 民 2nd

DEFINITION

People, subjects, citizen.

PRONUNCIATION

mín

SOUND WORD

Minion
Someone who is not important and who obeys the orders of a powerful leader.

COMPONENTS

口 MOUTH[41] + 氏 PLOW[345] FAMILY NAME

STORY

Once upon a time, a good king invented the PLOW. He then said, "With this new tool, I will now be able to feed the MOUTHS of all my **minions**, of all my *people*."

EXAMPLES

人民 (rén mín) The people. 农民 (nóng mín) Peasant. 国民 (guó mín) Citizen.

WANT A LITTLE MORE?

Usage frequency: Top 500.

347 兀 4th

DEFINITION

1. *Towering.*
2. *Bald.*
3. *Suddenly.*

PRONUNCIATION

wù

SOUND WORD

Steel wool

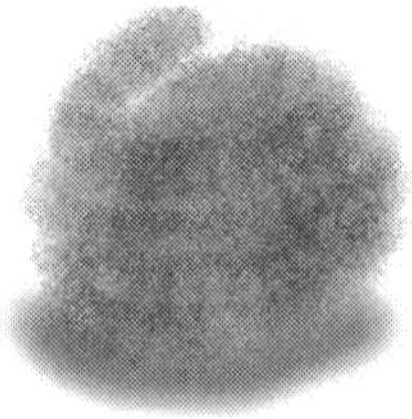

MNEMONICS

- *Pedestal.*
  Let's take this as the picture of a *pedestal* because of its shape.
- It is sometimes written 丌 when used as a building block.

STORY

Suddenly, the guy in charge of cleaning decides to scour the *towering pedestal* with a **steel wool** to make it as shiny as his *bald* head.

EXAMPLES

1. 兀立(wù lì) To stand upright rigidly.
2. 兀鹫(wù jiù) Bald vulture (griffon).
3. 突兀(tú wù) Suddenly.

WANT A LITTLE MORE?

- Learn to distinguish from 几 SMALL TABLE[229A].
- Usage frequency: Middle third.

348 元 2nd

DEFINITION

1. *Beginning; first.*
2. *Yuan* (Chinese monetary unit), *dollar.*
3. *Yuan dynasty* (1260-1368).

PRONUNCIATION

yuán

SOUND WORD

Eu anneau /y ano/
'He's got the ring.' Gollum will be the hook for this sound word. (See 'Special Sound Mnemonics,' page 493)

COMPONENTS

一 ONE[15] + 兀 PEDESTAL[347] towering

STORY

From the *beginning*, Gollum (**eu anneau**) always held his ONE 'precious' ring in high esteem, literally putting it on a PEDESTAL (the magic ring can be seen in the character, hovering over a PEDESTAL). No *dollar* or *yuan* amount could have convinced him to sell it.

EXAMPLES

1. 元始(yuán shǐ) Original.
2. 五十元(wǔ shí yuán) Fifty yuan. 美元(měi yuán) U.S. dollar.
3. 元朝(yuán cháo) Yuan (Mongol) dynasty.

WANT A LITTLE MORE?

Usage frequency: Top 500.

349 **弗** 2nd

DEFINITION

Not (literary).

PRONUNCIATION

fú

SOUND WORD

Foulard /fulaʁ/
French word for 'scarf.'

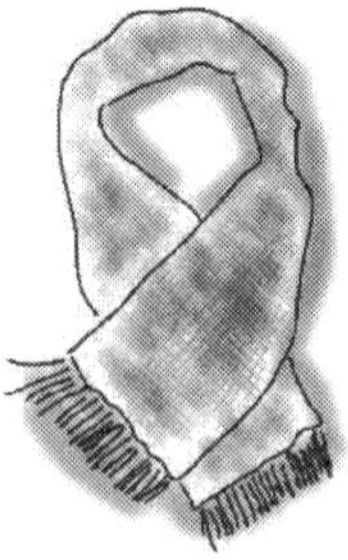

MNEMONICS

- *Dollar sign*; *one dollar*.
  Visually, this character looks like a *dollar sign* rotated around its vertical axis. As a building block, it also has the meaning of *one dollar*.
- It may sometimes appear with only one vertical stroke instead of two, the first vertical stroke being replaced by a 丿 SLIDE[4] at the bottom left: 弟.

STORY

I tell my good friend one day, "Thomas! Looks like an expensive ($$$) **foulard** you have around your neck!"
"Oh! I see you know your **foulards**… *Not*! Just *one dollar* at the dollar store!"

EXAMPLES

弗成(fú chéng) Not good. 弗克(fú kè) Unable to.

WANT A LITTLE MORE?

Usage frequency: Top third.

第

350 竹 2nd

DEFINITION

<u>*Bamboo*</u>.

PRONUNCIATION

zhú

SOUND WORD

<u>Jew</u>ish
Relating to the Jews, their culture or their religion.

MNEMONICS

- This is a pictogram of two *bamboo* trees side by side. Ancient form: .
- When used as a building block, it takes the following condensed form: ⺮. It looks like two children running one after another while holding a stick or a 𠂉 RIFLE[8] toy made of *bamboo*.
- *Armed man*.
Sometimes, only one element will appear in a character, like this: 𥫗. In that case, it means an *armed man* in the stories.

STORY

Two **Jewish** children are playing a war game, running after each other amongst *bamboo* trees, holding a toy gun made of *bamboo*.

EXAMPLES

竹竿 (zhú gān) Bamboo pole. 竹笋 (zhú sǔn) Bamboo shoots.

WANT A LITTLE MORE?

- This is the 118th of the 214 Kangxi radicals.
- Usage frequency: Top third.

351 **第** 4th

DEFINITION

Number (*no.*); a prefix placed before a number for ordering things.

PRONUNCIATION

dì

SOUND WORD

Caddie
A person who carries clubs for a golfer on the golf course.

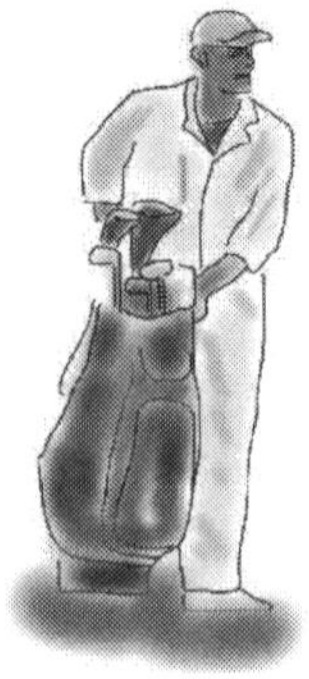

COMPONENTS

⺮ BAMBOO[350] + 弔 ONE DOLLAR[349] not

STORY

The other day, on hole *no.* 5, a par three, my **caddie** recommended I use neither an iron nor a wood, but a BAMBOO *no.* 8. “For good luck!” he said. Well, I shot a hole in one. I was so happy I gave him ONE DOLLAR.

EXAMPLES

第三人(dì sān rén) Third person. 第六感(dì liù gǎn) Sixth sense.

WANT A LITTLE MORE?

Usage frequency: Top 500.

352

公

1st

DEFINITION

Public, common.

PRONUNCIATION

gōng

SOUND WORD

Gong

COMPONENTS

八 EIGHT[55] + 厶 PRIVATE[10]

MNEMONICS

You can also remember it as the picture of a PRIVATE man, with his nose and drooping eyebrows, looking worried because he has to make a *public* declaration.

STORY

Every trading day at the New York Stock Exchange, an executive from a corporation stands behind the podium and pushes the button that makes a **gong** resonate, signaling the start of the trading session, when you can trade *common* stocks of *public* companies. Today's invited executive is a Chinese, who rang the **gong** EIGHT times. He then says in PRIVATE to the floor manager, "This is for good luck!"

EXAMPLES

公司 (gōng sī) Company, corporation. 公开 (gōng kāi) To make public. 公用电话 (gōng yòng diàn huà) Public telephone.

WANT A LITTLE MORE?

Usage frequency: Top 500.

353 **史** 3rd

DEFINITION

1. *History*.
2. *Surname*.

PRONUNCIATION

shǐ

SOUND WORD

Shish kebab
Pieces of meat and vegetables pushed on a skewer and cooked on a grill.

COMPONENTS

口 MOUTH[41] + 㕜 to HOLD A PEN IN HAND[72]

STORY

The *history* of the **shish kebab** goes like this: A long time ago, a historian was HOLDING A PEN IN HIS HAND, writing a *history* book when he saw a meaty, juicy bug walk across his desk. He skewered the insect with his pen and simply brought it up to his MOUTH.

EXAMPLES

1. 历史(lì shǐ) History records. 古代史(gǔ dài shǐ) Ancient history.

WANT A LITTLE MORE?

- It ranks amongst the top 100 Chinese surnames.
- Usage frequency: Top 500.

354 **吏** 4th

DEFINITION

Clerk, minor official, officer.

PRONUNCIATION

lì

SOUND WORD

Bruce Lee
The famous actor and martial artist.

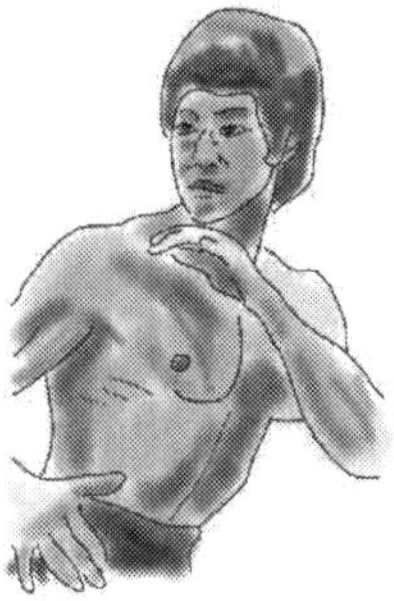

COMPONENTS

一 ONE[15] + 史 HISTORY[353]

STORY

Bruce Lee is sometimes called upon to clean out corrupted *officers* in the government. When asked to take care of a corrupted *minor official*, **Bruce Lee** always says, "Don't worry, it will be done. This ONE *clerk* is HISTORY!"

EXAMPLES

吏目 (lì mù) Government clerk. 吏员 (lì yuán) Minor official. 官吏(guān lì) Government officials. 澄清吏治(chéng qīng lì zhì) To clean out political corruption.

WANT A LITTLE MORE?

Usage frequency: Middle third.

355 **使** 3rd

DEFINITION

1. To *make*, *cause*, *enable*.
2. To *use*, *employ*.
3. *Messenger*, *envoy*.

PRONUNCIATION

shǐ

SOUND WORD

Shish kebab
Pieces of meat and vegetables pushed on a skewer and cooked on a grill.

COMPONENTS

亻 PERSON[23] + 吏 CLERK[354]

STORY

A forensic psychiatrist specialized in silencing lambs has just been accused of cannibalism. A CLERK sent as a *messenger* reports seeing in the house of the suspect a long metal shaft that the accused was planning to *use* for impaling three PERSONS one behind the other, in order to *make* a big human **shish kebab**.

EXAMPLES

1. 致使(zhì shǐ) To cause, result in. 这件事情使我很难过(zhè jiàn shì qíng shǐ wǒ hěn nán guò) This affair really makes me sad.
2. 使用(shǐ yòng) To use, employ. 这东西你会使吗?(zhè dōng xī nǐ huì shǐ ma) Can you use this thing?
3. 信使(xìn shǐ) Courier, messenger.

WANT A LITTLE MORE?

Usage frequency: Top 500.

356 **青** 1st

DEFINITION

1. *Blue-green*, *green*, *blue*.
2. *Young people*.

PRONUNCIATION

qīng

SOUND WORD

Chink
A small crack, a narrow opening or space. A small amount of light shining through a crack.

COMPONENTS

⺧ PLANT293 + 月 FLESH48

STORY

I am one of the *young people* who was selected to go into space. I am now on a mission and I am fighting a man in a spacesuit. At one point, I make a **chink** in his armor and I can see through the crack that his FLESH is *blue-green*. All of a sudden, a leaf comes out! I then realize I am fighting against an alien having the form of a PLANT!

EXAMPLES

1. 青菜(qīng cài) Green vegetables. 青石(qīng shí) Bluestone.
2. 青年(qīng nián) Youth, young people.

WANT A LITTLE MORE?

- This is the 174th of the 214 Kangxi radicals.
- Usage frequency: Top 500.

357 # 情 2nd

DEFINITION

1. *Feeling, emotion, passion.*
2. *Situation, circumstances.*

PRONUNCIATION

qíng

SOUND WORD

Cinque /tʃiŋkwe/
Italian for number 'five.' To make it more concrete, let's take this for a blue-green five-euro bill.

COMPONENTS

忄 HEART[321] + 青 BLUE-GREEN[356]

STORY

Two tramps are chatting in Rome. One of them says, "I am overcome with *emotions* right now. Can you imagine? We are in a much better *situation* now since I found this!" He then starts to dance and sing, 'What a *feeling*.'
The other tramp says, "Relax, Aldo. You'll have a HEART attack. This is just a BLUE-GREEN **cinque** euro note after all!"

EXAMPLES

1. 感情(gǎn qíng) Emotion, feeling. 热情(rè qíng) Enthusiastic, passionate.
2. 情况(qíng kuàng) Circumstances, situation.

WANT A LITTLE MORE?

Usage frequency: Top 500.

358

明

2nd

DEFINITION

1. *Bright*; *clear*, *obvious*.
2. To *understand*.
3. *Ming dynasty*.

PRONUNCIATION

míng

SOUND WORD

Mingle
To talk, chat with different people during a party or social event.

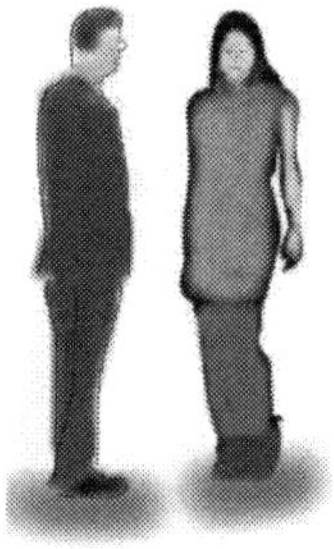

COMPONENTS

日 SUN & DAY[43] + 月 MOON[47]

STORY

Since the DAY the SUN got the *bright* idea to **mingle** with the MOON and ask the MOON to reside with him, it is not hard to *understand* that the night is way too dark and the DAY is way too *bright*!

EXAMPLES

1. 明天 (míng tiān) Tomorrow (literally 'bright day').
2. 明白 (míng bái) To understand.
3. 明朝 (míng cháo) Ming dynasty.

WANT A LITTLE MORE?

Usage frequency: Top 500.

359 **性** 4th

DEFINITION

1. *Sex, gender.*
2. *Nature, character.*
3. *Suffix* corresponding to *–ness*, *–ism* or *–ity*.
4. *Surname.*

PRONUNCIATION

xìng

SOUND WORD

Ki<u>ssing</u>

COMPONENTS

忄 MIND[321] + 生 BIRTH[188]

STORY

A sexologist explains to a couple worried about the sexual behavior of their 11-year-old son, "You know, this is human *nature* to think about **kissing** and *sex* once in a while during the day. But a teenage boy has been programmed from BIRTH to have it on his MIND all day! This unruli*ness* will die down somewhat with age, but that will really only stop the moment he'll be **kissing** the dust!"

EXAMPLES

1. 性别 (xìng bié) Sex, gender. 性爱 (xìng ài) Sexual love.
2. 性质 (xìng zhì) Nature, character.
3. 派性 (pài xìng) Factionalism. 爆炸性 (bào zhà xìng) Explosiveness, volatility.

WANT A LITTLE MORE?

Usage frequency: Top 500.

360

知

1st

DEFINITION

To *know*, *be aware*; *knowledge*, *information*.

PRONUNCIATION

zhī

SOUND WORD

Jerk
Just imagine an ignorant, cocky person who is inconsiderate and does stupid things.

COMPONENTS

矢 to SWEAR[88] + 口 MOUTH[41]

STORY

"I have *knowledge* that you SWEAR too much with your big MOUTH," says the boss to his employee.
"I do not say bad words, I SWEAR!"
"I *know* you SWEAR, this is not new *information*. No need to tell me…"
"**Jerk**!" mutters the employee under his breath.

EXAMPLES

知道 (zhī dào) To know, realize, be aware of. 知识 (zhī shí) Knowledge.

WANT A LITTLE MORE?

Usage frequency: Top 500.

361 **全** 2nd

DEFINITION

Whole, entire, all.

PRONUNCIATION

quán

SOUND WORD

Tuant
By aiming upwards. (See 'Special Sound Mnemonics,' page 490)

COMPONENTS

人 TENT[9] + 王 KING[19]

STORY

The KING has decided to go hunting fowl but since he hates sitting outside, he asked for a TENT to be set up for him. This way, he would sit in his TENT, killing (**tuant**) fowl by just shooting upwards through the opening. However, the TENT they brought was way too small and the KING, being fat and plump, took up the *whole* space, not able to move!

EXAMPLES

完全 (wán quán) Complete. 全国 (quán guó) The whole country; nationwide.

WANT A LITTLE MORE?

Usage frequency: Top 500.

362

丱

DEFINITION

† *Ponytails*.

Now a non-character used only as a building block.

PRONUNCIATION

Not applicable

SOUND WORD

Not applicable

MNEMONICS

This character depicts a child's hairstyle bound with two tufts of hair.

363 关[關] 1st

DEFINITION

1. To *turn off*, *shut*, *close*.
2. To *concern*, *involve*.
3. *Pass*, *barrier*.
4. *Key point*.
5. *Surname*.

PRONUNCIATION

guān

SOUND WORD

Guano
The excrement of seabirds. Just pronounce it **guan'**, to make it a one-syllable word. No Chinese character has the sound guán (second tone), so, there is no risk of confusion.

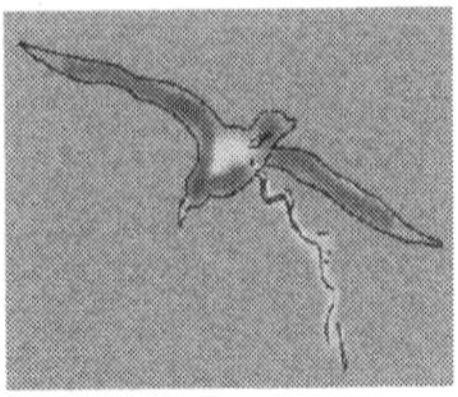

SIMPLIFIED COMPONENTS

丷 HORNS55 EIGHT + 天 HEAVEN31

TRADITIONAL COMPONENTS

[門 GATE119 + 2 x 幺 TINY227 + 丱 PONYTAILS362]

STORY

God says to a guy who just died and tries to be funny when he arrives, "You should not wear HORNS in HEAVEN, especially the plastic ones with flashing lights that you have on your head right now. *Turn* them *off* and take them off now if you want to pass the *barrier*! And *concerning* that smell… Is this **guan'**?"
"Yes. It's because when I was on earth, you, the HEAVEN guy, often dropped that stuff on my head. So, as a joke…"

["I guarantee you," says God, "that if you don't take those things off now, you won't pass the Pearl GATE! And undo the two TINY PONYTAILS on each side of your head. You look like a fool!"]

EXAMPLES

1. 关闭 (guān bì) To close, shut down.
2. 关系 (guān xì) To concern. 关于 (guān yú) About; concerning.
3. 把关 (bǎ guān) To guard a pass.
4. 关键 (guān jiàn) Key, crux.

WANT A LITTLE MORE?

Usage frequency: Top 500.

364 黑 1st

DEFINITION

Black; *dark*.

PRONUNCIATION

hēi

SOUND WORD

Hay

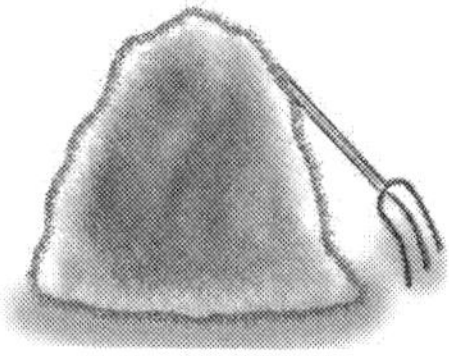

COMPONENTS

~里 RADAR246A HALF-KILOMETER + 灬 FIRE127

STORY

For 20 years in a row, this scientist at the RADAR station had been working night shifts, despite his repeated demands to have his share of day shifts. He's had it with this lifestyle! One *dark* moonless night, when the sky was pitch *black*, he put **hay** all around the base of the RADAR and set it on FIRE. The structure started to melt (this explains why the horizontal line inside the RADAR building block in the character is 'crumbling'), and the RADAR became a pile of *black* soot in no time.

EXAMPLES

黑夜(hēi yè) Night. 黑人(hēi rén) Black persons.

WANT A LITTLE MORE?

- This is the 203rd of the 214 Kangxi radicals.
- Usage frequency: Top third.

365A

占

1st

DEFINITION

To *tell fortunes*.

PRONUNCIATION

zhān

SOUND WORD

Jann
Let's think of a fortune teller named **Jann**.

COMPONENTS

卜 DIVINING ROD[18A] to PREDICT + 口 MOUTH[41]

STORY

Jann, the world-famous seer, raises her DIVINING ROD, opens her MOUTH and starts *telling fortunes* to the person sitting in front of her.

EXAMPLES

占星术 (zhān xīng shù) Astrology. 占卜 (zhān bǔ) To practice divination.

WANT A LITTLE MORE?

Usage frequency: Bottom third.

365B

占[佔]

4th

DEFINITION

To *occupy, take possession.*

PRONUNCIATION

zhàn

SOUND WORD

Azerbaijan [ɑːzərbaɪdʒɑːn] Country located between Armenia and the Caspian Sea. The stories mostly refer to the Nagorno-Karabakh War (1980 – 1994).

SIMPLIFIED COMPONENTS

卜 to PREDICT[18A] + 口 MOUTH[41]

TRADITIONAL COMPONENTS

[亻 HANDYMAN[23] MAN + to PREDICT + MOUTH]

STORY

"Anyone could have PREDICTED and verbalized with their MOUTH that the autonomous enclave of Nagorno-Karabakh in **Azerbaijan** that is presently *occupied* would become a source of conflict."

[Says the know-it-all HANDYMAN…]

EXAMPLES

侵占(qīn zhàn) To invade and occupy. 占领(zhàn lǐng) To occupy, capture.

WANT A LITTLE MORE?

Usage frequency: Top third.

366 点[點] 3rd

Definition

1. *Spots*, *specks*, *dots*; *a little bit*; *point*; *o'clock*.
2. To *call a name on a roll*.
3. To *ignite*.

Pronunciation

diǎn

Sound word

Dientes de león /djentez de leon/
Spanish for 'dandelion.'

Simplified components

占 to TELL FORTUNES[365A] +

灬 FIRE[127]

Traditional components

[黑 BLACK[364] + to TELL FORTUNES]

Story

To TELL FORTUNES, the old witch *ignites* a FIRE at precidely 12:00 *o'clock*, blows on **dientes de león** over the FIRE and interprets the various figures of *specks* and *dots* they produce.

[When she starts seeing BLACK spots, because of all the effort she exerted blowing on the **dientes de león**, she stops just *a little bit* and then repeats the procedure.]

Examples

1. 一点 (yī diǎn) Point; an hour, o'clock; a little, a small amount.
   一点八 (yī diǎn bā) 1.8. 五点半 (wǔ diǎn bàn) 5:30.
2. 点名 (diǎn míng) To call a roll.
3. 点火 (diǎn huǒ) To light a fire.

Want a little more?

Usage frequency: Top 500.

367 外 4th

DEFINITION

Outside, foreign, external.

PRONUNCIATION

wài

SOUND WORD

Hawaii

COMPONENTS

夕 EVENING[251] + 卜 to PREDICT[18A]

STORY

It's a beautiful EVENING here in **Hawaii**, as always. I am sitting *outside*, watching a game of soccer and the guy next to me PREDICTS that the final score will be **Hawaii** Five – 0 against the *foreign* team.

EXAMPLES

外边 (wài biān) Outside. 外国 (wài guó) Foreign country.

WANT A LITTLE MORE?

Usage frequency: Top 500.

368 片 4th

DEFINITION

1. *Slice*; *flat, thin piece*; measure word for *slices, sheets of paper, tablets, expanses of land or water*, etc.
2. *Photo, film.*

† Half of a tree, cut longitudinally.

PRONUNCIATION

piàn

SOUND WORD

Caspian Sea
The world's largest lake by surface, bounded by Kazakhstan, Russia, Azerbaijan and Turkmenistan.

MNEMONICS

Visually, it looks like a beach barman bringing you a bottle on a tray.

STORY

I am sitting on a beach of the **Caspian Sea**, taking *photos* of this vast *expanse of water* when a barman comes with a tray and asks, "Privyet, would you care for a bottle of vodka and a *slice* of caviar pizza?"

EXAMPLES

1. 唱片 (chàng piàn) Disc, record. 雪片 (xuě piàn) Snowflake.
2. 照片 (zhào piàn) Photograph, picture. 片子 (piān zǐ) Film, movie, record.

WANT A LITTLE MORE?

- This character is pronounced in the first tone in a few words related to photos, films and records.
- This is the 91st of the 214 Kangxi radicals.
- Usage frequency: Top 500.

369

丬 [爿]

2nd

DEFINITION

† Half of a tree, cut longitudinally.

PRONUNCIATION

qiáng

SOUND WORD

tShe hangs on
Imagine a tough, strong woman and tell yourself, "Bu**t she hangs on**!" (See 'Special Sound Mnemonics,' page 489)

MNEMONICS

Cupboard.
It originally depicted a strip of wood or half of a tree, cut longitudinally. Ancient form:  . Let's build something with this wood: a kitchen *cupboard*, seen from the side.

STORY

"She's a tough cookie. The conditions in the kitchen are very difficult bu**t she hangs on** around her *cupboards* all day."

WANT A LITTLE MORE?

- Note that the traditional character is almost the mirror image of 片 SLICE[368]. It is in fact the other half of the tree introduced in the previous entry.
- This is the 90th of the 214 Kangxi radicals.

370A

将[將]

1st

DEFINITION

1. *Will, shall* (future tense); *about to.*
2. *Used to position the object of a verb before it* (like 把 343A).

PRONUNCIATION

jiāng

SOUND WORD

The ANG
Any aviator from the organization. (See 'Special Sound Mnemonics,' page 486)

SIMPLIFIED COMPONENTS

丬 CUPBOARD369 + 夕 EVENING251 + 寸 STAPLE GUN160 INCH

TRADITIONAL COMPONENTS

[爿 CUPBOARD369 + 夕 MEAT48 + STAPLE GUN]

STORY

An aviator from **the ANG** has decided on his own to build new CUPBOARDS in the barracks. Every EVENING, while the other men of his garrison try to get some sleep, you can hear him use his STAPLE GUN until very late at night. One of the men is fed up with his antics and is *about to* explode. "This guy *will* die in my hands, that's for sure!

["He's dead MEAT!"]

EXAMPLES

1. 将来(jiāng lái) In the future.
2. 请将门关上(qǐng jiāng mén guān shàng) Please close the door.

WANT A LITTLE MORE?

Usage frequency: Top 500.

370B 将[將] 4th

DEFINITION

1. A *general*, *commander-in-chief*.
2. *Chess piece* (king).

PRONUNCIATION

jiàng

SOUND WORD

The big boss of the ANG
A tough, demanding general. (See 'Special Sound Mnemonics,' page 486)

SIMPLIFIED COMPONENTS

丬 CUPBOARD[369] + 夕 EVENING[251] + 寸 STAPLE[160] INCH

TRADITIONAL COMPONENTS

[爿 CUPBOARD[369] + ⺼ MEAT[48] + STAPLE]

STORY

The big boss of the ANG is asked by the *Commander-in-chief* to have a new CUPBOARD built in the *general*'s quarter. He convokes his men and says, "Here are wood planks and a box of STAPLES. Build our *general* a new CUPBOARD!" One of the men says, "But sir, this is EVENING…"

[The boss stares at him and says, "Well, you have a choice. You move your MEAT now or you lose your seat, because you will not be able to sit for a while after I am done with you!"]

EXAMPLES

1. 将领(jiàng lǐng) High-ranking military officer.
2. 逼将(bī jiàng) Checkmate (literally 'to compel the king to abdicate').

WANT A LITTLE MORE?

Usage frequency: Middle third.

370C

将[將]

1st

DEFINITION

To *invite*, *request*.

PRONUNCIATION

qiāng

SOUND WORD

Chiack
To deride with mockery or maliciously. (See 'Special Sound Mnemonics,' page 489)

SIMPLIFIED COMPONENTS

丬 CUPBOARD369 + 夕 EVENING251 + 寸 STAPLE160 INCH

TRADITIONAL COMPONENTS

[爿 CUPBOARD369 + 夕 BODY PART48 MEAT + STAPLE]

STORY

One EVENING, a guy *invites* his friends to come to his place to help him put up a CUPBOARD in the kitchen. While they hold the CUPBOARD, he fixes it to the wall with STAPLES. His friends start to **chiack** him, saying this will never hold.

[Of course, as soon as he *requests* them to release their end, the STAPLES do not hold up and the CUPBOARD falls with a bang on most of his BODY PARTS!]

EXAMPLES

将伯 (qiāng bó) To ask for assistance.

WANT A LITTLE MORE?

Usage frequency: Bottom third.

371

两 [兩]

3rd

DEFINITION

1. *Both, two; a few.*
2. *Ounce; 50 grams.*

PRONUNCIATION

liǎng

SOUND WORD

Liane gorilla
Gorilla swinging from one liane to another in a rainforest.

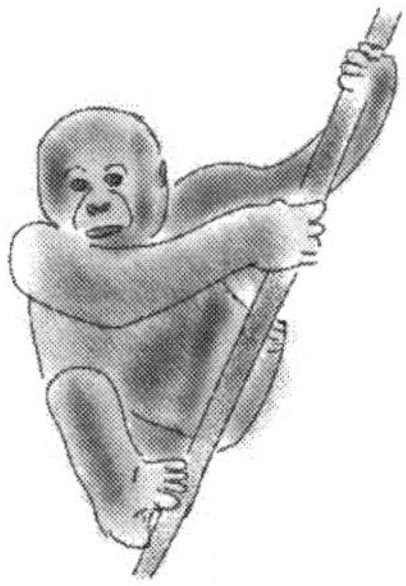

SIMPLIFIED COMPONENTS

一 ONE[15] + 冂 COVER[12] + 2 x 人 PERSON[23]

TRADITIONAL COMPONENTS

[ONE + 丨 STICK[1] + COVER + 2 x 入 to ENTER[22]]

STORY

Two **liane gorillas**, looking like *two* PERSONS, swing from ONE overhead branch above the vegetation COVER.

[ONE of the *two* **liane gorillas** hears *a few* sounds and warns the other. They then see a man walking with a STICK coming towards them. They *both* let themselves fall to the ground to hide by ENTERING the deep vegetation COVER. An *ounce* of prevention is worth *50 grams* of cure!]

EXAMPLES

1. 两旁 (liǎng páng) Both sides. 两手 (liǎng shǒu) Both hands. 两下子 (liǎng xià zǐ) A few times.
2. 英两 (yīng liǎng) Ounce. 市两 (shì liǎng) Weight equal to 50 grams.

WANT A LITTLE MORE?

Usage frequency: Top 500.

372A 间[間] 1st

DEFINITION

1. *Room, <u>space</u>.*
2. *Time duration.*
3. *Amongst, between.*

PRONUNCIATION

jiān

SOUND WORD

[i]**<u>The end</u>**
(See 'Special Sound Mnemonics,' page 485)

COMPONENTS

门[門] GATE[119] + 日 SUN[43]

STORY

(Add dramatic music for best effect) Outside, sirens have been blaring for a while, announcing an attack within *a short time* close to the *space* we are occupying. Me, my wife and our children are all in the same *room*, sitting *amongst* us. I suddenly see through our GATE a big flash of light as bright as a million SUNS. I tell my family, "This is **the end**…"

EXAMPLES

1. 房间 (fáng jiān) Room. 空间 (kōng jiān) Open air, sky, space.
2. 时间 (shí jiān) Time, duration.
3. 之间 (zhī jiān) Amongst, between. 中间 (zhōng jiān) Middle, in between.

WANT A LITTLE MORE?

Usage frequency: Top 500.

372B

间[間]

4th

DEFINITION

Interstice, interval, gap, space in between; to *separate*; to *sow discord, drive a wedge between.*

PRONUNCIATION

jiàn

SOUND WORD

Hygienist

As in dental **hygienist**, in that dreaded of all places: the dentist's chair.

COMPONENTS

门[門] GATE[119] + 日 SUN[43]

STORY

When I was a young kid, my dental **hygienist** tried to be cute by using metaphors with me, like "OK Billie, open your GATE. I will now turn on the big SUN and look inside the GATE. Oh, you have big *gaps* between your soldiers. Look at all the *space in between*. They don't seem to like each other. Did you *drive a wedge between* them?"

EXAMPLES

间隙(jiàn xì) Interval, gap. 间隔(jiàn gé) Intermission. 间隔成(jiàn gé chéng) To separate into. 间壁(jiàn bì) Next-door neighbor. 离间(lí jiàn) To sow discord.

WANT A LITTLE MORE?

Usage frequency: Bottom third.

373 问[問] 4th

Definition

To *ask*, *inquire*, *question*, *interrogate*; *problem*, *question*, *issue*.

Pronunciation

wèn

Sound word

Underwent
To have been submitted to, to have endured.

Components

门[門] GATE[119] + 口 OPENING[41]

Story

After his wife died in a strange way, my neighbor **underwent** a series of tough *questions* when he was *interrogated* by investigators. I still remember seeing a group of policemen barging in through the OPENING of his front GATE.

Examples

发问 (fā wèn) To ask a question. 查问 (chá wèn) To inquire about, question, interrogate. 问题 (wèn tí) Question, problem.

Want a little more?

Usage frequency: Top 500.

374 艮 3rd

DEFINITION

1. *Tough*, when talking of food (hard to chew) or of people: *tough guy*.
2. *Straightforward, blunt, stubborn.*

PRONUNCIATION

gěn

SOUND WORD

General /genəʁal/
Pronounced in German, with a hard 'G.' Let's picture a tough German **general** of World War II.

MNEMONICS

- This character used to depict a person with a big, threatening eye. Ancient form: .
- It may be written  when used as a building block.

STORY

The *tough* German **General** says *bluntly* at a dinner table, "Hey, officer! Tell the cook that his food is too *tough* to chew. Bring me something else!"
"Ja, mein **General**!"

EXAMPLES

1. 发艮 (fā gěn) Food (turnips, apples…) losing crispness.
2. 艮话 (gěn huà) Straightforward words.

WANT A LITTLE MORE?

- This is the 138th of the 214 Kangxi radicals.
- Usage frequency: Bottom third.

375 **很** 3rd

DEFINITION

Very, *extremely*, *quite*.

† To resist, be stubborn.

PRONUNCIATION

hěn

SOUND WORD

Henry VIII
The ruthless king of England (1491 - 1547), best remembered for his six marriages and the two wives he beheaded…

COMPONENTS

彳 to STEP FORWARD[192] + 艮 TOUGH GUY[374]

STORY

Henry VIII could be *very*, if not *extremely* brutal with people who opposed him. Take his second wife Anne Boleyn, for example. She was not afraid to STEP FORWARD and speak her mind. Apparently, she even said one day to the king, "I am not *quite* ready to spend the rest of my life with a man who cultivates an image of being a TOUGH GUY while he is not." One of her advisers rushed to her side and said, "Anne, have you lost your head?" Indeed she did, *very* shortly after…

EXAMPLES

很好(hěn hǎo) Very good. 怕得很(pà de hěn) To be very frightened.

WANT A LITTLE MORE?

Usage frequency: Top 500.

376

耳

3rd

DEFINITION

Ear.

PRONUNCIATION

ěr

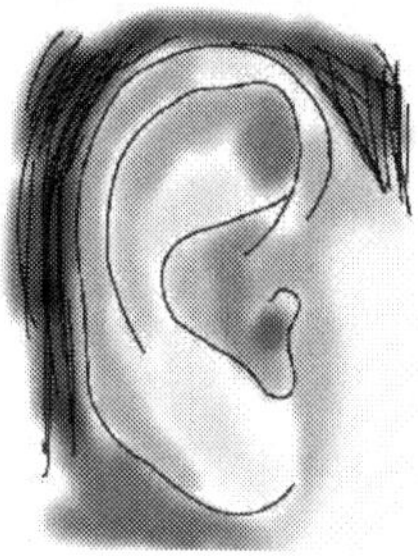

SOUND WORD

Auricular
Relating to the ear or hearing.

MNEMONICS

This is a pictogram of an ear. Ancient form: .

STORY

In a biology class, the instructor says, "Now, listen closely, because we will talk about the *ear* and all the potential **auricular** problems, like deafness." A student sitting at the back shouts, just to appear funny, "Could you repeat please? I did not hear!"

EXAMPLES

耳朵(ěr duǒ) Ear. 耳垂(ěr chuí) Earlobe.

WANT A LITTLE MORE?

- This is the 128th of the 214 Kangxi radicals.
- Usage frequency: Top third.

377 **取** $\vee$ 3rd

DEFINITION

1. To *take*, *grab*, *get*, *fetch*.
2. To *choose*.

PRONUNCIATION

qǔ

SOUND WORD

Turlutant /tʃyʁlytɑ̃/
French Canadian verb meaning 'singing a tune with specific wordless melody ornaments,' such as "tam tidelidelam."

COMPONENTS

耳 EAR[376] + 又 RIGHT HAND[71]

STORY

Walking slowly, the director looks at the room with all his employees, *chooses* one who was sitting calmly at his desk, *grabs* his EAR with his RIGHT HAND and, while **turlutant**, *takes* him all the way into his office.

EXAMPLES

1. 攫取(jué qǔ) To seize, grab. 取得(qǔ dé) To gain, obtain.
2. 拔取(bá qǔ) To choose, select.

WANT A LITTLE MORE?

Usage frequency: Top 500.

378 **最** 4th

DEFINITION

The most (indicator of superlative).

PRONUNCIATION

zuì

SOUND WORD

Venezuela /venedswela/
South American country over the equator, known in part for its sunny beaches. Pronounce it in Italian for a better sound match.

COMPONENTS

日 SUN[43] + 取 to TAKE[377]

STORY

To allow your skin to TAKE *the most* SUN, I recommend the beaches of **Venezuela**!

EXAMPLES

最多 (zuì duō) The most. 最后 (zuì hòu) Last, ultimate. 最近 (zuì jìn) Recently.

WANT A LITTLE MORE?

Usage frequency: Top 500.

379 亚[亞] 4th

DEFINITION

1. *Inferior*, *second*, *second-rate*.
2. *Asia*.

PRONUNCIATION

yà

SOUND WORD

Kayak

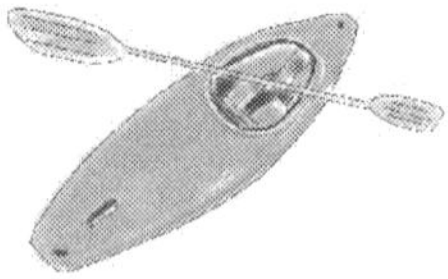

SIMPLIFIED COMPONENTS

一 ONE[15] + 业 INDUSTRY[185]

MNEMONICS

- *Drugstore*.
  The traditional character looks exactly like the *drugstore* sign in Europe.
- Another visual trick to remember the traditional character and its meaning of *second* is with the formula:
  1 (horizontal line on top) + (big plus sign) 1 (horizontal line at the bottom) = *Second*.

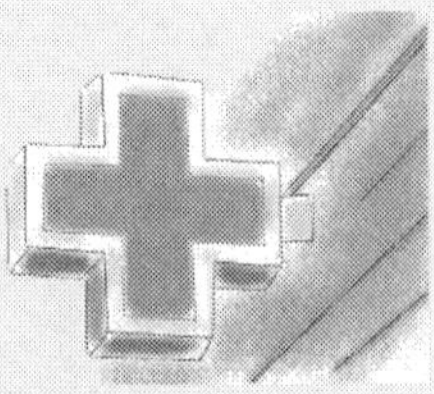

STORY

Once upon a time, there was ONE INDUSTRY in *Asia* that did not fare too well: the production of *second-rate* **kayak**.

[Because of the high number of accidents that resulted from the use of these **kayak**s of *inferior* quality, they had to compensate by building a high number of *drugstores*…]

EXAMPLES

1. 不亚于(bù yà yú) Second to none, not inferior to.
2. 东亚(dōng yà) East Asia.

WANT A LITTLE MORE?

Usage frequency: Top 500.

380A

并[並]

4th

DEFINITION

1. *And, furthermore.*
2. *Simultaneously, side by side, together with.*
3. *Not at all.*

PRONUNCIATION

bìng

SOUND WORD

Car bombing
A terrorist tactic, turning vehicles into weapons.

SIMPLIFIED COMPONENTS

丷 EIGHT[55] + 开 to OPEN[325]

TRADITIONAL COMPONENTS

[丷 DEVILISH[55] EIGHT + 亚 INFERIOR[379]]

STORY

I see a man filling EIGHT OPEN bottles standing *side by side* with some sort of liquid. I ask him what he is doing and he says, "Oh, nothing. I just prepare my next **car bombing** mission. I want these EIGHT bottles to detonate *simultaneously*…"

["Don't you think this is a DEVILISH plan?" I dare ask.
"*Not at all*!" he says. "I guess it appears DEVILISH but I only use material of INFERIOR quality, so it won't do much damage!"]

EXAMPLES

1. 并且(bìng qiě) And, besides, moreover.
2. 并排(bìng pái) Side by side. 一并(yī bìng) Together with all the others.
3. 并不(bìng bù) Not at all, by no means.

WANT A LITTLE MORE?

Usage frequency: Top 500.

380B

并[併]

4th

DEFINITION

To <u>*combine*</u>, *join*, *merge*, *amalgamate*.

PRONUNCIATION

bìng

SOUND WORD

Car bombing
A terrorist tactic, turning vehicles into weapons.

SIMPLIFIED COMPONENTS

丷 EIGHT[55] + 开 to OPEN[325]

TRADITIONAL COMPONENTS

[亻 HANDYMAN[23] MAN + EIGHT + to OPEN]

STORY

A man is trying to *join* EIGHT OPEN bottles of explosives for a **car bombing** attack.

[The HANDYMAN happens to walk by and says, "You seem to have trouble building your bomb. You just need to *combine* these two wires here…"]

EXAMPLES

合并(hé bìng) To merge, combine. 并入(bìng rù) To merge into. 火并(huǒ bìng) To open fight between factions.

WANT A LITTLE MORE?

Usage frequency: Top third.

381

物

4th

DEFINITION

Thing, object, matter.

PRONUNCIATION

wù

SOUND WORD

Steel <u>woo</u>l

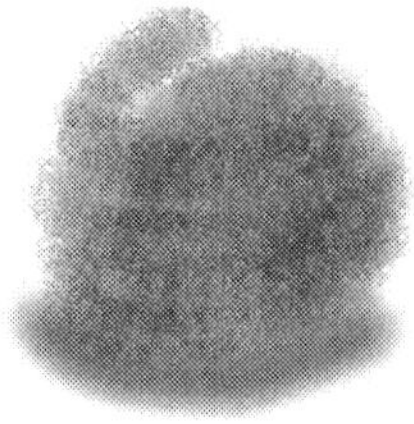

COMPONENTS

牜 COW[35] + 勿 NOT[81]

STORY

A sign next to an animal pen indicates, "Please do NOT feed the COWS with **steel wool** and other *objects*. They can't digest those *things*!"

EXAMPLES

动物(dòng wù) Animal. 物质(wù zhì) Matter, substance. 食物(shí wù) Food.

WANT A LITTLE MORE?

Usage frequency: Top 500.

382 **倠** 1st

DEFINITION

† Ugly face.

PRONUNCIATION

suī

SOUND WORD

Sway
To move slowly back and forth, or to cause (someone) to agree with you or to share your opinion.

COMPONENTS

亻 PERSON[23] + 隹 OSTRICH[310]

MNEMONICS

Superhero.
A PERSON dressed up in a bird suit, who **sways** in the air.

383A 应[應] 1st

DEFINITION

1. *Ought to, should, must.*
2. *Surname.*

PRONUNCIATION

yīng

SOUND WORD

Ink

SIMPLIFIED COMPONENTS

广 CASTLE[223] EXTENSIVE + ⺍ to HAUL UP[142]

TRADITIONAL COMPONENTS

[CASTLE + 雁 SUPERHERO[382] + 心 HEART[321]]

STORY

A hermit but prolific writer living in a CASTLE at the top of a mountain *must* HAUL UP his **ink** every month, otherwise, he would not have enough to write his books!

[Considering his advanced age and the condition of his HEART, he *should* ask the local flying SUPERHERO to help him with this task.]

EXAMPLES

1. 应该 (yīng gāi) Must, should, ought to. 应当 (yīng dāng) Should, ought to.

WANT A LITTLE MORE?

Usage frequency: Top 500.

383B

应[應]

4th

DEFINITION

1. To *answer, respond.*
2. To *promise, consent.*
3. To *apply.*

PRONUNCIATION

yìng

SOUND WORD

Flying

SIMPLIFIED COMPONENTS

广 EXTENSIVE[223] +

业 to UNCOVER[142]

TRADITIONAL COMPONENTS

[EXTENSIVE + 隹 SUPERHERO[382] +

心 HEART[321]]

STORY

"An EXTENSIVE plot to cause a commercial aircraft to crash has been UNCOVERED today. Three passengers, **flying** aboard the plane, had *consented* to incapacitate the pilots and stop the engines, which they did.

["Thankfully, the SUPERHERO took this cause to HEART and *responded* immediately when called. **Flying** under the plane, he was able to *apply* his power to carry and land the plane and its passengers safely."]

EXAMPLES

1. 答应 (dā yìng) To answer, reply. 反应 (fǎn yìng) To react, respond.
2. 应承 (yìng chéng) To agree, promise; consent.
3. 应用 (yìng yòng) To apply, use.

WANT A LITTLE MORE?

Usage frequency: Middle third.

384

吅

2nd

DEFINITION

† Clamors; to cry.

PRONUNCIATION

xuán

SOUND WORD

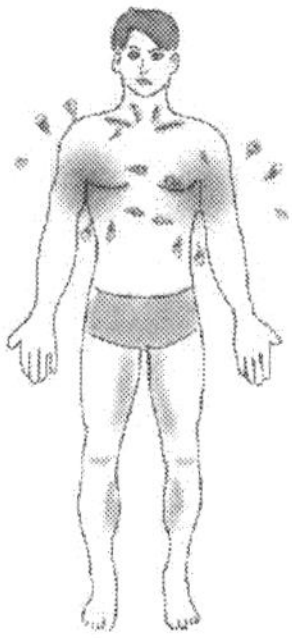

Suant
French verb meaning 'sweating,' from the armpits in this case. (See 'Special Sound Mnemonics,' page 492)

MNEMONICS

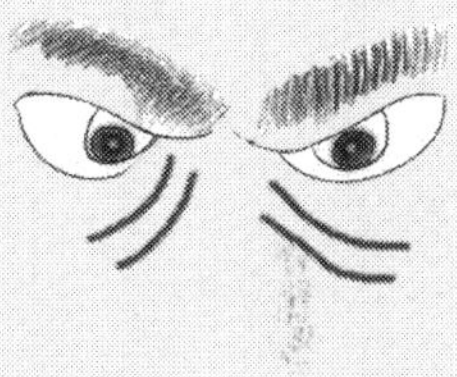

- *Angry eyes*.
  The character looks like two *angry eyes* looking at you.
- *Talkative*.
  Picture a person who speaks as if he had two 口 MOUTHS[41].

STORY

My boss, a very *talkative* man, has been shouting, with *angry eyes*, at an employee for the last hour to the point of sweating (**suant**) from his armpits. Two large sweat rings appear on the side of his shirt.

385 **单[單]** 1st

DEFINITION

1. *Single, alone.*
2. *List, form.*
3. *Sheet.*

PRONUNCIATION

dān

SOUND WORD

Dance

SIMPLIFIED COMPONENTS

丷 HORNY55 EIGHT + 田 FIELD195 + 十 TEN59

TRADITIONAL COMPONENTS

[吅 ANGRY EYES384 + FIELD + TEN]

STORY

Two guys are chatting in a bar.

"Look at this guy on the **dance** floor, doing his **dance** moves *alone* while there is a FIELD of at least TEN girls just waiting to be invited."
"I heard it's because he's too HORNY. Not a *single* girl wants to end up under the *sheets* with him. That's why he's still *alone* and not on the *list* of prospects."

[The 'dancer' overhears their conversation and looks at them with ANGRY EYES.]

EXAMPLES

1. 单独(dān dú) Alone.
2. 菜单(cài dān) Menu.
3. 被单(bèi dān) Bed sheet.

WANT A LITTLE MORE?

Usage frequency: Top 500.

386 战[戰] 4th

DEFINITION

War, *battle*; to *fight*.

PRONUNCIATION

zhàn

SOUND WORD

Azerbai<u>jan</u> [ɑːzərbaɪdʒɑːn] Country located between Armenia and the Caspian Sea. The stories mostly refer to the Nagorno-Karabakh War (1980 – 1994).

SIMPLIFIED COMPONENTS

占 to <u>OCCUPY</u>[365B] + 戈 <u>DAGGER AX</u>[90]

TRADITIONAL COMPONENTS

[單 <u>SINGLE</u>[385] + <u>DAGGER AX</u>]

STORY

As *war* broke out between **Azerbaijan** and Armenia, it came as a surprise to see soldiers running towards the enemy <u>OCCUPYING</u> their country with only a <u>DAGGER AX</u> in their hands to *fight* with.

[Needless to say, not a <u>SINGLE</u> one of those <u>DAGGER AX</u>-wielding soldiers made it out alive…]

EXAMPLES

战争(zhàn zhēng) War, warfare. 战役(zhàn yì) Battle. 作战(zuò zhàn) To fight.

WANT A LITTLE MORE?

Usage frequency: Top 500.

387A 曲 **1st**

DEFINITION

Bent, crooked, distorted.

PRONUNCIATION

qū

SOUND WORD

Tschüss /tʃʏs/
A German informal way of saying 'auf Wiedersehen,' meaning 'Bye, see ya.'

MNEMONICS

Just picture the low back of a plumber *bent* under the sink, where you can see his suspenders and part of his butt crack.

STORY

One of our sinks is leaking. So, my wife calls a plumber to fix it. I arrive in the kitchen and see him *bent* under the sink, in a *crooked* position, letting me see part of his behind. I tell my wife, "OK. I have seen enough. **Tschüss**!"

EXAMPLES

弯曲 (wān qū) Winding, wavy, curved. 曲解 (qū jiě) To distort.

WANT A LITTLE MORE?

Usage frequency: Top third.

387B

曲

3rd

DEFINITION

Tune, song; opera.

PRONUNCIATION

qǔ

SOUND WORD

Turluter /tʃyʁlyte/
French Canadian verb meaning 'to sing a tune with specific wordless melody ornaments,' such as "tam tidelidelam."

MNEMONICS

Note how the character also looks like a lectern on which you place the music sheets before a performance.

STORY

The orchestra is all set and the audience is looking forward to hear the *songs* of a world-class *opera* singer. Before the music starts, the French singer, standing in front of a lectern, says to the audience, "I don't know the lyrics of the *songs* I am about to sing tonight, so I will just **turluter**." And that's all he does during the whole show!

EXAMPLES

曲子 (qǔ zi) Tune, melody. **乐曲** (yuè qǔ) Musical composition.

WANT A LITTLE MORE?

Usage frequency: Top third.

388 **体[體]** 3rd

DEFINITION

1. *Body.*
2. *Substance.*

PRONUNCIATION

tǐ

SOUND WORD

Teetotaler
A nondrinker, someone who never drinks alcohol.

SIMPLIFIED COMPONENTS

亻 PERSON[23] + 本 BASIS[322]

TRADITIONAL COMPONENTS

[骨 BONE[209] + 曲 BENT[387A] + 豆 BEANS[332]]

STORY

A nutritionist speaks at a conference and says, "For a PERSON to have a healthy *body*, the BASIS is avoiding feeding it with toxic *substances*. This explains why **teetotalers** are usually healthier.

["In addition to being a **teetotaler**, your *body* and your BONES would be thankful if you spent more time BENT forward over a plate of BEANS rather than BENT backwards with a beer on your stomach."]

EXAMPLES

1. 身体(shēn tǐ) Body; health. 体力 (tǐ lì) Physical strength.
2. 物体(wù tǐ) Substance.

WANT A LITTLE MORE?

Usage frequency: Top 500.

389

政

4th

DEFINITION

Government, politics; political.

PRONUNCIATION

zhèng

SOUND WORD

Tarzan, king of the jungle

COMPONENTS

正 UPRIGHT[76A] + 攵 to HIT[220]

STORY

Tarzan, king of the jungle, being an honest member of his community, was the perfect candidate to become the *political* leader of the new 'green' *government*. Not only is he an UPRIGHT man, but he also has the strength to HIT hard when necessary to enforce the application of his environmental laws by the surrounding non-UPRIGHT monkeys.

EXAMPLES

政府 (zhèng fǔ) Government. 政治 (zhèng zhì) Politics; political affairs.

WANT A LITTLE MORE?

Usage frequency: Top 500.

390 # 美 3rd

DEFINITION

1. *Beautiful.*
2. *America.*

PRONUNCIATION

měi

SOUND WORD

Medication

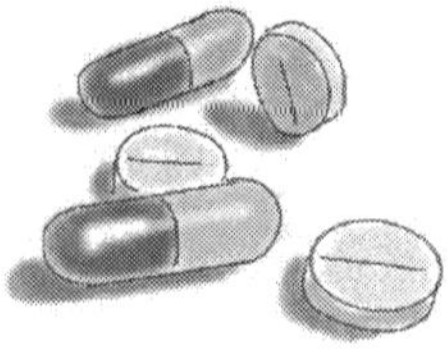

COMPONENTS

羊 SHEEP[37] + 大 BIG[27]

MNEMONICS

A BIG, fat SHEEP used to be a *beautiful* thing to have.

STORY

"The SHEEP raised in *America* are so BIG and *beautiful*!"
A die-hard naturalist says, "No wonder, with all the **medication** they feed them with!"

EXAMPLES

1. 美丽 (měi lì) Beautiful. 美发师 (měi fà shī) Hair stylist.
2. 美国 (měi guó) United States.

WANT A LITTLE MORE?

Usage frequency: Top 500.

Appendix 1: Chinese Initials and Finals

The pronunciation and spelling of Chinese characters are generally given in terms of initials (i.e. consonants) and finals (possible combinations of vowels and consonants). The following two tables describe the pronunciation of each Chinese initial and final in pinyin and how they are approximated in this series using the five European languages.

Table 1: Pronunciation of initials

Pinyin	Sound description	European equivalent
b	Not aspirated, between *b* and *p*.	*b*
c	Sounds like *t* followed by *s* (*cats*) or German *z* (*Zeitung*). Pronounced strongly aspirated.	English *ts* German *z*
ch	Strongly aspirated, as English or Spanish *ch* (*chin*, *chofer*) or Italian *ce* (*cenare*).	English *ch*, *tsh* Spanish *ch* Italian *ce*
d	t not aspirated, between *d* and *t*.	*d*
f	As English *f*.	*f*
g	k not aspirated, between *g* and *k*.	Hard *g*
h	Like Scottish *ch* (*loch*), English or German *h* (*Hund*), French or German *r* (*roue*, *raus*) and Spanish *j* (*jefe*).	English *h* French *r* Spanish *j* German *h*, *r*
j	Similar to the English pronunciation of the letter *G*, not aspirated.	English: Soft *j*, *g*. *Thee* for pinyin starting with ji. French *dj*. French or German *du* and *dü* for pinyin starting with ju. Italian soft *g*
k	Strongly aspirated *k*.	Hard *c*, *k*, *qu*
l	As English *l*.	l
m	As English *m*.	m

Table 1: Pronunciation of initials		
Pinyin	**Sound description**	**European equivalent**
n	As English *n*.	n
p	Strongly aspirated *p*.	p
q	Similar to an aspirated pinyin *j*. Sounds like English *ch* (*cheek*), Italian *c* (*cin cin*), Spanish *ch* (*bachiller*) and French Canadian *t* when followed by *u* (*tulipe*).	English *ch* French *t* for pinyin starting with qu Italian *ci* Spanish *ch*
r	Between English *r* and French *j* (*bonjour*).	English *r* French *j*
s	As English *s* (*sun*).	*s* and soft French *c*
sh	As English *s*, *ch* and *sh* (*sure*, *chandelier*, *shoe*) or French *ch* (*chêne*).	English *s*, *sh* French *ch* German *sch*
t	Strongly aspirated *t*.	*t*
w	As English *w* (*water*).	English *w*
x	A sound between *s* (*sea*) and *sh* (*shoe*).	English *s*, *c*, *sh* French *s*, *c*, *ch* Spanish *s*, *c* German *sch* and 'special' *s*
y	As in *yes*. Pronounced like English letter *e* when written yi and like French *u* when written yu.	English *e*, *i*, *y* French *u*, *eu*, *hu*, *hi*, *hy* (*h* is silent in French)
z	Sounds like *d* followed by *s* (*suds*) or Italian *z* (*pizza*).	English *ds*, *dz*, *z* Italian *z*
zh	Rather like English soft *j* or *g* (*joke*, *genetic*).	English soft *j*, *g* French *dj* Italian *g*

Table 2: Pronunciation of finals		
Pinyin	**Sound description**	**European equivalent**
a	Like English *a* in *father.*	*a*
ai	Like English *eye* or *aisle.*	English *ai*, *ay*, *eye*, *i* French *ail*, *aille* Italian *ai* Spanish *ai*, *ay* German *ai*, *ei*
an	As in *tan*, except when following an initial y-; it is then pronounced *yen.*	*an* in most languages + French *anne* and German *ahn*
ang	As in *angst.*	*anc*, *ang*, *ank* + French *agne*
ao	As in *how* or *cow.*	English *ao*, *ar*, *aw*, *ou*, *ow* French *ao*, *ar* Italian *ao*
e	Like *e* in *her* or *u* in *duh.*	English, French or German *e*
ei	As in *hay*, *eight* or the letter *a.*	English *a*, *ai*, *ay*, *e*, *ei* French *é*, *ez* Italian *e* Spanish *e*
en	As in *open*, *taken.*	*en*
eng	As in *open* with an appended *g.*	*eng* in most languages + English *ong*, *onk*, *ung*, *unk* and French *ogne*
er	As in *army.*	English *ar*, *aur*
i	Like *ee* in *bee* or *ea* in *tea.* When it follows initials z-, c-, s-, zh-, ch-, sh- or r-, it is either not pronounced, like pinyin zi where it sounds somewhat like *dzzzz*, or it sounds like an English vowel followed by the letter *r*, like *er* of *snatcher* or *ur* of *sure.*	English *e*, *ea*, *ee*, *er*, *or*, *ur* French *i*, *y* German *eu*

Table 2: Pronunciation of finals		
Pinyin	**Sound description**	**European equivalent**
ia	As in *yard.*	English *ea-a, e-a* Italian or Spanish *ia*
ian	Like *yen.*	English *ian, ien, eyenne* French *i-aine, ienne* Italian or Spanish *ien*
iang	Like *yang.*	English *ee-ang, ee-ank, e-hang, iang* French *i-ang, iant*
iao	As in *yowl* or *meow.*	English *e-ow, ee-ar, gnar, illar* French *i-a-eau, iao, iar, illard* Italian or Spanish *iao*
ie	As in *yes.*	English *ie* French *iait, ie, iè, illait* Italian *ie* Spanish *ie, ille*
in	As in *sin.*	*in* + French *ine*
ing	As in *bombing.*	*inc, ing, ink* + Italian *inq*
io, iu	As in *yoga* or *yo-yo.*	English *eo, ea-o, ee-o* French or Italian *io* + Spanish *illo*
iong	Like *young.*	French *ion*
o, ou	As in *so* or *dough.*	*o* in all languages + English *oa, ou, ough, ow* and French *eau*
ong	As in *young.*	English *ong, onk, oung, ung, unk* French *ogne, on* Italian *on*
u	Like English *oo,* as in *booby-trap*, except after initials j-, q-, x- and y- (as described below).	*u* in most languages + English *ew, oo* and French *aou, ou*
u, ü	When written with a diaeresis or after initials j-, q-, x- and y- with no diaeresis, it is pronounced like German *ü* (*Tschüss*) or French *u* (*tulipe*).	French *u* German *ü*

Table 2: Pronunciation of finals		
Pinyin	**Sound description**	**European equivalent**
ua	As in *suave.*	English *oua*, *ua*, *wa* French *oi*, *oua* Spanish *ua*
uai	Like English *why.*	English *ew-i*, *why*, *wi* French *ouaille* Spanish *uay*
uan	As in *Don Juan,* except after initials j-, q-, x- and y- (see below).	*uan* in most languages + English *wan* and French *ouan*, *ouanne*, *ou-en*
uan	After initials j-, q-, x- and y-, pronounced as French *u* + *an.*	French *uan*
uang	Like *Wang.*	English *ew-ang*, *ew-ank*, *u-ang*, *wang* French *ouen*, *ou-eng*, *ou-enk* Spanish *uanc*, *uang*
ue, üe	Sounds like French *u* + *è*, as in *duel.*	French *eu-e*, *uai*, *ue*, *uè*, *ué* German *ü-e*
ui	Like *way.*	*ue* in most languages + English *oe*, *ooey*, *ua*, *way* and French *oué*, *ouer*
un	Sounds like *u* + *en*, except after initials j-, q-, x- and y- (see below).	English *oon*, *un* French *oune* German *un*
un	After initials j-, q- and x-, pronounced as French *u* + *n.*	French *une*, *unne* German *ün*, *ühn*
uo	As in *duo, jewel.*	English *uo*, *wo* French *ou-eau* Italian *uo* Spanish *ullo*, *uo* German *u-ho*

Appendix 2: Special Sound Mnemonics

This section provides additional details for a few sound mnemonics.

Chuan

For this sound, the core image is the **Metabetchouan** River in the province of Quebec, Canada. It is 128 km (80 miles) long and offers rafting, canoeing, and fishing activities (google it!). The last part of its name, 'tchouan,' is the exact sound we're looking for. For an image, you can think of any river you know and it will do the trick.

The mnemonics are organized like this:

Metabetchouan /Metabɛtʃuan/

For the sound chuān (first tone), we are standing on the banks of the river.

Metabetchouan

For the sound chuán (second tone), we are riding a boat on the river.

Metabetchouan

For the sound chuǎn (third tone), we are swimming at the surface of the river.

Metabetchouan

For the sound chuàn (fourth tone), we are underwater, scuba diving.

Huo

Since this sound is not present in the five European languages selected, an approximation is needed. If we remove the middle 'l' from the French word 'rouleau' (roll), it gets very close to the sound we are looking for. This is the word we are going to use for the various tones of **huo**.

Rouleau /ʁulo/
First tone: Let's make this a roll used in steel plate rolling machines, where a steel plate is pinched between two rolls to shape it.

Rouleau pâte /ʁulo pɑt/
Second tone: Rolling pin. The exact French expression is 'rouleau à pâte,' but we drop the middle 'à' to make it a two-syllable utterance.

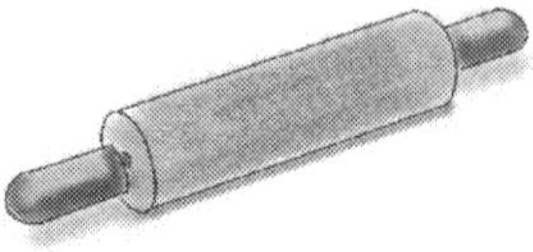

Rouleau compresseur /ʁulo kɔ̃pʁɛsœʁ/
Third tone: A steamroller.

Porte-rouleau /pɔʁt ʁulo/
Fourth tone: A toilet paper holder or just the little thingy with a spring in the middle that you insert in the center of the paper roll. Yea… the things we are ready to accept for having good mnemonics...

Ji-

There is no equivalent sound in the five European languages to accurately reflect the pinyin sounds beginning with **ji** followed by a vowel (**jia**, **jian**, **jie**, **jiu**, etc.). As such, in this book, **ji** will be replaced by the English 'the', which when followed by a vowel, is pronounced 'thee'. In our case, we will imagine being a foreigner having difficulty with the infamous English 'th' sound, and will replace it with the 'j' sound, thus pronouncing 'thee' like 'jee.' For example, 'the end,' pronounced 'jee end,' will be used for the first tone of pinyin **jian**. The sound word, when introduced, is preceded by a superscript j to remind you of this.

Jiang

This sound will be all about 'the ANG,' the Air National Guard. The Air National Guard (ANG) is the airforce component of each U.S. state.

ʲThe ANG

The sound jiāng (first tone) represents an aviator of the ANG.

ʲThe ANG missions

The sound jiǎng (third tone) stands for any mission they accomplish.

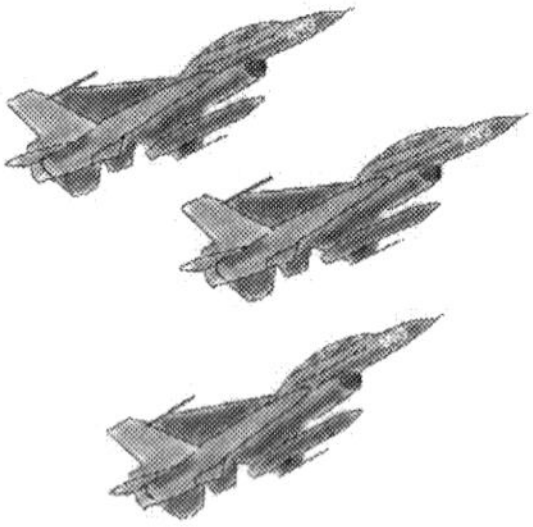

The big boss of ʲthe ANG

The sound jiàng (fourth tone) represents a tough, demanding officer.

Note that there is no second tone with this sound.

Ju

Pinyin sounds beginning with 'ju' are pronounced with the sound 'dj' followed by the French 'u' or the German 'ü.' The best approximation for the sound 'dj' in this case is French Canadian sound 'd'. This book uses French sound words beginning with the syllable 'du' or German sound words beginning with the syllable 'dü' to stand for the pinyin **ju** sound.

However, English, Spanish or Italian sound words beginning with the syllable 'du' stand for the pinyin **du** sound.

Mian

For this sound, in the second and third tones, a new fictitious word has emerged: **Mi-aine**. 'Aine' in French means 'groin.' **Mi-aine** would then translate to mid-groin. Just try not to use it to show off your French, because this expression has been made up just for this book.

Mi-aine slip /miɛn slip/
Second tone: Woman's underwear. A mi-aine slip is a woman's underwear that ends at the groin…

Mi-aine injury /miɛn ɪndʒri/
Third tone: Pain in the mid-groin (mi-aine) region due to an injury.

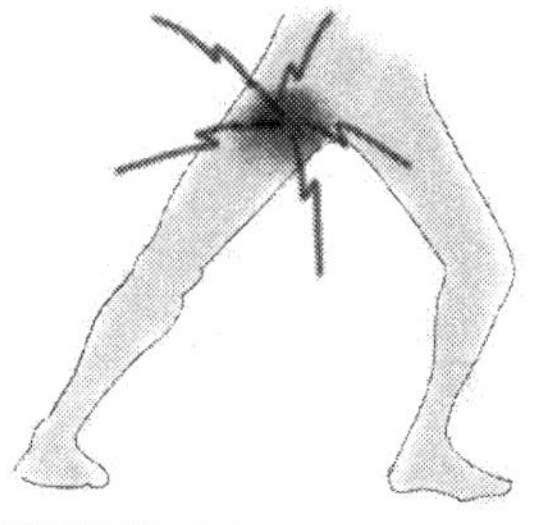

Qian

To introduce a needed 't' sound at the beginning of the sound word, two prefix expressions are used: 'Nothing but' or the French adjective 'petite' (small, little). The sound word is preceded by a superscript ᵗ to remind you of this.

ᵗChienne /t'ʃjɛn/

First tone: Chienne is a French word for 'female dog.' Think of the phrase, 'Nothing bu**t chienne**': 'nothing but female dogs' or 'peti**te chienne**': 'little female dog.'

ᵗCheyenne

Second tone: Think of the phrase, 'Nothing bu**t Cheyenne**.'

When the word Cheyenne appears by itself, just automatically add a 't' in front when you pronounce it in your mind.

ᵗCheyenne horses

Third tone: Think of the expression, 'nothing but Cheyenne horses.'

Picture horses ridden and used so well by the Cheyenne when they were introduced to them around 1730.

Qiang

For this very Chinese sound, we resort to rough approximations and to a prefix expression for the second and the third tones. The prefix expression in this case is 'But,' in order to introduce a needed 't' sound at the beginning of the sound word. The sound word is preceded by a superscript ᵗ to remind you of this.

Chiack
First tone: To chiack, to deride with mockery or maliciously. This is a rough approximation.

ᵗShe hangs on
Second tone: Imagine a tough, strong woman and tell yourself, "Bu**t she hangs on**!"

Do not pronounce the 'h' for a better sound representation.

ᵗShe hangs criminals
Third tone: Imagine a tough female law enforcer. "Bu**t she hangs criminals**!"

Do not pronounce the 'h' for a better sound representation.

Lychee hangover
Fourth tone: Getting a hangover by drinking too much lychee liquor.

Do not pronounce the 'h' for a better sound representation.

Quan

In pinyin, a 'u' following a 'q' is pronounced like the French 'u' or German 'ü.' The word that comes closest in pronunciation is the French word 'tuant' /tyɑ̃/ of the verb 'tuer' (to kill) in the progressive form, meaning 'killing' (there you go, an action verb that is easy to remember!). The killing is done preferably with a big rifle. The tones are differentiated by the aiming angle of the rifle, as described below.

For quān (first tone), we imagine a shooter aiming his gun vertically at the sky, killing (**tuant**) airplanes (imagine the futility of it all!).

For quán (second tone), the rifle is aimed upwards, at an angle, just like the accent on the á, **tuant** fowl.

For quǎn (third tone), the shooter is aiming horizontally at a moving target on the ground, similar to a dog jumping up and down, like the shape of the accent on ǎ.

Finally, for quàn (fourth tone), the rifle is aimed downward, for shooting fish in a lake or a man on the ground.

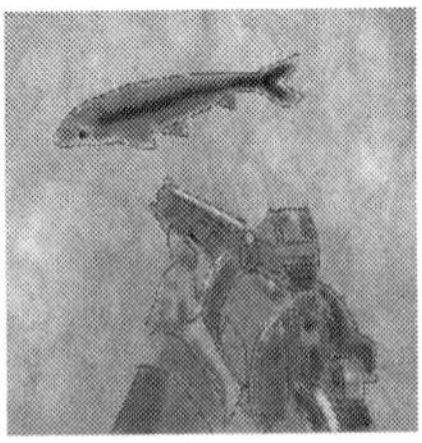

Sheng

Sheng is one of those sounds that are hard to come by in European languages. So, we need to rely on a rough approximation.

In French, 'I bleed' is translated by 'Je saigne' /ʒə sɛɳ/. When said rapidly, the French often drop the first 'e' and end up with the contraction 'j'saigne' /ʃɛɳ/ which is, although not a perfect match, quite close to **sheng**. The four tones will be represented by a variation of the French expression equivalent to 'Bleeding from,' moving sequentially from the head to the feet. This is graphic enough to make good mnemonics!

J'saigne (de la tête)
First tone: I bleed from the head, bleeding from the head.

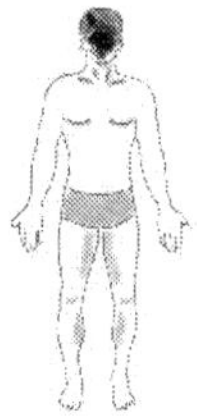

J'saigne (du thorax)
Second tone: Bleeding from the chest or thorax.

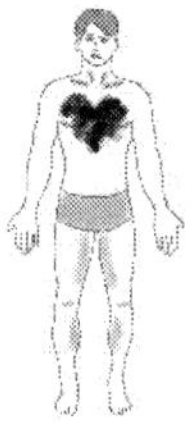

J'saigne (à l'aine)
Third tone: Bleeding from the groin.

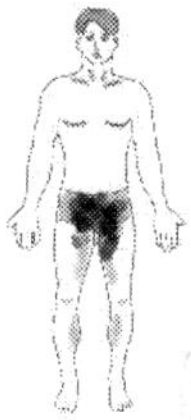

J'saigne (des pieds)
Fourth tone: Bleeding from the feet.

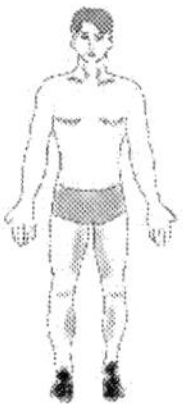

Xuan

The only word that comes close to this sound is the present participle 'suant' /syɑ̃/ (sweating) of the French verb 'suer' (to sweat). We will proceed as follows:

Suant (from the head)
xuān (first tone) is represented by a person sweating from the head (picture beads of sweat on the face).

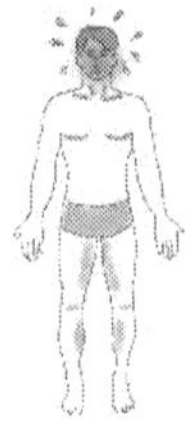

Suant (from the armpits)
xuán (second tone) is represented by a person sweating from the armpits.

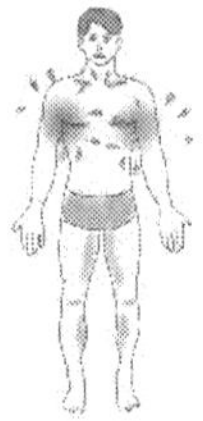

Suant (from the groin)
xuǎn (third tone) represents a person sweating from the groin, rather a person wetting his or her pants.

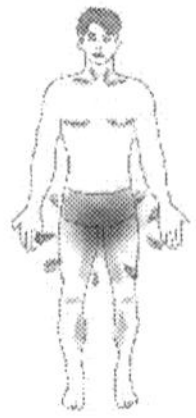

Suant (from the feet)
xuàn (fourth tone) represents a person sweating from the feet (picture very smelly feet).

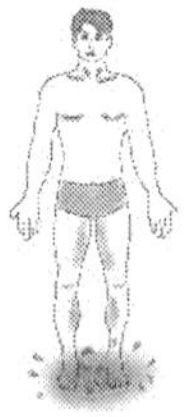

Yuan

We need to rely on the French 'u' for this sound. In French, the phrases 'he has got' or 'he's had' is translated by 'il a eu,' where 'eu' is pronounced like the French 'u' or the German 'ü.' Therefore, 'il a' will be the helping prefix and everything that follows will form the sound word. For example, for yuán, we use 'il a eu l'anneau' (he's got the ring; he's had the ring). We just eliminate or ignore the middle article (l') with this approach, ending up with **eu anneau** as the sound word. By the way, who's got the ring? Gollum, of course!

Yue

This sound is characteristically Chinese and we must get creative to find an equivalent in French (because it is pronounced with the French 'u' followed by the French 'e'.)

For yuē (first tone), we use the French expression '**eu E**' /y ə/, as in the sentence 'Il a **eu E**': 'He's got an E,' on his report card.

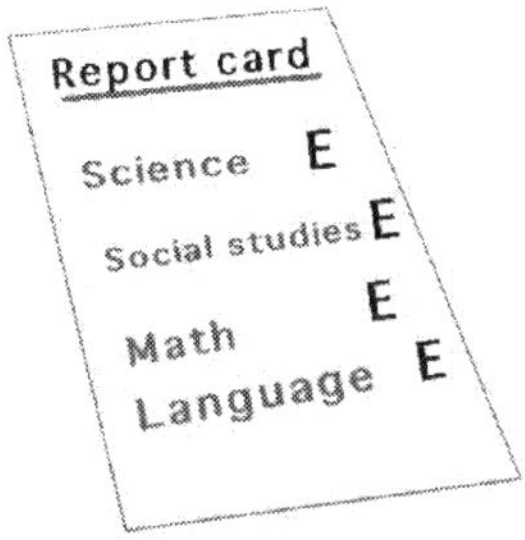

For yuè (fourth tone), we use the French adjective **feuillu** /fœjy/, which means 'leafy, deciduous,' referring here to a tree shedding foliage at the end of the growing season, as opposed to an evergreen tree. It can also be used as a noun when talking about those trees ('un feuillu'). Just add a French 'e' sound in your mind at the end of the sound word. It should sound like '**feuillu-e**.'

Zao

For the second and third tone of this sound, we use a prefix word to introduce a needed 'd' sound at the beginning of the sound word, namely 'Bad' and 'Goddamned'. The sound word is preceded by a superscript d to remind you of this.

[d]Sour wine
Second tone: Think 'Ba**d sour** wine.'

[d]Sarcoma
Third tone: A type of cancer. Think 'Goddamne**d sarcoma**.'

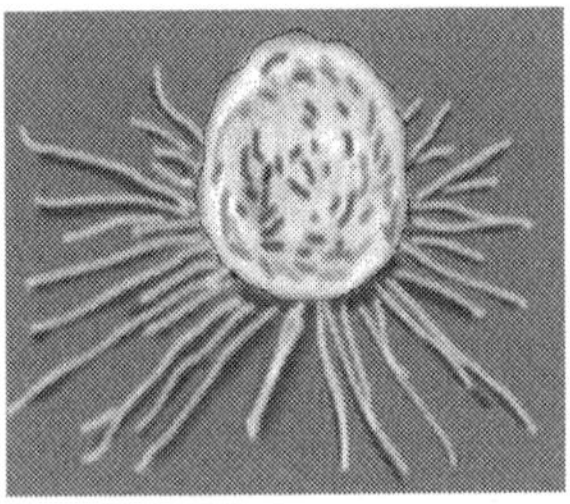

Zhua

For the first and third tone of this sound, we use a prefix word to introduce a needed 'd' sound at the beginning of the sound word. The prefix word is the French feminine adjective 'grande,' meaning 'great.' The sound word is preceded by a superscript **d** to remind you of this.

^{d}Joie
First tone: Think 'Gran**de joie**' /gʁɑ̃d'ʒwa/, which means 'great joy.'

^{d}Jouabilité
Third tone: Think 'gran**de jouabilité**' /gʁɑ̃d'ʒwabilite/, which means 'great playability,' or the ease by which a game can be played.

APPENDIX 3: 214 KANGXI RADICALS

#	Char.	Pinyin	Definition
1	一	yī	One
2	丨	gǔn	Stick
3	丶	zhǔ	Dot
4	丿	piě	Left-falling stroke
5	乙	yì	Second
6	亅	jué	Hook
7	二	èr	Two
8	亠	tóu	Lid
9	人	rén	Man
10	儿	ér	Child, legs
11	入	rù	To enter
12	八	bā	Eight
13	冂	jiǒng	Long cover
14	冖	mì	Top cover
15	冫	bīng	Ice
16	几	jī	Small table
17	凵	qiǎn	Pit
18	刀	dāo	Knife
19	力	lì	Power
20	勹	bāo	To wrap
21	匕	bǐ	Spoon
22	匚	fāng	Box

#	Char.	Pinyin	Definition
23	匸	xì	Box
24	十	shí	Ten
25	卜	bǔ	To predict
26	卩	jié	Kneeling person
27	厂	hàn	Cliff
28	厶	sī	Private
29	又	yòu	Again
30	口	kǒu	Mouth
31	囗	wéi	Enclosure
32	土	tǔ	Earth
33	士	shì	Scholar
34	夂	zhǐ	To walk slowly
35	夊	suī	To walk slowly
36	夕	xī	Evening
37	大	dà	Big
38	女	nǚ	Woman
39	子	zǐ	Child
40	宀	mián	Roof
41	寸	cùn	Inch
42	小	xiǎo	Small
43	尢	wāng	Lame
44	尸	shī	Corpse

#	Char.	Pinyin	Definition
45	屮	chè	Sprout
46	山	shān	Mountain
47	川	chuān	River
48	工	gōng	Work
49	己	jǐ	Oneself
50	巾	jīn	Towel
51	干	gān	Dry
52	幺	yāo	Tiny, cocoon
53	广	guǎn	Extensive
54	廴	yǐn	Long Stride
55	廾	gǒng	Two hands
56	弋	yì	To shoot
57	弓	gōng	Bow
58	彐	jì	Pig snout
59	彡	shān	Hair
60	彳	chì	To step forward
61	心	xīn	Heart
62	戈	gē	Dagger ax
63	户	hù	Door
64	手	shǒu	Hand
65	支	zhī	Branch
66	攵	pū	To hit
67	文	wén	Language
68	斗	dǒu	Cup-shaped
69	斤	jīn	Ax

#	Char.	Pinyin	Definition
70	方	fāng	Square
71	无	wú	Not
72	日	rì	Sun
73	曰	yuē	To say
74	月	yuè	Moon
75	木	mù	Tree
76	欠	qiàn	To lack
77	止	zhǐ	To stop
78	歹	dǎi	Bone fragment
79	殳	shū	Weapon
80	毋	wú	Do not
81	比	bǐ	To compare
82	毛	máo	Fur
83	氏	shì	Clan
84	气	qì	Steam
85	水	shuǐ	Water
86	火	huǒ	Fire
87	爪	zhǎo	Claw
88	父	fù	Father
89	爻	yáo	Mesh
90	爿	qiáng	Half tree
91	片	piàn	Slice
92	牙	yá	Tooth
93	牛	niú	Cow
94	犬	quǎn	Dog

#	Char.	Pinyin	Definition
95	玄	xuán	Mysterious
96	玉	yù	Jade
97	瓜	guā	Melon
98	瓦	wǎ	Tile
99	甘	gān	Sweet
100	生	shēng	Life
101	用	yòng	To use
102	田	tián	Field
103	疋	pǐ	Bolt of cloth
104	疒	chuáng	Sickness
105	癶	bò	To straddle
106	白	bái	White
107	皮	pí	Skin
108	皿	mǐn	Dish
109	目	mù	Eye
110	矛	máo	Spear
111	矢	shǐ	Arrow
112	石	shí	Stone
113	示	shì	Altar
114	禸	rǒu	Rump
115	禾	hé	Grain
116	穴	xué	Cave
117	立	lì	To stand
118	竹	zhú	Bamboo

#	Char.	Pinyin	Definition
119	米	mǐ	Rice
120	糸	mì	Silk
121	缶	fǒu	Jar
122	网	wǎng	Net
123	羊	yáng	Sheep
124	羽	yǔ	Feather
125	老	lǎo	Old
126	而	ér	And
127	耒	lěi	To plow
128	耳	ěr	Ear
129	聿	yù	Writing brush
130	肉	ròu	Meat
131	臣	chén	Minister
132	自	zì	Self
133	至	zhì	To arrive
134	臼	jiù	Mortar
135	舌	shé	Tongue
136	舛	chuǎn	To oppose
137	舟	zhōu	Boat
138	艮	gèn	Tough
139	色	sè	Color
140	艸	cǎo	Blades of grass
141	虍	hǔ	Tiger
142	虫	chóng	Insect

#	Char.	Pinyin	Definition
143	血	xuè	Blood
144	行	xíng	To go
145	衣	yī	Clothes
146	襾	yà	West
147	見	jiàn	To see
148	角	jiǎo	Horn
149	言	yán	Speech
150	谷	gǔ	Valley
151	豆	dòu	Bean
152	豕	shǐ	Pig
153	豸	zhì	Beast of prey
154	貝	bèi	Shell
155	赤	chì	Red
156	走	zǒu	To walk
157	足	zú	Foot
158	身	shēn	Body
159	車	chē	Cart
160	辛	xīn	Bitter
161	辰	chén	Morning
162	辵	chuò	To go hesitantly
163	邑	yì	City
164	酉	yǒu	Alcohol
165	釆	biàn	To distinguish
166	里	lǐ	Village

#	Char.	Pinyin	Definition
167	金	jīn	Gold
168	長	cháng	Long
169	門	mén	Gate
170	阜	fù	Mound
171	隶	lì	Slave
172	隹	zhuī	Short-tailed bird
173	雨	yǔ	Rain
174	青	qīng	Blue-green
175	非	fēi	Not
176	面	miàn	Face
177	革	gé	Leather
178	韋	wéi	Tanned leather
179	韭	jiǔ	Leek
180	音	yīn	Sound
181	頁	yè	Head
182	風	fēng	Wind
183	飛	fēi	To fly
184	食	shí	To eat
185	首	shǒu	Chief
186	香	xiāng	Fragrant
187	馬	mǎ	Horse
188	骨	gǔ	Bone
189	高	gāo	Tall
190	髟	biāo	Long hair

#	Char.	Pinyin	Definition
191	鬥	dòu	To fight
192	鬯	chàng	Sacrificial wine
193	鬲	lì	Cauldron
194	鬼	guǐ	Ghost
195	魚	yú	Fish
196	鳥	niǎo	Bird
197	鹵	lǔ	Brine
198	鹿	lù	Deer
199	麥	mài	Wheat
200	麻	má	Hemp
201	黃	huáng	Yellow
202	黍	shǔ	Millet

#	Char.	Pinyin	Definition
203	黑	hēi	Black
204	黹	zhǐ	Embroidery
205	黽	mǐn	Frog
206	鼎	dǐng	Tripod
207	鼓	gǔ	Drum
208	鼠	shǔ	Rat
209	鼻	bí	Nose
210	齊	qí	Equal, even
211	齒	chǐ	Tooth
212	龍	lóng	Dragon
213	龜	guī	Turtle
214	龠	yuè	Flute

Appendix 4: Heavenly Stems & Earthly Branches

In ancient China, heavenly stems and earthly branches were used to form a calendar system based on a sexagenary cycle. Nowadays, heavenly stems are mostly used in enumerations while earthly branches are used for the 12 animals of the Chinese zodiac.

Heavenly stems			
#	**Char.**	**Pinyin**	**Definition**
1	甲	jiǎ	First
2	乙	yǐ	Second
3	丙	bǐng	Third
4	丁	dīng	Fourth
5	戊	wù	Fifth
6	己	jǐ	Self
7	庚	gēng	Age of a person
8	辛	xīn	Hardship
9	壬	rén	Burden
10	癸	guǐ	Menstruation

Earthly branches			
#	**Char.**	**Pinyin**	**Zodiac animal**
1	子	zǐ	Rat
2	丑	chǒu	Ox
3	寅	yín	Tiger
4	卯	mǎo	Rabbit
5	辰	chén	Dragon
6	巳	sì	Snake
7	午	wǔ	Horse
8	未	wèi	Sheep
9	申	shēn	Monkey
10	酉	yǒu	Rooster
11	戌	xū	Dog
12	亥	hài	Pig

Appendix 5: Order for Writing Chinese Characters

Although this series does not show you how to write characters but rather how to read them, having some basic notions regarding the order in which strokes are written is useful. The reason is because this order is reflected in the order in which the building blocks are presented and listed under each character. Basically, all you need to know is this. When writing a Chinese character:

- Horizontal strokes are written before vertical strokes.
- A character is written from left to right.
- A character is written from top to bottom.
- When a character is framed in a box, the top of the box is written first, the content is written next and the box is closed last.
- In symmetrical characters, the middle is written before the sides.

Index 1: Character Meanings (Real and Fictitious)

Definitions (real and fictitious) associated with each character or building block (with the exception of non-characters) are listed below, along with the character sequence number. Fictitious meanings are indicated by an asterisk *.

7

7-9 p.m. 戌 225

9

9-11 a.m. 巳 299

A

A few, several 些 317
A little bit 点[點] 366
Ability 才 84
Above 上 122
Abundance 八 55
Accompanying action 着[著] 205A
Act, to 为[為] 146A
Action in progress 着[著] 205A
Advance, go forward, to 进[進] 311
Adverbial particle 地 128B
Affected by, to be 着[著] 205C
Africa 非 80
Again 又 71
Again 重 262B
Age 年 207
All 全 361
All 都 285A
All around 八 55
Almost 几[幾] 229A
Alone 单[單] 385
Already 已 300
Also 也 94
Also 又 71
Also 还[還] 308A
Altar 示 233
Although 然 259
America 美 390
Amidst 中 121
Among, between 间[間] 372A
Ancestor 示 233
Ancient 古 116
And 和 148A
And 而 191
And, furthermore 并[並] 380A
And, together with 与[與] 342
Angry eyes * 吅 384
Animals 只[隻] 328B
Answer, respond, to 应[應] 383B
Answer, to 对[對] 187
Appearance 样[樣] 319
Apply, attach, to 着[著] 205D
Apply, to 应[應] 383B
Appropriate 当[當] 290B
Armed man * 350
Armless child * 了 83A
Army 军[軍] 338
Arrive, reach a place, to 到 151
Arrive, to 来[來] 145
Arrow 弋 89
Arrow 矢 88
As if 如 284
Ashtray * 臼 46
Asia 亚[亞] 379
Ask, inquire, to 问[問] 373
Aspect, side 面 295A
Assemble, meet, gather, to 会[會] .. 182A
Assorted 什 276B
At a given time or place 当[當] 290A
Awesome 牛 35
Ax 斤 256

B

Backsaw * 乍 243
Bald 兀 347
Bamboo 竹 350
Barbed wire * 111

Barley 麦[麥].. 294
Baseball * 九.. 58
Basis, foundation 本.. 322
Battle 战[戰].. 386
Be able to, to 会[會].. 182A
Be capable, to 能.. 189
Be, to 是.. 78
Beans 豆.. 332
Bear 熊.. 190
Beautiful 美.. 390
Because 因.. 327
Because of 为[為].. 146B
Become, to 为[為].. 146A
Become, to 成.. 268
Beg, to 乞.. 14
Beginning 元.. 348
Beginning, first 头[頭].. 333
Believe, suppose, to 想.. 330
Below 下.. 123
Bent 曲.. 387A
Bent in half * 乚.. 296
Beret * ノ.. 4
Big 大.. 27
Bind, tie, to 束.. 261
Black 黑.. 364
Blade 刃.. 110
Blade of grass 屮.. 40
Blame, to 斥.. 257
Blue-green 青.. 356
Boar 豕.. 38
Boat anchor * 于[於].. 199
Boats 只[隻].. 328B
Body 体[體].. 388
Body part * 肉.. 48
Bolt of cloth 疋.. 77
Bone 骨.. 209
Bone fragment 歹.. 252
Books 本.. 322
Both 两[兩].. 371
Bother, to 麻.. 279
Bow 弓.. 215
Bow down, to * 卩.. 297
Bow-shaped 弓.. 215
Breasts 母.. 334
Breed, species 种[種].. 263A
Briefly 一.. 15
Bright 明.. 358
Broom head * ヨ.. 39
Buddhist temple 寺.. 161
Bug 虫[蟲].. 230
Bull's-eye 的.. 69C
Bunch * 勹.. 67
Bundle 束.. 261
But 但.. 326
But 可.. 155
But 而.. 191
Butcher * 刖.. 323
By means of 以.. 152

C

Cage * 冂.. 12
Call a name on a roll, to 点[點].. 366
Can 可.. 155
Can do 能.. 189
Can(v) 会[會].. 182A
Capability 能.. 189
Capital 京.. 172
Capital (finance) 本.. 322
Capital city 都.. 285B
Car 车[車].. 337
Cart, chariot 车[車].. 337
Cash, to 兑[兌].. 158
Castle * 广[廣].. 223
Catch fire, to 着[著].. 205C
Category 门[門].. 119
Catty 斤.. 256
Cause 因.. 327
Cause 由.. 217
Cause, enable, to 使.. 355
Ceiling * 一.. 15
Center 中.. 121
Center 心.. 321
Chief 长[長].. 237B
Chief 首.. 248
Child 儿[兒].. 52
Child 子.. 82
Chinese inch 寸.. 160
Choose, to 取.. 377
Choose, to 采[採].. 143A
Chop, cut, to 七.. 57
Christmas carols choir * 同.. 286A
Church *.. 140
Citizen 民.. 346
City wall 阝.. 107
Clam, mussel 贝[貝].. 287

Clan, family 氏 345
Classics, scripture 经[經] 273
Claw 爪 138A
Clerk 吏 354
Cliff 厂[廠] 222
Clothes 衣 234
Clothes hamper * 其 274
Cloud 云[雲] 180A
Cloudy 云[雲] 180A
Coat hook * 7
Cobra * 巴 301
Cocoon 幺 227
Coerce, to 要 165B
Combine, to 并[併] 380B
Come into existence, to 发[發] 239A
Come, to 来[來] 145
Common 公 352
Complete 十 59
Completion of a verbal action 到 151
Computer * 里 246A
Concern, involve, to 关[關] 363
Conform with, to 入 22
Consider, treat as, to 当[當] 290B
Control, restrain, to 束 261
Cork 覀 163
Corner * 6
Corpse 尸[屍] 254
Correct, just right 正 76A
Correct, right 然 259
Could 可 155
Country 国[國] 149
Couple, pair 对[對] 187
Courses of study 门[門] 119
Cover 冂 12
Cover 冖 11
Cow 牛 35
Cowboy hat * 亠 49
Cowrie 贝[貝] 287
Crooked, distorted 曲 387A
Cross * 十 59
Cross, to 过[過] 211
Crown * 冖 11
Crutches * 九 173
Cubes of food 丁 153
Culture 文 101
Cupboard * 丬[爿] 369
Custom, manner 风[風] 231

D

Dagger ax 戈 90
Dangerous * 乂 99
Dark 黑 364
Dart 矢 88
Dawn 旦 193
Day 天 31
Day 日 43
Daybreak 旦 193
Dead 死 253
Defend, to 戍 226
Demand, to 要 165B
Department 门[門] 119
Destroy, to 戌 225
Determine, to 定 305
Develop, to 发[發] 239A
Devilish * 丷 55
Did it 了 83A
Die young, to 夭 32
Die, to 死 253
Direction 向 166
Direction 方 198
Direction 面 295A
Dirt 土 85
Divide, to 分 306A
Divining rod * 卜 18A
Do, to 作 244
Do, to 做 245
Doer 者 203
Dog 犬 29
Dog collar * 丿 4
Dollar 元 348
Dollar sign * 弗 349
Dome * 170
Door 户[戶] 255
Doorway 门[門] 119
Dot 丶 3
Down 下 123
Draft document 艹 131
Drag, to * 240
Dramas 出 177
Drive a vehicle, to 开[開] 325
Drive a wedge between, to 间[間] ... 372B
Drop 丶 3
Drudge, to * 者 203
Drugstore * 亚[亞] 379

Dry 干[乾] 133B
Dusk 夕 251

E

Each other 相 329A
Ear 耳 376
Early 早 130
Earth 地 128A
Edible roots 卜 18B
Eiffel tower * 高 171
Eight 八 55
Elbow * 厶 10
Elder brother 兄 157
Elderly 丈 28
Emit, to 发[發] 239A
Encircle, to 口 42
Enclose, to 口 42
Enclosure 口 42
Enter, to 入 22
Enter, to 进[進] 311
Entire 全 361
Entirely 都 285A
Especially 尤 174
Esteem, to 尚 168
Eternity 永 318
Evening 夕 251
Examine, appraise, to 相 329B
Exceed, to 出 177
Excessively 太 30
Exchange (money), to 兑[兌] 158
Exist, live, to 在 86
Exit, to 出 177
Experience (marker) 过[過] 211
Experienced 老 202
Extend, spread, to 乍 243
Extensive 广[廣] 223
External 外 367
Extremely 很 375
Extremely 甚 275
Eye 目 200

F

Face 面 295A
Factory 厂[廠] 222
Fall asleep, to 着[著] 205C
Family 家 260
Family name 氏 345
Famous, prominent 著 204
Fault, mistake 尤 174
Feeling, emotion 情 357
Fell a tree, to 采[採] 143A
Fetus 巳 299
Fief 采[埰] 143B
Field 田 195
Field hockey stick * 265
Fifth 戊 224
Fight, to 战[戰] 386
Films 部 315
Finish, complete, to 成 268
Finish, to 了 83B
Fire 火 127
First month of the lunar year 正 76B
Fishhook * 乙 13
Five 五 54
Fix, to 定 305
Flame 火 127
Flat cap * 冖 5
Flat, thin piece 片 368
Flee, to 亡 51
Floor * 一 15
Flower * 艹 131
Follow, to 从[從] 216
Footprint 止 75
For nothing, in vain 白 45
For the first time 乍 243
For the sake of 为[為] 146B
Force 力 108
Foreign 外 367
Forest 森 278
Forever 永 318
Former 前 324
Four 四 53
Fourth 丁 153
Frame, to 口 42
France 法 282
Free of charge 白 45
Friend 友 212
From 由 217
From a point on 以 152
From, by, than, out of 于[於] 199
From, since 从[從] 216

G

Gap, space in between 间[間] 372B
Garrison 戍 226
Gate 门[門] 119
Gathering * 178
Gender 性 359
General, commander-in-chief 将[將] 370B
Generation 世 63
Gentle, mild 和 148A
Get, fetch, to 取 377
Get, to 得 194B
Give back, repay, to 还[還] 308B
Give birth, to 生 188
Give, to 与[與] 342
Glass bell * 冂 12
Gloomy 森 278
Go down, to 下 123
Go over, to 过[過] 211
Go upwards, to 上 122
Go, leave, to 去 281
Go, travel, walk, to 行 250A
Gold 金 124
Good 好 312A
Good fortune 幸 134
Government 政 389
Gown * 235
Grab, to 取 377
graceful, supple 夭 32
Grain 禾 136
Grass 艹 131
Grazing cows * 61
Great Dane * 大 27
Great-grandfather 曾 181B
Great-grandson 曾 181B
Grip, to 爪 138A
Ground 土 85
Ground 地 128A
Ground level * 一 15
Group, circle of people 林 277
Grow, develop, to 长[長] 237B
Guard, to 把 343A
Guardian angel * 己 298

H

Hair (human head) 发[髮] 239B
Hair (on the head) 彡 103
Hairy head * 头[頭] 333
Half-kilometer 里 246A
Hand 手 73
Hand broom * 彐 39
Hand holding something 聿 264
Handle 把 343B
Handyman * 人 23
Hard, strong 固 117
Hardship 辛 135
Harmony 和 148A
Hat * 冖 11
Haul up, to * 142
Have to do with, to 干 133A
Have, possess, to 有 87
He 他 95
He, she, it 其 274
Head 头[頭] 333
Head 首 248
Head (human) 页[頁] 331
Headless horse * 与[與] 342
Heart 心 321
Heaven 天 31
Heavenly stems 干 133A
Heavy 大 27
Heavy 重 262A
Helmet * 冂 12
Hemp 麻 279
Her 她 96
Herb 艹 131
High 高 171
Him 他 95
Him, her, it (Classical Chinese) 之 206
Himself, herself 自 201
His, her, its, theirs 其 274
History 史 353
Hit, to 攵 220
Hobby 好 312B
Hold a meeting, to 开[開] 325
Hold a pen in hand, to * 72
Hold, grasp, to 把 343A
Home 家 260
Hook * 乙 13
Hooked, to be * 乙 13

Horizon * 一 15
Horns * ⺌ 55
Horse *马[馬]* 36
Hot pepper * 辛 135
House 宀 50
Household 户[戶] 255
Houses, schools 所 258
How many 几[幾] 229B
How much 几[幾] 229B
However 但 326
However 可 155
However, but 然 259
Human legs * 儿 52
Hundred 百 64
Husband 丈 28
Husband 夫 33

I

I 我 91
I-beam * 工 271
Ice 冰 129
Icy 冰 129
Idea 意 339
If 如 284
Ignite, to 点[點] 366
Important 要 165A
Important 重 262A
In addition 还[還] 308A
In front 前 324
In order to 以 152
In pain * 卫 296
In reality 的 69B
In the middle of my walk * 行 250A
In the past 曾 181A
In, at, to 于[於] 199
Inch 寸 160
Incident 故 242
Incident, event 事 267
Income 入 22
Individual *个[個]* 118
Industry 业[業] 185
Inferior, second-rate 亚[亞] 379
Inflexible, rigid 死 253
Insect 虫[蟲] 230
Inside *内[內]* 24
Inside 里[裡] 246B
Insignificant 麽[麼] 280B
Intention 意 339
Interior *内[內]* 24
Interrogative suffix 么[麼] 280A
Interstice, interval 间[間] 372B
Introduce object of main verb 将[將] 370A
Invite, request, to 将[將] 370C
Issue, to 发[發] 239A
It 它 98
It 牠 97

J

Jade 玉 21
Jaw 呙[咼] 210
Jaws of life * 341
Jester hat * 141
Join in the singing, to 和 148B
Join, merge, to 并[併] 380B
Jumping sheep * 羊 37
Just 就 175
Just now 才 84

K

Key point 关[關] 363
Kilt * 236
Kind, type 种[種] 263A
King 王 19
King (chess piece) 将[將] 370B
Knead, to 和 148C
Knife 刀 109
Know, to 知 360
Knowledge, information 知 360

L

Lace * 爻 100
Lack 无[無] 340
Ladle 勺 68
Lame 尢 173
Lane, alley 同 286B
Language 文 101
Law, rule 法 282
Learn, to 学[學] 283
Left hand 70
Left-falling stroke 丿 4
Length 长[長] 237A
Liable to, to be 好 312B

Lid * 冖 11
Life 生 188
Like that, thus 然 259
Like, be fond of, to 好 312B
Limping man * 丈 28
Line of business 行 250B
Line, column of print 行 250B
Lines 爻 100
Lining 里[裡] 246B
List, form 单[單] 385
Lit, to be 着[著] 205C
Literature 文 101
Little 寸 160
Located at, in, on, to be 在 86
Location 面 295A
Long 长[長] 237A
Long cover 冂 12
Long hair 髟 238
Look after, to 看 304B
Look for, to 找 92
Looks, appearance 相 329B
Lord 主 20
Lose, to 亡 51
Loud 大 27
Luck 幸 134

M

Machine 机[機] 344
Machines 部 315
Main 主 20
Main 大 27
Major 大 27
Make a fortune, to 发[發] 239A
Make progress, to 彳 192
Make trouble, to 和 148D
Make, to 作 244
Make, to 做 245
Maker 者 203
Male 丁 153
Man 丁 153
Man 人 23
Manage, to 经[經] 273
Manner 样[樣] 319
Manure * 釆 144
Many, a lot of 多 269
Marker for pre-verbal objects 把 343A
Married woman 太 30
Mask *, hood * 冂 12
Master 主 20
Matter 物 381
Matter, affair 事 267
Maybe, possibly 或 93
Me 我 91
Meaning 意 339
Measuring spoon * 勺 68
Meat 肉 48
Meeting 会[會] 182A
Melon 瓜 139
Mesh * 爻 100
Messenger, envoy 使 355
Metal 金 124
Metallic 金 124
Meter 米 137
Method 法 282
Metropolis 都 285B
Middle 中 121
Military 军[軍] 338
Mind 心 321
Ministry, department 部 315
Minor official 吏 354
Miss, long for, to 想 330
Mix with water, to 和 148C
Mix, blend, stir, to 和 148D
Model, pattern 样[樣] 319
Moment 会[會] 182B
Money 贝[貝] 287
Month 月 47
Moon 月 47
Mortar 臼 46
Mortar-shaped 臼 46
Mosque 寺 161
Extremely 150
Mother 母 334
Mound 阜 106
Mound 阝 106
Mountain 山 176
Mouth 口 41
Move, to 动[動] 292
Moves 着[著] 205B
Muscle, flesh 肉 48
Must 得 194C
Mutually 相 329A
Myself 自 201

N

Nail 钉[釘] 154A
Nail * 丁 153
Nail, to 钉[釘] 154B
Nail, to * 丁 153
Nation 国[國] 149
Nature, character 性 359
Need to, have to, to 得 194C
Needle * 十 59
Negligible 幺 227
Next 下 123
Nine 九 58
No 不 79
Noise 音 314
Nominal localizer 头[頭] 333
Nose 自 201
Nose * 厶 10
Not 不 79
Not 弗 349
Not (negative prefix for verbs) 没[沒] 291A
Not at all 并[並] 380A
Not have 没[沒] 291A
Not, do not 勿 81
Not, nin-, un- 非 80
Nothing, none 无[無] 340
Noun suffix 儿[兒] 52
Noun suffix 子 82
Noun suffix 巴 301
Now 现[現] 289
Number (no.) 第 351
Numerous 广[廣] 223

O

O'clock 点[點] 366, 366
Oat 麦[麥] 294
Object 物 381
Observe, to 见[見] 288
Obtain, to 得 194B
Obvious 明 358
Obvious, clear 白 45
Occidental, western 西 164
Occupation 丁 153
Occupy, take possession, to 占[佔] . 365B
Occur, to 出 177
Octopus * 八 55
Of 的 69A
Of (Classical Chinese) 之 206
Of course 固 117
Offend, to 干 133A
Offer, to 与[與] 342
OK 行 250A
Old man 老 202
Older brother 哥 156
On purpose 故 242
One 一 15
One dollar * 弗 349
One of a pair of things 只[隻] 328B
One's own 本 322
Oneself 自 201
Only then 才 84
Only, merely 但 326
Open, to 开[開] 325
Opening 口 41
Openly 敞 221
Opera 曲 387B
Opportunity 机[機] 344
Oppose, to 对[對] 187
Or 或 93
Origin 本 322
Original, former 故 242
Ostrich * 隹 310
Ought to 应[應] 383A
Ounce 两[兩] 371
Outside 外 367
Outstanding 尤 174
Over 上 122
Ox 牛 35
Oxen, livestock 头[頭] 333

P

Page 页[頁] 331
Parasol * 9
Part, fraction 分 306A
Pass (time), to 过[過] 211
Pass through, to 经[經] 273
Pass through, to 贯[貫] 335
Pass, barrier 关[關] 363
Pavement * 行 250A
Pedestal * 兀 347
People 民 346
Perhaps 或 93
Period 时[時] 162

Perish, to 亡 51
Perpetual 永 318
Person 人 23
Persons 个[個] 118
Persuade, to 说[說] 159B
Photo, film 片 368
Photograph 相 329B
Pick, to 采[採] 143A
Picket fence * 61
Pierce, to 贯[貫] 335
Pig 豕 38
Pig snout ヨ 39
Pit bull * 犬 29
Pitchfork * 中 40
Place 地 128A
Place 所 258
Place 方 198
Plant * 293
Plant, cultivate, to 种[種] 263B
Plays 出 177
Plow * 氏 345
Plural marker 们[們] 120
Pockmarked 麻 279
Podium * 105
Poems, songs 首 248
Pole * 丨 1
Political 政 389
Politics 政 389
Ponytails 362
Possibility 了 83B
Possibility 得 194A
Power 力 108
Precisely, indeed 就 175
Predict, to 卜 18A
Present 现[現] 289
Previous 上 122
Previous 前 324
Prime minister 相 329B
Princess * 睘 307
Principal 主 20
Principle, doctrine 道 249
Principle, theory 理 320
Private 厶 10
Problem, issue 问[問] 373
Produce, to 出 177
Profession 行 250B
Profession, occupation 业[業] 185
Progress, to 彳 192
Projectile * 殳 232
Promise, consent, to 应[應] 383B
Public 公 352
Python * 也 94

Q

Question, interrogate, to 问[問] 373

R

Radar * 里 246A
Rain 雨 179
Rain, to 雨 179
Raw, unripe 生 188
Real 实[實] 336
Reason 因 327
Reason 由 217
Reason, cause 故 242
Reason, logic 理 320
Reject, to 斥 257
Remove, to 去 281
Repeat, to 重 262B
Return, come back, to 还[還] 308B
Rice 米 137
Rifle * 8
Right away 就 175
Right hand 又 71
Rise, get up, to 起 303
River 川 270
Road * 辶[辵] 104
Robe 衣 234
Roof 宀 50
Roots, stems 本 322
Row 行 250B
Rumors 风[風] 231
Rump 内 196
Run away, to * 方 198
Running sheep * 羊 37

S

Same, similar 同 286A
Say, communicate, to 道 249
Say, state, to 云 180B
Say, to 说[說] 159A

Scissors * 乂 99
Scorpion 万[萬] 197
Search for, to 找 92
Second 乙 13
Second 亚[亞] 379
Section, part, division 部 315
See, look at, to 看 304A
See, to 见[見] 288
Seed 子 82
Seed 种[種] 263A
Self 己 298
Send out, to 发[發] 239A
Send, to 着[著] 205D
Separate, divide in half, to 八 55
Serve as, to 当[當] 290A
Set up, to 立 112
Seven 七 57
Several 几[幾] 229B
Sew on, to 钉[釘] 154B
Sex 性 359
Shall, will 要 165A
Shampoo * 发 239A
She 她 96
Shears * 乂 99
Sheep 羊 37
Sheet 单[單] 385
Sheets of paper 片 368
Shellfish 贝[貝] 287
Shelter * 冂 12
Shepherd * 着[著] 205A
Shield 干 133A
Shoot, to 弋 89
Should, must 应[應] 383A
Should, ought to 当[當] 290A
Shovel * 而 191
Show, appear, to 现[現] 289
Show, reveal, to 示 233
Shut, to 关[關] 363
Side 方 198
Side by side 并[並] 380A
Silk thread 糸 228
Silky * 糸 228
Single 单[單] 385
Situation, circumstances 情 357
Six 六 56
Skeleton 冎 208
Skirt * 236
Sky 天 31
Slice 片 368
Slide * 丿 4
Slide, to * 丿 4
Sling * 殳 232
Sling, to * 殳 232
Slit * 一 15
Small 小 167
Small table 几[幾] 229A
Small thing * 丶 3
Small, indefinite amount 些 317
Soil, earth 土 85
Solid 固 117
Solid 实[實] 336
Some 些 317
Son, daughter 儿[兒] 52
Sound 音 314
Space 间[間] 372A
Spacious 敞 221
Speak, say, talk, to 曰 44
Speak, say, to 言 102
Speak, to 说[說] 159A
Speaking mouth * 曰 44
Speech 言 102
Spicy, hot 辛 135
Spit out, to 咅 313
Spoon 匕 66
Spoon guy * 匕 66
Spots, specks 点[點] 366
Sprout 由 217
Sprout, to 由 217
Square 方 198
Squash 瓜 139
Stand, to 立 112
Standing grain 禾 136
Standing hanger * 尔[爾] 183
Standing with the legs spread apart * 癶 214
Staple * 寸 160
Staple gun * 寸 160
Staple, to * 寸 160
Start, begin, to 起 303
Start, to 开[開] 325
Step forward, to 彳 192
Stick * 丨 1
Stick * 亅 2
Still, yet, even 还[還] 308A
Stop, cease, to 已 300
Stop, to 止 75

Straight 正 76A
Straighten, to * 疋 76A
Straightforward, blunt 艮 374
Stream 川 270
Strength 力 108
Strike, to 攵 220
String together, to 贯[貫] 335
Stripes 彡 103
Stubborn 艮 374
Study, to 学[學] 283
Subjects 民 346
Subscribe, order, to 定 305
Substance 体[體] 388
Substantive suffix 头[頭] 333
Successful result of a verb 着[著] 205C
Such as, like 如 284
Suddenly 乍 243
Suddenly 兀 347
Suffix (–ness, –ism or –ity) 性 359
Suffix for profession 家 260
Suitable, adequate 当[當] 290B
Sun 日 43
Sunflower * 早 130
Superhero * 隹 382
Surface 面 295A
Surname 氏 345
Swear, to 矢 88
Sword * 戈 90

T

Take a shower, to * 友 213
Take, to 取 377
Talent 才 84
Talkative * 吅 384
Tall * 169
Taoism 道 249
Target 的 69C
Telephone pole * 34
Tell fortune, to 卜 18A
Tell fortunes, to 占 365A
Ten 什 276B
Ten 十 59
Ten past ten * 132
Ten thousand 万[萬] 197
Tender 夭 32
Tennis court * 田 195
Tent * 9
Terracotta warrior * 曾 181A
That 那 114
That, such 其 274
That's right 对[對] 187
The most 最 378
There is, there are 有 87
Therefore 所 258
These 这[這] 113
Thing 物 381
Things 个[個] 118
Things with handles 把 343A
Think that, to 看 304A
Think, to 想 330
Third 丙 25
Thirty 卅 62
This 这[這] 113
This, these 此 316
Those 那 114
Thou 尔[爾] 183
Thought 意 339
Thousand 千 65
Thread 糸 228
Three 三 17
Throwing star * 戊 224
Thus 尔[爾] 183
Tie up, to 勹 67
Tightrope walker * 才 84
Time 时[時] 162
Time duration 间[間] 372A
Timex time * 132
Tingling 麻 279
Tiny 幺 227
Together 同 286A
Together 起 303
Together with 并[並] 380A
Tone 音 314
Top cover 冖 11
Touch, contact, to 着[著] 205D
Touch, to 着[著] 205C
Tough 艮 374
Tough guy 艮 374
Towards 向 166
Tower crane * [巠] 272
Towering 兀 347
Tree 木 125
Tricks 着[著] 205B

Troops 部 315
True 实[實] 336
Trunk (tree, body) 干[幹] 133C
Try to find, to 找 92
T-shaped * 丁 153
Tune, song 曲 387B
Tuque * 冖 11
Turn into, to 成 268
Turn off, to 关[關] 363
Turn the soil over, to * 干 133A
Turning stroke ㇇ 5
Twenty 廿 60
Two 两[兩] 371
Two 二 16
Two hands 廾 74
Type, kind 样[樣] 319

U

Umbrella * 9
Uncork, to * 覀 163
Uncover, to * 142
Under 下 123
Understand, to 了 83B
Unfamiliar 生 188
Union, group, association 会[會] 182A
Units of length, weight, money, time 分 306A
Until 至 150
Up to 到 151
Up to 至 150
Upright 正 76A
Use, employ, to 使 355
Use, to 用 247
Using 以 152

V

Value, to 尚 168
Vehicle 车[車] 337
Verb suffix 得 194A
Very 很 375
Vicious 歹 252
Village 里 246A
Vomit, to 音 313
Vow, to 矢 88

W

Walk slowly, to 夂 219
Walk, to 走 302
Walking legs * 儿 52
Walkway * 行 250A
Want to, plan to, to 想 330
Want, to 要 165A
War 战[戰] 386
Wasp * 彡 103
Water 水 126
Watery 水 126
Way, path 道 249
Wear clothes, to 着[著] 205D
Weather 天 31
Well (source) 井 309
West 西 164
What, that which 所 258
What? 么[麼] 280A
What? 什 276A
What? 哪 115
Whatever 么[麼] 280A
Wheat 麦[麥] 294
Where? 哪 115
Which? 哪 115
White 白 45
Whole 全 361
Whole, all 一 15
Wicked 歹 252
Wild dog * 犬 29
Will, shall 将[將] 370A
Wind 风[風] 231
Window 口 41
Winery * 芈 186
Wish, desire, to 意 339
Witch hat * 亠 49
With 同 286A
With 和 148A
Woman 女 26
Wood 木 125
Wooden 木 125
Woods, grove 林 277
Word 言 102
Work 工 271
Work, do, manage, to 干[幹] 133C
Works of literature 部 315
World 世 63
Worm 虫[蟲] 230

Wrap, to 勹 67
Wristwatch * 132
Write books, to 著 204
Writing brush 聿 266

Y

Yard, depot 厂[廠] 222
Year 年 207
Yes 是 78
Yet 而 191
You 你 184
Young people 青 356
Yuan (Chinese monetary unit) 元 348
Yuan dynasty 元 348

Z

Zipper * 王 19
Zorro * 之 206
Zzzz... * 之 206

Index 2: Character Pronunciations, Ordered by Pinyin

Pronunciations in pinyin of the characters and building blocks are listed below, along with the character sequence number. Some characters have more than one pronunciation.

bā 八 55
bā 巴 301
bá 犮 213
bà 把 343B
bǎ 把 343A
bái 白 45
bǎi 百 64
bàn 办[辦] 147
bāo 勹 67
bèi 贝[貝] 287
běn 本 322
bǐ 匕 66
biàn 釆 144
biāo 髟 238
bīng 冰 129
bǐng 丙 25
bìng 并[併] 380B
bìng 并[並] 380A
bō 癶 214
bo 卜 18B
bǔ 卜 18A
bù 不 79
bù 部 315
cái 才 84
cǎi 采[採] 143A
cài 采[埰] 143B
cǎo 草/艹 131
céng 曾 181A
chǎng 厂[廠] 222
chǎng 敞 221
cháng 长[長] 237A
chē 车[車] 337
chè 屮 40
chéng 成 268
chì 彳 192
chì 斥 257
chóng 虫[蟲] 230
chóng 重 262B
chū 出 177
chuān 川 270
chuò 辶[辵] 104
cǐ 此 316
cóng 从[從] 216
cùn 寸 160
dà 大 27
dǎi 歹 252
dān 单[單] 385
dàn 旦 193
dàn 但 326
dàng 当[當] 290B
dāng 当[當] 290A
dāo 刀 109
dào 到 151
dào 道 249
de 得 194A
dé 得 194B
de 的 69A
de 地 128B
děi 得 194C
dí 的 69B
dì 的 69C
dì 地 128A
dì 第 351
diǎn 点[點] 366
dīng 丁 153
dìng 钉[釘] 154B
dīng 钉[釘] 154A
dìng 定 305
dòng 动[動] 292
dōu 都 285A
dòu 豆 332
dū 都 285B
duì 对[對] 187
duì 兑[兌] 158
duō 多 269
ér 儿[兒] 52
ér 而 191
ěr 尔[爾] 183
ěr 耳 376
èr 二 16
fā 发[發] 239A
fà 发[髮] 239B
fǎ 法 282
fāng 方 198
fēi 非 80
fèn 分 306B
fēn 分 306A
fēng 风[風] 231
fū 夫 33
fú 弗 349
fù 阜/阝 106
gān 干 133A
gàn 干[幹] 133C
gān 干[乾] 133B
gāo 高 171
gē 戈 90
gē 哥 156
gè 个[個] 118
gěn 艮 374
gōng 工 271
gōng 弓 215
gōng 公 352
gǒng 廾 74
gǔ 古 116
gǔ 骨 209
gù 固 117
gù 故 242
guā 瓜 139
guǎ 冎 208
guān 关[關] 363
guàn 贯[貫] 335
guǎng 广[廣] 223
gǔn 丨 1
guō 呙[咼] 210

guó 国[國]..............149
guò 过[過]..............211
hái 还[還]..............308A
háng 行..............250B
hào 好..............312B
hǎo 好..............312A
hé 禾..............136
hé 和..............148A
hè 和..............148B
hēi 黑..............364
hěn 很..............375
hòu 后[後]..............241
hù 户[戶]..............255
huán 还[還]..............308B
huán 睘..............307
huáng 黄[黃]..............218
huì 会[會]..............182A
huǐ 会[會]..............182B
huó 和..............148C
huò 和..............148D
huǒ 火..............127
huò 或..............93
jī 机[機]..............344
jǐ 几[幾]..............229B
jī 几[幾]..............229A
jǐ 己..............298
jì 彐..............39
jiā 家..............260
jiàn 间[間]..............372B
jiān 间[間]..............372A
jiàn 见[見]..............288
jiàng 将[將]..............370B
jiāng 将[將]..............370A
jié 卩..............297
jié 㔾..............296
jīn 斤..............256
jīn 金..............124
jìn 进[進]..............311
jīng [巠]..............272
jīng 京..............172
jīng 经[經]..............273
jǐng 井..............309
jiōng 冂..............12
jiǔ 九..............58
jiù 臼..............46
jiù 就..............175
jué 亅..............2
jūn 军[軍]..............338
kāi 开[開]..............325
kàn 看..............304A
kān 看..............304B
kě 可..............155
kǒu 口..............41
kuài 会[會]..............182C
lái 来[來]..............145
lǎo 老..............202
le 了..............83A
lǐ 里..............246A
lǐ 里[裡]..............246B
lǐ 理..............320
lì 力..............108
lì 立..............112
lì 吏..............354
liǎng 两[兩]..............371
liǎo 了..............83B
lín 林..............277
liù 六..............56
má 麻..............279
mǎ 马[馬]..............36
mài 麦[麥]..............294
me 么[麼]..............280A
méi 没[沒]..............291A
měi 美..............390
mén 门[門]..............119
men 们[們]..............120
mǐ 米..............137
mì 冖..............11
mián 宀..............50
miàn 面..............295A
miàn 面[麵]..............295B
mín 民..............346
míng 明..............358
mó 麽[麼]..............280B
mò 没[沒]..............291B
mǔ 母..............334
mù 木..............125
mù 目..............200
nǎ 哪..............115
nà 那..............114
nèi 内[內]..............24
néng 能..............189
nǐ 你..............184
nián 年..............207
niàn 廿..............60
niè 聿..............264
niú 牛..............35
nǚ 女..............26
pǐ 疋..............77
piàn 片..............368
piě 丿..............4
pǒu 咅..............313
pū 攵..............220
qī 七..............57
qí 其..............274
qǐ 乞..............14
qǐ 起..............303
qiān 千..............65
qián 前..............324
qiāng 将[將]..............370C
qiáng 丬[爿]..............369
qīng 青..............356
qíng 情..............357
qǔ 曲..............387B
qū 曲..............387A
qǔ 取..............377
qù 去..............281
quán 全..............361
quǎn 犬..............29
rán 然..............259
rén 人..............23
rèn 刃..............110
rì 日..............43
róu 内..............196
ròu 肉..............48
rú 如..............284
rù 入..............22
sà 卅..............62
sān 三..............17
sēn 森..............278
shān 彡..............103
shān 山..............176
shàng 上..............122
shàng 尚..............168
sháo 勺..............68
shén 什..............276A
shèn 甚..............275
shēng 生..............188
shí 什..............276B
shī 尸[屍]..............254
shí 十..............59
shí 时[時]..............162
shí 实[實]..............336
shǐ 史..............353
shǐ 矢..............88

shǐ 豕........................38
shǐ 使........................355
shì 氏........................345
shì 示........................233
shì 世........................63
shì 事........................267
shì 是........................78
shǒu 手........................73
shǒu 首........................248
shū 殳........................232
shù 戍........................226
shù 束........................261
shuǐ 水........................126
shuì 说[說]............159B
shuō 说[說].......... 159A
sī 厶........................10
sī 糸........................228
sǐ 死........................253
sì 巳........................299
sì 四........................53
sì 寺........................161
suī 隹........................382
suǒ 所........................258
tā 他........................95
tā 它........................98
tā 她........................96
tā 牠........................97
tài 太........................30
tǐ 体[體]..................388
tiān 天........................31
tián 田........................195
tóng 同................ 286A
tòng 同................286B
tóu 头[頭]..............333
tóu 亠........................49
tǔ 土........................85
wài 外........................367
wàn 万[萬].............197
wáng 亡........................51
wáng 王........................19
wāng 尢........................173
wéi 囗........................42
wéi 为[為]........... 146A
wèi 为[為]............146B
wén 文........................101
wèn 问[問].............373
wǒ 我........................91
wú 无[無]...............340
wǔ 五........................54
wù 兀........................347
wù 勿........................81
wù 戊........................224
wù 物........................381
xī 夕........................251
xī 西........................164
xià 下........................123
xiàn 现[現].............289
xiàng 相...............329B
xiāng 相...............329A
xiǎng 想........................330
xiàng 向........................166
xiǎo 小........................167
xiē 些........................317
xīn 心........................321
xīn 辛........................135
xíng 行................250A
xìng 幸........................134
xìng 性........................359
xiōng 兄........................157
xióng 熊........................190
xū 戌........................225
xuán 吅........................384
xué 学[學]..............283
yà 覀........................163
yà 亚[亞]................379
yán 言........................102
yáng 羊........................37
yàng 样[樣]............319
yāo 幺........................227
yāo 夭........................32
yáo 爻........................100
yào 要................165A
yāo 要................165B
yě 也........................94
yè 业[業]................185
yè 页[頁]................331
yī 一........................15
yī 衣........................234
yǐ 乙........................13
yǐ 已........................300
yǐ 以........................152
yì 乂........................99
yì 弋........................89
yì 意........................339
yì 卩........................107
yīn 因........................327
yīn 音........................314
yìng 应[應]...........383B
yīng 应[應]...........383A
yǒng 永........................318
yòng 用........................247
yóu 尤........................174
yóu 由........................217
yǒu 友........................212
yǒu 有........................87
yòu 又........................71
yú 于[於]...............199
yǔ 与[與]...............342
yù 雨........................179
yù 玉........................21
yù 聿........................266
yuán 元........................348
yuē 曰........................44
yuè 月........................47
yuè 刖........................323
yún 云................180B
yún 云[雲]...........180A
zài 在........................86
zǎo 早........................130
zēng 曾................181B
zhà 乍........................243
zhān 占................365A
zhàn 占[佔]..........365B
zhàn 战[戰]............386
zhǎng 长[長].........237B
zhàng 丈........................28
zhǎo 爪................138A
zhǎo 找........................92
zháo 着[著]..........205C
zhāo 着[著]..........205B
zhé 乛........................5
zhě 者........................203
zhè 这[這]..............113
zhe 着[著]............205A
zhèng 正................76A
zhēng 正................76B
zhèng 政........................389
zhī 之........................206
zhǐ 只................328A
zhī 只[隻]............328B
zhī 知........................360

zhǐ 夂 219
zhǐ 止 75
zhì 至 150
zhōng 中 121
zhòng 种[種].........263B
zhǒng 种[種].........263A
zhòng 重 262A
zhǔ 丶 3
zhú 竹 350
zhǔ 主 20
zhù 著 204
zhuǎ 爪 138B
zhuī 隹 310
zhuó 着[著]..........205D
zhuó 丵 186
zǐ 子 82
zì 自 201
zǒu 走 302
zuì 最 378
zuò 作 244
zuò 做 245

42909137R00296

Made in the USA
Middletown, DE
18 April 2019